United States History and Government

A Review Text

Authors:

Paul Stich
Wappingers Central Schools
Wappingers Falls, New York

Susan F. Pingel
Skaneateles Central Schools
Skaneateles, New York

John Farrell
New York Archdiocesan Schools
Cardinal Spellman High School, Bronx, NY

Editors:

Wayne Garnsey and **Paul Stich**
Wappingers Central Schools

Cover Design, Illustrations, and Artwork:

Eugene B. Fairbanks
John Jay High School
Hopewell Junction, New York

N & N Publishing Company, Inc.
18 Montgomery Street   Middletown, New York 10940
(914) 342 - 1677

Dedicated to our students, with the sincere hope that

United States History and Government - A Review Text

will further enhance their education and better prepare them
with an appreciation and understanding
of the historical events and people that have shaped our country.

Special Credits

Thanks to the many teachers that have contributed their knowledge, skills, and years of experience to the making of our review text.

To these educators, our sincere thanks
for their assistance in the preparation of this manuscript:

Cindy Fairbanks
Kenneth Garnsey
Bonnie Kieffer
Virginia Page
Victor Salamone
Gloria Tonkinson

Special thanks to our understanding families

United States History and Government - A Review Text was produced
on a Macintosh II and LaserMax 1000.

The Apple application *MacWrite II* and *Canvas* by Deneba Software were
used to produce text, graphics, and illustrations. Original line drawings were
reproduced on a Microtek MSF-300ZS scanner and modified with *DeskPaint*
by Zedcor. Formatting, special design, graphic incorporation, and page layout
were accomplished with *Ready Set Go!* by Manhattan Graphics. Special technical assistance was provided by Frank Valenza and Len Genesee of Computer Productions Unlimited, Newburgh, N.Y.

Thank you for your excellent software, hardware, and technical support.

SAN # 216 - 4221   ISBN # 0935487-21-2

Printed in the United States of America
67890 BM 09876543

Table Of Contents

Unit One: Constitutional Foundations .... **Page 6**
  I.   **The Constitution** **8**
      A. Foundations 8
      B. Constitutional Convention 13
      C. The Bill of Rights 17
      D. Basic Structure and Function of Government 20
      E. Implementing the New Constitution 28
  II. **The Constitution Tested** **39**
      A. Constitution Stress and Crisis 39
      B. Constitution in Jeopardy: American Civil War 47

Unit Two: Industrialization Of The United States .... **Page 52**
  I.   **The Reconstructed Nation** **54**
      A. Reconstruction Plans 54
      B. The North 58
      C. The New South 59
      D. The Grant Era 62
      E. The End of Reconstruction 66
      F. Impact of Civil War and Reconstruction 67
  II. **The Rise of American Business, Industry, & Labor** **70**
      A. Technology and World Industrialization 70
      B. Pre-Civil War Industrial Growth: Textiles and Iron 71
      C. Business Organizations 72
      D. Major Areas of Growth in Business and Industry 76
      E. Representative Entrepreneurs: Wealth and Effort 78
      F. Business and Government Practices 82
      G. Labor Unionization 83
  III. **Adjusting Society to Industrialism** **90**
      A. Impact of Industrialization on People 90
      B. The Immigrant and Changing Patterns 97
      C. The Last Frontier (1850 - 1890) 103
      D. Retrospective: American Society 109

Unit Three: The Progressive Movement .... **Page 114**
  I.   **Reform in America** **116**
      A. The Reform Tradition: A Review 116
      B. Pressures for Reform 117
      C. Progress: Social and Economic Reform 120
      D. Progressivism and Governmental Action 123
  II. **America Reaching Out** **132**
      A. The Industrial - Colonial Connection 132
      B. An Emerging Global Involvement 135
      C. Restraint and Involvement (1914 - 1920) 142
      D. Wartime Constitutional Issues 146
      E. Search for Peace and Arms Control (1914 - 1930) 147

Unit Four: At Home And Abroad .... **page 154**
  I.   **War Economy and Prosperity (1917 - 1929)** **156**
      A. War Economy 156

    B.   The Twenties: Business Boom or False Prosperity? 159
    C.   Consumerism and the Clash of Culture 163
  II.   **The Great Depression** **167**
    A.   Onset of the Depression.. 167
    B.   Franklin D. Roosevelt and the New Deal 169

Unit Five: **The U.S. In An Age Of Global Crisis**.................................... *Page 184*
   I.   **Peace in Peril (1933 - 1950)** **186**
    A.   Isolation and Neutrality 186
    B.   Failure of Peace: Triumph of Aggression 191
    C.   The United States in World War II 195
  II.   **Peace with Problems (1945 - 1955)** **207**
    A.   International Peace Efforts 207
    B.   Expansion and Containment: Europe................................ 208
    C.   Containment in Asia.. 215
    D.   Cold War at Home 217

Unit Six: **A World In Uncertain Times (1950's - 1990's)** .... *Page 222*
   I.   **Toward a Post–Industrial World** **224**
    A.   Change Within the United States.................................... 224
    B.   In the World 228
  II.   **Containment and Consensus (1945 - 1960)**.............................**234**
    A.   Eisenhower Foreign Policies 234
    B.   Domestic Politics and Constitutional Issues......................... 238
    C.   People: Prosperity and Conservatism................................ 244
 III.   **Decade of Change: 1960's** **248**
    A.   The Kennedy Years.. 248
    B.   Lyndon Johnson and the Great Society............................. 253
  IV.   **Limits of Power: Turmoil at Home and Abroad** **265**
    A.   Vietnam: Sacrifice and Turmoil...................................... 265
    B.   Pres. Johnson: Abdication and Peace Overtures 268
   V.   **Trend Toward Conservatism (1972 - 1985)**.............................**271**
    A.   Nixon as President (1969 - 1974) 271
    B.   The Ford and Carter Presidencies 279
    C.   The New Federalism... 287
    D.   New Approaches to Old Problems....................................... 289
    E.   Renewed United States Power Image 292
    F.   Trade Imbalance and Divesting... 294
    G.   United States - Soviet Relations 296
    H.   Iran Contra Affair... 297
  VI.   **America in the 1990's** **299**
    A.   Bush Presidency 299
    B.   Domestic Issues 299
    C.   Foreign Issues 300

Appendices .... *Page 306*
   I.   The Enduring Constitutional Issues Chart 306
  II.   The Constitutional Amendments 308
 III.   Glossary and Index.. 309
  IV.   Examination Strategies 342
   V.   Practice Examinations, Answers, Explanations 343

How To Use This Book

United States History and Government - A Review Text has been written and illustrated to provide the fundamental information necessary to prepare you for your final examination in United States history.

United States History and Government - A Review Text begins with an overview of the structure and evolution of U.S. Constitutional government up to 1865. The history of the U.S. is then traced with a special focus on key constitutional themes, which scholars call the *"13 Enduring Issues"* of our democracy.

Thirteen Enduring Issues

1. National Power - limits and potentials
2. Federalism - the balance between nation and state
3. The Judiciary - interpreter of the Constitution or shaper of policy
4. Civil Liberties - balance between government and the individual
5. Rights of the Accused and Protection of the Community
6. Equality - its definition as a Constitutional value
7. The Rights of Women under the Constitution
8. Rights of Ethnic and Racial Groups under the Constitution
9. Presidential Power in Wartime and Foreign Affairs
10. Separation of Powers and the Capacity to Govern
11. Avenues of Representation
12. Property Rights and Economic Policy
13. Constitutional Change and Flexibility

Since these issues are the core of the course, you should center your attention on them. Throughout the book, we have used a special icon (at right) to designate discussion of these issues. An appendix at the end of the book has suggested procedures for a year-end review, and we have again listed examples of the *"Thirteen Enduring Constitutional Issues."*

Enduring Issues **13**

We suggest that you use these procedures to prepare for the exams:

1. Look at each Unit divider. Review your understanding of how the illustrations, list of terms, and events on the time-line are related.
2. Read each section of the Unit material. Answer all the drill questions that follow. Obtain the correct answers from your teacher.
3. Re-read the section and re-answer the questions missed the first time. (All questions are based on the style and format of recent state examinations).
4. Use the Glossary to check the terms and concepts used on state examinations. List the terms of which you are unsure. Look them up in the appropriate section and write out the meaning and an example.
5. Review the "Examination Strategies" section, then take the practice examination at the end of the book. Check the answers with your teacher. Concentrate your efforts on re-reading the text sections and glossary terms on which you did poorly.

Unit One

Constitutional Foundations

for the United States Democratic Republic

1700	1750	1790
· Enlightment	·Albany Plan ·Declaration of	·U.S. Constitution
·Locke ·Montesquieu ·Rousseau	Independence	·Bill of Rights
	· Articles of Confederation	

Unwritten Constitution
Separation of Power
Limited Government
Manifest Destiny
Judicial Review
States' Rights
Due Process
Mercantilism
Sectionalism
Compromise
Sovereignty
Federalism
Neutrality
Secession
Republic
Suffrage

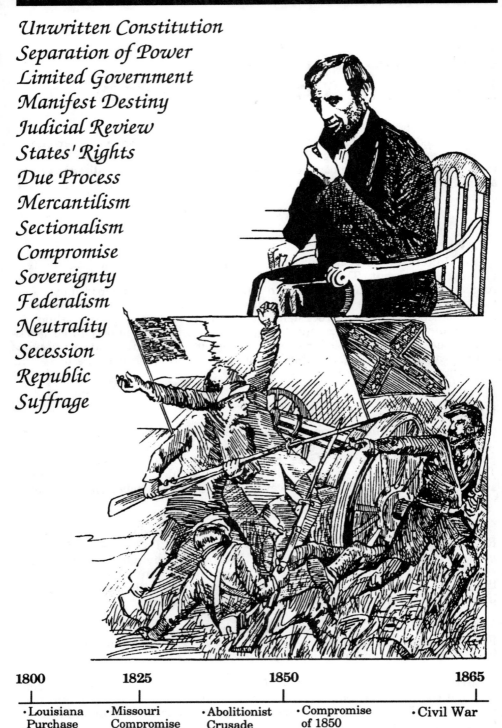

1800	1825	1850	1865

· Louisiana Purchase
· Missouri Compromise
· Abolitionist Crusade
· Compromise of 1850
· Civil War

· Tariff Conflict
· Mexican War
· Dred Scott decision

I. The Constitution:
Bulwark of American Society

The United States is the first nation in modern times to have a government designed and run according to democratic principles. Those principles came from many earlier democratic traditions. America's colonial experience altered some of these traditions. The experiences of the young nation changed others.

A. Foundations

The United States Constitution is the world's oldest functioning written plan of government. The document's ideas flow from several sources: the Ancient World, the European Enlightenment, Native-American Indians, and Colonial America. The long tradition of western political thought traces back to the ancient **Greeks** (direct democracy, juries, and salaries for public officials) and **Romans** (representative government, vetoes, and codified law). These ideas were Anglicized over several centuries in Britain and were part of the **Anglo-Saxon** legal system brought to the English colonies of North America.

Enlightenment Thought

The European Enlightenment, or "Age of Reason," of the 17th and 18th centuries provided much of the rationale for instituting a new republican form of government in the United States. Educated Americans such as John Adams, Thomas Jefferson, and James Madison, knew the ideas of classical thinkers such as **Plato** and **Aristotle**. However, later European scholars' works also influenced the founders.

John Locke (1632-1704), motivated by England's Glorious and Puritan Revolutions, set out important theories in his *Two Treatises on Government*. His beliefs: an optimistic and rational view of human nature; natural rights (life, liberty, and property); that government's authority stems from the people (social contract); that government may be abolished or redesigned if it does not meet the peoples' needs (right of revolution).

Voltaire (1694-1778) was the leading intellectual figure of the French Enlightenment. He advocated religious tolerance, growth of material prosperity, natural rights, and abolition of torture.

Baron de Montesquieu (1689-1755), another French "philosophe," contributed the idea that power in the modern state must be limited, and that the best device for this is to separate powers within governments. Montesquieu promoted separation of government functions (legislative, executive, and judicial branches).

Jean-Jacques Rousseau (1712-1778) expanded Locke's ideas and made them more popular. Rousseau spoke against the contemporary theory of the divine right of kings. He favored democratic self-rule. Rousseau wrote that government flowed from a social contract among the people. Under this contract, rulers served the wishes of the people.

Native-American Contribution

Not all of America's political ideas came from the Old World. The people of the Seneca, Cayuga, Onondaga, Oneida, Mohawk, and Tuscarora nations had set up a **Haudenosaunee Union**, that is better known as the **Iroquois Confederation**, to deal with common problems.

A **confederacy** is a loose union with individual members retaining almost full independence except for the few powers that they delegate to the central authority. The Iroquois Confederation was based on matrilineal kinship and ignored social classes. There are several indications that the Native-American ideas of confederation and minimizing social hierarchy were highly influential in organizing governments at the time of American independence.

The **Albany Plan of Union** (1754) was an attempt to organize British colonial defenses against the French. Colonial representatives met with the delegates of the Iroquois to discuss a plan for union. Sponsored by Benjamin Franklin, it called for a general colonial government with elected representatives. The plan failed because of inter-colonial jealousy, lukewarm response from the Crown, and refusal of the Iroquois to offer a firm commitment.

The **Articles of Confederation** (1781-89) was the first national government for the United States and reflected the Iroquois idea of **federalism** (division of power between member units [states] and a central government).

The **U.S. Constitution** (1789) also reflected the Haudenosaunee-Iroquois on class discrimination. The central governing council of the Five Iroquois Nations recognized no formal social rankings. The **federal union** under the U.S. Constitution prohibited the granting of titles of nobility and mentioned no social rank among governing representatives.

Colonial Experience

Nearly two hundred years under British colonial rule influenced America more than the other elements. Britain's thirteen colonies on the Atlantic seaboard evolved from several different situations. A comparison of them shows more similarities than differences.

Written law, elected legislatures, and separation of government power among the branches reflect common Anglo-Saxon traditions. Not all colonial experiences were democratic. Royal governors and the British Crown exerted powerful vetoes on colonial legislatures. Property and religious qualifications restricted those who were eligible to vote.

Revolution And Declaration Of Independence

The colonists declared independence from Britain in 1776. Jefferson's *Declaration* draws on many of the ideas mentioned above. The *Declaration* itself did not set up a framework for a new government. However, it proclaims a basic philosophy that reflects later designs for the American government, including the U. S. Constitution.

In 1763, the expense of the **Seven Years' War** with France (called the "French and Indian War" in America) caused the British to tighten the **mercantile system**. Under mercantilism, the purpose of having colonies was to supply wealth and markets for the mother country. This led to conflict. The colonists' economic life had not been restricted in the preceding generations. Revenue acts such as the **Stamp Act** (1765), and the **Townshend Acts** (1767) drew fierce protests of "taxation without representation." The **Tea Act** (1772) drew such a violent response that Prime Minister Lord North retaliated with a punitive series of laws which Bostonians labeled the **Intolerable Acts** (1774).

These acts prompted the colonists to call the **First Continental Congress**. It pledged loyalty to the king, but issued a detailed list of grievances. Fighting broke out in Massachusetts. At the **Second Continental Congress**, **John Adams** of Massachusetts led the call for a complete break with England. Full support was not easily forthcoming. On 7 June 1776, Virginia's **Richard Henry Lee** proposed that the colonies *"...are, and of right ought to be, free and independent states."* Members of Congress wanted a written statement to rally the people. Adams joined **Benjamin Franklin**, Virginia's **Thomas Jefferson**, New York's **Robert Livingston**, and Connecticut's **Roger Sherman** in composing one. Jefferson did most of the writing.

The *Declaration of Independence* has three main parts:

- **A Proclamation of Democratic Ideals**, embodying the ideas of John Locke, proclaims the equality of men; their *"... unalienable Rights ...[to] Life, Liberty, and the Pursuit of Happiness ...;"* that government draws its authority from the consent of the governed (the people); and that *"... whenever any form of government becomes destructive to these ends, it is the Right of the People to alter or abolish it."*

- **A Statement of Grievances** against King George III of England is detailed in the second section.

- **A Concluding Statement** incorporated Richard Henry Lee's resolution in declaring the break with Britain.

The Declaration implemented radical elements of Enlightenment thinking for the first time. It has since become the source of inspiration for other revolutionary movements, including the French Revolution of 1789, the Latin American independence movements of the early 1800's, and the African and Asian nationalist movements of the 20th century. Its preamble proclaims universal ideas that America has still not attained.

The Articles Of Confederation

This first system of national government for the United States was drawn up during the American Revolution by the Continental Congress. It was in effect from 1781 to 1789, a time which historians now call the "Critical Period" in U.S. History. It formed a **confederation** in which most of the **sovereignty** (power) was retained by the states. The central authority was extremely limited, had no executive or judiciary, and gave little power to the legislative branch (Congress). There were some achievements: it successfully concluded the Revolutionary War, negotiated a favorable end to the war **(Treaty of Paris, 1783)**, and created a model for admission of new territories **(Northwest Ordinance)**. However, it was too weak to give the new nation the firm basis for growth that it needed. The following table summarizes these weaknesses, and how the new Constitution of 1787 remedied them.

Weaknesses Of The Articles	Constitutional Changes
• Unicameral legislature; each state had equal vote no matter size of population	• Bicameral legislature; representation proportional in House, states equal in Senate
• Two-thirds majority needed to pass laws	• Simple majority can pass laws
• No control of interstate or foreign trade	• Congress regulates interstate and foreign commerce.
• Congress could levy but could not collect taxes	• Congress could levy and collect taxes
• No executive department to enforce laws	• Executive department headed by a single president.
• No national judicial branch, only individual state courts	• National judiciary, headed by a Supreme Court
• Unanimous vote of states needed to amend the constitutional structure.	• Two-thirds vote of Congress, then three-fourths of the states must approve.

Questions

1 A federal union differs from a confederation in that a federal union has
   1 a stronger central government.
   2 less power than a confederation over member states.
   3 no power to tax the member states.
   4 all power concentrated in the central authority.

2 An Enlightenment idea found in American governmental structure is government by
   1 confederation.
   2 direct democracy.
   3 consent of the governed.
   4 divine right.

3 The influence of western political philosophy on American government indicates it is the product of
   1 the ideas of the European Enlightenment exclusively.
   2 the Haudenosaunee-Iroquois confederate structure.
   3 the various forms of colonial governments.
   4 a combination of Old and New World influences.

Base your answer to question 4 on the 1775 verse below:

> We have an old mother
> That ill-tempered has grown.
> She snubs us such as children
> That scarce walk alone;
> She forgets we're grown up
> And have a sense of our own.

4 This verse describes the American colonial dissatisfaction with the British policy of
   1 refusing to defend the colonies in the French and Indian War.
   2 granting the colonial assemblies the power to tax.
   3 forbidding slavery in the colonies.
   4 tightening up colonial mercantile regulations.

5 A major reason why the Articles of Confederation was abandoned as the central form of U.S. government was that it
   1 placed too many restrictions on the activities of individual states.
   2 did not give the central government enough power to rule effectively.
   3 denied citizens the right to vote directly for chief executive.
   4 denied states the right to regulate their own commerce.

6 Achievements under the Articles of Confederation included
   1 a statement of John Locke's basic philosophy of government.
   2 self-government for the Iroquois.
   3 establishment of a national court system.
   4 successful conclusion of the Revolutionary War.

7 A common trait of American colonial governments was
   1 executive control of finances.
   2 unwritten constitutions with Bills of Rights.
   3 appointed legislatures.
   4 executive, legislative, and judicial branches.

8   Which grouping is in the correct chronological order?
   1   Declaration of Independence, U.S. Constitution, Art. of Confederation
   2   U.S. Constitution, Declaration of Independence, Art. of Confederation
   3   Art. of Confederation, Declaration of Independence, U.S. Constitution
   4   Declaration of Independence, Art. of Confederation, U.S. Constitution
9   Thomas Jefferson's use of the phrase *"... certain unalienable Rights ...*
Life, Liberty, and the Pursuit of Happiness ..." in the Declaration of
Independence illustrates his familiarity with the
   1   political legacy of ancient Rome.
   2   governmental structures of Montesquieu.
   3   philosophy of John Locke.
   4   Haudenosaunee or Iroquois political system.
10   Under the Articles of Confederation,
   1   the states were the ultimate source of authority and power.
   2   the national government had absolute sovereignty.
   3   new legislation was passed by simple majority.
   4   a unanimous decision was needed to levy taxes.

B. Constitutional Convention

In 1787, Congress authorized a convention to meet in Philadelphia for the purpose of revising the Articles of Confederation. However, the delegates decided to draft an entirely new form of government and produced a document which became the *United States Constitution*.

Representation And Process

Fifty-five white, male delegates, mostly lawyers, large landholders, and a few merchants and bankers from twelve states (Rhode Island refused to send a delegation) met that summer in Philadelphia. It was an impressive gathering. **George Washington** was chosen to preside. Influential supporters of a more powerful government included: **James Madison** and **Edmund Randolph** of Virginia, **Alexander Hamilton** of New York, and **James Wilson** of Pennsylvania. The proceedings were secret. Madison's notes are our main source of knowledge of how they created the Constitution.

Some delegates, such as **Robert Yates** and **John Lansing** of New York, left in the midst of the convention rather than lend their presence to an unauthorized reforming of the national government. Others, such as **Edmund Randolph** and **Eldridge Gerry** of Massachusetts, refused to sign. The common people, small farmers, and frontiersmen were not well represented. Thomas Jefferson and John Adams were away on diplomatic missions. Old revolutionaries, such as **Governor Clinton** of New York, **Patrick Henry** of Virginia, and **John Hancock** of Massachusetts were suspicious and later led the opposition against ratification.

At the convention, delegates generally agreed to the need for:
- a stronger central government
- better guarantees of property rights
- executive and judicial branches
- legislative power to tax, regulate commerce, and raise an army

Conflict And Compromise

There were also many long arguments about how these general points of agreement would be implemented. The Constitution has been called a "bundle of compromises." The major compromises were:

The Great Compromise. Representation in Congress was a problem. Virginia led the states with large populations in calling for the representatives to be apportioned by the number of people a state had. Small states, such as New Jersey, wanted the number of representatives per state to be equal. After a number of heated debates, Connecticut offered a compromise for a **bicameral legislature** with equal state representation in the upper house (**Senate**) and representation in the lower house by population (**House of Representatives**).

Three-Fifths Compromise. The Southern states with sizable slave populations wanted slaves counted in determining their representation in the House but not for taxation. The Northern states felt slaves (considered as property) should be taxed but not represented. It was finally agreed that five slaves would be counted as only three persons for both purposes.

Slave Trade. Slavery again became an issue when its opponents tried to have it abolished. They succeeded in having the importation of slaves forbidden after 1808, but slavery itself was allowed to continue.

Tariffs. Southern agricultural exporters disapproved of any federal tariffs. Northern business interests wanted tariffs as protection against foreign competition. Congress was given authority to tax imports but forbidden to tax exports.

The Presidency. Proposals on term of office ranged from three years to life. Some delegates wanted direct election, but some mistrusted the people. Compromises worked out four year terms and indirect elections through the "electoral college" system.

The Document

The final document contained seven brief articles that outline governmental structure but left much room for flexible interpretation of power. Careful attention was paid to keeping power limited within each branch, and procedures were included for each of the branches to block the others from overstepping their bounds. Several provisions deserve special focus:

- **The Preamble** lists the purposes of the U.S. government: *"... to form a more perfect union, establish justice, insure domestic tranquillity, provide for the common defense, promote the general welfare, [and] secure the blessings of liberty ..."*

- **Limited Government** is a principle provided by the Constitution detailing what the national and state governments can and cannot do.

- **Representative Government** provides a process by which the people directly and indirectly choose their leaders.

- **Federalism** is a compromise between unitary concentration of power and decentralized confederate structure. A federal union provides a dual system with states recognizing the overall sovereignty of the national government while retaining their power in local matters.

- **Separation of Power** is assured by assigning different functions to three distinct, but co-equal branches: legislative, executive, judicial.

- **A System of Checks and Balances** gives each branch powers to insure that the other branches will not illegally expand their powers.

Ratification

The convention decided to include an article which set up the procedure for ratification of the new government, rather than leave such an important detail to Congress. Article VII required ratification, not by all the states, but only nine. Since the government would be changed considerably by the new constitution, ratification became a controversial issue in the new nation.

Federalists, supporters of the new constitution, were mainly from the business and propertied interests. They were well-organized and financed. Their arguments were that a strong, stable government was the key to peace and economic growth, and that personal liberty would be guaranteed by state constitutions.

Anti-Federalists were the less well-to-do and less educated who were not able to offer strong arguments but feared a conspiracy. Some were prominent figures, such as Patrick Henry and Thomas Jefferson. Others were frontiersmen, laborers, and yeoman farmers.

Anti-Federalists were not a cohesive group. Some wanted only the addition of a Bill of Rights. Others feared a loss of local power to a tyrannical central government.

In the ratification campaigns in Pennsylvania and several less populous states, the Federalists were able to rush through voting before their opponents could become organized. In the more populous states, the process was drawn out, and passage came by much smaller margins.

A bitter ratification battle raged in New York State. New York's geographic position made it critical to keeping the new union together. The ratifying convention was held in Poughkeepsie. John Lansing, Robert Yates, and Governor George Clinton led the anti-federalist forces. The Federalists were better organized. A narrow victory made New York the 11th state to ratify the Constitution.

The Federalists won New York by a narrow 30-27 margin. Earlier, **Hamilton** and **John Jay** had joined **Madison** in writing a series of eighty-five persuasive articles published in newspapers throughout the states under the pen-name "Publius." They were later collected and published as the *Federalist Papers*. They are still considered among the best analyses of the American constitutional system.

Questions

1   Federalism is best defined as a system of government based on
   1   branches within a government checking each other's power.
   2   written guarantees of personal civil liberties.
   3   passage of legislation by majority vote.
   4   division of power between levels of governments.

2   Which is the best example of the concept of checks and balances?
   1   The Senate passes a tax bill approved by the House of Representatives.
   2   The President sends an envoy to negotiate a peace settlement in the Middle East.
   3   A U.S. District Court hears a case involving drug smuggling from Columbia.
   4   The Senate ratifies an arms treaty made by the President with Russia.

3   The system of federalism was adopted by the writers of the United States Constitution due primarily to their fear of
   1   powerful radical groups.
   2   an overly strong national judiciary.
   3   aggressive foreign leaders.
   4   an overpowering central government

Use the cartoon below to answer questions 4 and 5:

On the erection of the eleventh PILLAR of the great National Dome, we beg leave most sincerely to felicitate "our Dear Country."

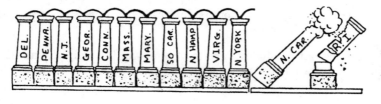

The foundation is good - it may yet be saved.

4   The "dome" mentioned in the cartoon's text refers to the
   1   dome of the U.S. Capital building in Washington, D.C.
   2   new structure of government under the Articles of Confederation.
   3   new federal union formed under the U.S. Constitution.
   4   influence of newspapers and public opinion on government.

5   Which phrase from the Revolutionary era would be most similar to the ideas expressed in the cartoon?
   1   "Thirteen staves and never a hoop will not make a barrel."
   2   "Taxation without representation is tyranny."
   3   "… Life, Liberty. and the Pursuit of Happiness…"
   4   "Give me Liberty, or give me death."

6   Which is the basic principle underlying the United States Constitution?
   1   The executive branch should determine the type of government the nation has.
   2   Interests of the state are more important than those of the citizens.
   3   Government must maintain law and order by any means.
   4   The basic source of power rests in the people.

7   At the Constitutional Convention, slavery was an issue in both the Slave
    Trade Compromise and the
    1   Connecticut Plan.   3   Great Compromise.
    2   Three-Fifths Compromise.   4   Presidential Compromise.
8   Which group dominated the Constitutional Convention?
    1   frontiersmen   3   city laborers
    2   yeoman farmers   4   lawyers
9   Article II of the Constitution states that the President *"...shall nominate,
    and by and with the consent of the Senate, shall appoint ...judges of the
    Supreme Court..."* This passage illustrates the governmental principle of
    1   judicial review.   3   checks and balances.
    2   federalism.   4   representative government.
10 *"The proposed Constitution, so far from implying an abolition of the State
    governments, makes them constituent parts of the national sovereignty, by
    allowing them a direct representation in the Senate, and leaves in their
    possession certain exclusive and very important portions of their sovereign
    power."* - Publius
    The author of this statement believed the
    1   Articles of Confederation was superior to the Constitution.
    2   states' power was properly preserved in the Constitution.
    3   fears of the Anti-Federalists were well founded.
    4   power of the central government as too weak compared to the states.

C. The Bill Of Rights

One of the major Anti-Federalist criticisms of the Constitution
was its lack of specific guarantees of individual civil liberties.
Opponents felt that the enumerated powers of Congress were
too open to interpretation and would lead to laws that could infringe on citizens rights.

Enduring Issues 4

Reacting to these arguments, Congressman James Madison offered a group
of amendments to safeguard personal freedom. Madison's ideas became the
basis for ten amendments proposed and sent to the states for ratification by
the first Congress in 1789. Officially adopted in 1791, these first ten amendments to the Constitution became known as the **Bill of Rights**.

Two basic steps are required to amend the Constitution:

1. Proposed amendments can be offered by either two-thirds vote of Congress, or by a special national convention called by Congress at the request of
two-thirds of the state legislatures. (The latter procedure has never been
used.)

2. Proposed amendments must then be ratified either by:

a) sending them to the state legislatures, three-fourths of which are
    needed for ratification; or

b) setting up special conventions in the states in which case three-
    fourths of them must approve the amendment for it to become part of
    the Constitution.

The Bill of Rights was originally intended to guarantee citizens protection from abuse by the national government. State constitutions listed their own guarantees for their citizens.

The Bill of Rights has not changed in 200 years. However, the Federal courts interpreted its ideas in different ways over the years. In our own times, court rulings apply Bill of Rights guarantees to protect individuals from the actions of state governments. A later amendment, the 14th, (see page 55) guarantees of equal protection of the laws for all citizens. The Federal courts use the 14th to make sure the Bill of Rights is fairly and properly applied to all citizens.

Major Provisions Of The Bill Of Rights

Amendment	Protection Against:
I..................	Congressional laws infringing on freedoms of speech, press, peaceful assembly; free exercise of religion or separation of church and state.
II................	Congressional laws infringing on the right to bear arms.
III..............	Congressional laws quartering troops in private homes in peacetime.
IV..............	Unreasonable searches, seizures; warrants only on probable cause.
V................	Abuse in legal proceedings. It requires: 1. indictment by grand jury in felony cases 2. no double jeopardy (being tried a second time after acquittal) 3. self-incrimination cannot be forced 4. due process must be used (proper and equal legal procedures) 5. property cannot be taken without just compensation
VI..............	Abuse of accused citizens. It requires: 1. speedy and public trial 2. impartial jury of peers 3. informing of charges 4. confrontation by accusers 5. calling of supportive witnesses 6. guarantee of counsel
VII.............	Jury trials being denied in certain civil (non-criminal) cases.
VIII...........	Excessive bail; cruel, or unusual punishment.
IX..............	Other rights not listed in the Constitution being denied.
X................	Powers not listed in the Constitution being denied to the states. (As part of the theory of federalism, powers not specifically assigned to the central government are reserved for the states.)

Protection for the **reserved powers** of states in the 10th Amendment is modified by two of Article I's sections: one places many specific restrictions on the states, and the famous **elastic clause** in section eight gives Congress a great deal of **implied power** to do things not restricted in the Constitution.

Many of the **civil liberties** granted in the Bill of Rights flow directly from problems encountered during the colonial experience; for example, the 4th Amendment was drawn up in response to the British authorities' use of "blanket" search warrants (writs of assistance).

Questions

1   Legal authorities must obtain search warrants in the U.S. because
     1   a person can be assumed guilty until proven innocent.
     2   governments have been known to abuse their power.
     3   the crime rate is very high.
     4   criminals are pampered by our government.

Use the following quotation to answer questions 2 and 3:

"... a constitution does not in itself imply any more than a declaration of the relationship which the different parts of the government bear to each other, but does not, in any degree, imply security to the rights of the individual." -Agrippa (20 January 1788)

2   The author, "Agrippa," is expressing the feeling that constitutions
     1   are useless against tyranny.
     2   simply outline the connections among government branches.
     3   are written guarantees of individual freedom.
     4   provide security for the entire society.
3   The author was most likely a
     1   supporter of Madison, Hamilton, and Jay.
     2   Federalist.
     3   proponent of a three branch government.
     4   member of the Anti-Federalists.
4   In the United States, legal driving ages differ from state to state. This illustrates
     1   the reserved power principle.
     2   checks and balances.
     3   the right of due process in criminal cases.
     4   protection against double jeopardy.
5   Opponents of capital punishment argue that it violates protections against
     1   the reserved power principle.
     2   established religions.
     3   the right of due process in criminal cases.
     4   cruel and unusual punishment.
6   A major objection to the U.S. Constitution when it was presented for ratification in 1787, was that the Constitution
     1   reserved too much power for the states.
     2   contained too many compromises.
     3   required the approval of all the states to ratify it.
     4   provided insufficient guarantees of civil liberties.

7   The Bill of Rights provides that Congress must
    1   guarantee each state a republican form of government.
    2   not issue titles of nobility.
    3   not grant writs of assistance.
    4   have unlimited power to prosecute criminals.
8   Which is the basic reason that the Bill of Rights was added to the Constitution?
    1   Local governments needed a clear listing of their powers.
    2   There was a need for a stronger central government.
    3   Individuals needed protection from possible abuses of government power.
    4   The powers of Congress were not sufficiently defined in the original Constitution.
9   The practice of a trial before a jury of one's peers is based primarily on the assumption that
    1   peer groups have a better understanding of the legal process than do appointed judges.
    2   having a background similar to that of the accused helps in making fair verdicts.
    3   trials can be conducted faster if the jury is carefully selected.
    4   decisions reached by a peer group are less likely to be overturned by a higher court.
10 Which attitude led to the inclusion of the Bill of Rights in the U.S. Constitution?
    1   mistrust of states' rights
    2   distrust of the common people
    3   fear of intellectual and religious diversity
    4   suspicion of the power of government

D. Basic Structure
And Function Of Government

The writers of the Constitution were cautious about letting voters directly elect all national government officials. Under the original Constitution, the people directly chose *only* their local member of the House of Representatives. Senators, the President and Vice-President, and Federal judges were chosen indirectly. The founders had doubts about the education and wisdom of the general population in 1787. The Constitution framers believed that voters are easily swayed.

Because of the uncertainty about people and power, the federal powers were separated into three branches. **Each of the three branches of the Federal government has a primary purpose according to Constitutional design.**

The Congress (Article I)

The founders described Congress in Article I of the Constitution. It writes the nations' laws. It is the "peoples' branch" because the legislature is the gathering place for the ideas of the nation. The 17th Amendment (direct election of Senators) and the 20th Amendment (moving the date for starting sessions of Congress to January) changed Congress' structure and operation.

The table that follows indicates its basic structure:

House of Representatives (change)	Senate (continuity)
Membership: • Total of 435 (set by law); each state's delegation is determined by its population relevant to the others	• 2 per state (currently 100 from 50 states)
Qualifications: • At least 25 years of age, U.S. citizen for 7 years, resident of state represented	• At least 30 years of age, U.S. citizen for 9 years, resident of state represented
Term: • 2 years, entire House must be elected every two years	• 6 years with staggered elections, one-third of the members elected every 2 years.
How Elected: • Directly by the voters of a district	• Directly by voters of a state (17th Amendment). Originally, state legislature chose them
Presiding Officer: • Speaker of the House elected by the members (voting along party lines)	• Vice-President of the U.S. is assigned as "President of the Senate," a "President Pro-Tempore" is also chosen by the membership
Special Powers: • Brings impeachment charges • May choose President if there is no majority in the electoral system • Must start all revenue bills	• Acts as jury in impeachment trials (two-thirds vote needed) • May choose the Vice Pres. if there is no majority in the electoral system • Must ratify treaties with foreign nations by two-thirds vote • Must approve Presidential appointments (majority needed)

Congressional Power is basically derived from the seventeen powers **enumerated** or **delegated** in Section 8 of Article I of the Constitution, including:

• levying and collecting taxes	• borrowing on the credit of the U.S.
• declaring war	• establishing immigration rules
• maintaining the court system	• maintaining a postal system
• regulating interstate and foreign commerce	• governing patents and copyrights
• coining money and punishing counterfeiters	• maintaining an army and navy

The eighteenth power listed in Article I, Section 8 is the famous **"elastic clause."** It allows Congress to stretch the meaning of the other seventeen powers to cover new situations. The elastic clause states that *"...to make all laws necessary and proper to carry into effect the foregoing powers..."* The doctrine of **implied power** that it created has both proponents (**loose constructionists**) and enemies (**strict constructionists**). To this day, it continues to cause some of the deepest controversies in our society.

Another type of power in the constitutional structure is **concurrent power**. This is the idea of shared power. All governments must have two powers operate. They must have the power to enforce their laws. (States and local governments have police power). Governments also need **revenue** (income) to operate. To get revenue, taxes are necessary and so are tax collection agencies.

The Constitution delegates these powers to the national government, and the 10th Amendment also reserves these powers for the states.

Certain powers are specifically denied to the Federal government: suspending **writs of habeas corpus** (speedy arraignment), except in times of rebellion and invasion; passing **bills of attainder** (legislative acts declaring people guilty without trials) or **ex post facto laws** (laws that declare an act a crime, after the act has been done); levying **direct taxes** on people (16th Amendment - Income Tax is an exception); **taxing exports; spending money without appropriation**; and **granting titles of nobility**.

How a Bill Becomes a Law: Proposed legislation ("bill") goes through a lengthy process before being adopted. Below is a pictorial representation of the process. [Note: Legislation process on revenue bills can only be started in the House.]

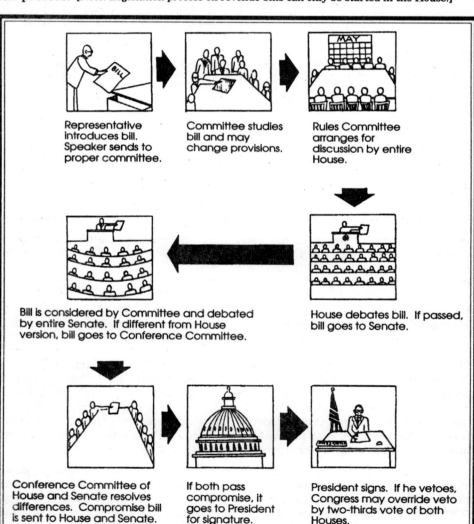

Representative introduces bill. Speaker sends to proper committee.

Committee studies bill and may change provisions.

Rules Committee arranges for discussion by entire House.

Bill is considered by Committee and debated by entire Senate. If different from House version, bill goes to Conference Committee.

House debates bill. If passed, bill goes to Senate.

Conference Committee of House and Senate resolves differences. Compromise bill is sent to House and Senate.

If both pass compromise, it goes to President for signature.

President signs. If he vetoes, Congress may override veto by two-thirds vote of both Houses.

The Presidency (Article II)

The executive branch is outlined in Article II and the 12th, 20th, 22nd, 23rd, and 25th Amendments. The qualifications are simple. A person must be at least 35 years of age, a native born citizen, and a resident of the U.S. for at least 14 years. The term of office is four years, and a President can be removed from office for "high crimes and misdemeanors" by impeachment procedures. (Official charges are brought by the House of Representatives, and a trial takes place in the Senate, with a two-thirds vote necessary to remove.)

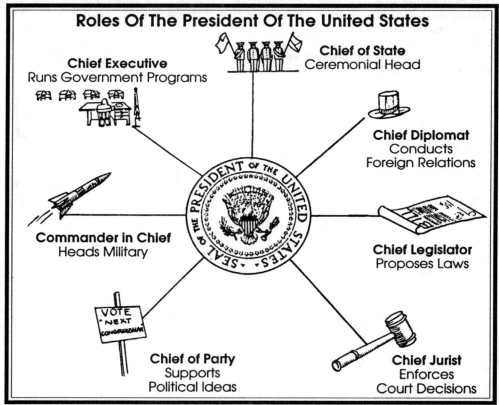

There is much more to the Presidency than the Constitution outlines. Much about the office has evolved over time. For example, almost every President since George Washington has had to **campaign** for the office. This has become an difficult task in modern times. Candidates often begin years before the election. Up to the first quarter of the 19th century, **caucuses** of party leaders chose candidates. Today, a complex system of local caucuses and primary elections choose delegates to national party nominating conventions. The delegates then officially nominate party candidates at the conventions.

| Enduring Issues 13 | The Constitution provides for indirect election of the President and the Vice-President by special officers called **Electors of the President**. (Taken together, this group is often referred to as the "Electoral College"). Each state is entitled to a number of |

electors equivalent to its total Congressional delegation (Representatives + 2 Senators). U.S. territories do not have electors, but the **23rd Amendment** granted the District of Columbia a minimum of three. The rules by which these electors are chosen are set by each state.

To win the presidency, a candidate must receive a majority (270) of the 538 electoral votes. If a party's candidate wins the popular vote in a state by a majority, all of the state's electors will be from that party (and they customarily cast a "rubber stamp" vote for their party's candidate).

It is possible to win a national majority of the public's votes but not win in critical states and thereby lose the presidency. It happened to Andrew Jackson in 1824, and to Grover Cleveland in 1888. The possibility of winning certain very populous states (California, New York, Texas), with their high electoral votes, makes candidates spend more time and money campaigning in them and sometimes ignore other states.

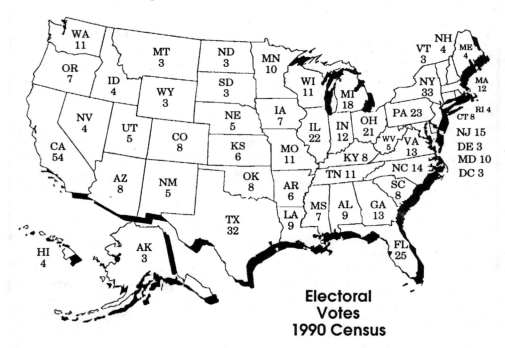

**Electoral
Votes
1990 Census**

If a vacancy occurs through the President's death, retirement, or resignation, the Vice-President takes over. If there is no Vice-President to succeed the President, Congress can set the order of succession. In 1947, it set up the **Presidential Succession Act** (President - Vice President - Speaker of the House - President Pro Tempore of the Senate - then Secretaries of the Cabinet, starting with the Secretary of State).

However, the adoption of the **25th Amendment** (1967) makes it unlikely that there will be a vacancy in the Vice-Presidency. This is called the **Presidential Disability and Succession Amendment**. It requires the President, with the approval of both houses of Congress, to nominate a new Vice-President if that office becomes vacant. It also says that in the event of the disability of the President, the Vice-President may become "Acting President."

Presidential Powers

Constitutional	Extra-Constitutional
• Appoints all important gov't. officials • Commander-in-Chief • Grants pardons and reprieves • Recommends legislation • Delivers State of the Union address • Executes federal laws and programs • Receives ambassadors • Makes treaties with foreign nations • May call special sessions of Congress	• Head of political party • World Leader • Voice of the People • Domestic emergency actions • Manager of Economic Prosperity

The 20th Amendment (1933) set the inauguration of the President as the January 20th after election. The President takes an oath to "preserve, protect, and defend the Constitution of the United States of America."

The Judicial Branch (Article III)

The founders described the national courts in Article III of the Constitution. They interpret the nations' laws. The Constitution only refers to one court by name - **The Supreme Court of the United States**. Congress had to pass laws to create other courts in the Federal system. The first Congress did this under the Judiciary Act of 1789. All federal judges are appointed by the President for life tenure and must be approved by the Senate. They serve while in "good behavior," and are subject to the same Congressional impeachment process as the President. The diagram below shows the current Federal court system.

The Supreme Court's main power is **judicial review** (the Court's power to examine local, state, and federal statutes and governmental actions and decide if they violate the United States Constitution).

If the Supreme Court finds such a conflict, it will declare a law or action null and void or **unconstitutional**. This power is not specified in Article III.

This power was assumed by the Court in the famous ***Marbury v. Madison*** decision under Chief Justice John Marshall in 1803. It is a unique power in government and has often been the center of controversy in American history.

Enduring
Issues

3

Supreme Court of the United States
1 Chief Justice & 8 Associate Justices
(has original & appellate jurisdiction
hearings on constitutional issues)

U.S. Circuit Courts of Appeal (11)
(have only appellate jurisdiction -
operate as hearing panels - decisions
are final in most cases)

U.S. District Courts (94)
(have original jurisdiction - operate
using normal jury trial procedure)

The Federal Bureaucracy

Beyond the basic elements of government described in the Constitution, a broader structure of power has evolved since 1789. Today, there are several million people working for a government that has grown in size and scope, especially in our own times. The "bureaucrats" are the civil servants and appointees who do everything from delivering the mail to processing your income tax returns. Without this army of workers, the President could not hope to carry out the numerous programs that Congress has set up.

Paid Civilian Employees Of The United States Government*			
1816	4,837	1945	3,816,310
1861	36,672	1960	2,421,000
1881	100,000	1970	2,881,000
1935	780,582	1985	3,021,000

* If military employment was added, the figure for 1985 would be over 5.1 million. (Source: Historical & Statistical Abstracts of U.S.)

Comparison To New York State Government

Most states copied the Federal government structure. New York State's structure is an example:

- **republican form** (representative democracy) as required by the U.S. Constitution

- **written constitutions** outlining powers and limits of branches

- **three branches**

- **bicameral legislatures (N.Y.S. Senate** is upper house, **Assembly** is lower house

- **Bills of Rights**

Of course, states entered the union at different times. Every one of the fifty states have some different government characteristics. New York State has these differences:

- The Governor may veto individual parts of the state's budget as proposed by the legislature. This is a **line-item veto**, whereas the President of the U.S. has only a "blanket" veto.

- The N.Y.S. Constitution can be changed by an amendment passing in two sessions of the Legislature, then being voted on in a **referendum** (general election).

Since New York State ranks second in population and is a leading financial, industrial, and agricultural center, many of the state's leaders have gone on to become candidates for the Presidency. Included in this group are: George Clinton, Aaron Burr, DeWitt Clinton, Martin Van Buren, Millard Fillmore, Samuel Tilden, Grover Cleveland, Theodore Roosevelt, Alfred E. Smith, Franklin Roosevelt, Thomas E. Dewey, and Nelson Rockefeller.

Comparison To Other National Governments

The table below indicates some of the basic similarities and differences between our national government and those of Great Britain and the China.

Characteristic	U.S.A.	Great Britain	China
Type	representative democracy	representative democracy	totalitarian
Organization	federal	unitary	unitary
Executive	President elected independently	Prime Minister chosen by Parliament	Premier selected by Communist Party oligarchy
Constitution	written: guaranteed civil liberties	unwritten: common law plus precedent plus documents (Magna Carta)	no written guarantee of civil liberties
Political Parties	2 major (Democrat and Republican plus several minor	2 major (Labour and Conservative) plus several minor	only Communist Party is allowed

Questions

1 The U.S. and Great Britain are democracies because in each country
 1 the government maintains a national court system.
 2 power rests with citizens and is exercised by representatives.
 3 the executive branch can veto laws passed by the legislative.
 4 the chief executive is elected directly by the people.
2 In 1787, the authors of the Federal Constitution originally provided for an indirect rather than direct election of United States Presidents and Senators primarily because they believed that
 1 only the upper classes should be given citizenship.
 2 the people could not be fully trusted.
 3 the checks and balances system could not be fully trusted.
 4 the electoral college should control elections for both.
3 Which exercises the most direct influence on proposed legislation?
 1 Congressional committees
 2 Electoral College
 3 President
 4 Supreme Court
4 A similarity between the United States Constitution and the New York State Constitution is that both
 1 the Governor and the President are directly elected by the people.
 2 provide for constitutional change by vote of the people.
 3 divide and limit power among three separate branches.
 4 the Governor and the President have line-item veto power.

5   The American and British systems of government differ in that the American chief executive is
    1   appointed.
    2   elected independently from other branches.
    3   chosen by the legislature.
    4   elected directly by the citizens.
6   The founding fathers seemed to believe the people's wishes would be most directly expressed in the
    1   Presidency.   3   Senate.
    2   Judiciary.   4   House of Representatives.
7   The Constitution of the United States provides that revenue bills
    1   be mentioned in the President's State of the Union Address.
    2   must be approved by a two-thirds vote of the Senate.
    3   are subject to line-item veto by the President.
    4   can only start in the House of Representatives.

Use the chart below to answer questions 8 and 9:

Paid Civilian Employees Of The U.S. Government*	
1816..........................4,837	1945.................3,816,310
1861......................36,672	1960.................2,421,000
1881.....................100,000	1970.................2,881,000
1935....................780,582	1985.................3,021,000

* If military employment was added, the figure for 1985 would be over 5.1 million.
(Source: Historical & Statistical Abstracts of U.S.)

8   The chart indicates the
    1   total number of federal, state, and local government employees.
    2   non-military national bureaucracy since 1816.
    3   civilian and military government work force.
    4   national and state civil service growth for more than 170 years.
9   Which statement is best supported by information in the chart?
    1   The growth stabilized after World War I.
    2   The bureaucracy grew at its fastest rate in the 1861-81 period.
    3   The size of the federal bureaucracy has grown.
    4   The current trend in growth stems from World War II.
10 The President of the United States is exercising extra-Constitutional powers when he
    1   appoints a new ambassador to Ireland.
    2   increases naval forces in the Persian Gulf region.
    3   helps a Senator campaign for re-election.
    4   sends a State of the Union Address to Congress.

E. Implementing The New Constitution

During the Era of the New Republic (1789-1825), the theories behind the new Constitution became reality. A new structure of government based on a federal union began operation. The actions of the early Presidents and other political and governmental figures set **precedents** (procedures based on tradition) still in effect today. Taken together, these precedents make up "**the unwritten constitution.**"

Creating Domestic Stability: Hamilton's Financial Plan

Enduring Issues
12

Washington's Secretary of the Treasury, Alexander Hamilton, had the formidable challenge of putting the shaky U.S. economy on a firm footing. His basic goals were to: establish the credit of the U.S. among the other nations; provide a sound currency; strengthen the central government; and secure the support of the propertied classes. To do this, Hamilton proposed:

- **repaying the foreign debt**
- **assuming debts** still unpaid by states from the Revolutionary War
- **raising revenue** through **excise taxes** on luxury items (liquor and jewelry) and **tariffs**
- imposing a **protective tariff** to encourage domestic industries
- **creating a Bank of the United States** to coordinate public and private financial activities

These proposals passed after much debate and **log-rolling** (trading of votes in Congress). One of the most controversial actions was the creation of a national bank (The Bank of the United States). Opponents, **strict constructionists** (taking the Constitution literally), claimed Congress had no power to do this. **Loose constructionists** argued that the "elastic clause" (see page 21) allowed the bank, because it was "necessary and proper" to carry out Congress' responsibility, to stabilize the economy.

Development Of The Unwritten Constitution: Washington, Adams, And Jefferson

The first three Presidents of the United States (Washington, John Adams, Jefferson) set several political traditions that became part of the unwritten constitution. Illustrations of precedents range from the Cabinet and political parties to judicial review and lobbying.

The Cabinet

Although the Constitution mentioned establishing "executive departments," no reference was made of an advisory group for the heads of the departments. George Washington established the idea after naming **Hamilton** as head of the Treasury, **Jefferson** as Secretary of State (foreign affairs), **Edmund Randolph** as Attorney General (Justice Department), and **Henry Knox** as Secretary of War. Washington called on them as an advisory committee when making executive decisions, and subsequent presidents have followed the precedent. Hamilton and Jefferson often disagreed on policy issues, including how loosely the Constitution could be interpreted.

Current U.S. Departments Under The President	
1. State - 1789	8. Defense - 1947
2. Treasury - 1789	9. Housing & Urban Development - 1965
3. Justice (Attorney General)-1789	10. Transportation - 1966
4. Interior (federal lands) - 1849	11. Energy - 1977
5. Agriculture - 1889	12. Health & Human Services - 1977
6. Commerce - 1903	13. Education - 1979
7. Labor - 1913	14. Veterans Affairs - 1989

Political Parties

Groups of individuals began to organize for common goals, such as:

- electing officials
- influencing the public
- conducting campaigns
- framing solutions to political issues
- monitoring the other groups in power

The founding fathers had indicated a certain distaste for **partisan** politics, or government by **competing factions**, but such groups began forming almost immediately. The first two political parties formed during Washington's administration.

The Federalists	The Democratic-Republicans*
Leaders: Hamilton, Adams	**Leaders:** Jefferson, Madison
Advocated: • loose construction • stronger central gov't. • central control of economic affairs, pro-National Bank & protective tariffs	**Advocated:** • strict construction • stronger state gov'ts. • less central control of economic affairs; against Bank & high tariffs
Supporters: Wealthy & propertied groups merchants & manufacturers	**Supporters:** "Common People" - small farmers, city labor, frontier people
Foreign Affairs: pro-British	**Foreign Affairs:** pro-French

(*For a while after 1800, the group was called "Republicans," but is no relation to the Republican Party of today which formed in the 1850's. By the 1830's, the group was to take the permanent name of "Democrats.")

Suppressing Rebellion

In 1794, western Pennsylvania distillers and farmers seized federal marshals trying to arrest them for evading the excise tax. Hamilton persuaded Washington to let him lead a militia against the "insurrection." There was no fighting. Only a few were arrested and later pardoned. While an overreaction, **"The Whiskey Rebellion"** did demonstrate the power of the federal government to enforce the law. It also pushed many frontier people toward the Democratic-Republicans who had opposed the use of such force.

Judicial Review

Judicial review was a fourth major precedent of the unwritten constitution to emerge in this early period. It emerged from a Supreme Court decision involving appointments made as Federalist President John Adams left office in 1801. The new Democratic-Republican President, Thomas Jefferson, told Secretary of State James Madison not to deliver the appointments. One of the appointees, William Marbury sued Madison. Madison (and Jefferson) won the case, but in the *Marbury v. Madison* (1803) decision, Chief Justice John Marshall

Enduring Issues
3

overturned a Congressional act (Judiciary Act of 1789). This established the precedent for the power of judicial review. Marshall went on to use the power in a number of famous cases, and of course, it remains the Supreme Court's major power to this day.

Year	Decision	Significance
1810	*Fletcher v. Peck*	Supreme Court established its power to review state laws.
1819	*Dartmouth College v. Woodward*	Set precedent that states may not pass laws impairing private contracts
1819	*McCulloch v. Maryland*	Upheld the constitutionality of the Bank of the United States by denying Maryland's attempt to tax a federal institution.
1824	*Gibbons v. Ogden*	Established broad interpretation of the federal government's authority over interstate commerce.

Executive And Congressional Interpretation

Enduring Issues **10**

Another precedent set by Washington was his reluctance to be constantly called to task over his decisions by Congress. He limited how often his cabinet officers appeared to testify before Congress, underlining the independence and separation of the executive branch. How far the President could carry this idea of "executive privilege" is still questionable as we have learned from the "Watergate" and "Iran-Contra" affairs in our own times.

Lobbying

Enduring Issues **11**

Using the First Amendment's "right to petition" clause, many early groups began the practice of trying to influence government officials to see their side of an issue. These outside pressure groups now exercise tremendous influence on Congress. Today, there are an estimated 7,000 hired agents (lobbyists) in Washington D.C. representing virtually every major business, economic group, foreign nation, and other special interests. Many believe that lobbyists present Congressmen with vital information they would not otherwise be able to obtain. Opponents indicate the information is always biased, and that lobbyists may lean toward unethical behavior (bribes) to get their way. A number of laws have been passed to monitor and control this practice. Lobbyists must now register with the federal government and publicly report their financial activities.

Precedents In Foreign Policy: Washington Through Monroe

Foreign policies instituted by the early presidential administrations set precedents for America's behavior in the world that would last into the 20th century.

Neutrality

Realizing that the U.S. was militarily and economically weak, President Washington adopted policies which kept the nation out of volatile European politics. While the Atlantic provided realistic protection in a time of slow-

Enduring Issues 9

moving transportation, America was still surrounded by British and Spanish possessions. France's revolutionary politics had wide-ranging effects. While seeking political neutrality, the U.S. was economically linked to these major powers. In order to avoid being drawn into the conflicts between Britain and France, Washington issued a **Proclamation of Neutrality** in 1793. Later, as he left the Presidency, Washington advised the new nation to *"steer clear of permanent alliances with any portion of the foreign world."* This became a cornerstone of the long-standing American isolationist tradition.

John Adams, the second President, continued this policy but only narrowly avoided serious problems with Britain and France. The two political parties often took sides in the Anglo-French struggles. The third President, Thomas Jefferson, urged *"peace, commerce, and honest friendship with all nations, entangling alliances with none,"* but came very close to war with Britain (see "Embargo" below).

Economic Pressures

In this early period, America's economic needs often determined the path it took in world political affairs:

Jay's Treaty (1794). Britain did not live up to its promises in the Treaty of Paris (1783) which ended the American Revolution. British troops remained in the western regions of the U.S. The British also ignored financial claims of American merchants. In its war France, British commanders harassed U.S. ships and impressed American seamen into the British Navy. (Impressment means forced service or draft.) Washington sent Chief Justice John Jay to try to settle these problems. Relations with Britain improved slightly, but Jay made many concessions, and the treaty was very unpopular.

Pinckney's Treaty (1794). Ambassador Charles Pinckney negotiated a useful treaty with Spain. It settled American rights on the Mississippi. Western farmers received the **right of deposit** to ship goods through the Spanish port of New Orleans safely.

Enduring Issues 9

Jefferson's Embargo (1807). As the Napoleonic Wars broke out in Europe in the early 19th century, Britain blockaded the continent, and American Atlantic trade suffered. The British continued to badger U.S. ships and sailors, while the French launched a counter blockade of the British Isles. Increasing tensions finally led President Jefferson to get Congress to pass an Embargo Act, forbidding all U.S. foreign trade. It was extremely unpopular with trading interests and was repealed in favor of a law which only restricted trade with Britain and France.

War of 1812. President Madison (1809-17) eventually failed in his diplomatic attempts to avoid the U.S. being drawn into the increasingly hostile Napoleonic Wars. A group of young Western and Southern Congressmen (John C. Calhoun and Henry Clay) blamed the British for inciting the Indians in their region and patriotically called for war. There was an underlying desire to take British lands from Canada.

These **War Hawks** managed to get control of Congress and declare war against Britain. The war consisted of numerous skirmishes and a few major water battles on the Great Lakes. American forces burned the Canadian capital, Kingston, and the British retaliated by burning Washington, D.C. No headway was made and the Treaty of Ghent (1814) largely indicated the war was a draw.

Territorial Expansion

The War of 1812 did increase interest in western lands, both in settlement and investment.

This spurred road and canal building. The **Cumberland (National) Road** was financed by Congress, and New York State built the **Erie Canal** making Buffalo a major western port by connecting it to Albany and New York City.

The territorial map below shows the rapid growth of the U.S. in the first half of the 19th Century. Expansion was almost an obsession with many Americans at the time.

By the 1840's expansionists spoke of America's "divine mission" to spread democracy from "sea to shining sea." An examination of the chart on the next page reveals that this **Manifest Destiny** idea became one of the primary reasons for our contact with other nations.

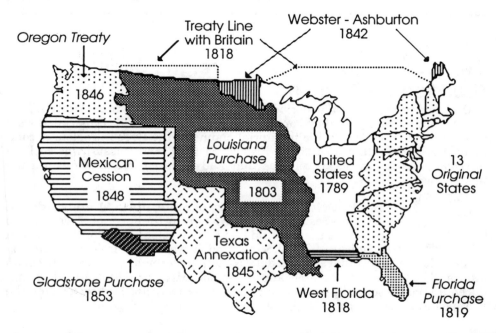

U.S. Territorial Expansion

1803	Louisiana	• Purchased from France for $15 million; Doubled U.S. territory, secured port of New Orleans.
1818	Northern Border	• Set western U.S.-Canadian border at 49th parallel; exchange of territory in Great Lakes.
1818	Western Florida	• Indian uprising quelled by General Andrew Jackson; U.S. claimed Spanish lands.
1819	Florida	• Adams-Onis Treaty: U.S. paid $5 million for Florida peninsula; U.S. gave up claim to Texas 42nd parallel as boundary with Spanish Mexico.
1842	Northern Maine	• Webster-Ashburton Treaty settled disputed boundary with Great Britain.
1845	Texas	• An independent republic since 1836, Congress agreed to Texans' request to be annexed.
1846	Oregon	• Treaty with Britain extended the 49th parallel border from the Rockies to the Pacific.
1848	Mexican Cession	• War broke out with Mexico over Texan boundary; U.S. paid $13 million for southwest region which included New Mexico, Arizona, California, Utah, Nevada, and Colorado.
1853	Gadsden Purchase	• Bought from Mexico to complete a southern transcontinental rail line.

Democratic Idealism In Foreign Policy:
The Monroe Doctrine

Also during this national period, the fifth President, **James Monroe**, set another major foreign policy cornerstone in place. In 1823, Imperial Russia was intruding on U.S. Pacific territorial claims in the Oregon region. A combined European alliance (Austria, France, Prussia, and Russia) was seeking to reclaim Latin American colonies that had declared independence during the Napoleonic Wars.

Enduring Issues 9

President Monroe's Secretary of State, **John Quincy Adams**, urged the President to take action in the form of a warning to Europe that there would be no more colonization of the Western Hemisphere. The U.S. pledged it would not interfere with existing colonies, and reiterated its determination to remain aloof of European affairs. The statement became known as the **Monroe Doctrine**. It introduced a U.S. presence in world affairs and was successful in discouraging the European alliance. It continues as a major element in U.S. policy.

Questions

1 Which is part of the *unwritten constitution?*
  1 bicameral legislatures
  2 political parties
  3 the elastic clause
  4 the electoral college

2 The purpose of Alexander Hamilton's financial plans was to
  1 create a stable economy.
  2 balance the budget.
  3 rule through a bureaucracy.
  4 tax the rich.

3 The precedent of judicial review was set in
  1 *Gibbons v. Ogden*
  2 *Fletcher v. Peck*
  3 *McCulloch v. Maryland*
  4 *Marbury v. Madison*

Base your answers to questions 4-6 on the speaker statements below.

SPEAKER A: Government could not function very well without them. The flow of information they provide to Congress and the federal agencies is vital to our democratic system.

SPEAKER B: Yes, but the secrecy under which they generally operate makes me suspicious that they are influencing lawmakers in improper ways.

SPEAKER C: Don't forget that they not only try to influence government opinion, but they try to shape national public opinion to create a favorable climate for their viewpoint.

SPEAKER D: That's true. Any politician who ignores 40,000 letters from members of these groups does so at great risk. We have to pay attention to them whether we accept their views or not.

4 Which group are the speakers discussing?
  1 lawyers
  2 reporters
  3 lobbyists
  4 bureaucrats

5 Which speaker is most concerned with the impact on democratic government of the methods used by this group?
  1 A   3 C
  2 B   4 D

6 Which speaker implies that lawmakers frequently have to deal with subjects about which they know very little?
  1 A   3 C
  2 B   4 D

7 A Democratic-Republican most probably favored
  1 loose construction using the elastic clause.
  2 high protective tariffs.
  3 strong states' rights.
  4 the Bank of the United States.

8　George Washington chose able-bodied, intelligent men to serve as the first heads of the first executive departments. The disagreements between two of those men, Hamilton and Jefferson, led to
　1　development of the nation's first two political parties.
　2　an amendment to abolish cabinets.
　3　war between the U.S. and France.
　4　an embargo on foreign trade.

9　Which of the following *first* applied the idea of judicial review to state laws?
　1　McCulloch decision
　2　Marbury decision
　3　Fletcher v. Peck
　4　Louisiana Purchase

10　The institution of traditions such as judicial review, the President's Cabinet, and political parties illustrates the
　1　inadequacy of the Constitution in dealing with changes and conflicts.
　2　debt America owes to the Federalists and Democratic-Republicans.
　3　flexibility of the American governmental system.
　4　concept of strict construction of the Constitution.

11　Any part of the *unwritten constitution* may formally become part of the U.S. Constitution by
　1　Congressional statute.
　2　amendment.
　3　tradition.
　4　referendum.

12　In the United States, the exercise of the power of judicial review requires
　1　amending the Federal Constitution.
　2　interpreting the Federal Constitution.
　3　applying the elastic clause to the Constitution.
　4　distributing power outlined in the Constitution.

13　*"The great rule of conduct for us in regard to foreign nations is, in extending our commercial relations, to have with them as little political connection as possible."*
　Which foreign policy flows from these words of President Washington?
　1　supporting a particular faction in an internal conflict
　2　entering into trade agreements with other nations
　3　providing military aid to developing nations
　4　signing a mutual defense pact

14　Jefferson's embargo policy can best be explained as
　1　favoring the British over the French.
　2　favoring the French over the British.
　3　an attempt to keep out of the Napoleonic Wars.
　4　a violation of loose construction of the Constitution.

15　A study of early United States territorial acquisitions and treaties illustrates
　1　the lack of European nations that had interests in North America.
　2　land was acquired through force and negotiation.
　3　a failure of democracy to grow with geographic expansion.
　4　that early Presidents were constrained by strict interpretation of the Constitution.

16 The policy exhibited in the cartoon above is known as
   1   the Monroe Doctrine.
   2   the Embargo Act.
   3   Manifest Destiny.
   4   the Whiskey Rebellion.
17 The events surrounding the War of 1812
   1   forced Americans to seek defense alliances.
   2   increased interest in western lands.
   3   stopped European nations from settling colonies.
   4   were caused by strict construction of the Constitution.
18 The 19th century belief in a "divine mission" to expand U.S. territory is known as
   1   the Monroe Doctrine.
   2   strict constructionism.
   3   Manifest Destiny.
   4   neutrality.
19 The Monroe Doctrine was instituted because
   1   America wished to justify its policy of territorial expansion.
   2   European powers appeared to threaten the security of the Western Hemisphere.
   3   U.S. military power was superior to that of any European Alliance.
   4   the country desired to remain neutral in the Napoleonic Wars.

Essays

1   Since the United States Constitution was written, many generalizations have been made about it. Some of these generalizations are:

   •   The strength of the Constitution rests on its flexibility.
   •   The Constitution is basically an economic document.
   •   The Constitution is a "bundle of compromises."
   •   The Constitution has both divided and limited the powers of government.
   •   The Constitution combines European tradition and American colonial experiences.

   Choose THREE of the generalizations listed above. For EACH ONE chosen, discuss the extent to which the generalization is accurate, and use TWO specific examples to support your position. [5,5,5]

2   There are many political institutions in the United States that were not part of the original Constitution. These are referred to as part of the *unwritten constitution* and include:
- political parties
- the cabinet
- judicial review
- lobbyists

Choose THREE of the topics above and for EACH ONE define and give a specific historic example of the concept in action, and discuss a problem with the institution. [5,5,5]

3   A new nation has to deal with many political, economic, social, and international crises.
   a   Identify and describe TWO crises the U.S. faced during the period 1789-1825. [9]
   b   Discuss the methods America used to deal with EACH crisis and evaluate their success. [6]

4   The Articles of Confederation were in effect for almost nine years from 1781 to 1789.
   a   Describe the type of government formed under the Articles of Confederation. [3]
   b   Identify TWO reasons why this document lasted only nine years. [6]
   c   Explain how the situations in "b" were finally resolved. [6]

5   Certain theories at work in the first half of the 19th century led to the "Manifest Destiny" and the "Monroe Doctrine." For EACH of these policies,
   a   Explain the theory behind the policy. [8]
   b   Give an example of the policy being implemented. [3]
   c   Assess effect of the policy on the development of the U.S. [4]

6   George Washington, Thomas Jefferson, and James Madison left indelible marks on the future of government and politics. Discuss what EACH of these presidents did to influence the future of the American political system. [5,5,5]

7   The ideas that form the basis of the American governmental tradition have come from a number of different sources, including:
- Voltaire
- The Iroquois
- John Locke
- Montesquieu
- Jean-Jacques Rousseau

Choose THREE of the above, describe the ideas of each and show how their ideas were adapted in the U.S. political structure. [5,5,5]

II. The Constitution Tested

A. Constitutional Stress And Crisis
Developing Sectional Differences And Philosophies

The short-lived **"Era of Good Feeling"** followed the War of 1812. It was a period of national unity and political cooperation. President Monroe ran unopposed in 1820, and he received all but one electoral vote. Nevertheless, there were differences of opinion which would soon cause deep divisions among the sections of the country and their leaders. Bitter debates over the power of the central government, states' rights, and slavery would eventually lead to civil war.

The "Era of Good Feeling" soon fell victim to **sectionalism**, giving primary loyalty to a state or region rather than to the nation as a whole. In the South, advocates of **states' rights** proclaimed the states were supreme over the Federal government. The varied life-patterns which emerged in the United States after the War of 1812 were responsible for the sectional differences:

- The commercial **North** favored policies which would protect its industries from foreign competition, increase trade, and provide a strong banking system.
- The agricultural **South** hoped to increase its cotton exports and generally favored less interference from the Federal government.
- The agricultural **West** wanted Federal protection and transportation improvements but was against regulated banking.

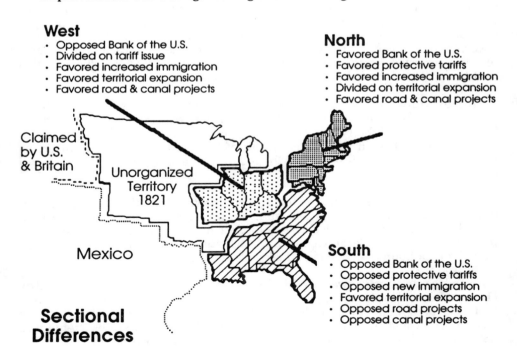

West
- Opposed Bank of the U.S.
- Divided on tariff issue
- Favored increased immigration
- Favored territorial expansion
- Favored road & canal projects

North
- Favored Bank of the U.S.
- Favored protective tariffs
- Favored increased immigration
- Divided on territorial expansion
- Favored road & canal projects

Claimed by U.S. & Britain

Unorganized Territory 1821

Mexico

South
- Opposed Bank of the U.S.
- Opposed protective tariffs
- Opposed new immigration
- Favored territorial expansion
- Opposed road projects
- Opposed canal projects

Sectional Differences

Enduring Issues 2

In 1828, Congress passed a very high protective tariff (called the "**Tariff of Abominations**" in the South). While its aim was to protect infant northern industries from foreign competition, Southerners felt the tariff could ruin their economy. High rates would increase the cost of foreign manufactured goods in the South and lead to retaliation by foreign nations raising their tariffs against southern cotton exports.

John C. Calhoun, a senator from South Carolina and later Jackson's Vice-President, secretly wrote the famous *South Carolina Exposition and Protest* denouncing the Tariff of 1828. Calhoun's doctrine of nullification held that states could declare acts of the Federal government unconstitutional, making such laws *"null and void"* in that state. If all else failed in such a controversy, Calhoun declared that states have the *"right to secede"* or leave the Union. This doctrine was in direct opposition to Article VI of the U.S. Constitution, known as the **supremacy clause**. This article makes clear that laws made by the Federal government must be adhered to by the states, and that states cannot pass laws that contradict federal law.

Other leaders rejected Calhoun's arguments. **Senator Daniel Webster** of Massachusetts, debating **Robert Y. Hayne**, successor to Calhoun's Senate seat, defended the power of the federal government stating that it is an agent of the people, not of individual states. Webster repeated Madison's point that only the Supreme Court could declare laws unconstitutional. He added that if the states could nullify federal laws, the Union would become a mere "rope of sand."

This debate over the balance of power between state government and federal government was not new. The writers of the Constitution had argued over it at length. The system of balance of power became known as the **principle of federalism**. In a federal system, power is divided. Delegated to the federal government are certain broad powers. The powers to take care of local matters are reserved for the states. However, the Constitution clearly indicates that the power of the federal government is supreme.

Andrew Jackson, born in the South and raised in the West, came into office as a hero of the common man. As an agrarian Westerner, he despised the "old aristocracy" of the North, that is, the powerful banking and financial interests who controlled the central Bank of the United States. However, as President, he was sworn to defend the federal Constitution in the controversy over the tariff.

At a reception, Jackson let his feelings be known in an official toast, saying, "Our Federal Union, it must and shall be preserved." The South Carolina state legislature officially declared the tariff null and void in 1832. Jackson prepared to send federal troops into the state to enforce the law. Vice-President Calhoun resigned over Jackson's actions.

Armed confrontation was avoided by a compromise offered by **Senator Henry Clay** of Kentucky. Clay introduced a bill to gradually reduce the tariff to levels acceptable to both North and South. This compromise bill was passed. The constitutional crisis subsided, but the issue of states' rights was not resolved. It would plague the nation for another generation.

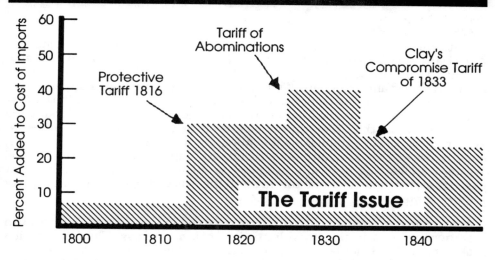

The South did succeed in its opposition to the powerful financial interests of the Bank of the United States. This time President Jackson took the South's side, agreeing that the Bank was a financial monopoly and made life difficult for debt-ridden farmers. In the eyes of the Southerners, the Bank was a corrupt tool of northern financiers which kept interest rates high and made borrowing difficult for agricultural interests. In its place, they wanted state chartered banks more sensitive to the needs of each region.

The Bank's charter was not up for renewal until 1836, but Whig candidate Henry Clay and his supporters tried to have it renewed in 1832, making it an issue in Jackson's bid for re-election. Many originally questioned the authority of Congress to set up such a national bank, saying the power was not specifically mentioned in the Constitution.

In his *McCulloch v. Maryland* decision in 1819, **Chief Justice John Marshall** said that Congress is given **implied power** in the Constitution's Article I, Section 8 to do what is *"necessary and proper"* to carry out its **delegated powers**. According to Marshall, the Bank of the United States was a constitutionally proper use of the **elastic clause**. In the same case, Marshall also ruled on the supremacy of the federal law, saying that the state of Maryland had no right to interfere with the functioning of a federal agency like the Bank.

> Enduring
> Issues
> **3**

Despite all this, the Bank died at the hands of President Jackson. Early in 1832, he vetoed the recharter bill, indicating his interpretation was that the Bank was a misuse of government power to create privileges for the rich at the expense of *"the humble members of the society."*

In actuality, the Bank did provide some economic stability for the country. Ultimately, the Bank veto proved to be a disaster. Unregulated, the **"wildcat" state banks** proceeded to issue paper securities of little value. They made unwise loans and speculated in Western lands with depositors' money. When Jackson left office in 1837, the country was already in the midst of a long and dismal depression caused by his Bank veto.

Growth Of Democracy

Just prior to and during the presidency of Andrew Jackson, the number of Americans able to take part in the democratic process increased dramatically. When the Constitution took effect in 1789, most of the original thirteen states required voters and candidates to own a **specific amount of property** in order to participate in the democratic process. This began to change in the first half of the 19th century, as frontier states beyond the Appalachian Mountains were admitted to the Union. In these states nearly everyone owned property. With no aristocratic establishment dominating the economic and political life, equality was closer to reality. As a result, **suffrage** (the right to vote) in the Western states was generally extended to all white males. By 1830, most eastern states had followed the lead of the west, dropping most property requirements.

Another major area of political reform emerged in the "**Age of Jacksonian Democracy**" was in the **presidential election process**. The Constitution makes mention of neither political parties nor how presidential candidates are selected. Soon after the Constitution was adopted, a two party system emerged. Prior to 1828, candidates for the presidency were selected by **party caucuses** (leadership groups) in Congress. The general party membership played no part in the selection process. Voters began to demand a greater voice in party affairs.

Beginning in 1832, a new system began to emerge: the **national nominating convention**. Another reform was in how **Electors of the President** were chosen. The Constitution left this up to the states. In most states before the 1830's, the caucuses in the state legislatures chose the Electors. By the 1830's, most states were letting the people *vote directly* for the Electors.

These election reforms greatly increased the interest in Presidential politics among average citizens. Campaigning among the masses became necessary if a candidate wanted to gain support of the increasing number of voters.

Year	Popular Vote	% of Total Population Voting
1824	356,000	3.3 %
1828	1,155,000	9.5 %
1840	2,404,000	14.1 %

From the chart on the left, it is evident that while the popular vote was increasing, most people still did not go to the polls. The political reforms affected only **white males**. It would be many decades before women, blacks, or Native-Americans would be permitted to cast ballots.

Democracy bypassed Native Americans in the 19th century. As the frontier moved westward, settlers put increasing pressure on the federal government to remove the Indians from the land. Previously, the government had officially dealt with the Indians as if they were separate foreign nations, making treaties which were often broken. President Jackson proposed that they should be moved to a special **Indian Territory**, west of the Mississippi (the location of the present state of Oklahoma). Here, he claimed they would be free to practice their own ways and free of harassment by white settlers. Those Indian nations refusing to go peacefully were to be forcibly moved by the U.S. Army.

The Cherokee Nation sought to fight this **removal policy** in the U.S. Supreme Court. Despite the fact that Chief Justice Marshall ruled *(Worcester v. Georgia)* the state of Georgia could not take their lands, Congress took no supportive action for the Cherokee, and the takeover and forced removals continued. By the 1850's, settlers were streaming across the Mississippi and more restrictions and violence were in store for the Native Americans.

> Enduring
> Issues
> **8**

The Great Constitutional Debates

At the time the Constitution was written, many people believed that the institution of slavery would become unprofitable and gradually die out in the U.S. While this is what occurred in the North, the South saw the demand for slaves increase in the last decade of the 18th century and the early decades of the 19th century. The invention of the cotton gin, the expansion of territory, and the increased demand in the north and overseas for cotton cloth, all contributed to this rejuvenation of slavery. Article I, Section 9 of the Constitution officially ended the slave trade, but not slavery itself, in 1808.

As the sectional differences grew after 1820, slavery became a thorny issue, increasing the animosity among Northerners, Southerners, and Westerners. As with the tariff issue, legislative compromises on slavery played an important part in keeping peace among the sections between 1820 and 1850. Two specific issues related to the controversy were balancing the Senate representation between free and slave states, and allowing slavery in new Federal territories.

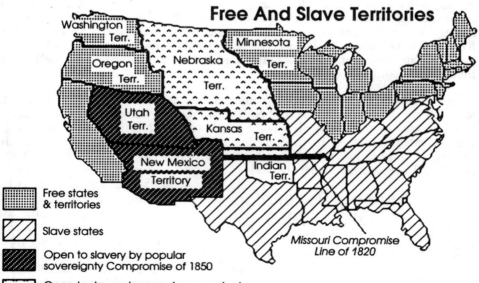

Free And Slave Territories

Free states & territories

Slave states

Open to slavery by popular sovereignty Compromise of 1850

Open to slavery by popular sovereignty Kansas-Nebraska Act 1854

Missouri Compromise Line of 1820

Southern states demanded that the states allowing slavery be balanced with those having abolished it so that there would be equal representation in the U.S. Senate. The free states of the North had almost twice the population of the slave states of the South. Therefore, control of the House of Representatives was never at issue.

In 1820, the question of the admission of Maine as a new free state aroused the South. **Henry Clay** offered the **Missouri Compromise**. Missouri would

Enduring Issues 1

be allowed to enter the Union as a slave state. Simultaneous free state - slave state admissions would continue for thirty years. By the compromise, territories north of 36°30" latitude would henceforth be considered free, those to the south, slave.

In the late 1840's, the new lands acquired in the **Mexican War** re-opened the controversy. An aging Clay once again offered a compromise solution, **The Compromise of 1850**. California would be admitted as a free state, but the slavery question in the rest of the new southwest territories would be determined by vote of the inhabitants, or what became known as "popular sovereignty." Runaway slaves could be hunted down and captured more rapidly in the north by a new **Fugitive Slave Law**. However, Clay's solution would be very short lived.

Abolitionism was on the rise. An increasing number of Americans began to oppose slavery as a moral wrong which violated religious teaching and basic human rights stated in the *Declaration of Independence*. These reformers wanted it abolished throughout the United States. Abolitionists fell into two categories: moderate and extreme. **Moderate abolitionists** wanted gradual elimination of slavery. They realized that the South was economically dependent and politically committed to slavery, and attempted to seek compromise solutions. **Extreme abolitionists** wanted an immediate end to slavery with no economic compensation to owners. They argued that because slavery was such a horrible wrong, it had to be ended regardless of the consequences. **William Lloyd Garrison**, a leading militant abolitionist, constantly stirred up the controversy through his newspaper, *The Liberator*. **Frederick Douglass**, a former slave, was somewhat more moderate. However, in his frequent lecture tours throughout the country, he called for immediate abolition.

The extremists gained little popular support. Northern textile interests feared a rise in cotton prices, and Northern laborers feared a drop in wages if freed slaves began to enter the labor market. Most Northerners could accept gradual abolition, first in the territories, then slowly in the states. Southerners, of course, rejected any talk of abolition. Prior to 1830, some in the South did accept the moderate idea of gradual elimination, but a series of aborted minor **slave revolts** (the most notable by **Nat Turner** in Virginia) plus the vehement writings of Garrison, turned many away from the idea. Most Southerners defended the institution of slavery. They pointed out that black slaves had been civilized by their white masters who christianized them, educated them, and gave them better living conditions than many northern factory workers. Of course, economic

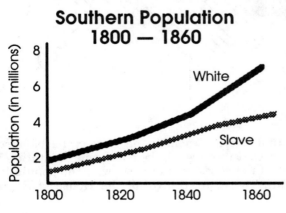

Southern Population 1800 — 1860

Population (in millions)

White

Slave

1800   1820   1840   1860

prosperity in the South depended on labor-intensive cotton exports. Actually, less than 25% of white Southerners owned slaves. Nevertheless, nearly all white Southerners supported the system because they someday hoped to own slaves, or because such an inferior status system had become an accepted part of their culture.

Abolitionists attempted to smuggle runaway slaves out of the South and into Canada by means of the **"Underground Railway,"** a series of secret "safe-houses," where runaways could hide in the daytime and receive care. **Harriet Tubman**, a former slave, was one of the most active organizers of the movement. Although relatively few slaves managed to escape, Southerners were enraged when many Northern states refused to enforce the **Fugitive Slave Law**. The sides in the slavery argument became more rigidly drawn in the 1850's. More extreme abolitionists and "hard-line" states' rights positions made compromise less and less feasible.

In the North, the abolitionist crusade gained momentum after the publication of Harriet Beecher Stowe's 1852 propaganda novel of harsh treatment on the plantations, *Uncle Tom's Cabin*. In 1854, when Congress passed the Kansas-Nebraska Act to allow the slavery issue to be settled by popular sovereignty, militant pro- and anti-slavery groups rushed to the territory, leading to five years of intermittent bloodshed. The Supreme Court fanned the flames of controversy in its 1857 *Dred Scott v. Sanford* decision. The Court, in a rare display of **judicial activism** for the time, ruled that slaves were property. Since the **5th Amendment** to the Constitution forbids Congress from depriving citizens of life, liberty, or property without due process of law, the Missouri Compromise and other actions taken to forbid slavery in some areas were unconstitutional. All territories were now open to slavery. Pro-slavery groups praised the decision, abolitionists urged disobedience to the court's ruling.

> Enduring Issues
>
> **3**

The two national political parties of the era, the Democrats and the Whigs, tried to avoid alienating sections by refusing to take a stand on the slavery issue. As a result, abolitionists were drawn first to a **Free Soil Party** and to what would become the modern **Republican Party**. The Republicans were relatively moderate in opposing the extension of slavery into the new territories. By 1860, the Democrats were so badly split into many different factions that the Republicans were able to gain enough electoral votes in the North to elect their candidate, **Abraham Lincoln** of Illinois.

Once again led by South Carolina, the Southern states decided that the policies of the Republicans under Lincoln would ruin the South, and one by one, began to secede from the United States of America. By May of 1861, eleven states had seceded and formed a loosely organized new nation called the **Confederate States of America** with former Senator **Jefferson Davis** of Mississippi as their President. When the secessions began in December of 1860, **James Buchanan** was still the **"lame-duck"** President of the U.S. He declared the actions by the Southern states unconstitutional, but claimed the Constitution gave him no power to stop the states from seceding. It is doubtful that Buchanan could have done anything to bring about a peaceful solution to the problem.

> Enduring Issues
>
> **2**

Lincoln was inaugurated in March of 1861. His inaugural address indicated that he wished to preserve the Union. He promised not to interfere with slavery in the states where it already existed. The South rejected Lincoln's offers. Federal forts in the South were attacked, and the tragedy of the American Civil War had begun.

Questions

1   A major reason for the growth of sectionalism during the 1820's was the
    1   treatment of the Indians by the Federal government.
    2   differing economic activities of each section.
    3   inequality created by the electoral college system.
    4   dispute over the active role of the U.S. in world affairs.

2   The "supremacy clause" of Article VI of the Constitution states that
    1   individual states will be permitted to declare Federal laws unconstitutional.
    2   the governor of each state has the ultimate decision on enforcing Federal laws.
    3   the Supreme Court can override Presidential vetoes.
    4   states are bound to obey all laws made by the Federal government.

3   In *Dred Scott v. Sanford,* the U.S. Supreme Court ruled that the Federal government could not prohibit slavery in the territories because the
    1   territories were under the jurisdiction of state governments.
    2   Constitution states that slavery is permitted in territories.
    3   Constitution permits popular sovereignty to settle the slavery question.
    4   Congress may not take personal property without due process.

4   The South objected to the 1828 "Tariff of Abominations" because the tariff
    1   encouraged increased trade with nations that had outlawed slavery.
    2   placed taxes on agricultural exports grown in the South.
    3   increased the cost of imported manufactured goods and could cause economic ruin of Southern plantation agriculture.
    4   increased the power of the Bank of the United States by giving it more funds.

5   Armed confrontation in the Constitutional crisis over the Tariff of 1828 was avoided when Henry Clay
    1   proposed a gradual reduction in the tariff rates.
    2   proposed the Missouri Compromise.
    3   agreed to change the "Supremacy Clause" of the Constitution.
    4   traded lower tariff rates for re-chartering the Bank of the United States.

6   During the 19th century, the expansion of the population affected the lives of American Indians in that most of them
    1   moved to urban areas in large numbers.
    2   sought to form alliances with other groups working for civil rights.
    3   were forced to leave their ancestral lands by the government.
    4   chose to adopt the culture of the white settlers.

7   Slavery did not become a lasting institution in the Northern states primarily because
    1   it was always considered morally wrong by the people there.
    2   anti-slavery societies were formed in the North.
    3   traders never brought any slaves to the North.
    4   it was unprofitable on small farms of the North.

8　The growth in democratic procedures in the 19th century can best be attributed to the
  1　equality of the Western frontier.
  2　social structure of the Southern plantations.
  3　increasing numbers of European immigrants.
  4　inability of the federal government to control controversies.
9　When Southern states began seceding in 1860-1861, President Buchanan
  1　ordered a military invasion which began the Civil War.
  2　suspended civil liberties in the border states allowing slavery.
  3　did nothing, fearing he might violate the Constitution.
  4　asked the Supreme Court to order the states back into the Union.
10　Southern defenders of slavery said that most slaves
  1　received a quality education.
  2　were better cared for than Northern factory workers.
  3　would be set free after a particular period of service.
  4　were allowed to take part in the political process.

B. Constitution In Jeopardy:
The American Civil War

While slavery was a leading cause of the Civil War, it was by no means the only cause. The issue of states' rights, differing economic and cultural patterns, the territorial expansion issue, and the rising power of the industrial North all contributed to the breakdown of unity. While initially fighting to preserve the Union, the North was later led by Lincoln into making abolition of slavery a major aim. Slavery was abolished at the end of the war, but bitterness between North and South remained long after the last shot was fired.

The United States:
Society Divided

As hostilities began, volunteers from both North and South rushed to join their respective armies. The most difficult decisions were made by those in the **border states** where slavery existed, but which remained loyal to the Union. Although much of the population leaned toward the Confederate side, Lincoln was able to convince them, sometimes by force, to remain in the Union.

People were mainly loyal to their section but support was by no means unanimous. It is doubtful that a majority of Southerners really favored secession, and a large number joined the Union forces. While most Northerners were willing to fight to preserve the Union, the goal of abolishing slavery was not universally supported.

Others in the North, called "**Copperheads**," demanded an immediate, negotiated settlement. Desertions were heavy on both sides.

States loyal to the Union

Border states remained in Union

Confederate States of America

Territories

War Between The States
1861 — 1865

Wartime Measures:
Unity, Stability, And Security

For the most part, President Lincoln acted within Constitutional guidelines as Commander-in-Chief, but he did exceed his authority on a number of occasions. Congress was not in session when the South began hostilities, and Lincoln did not call a special session. Most Americans realized the need for quick action, and did not question Lincoln's actions. Ultimately, Congress gave its approval to most of his actions, although his arbitrary implementation of martial law in the border states was later ruled unconstitutional by the Supreme Court (***Ex parte Milligan***, 1866).

Enduring Issues 9

Congress also stretched its powers by using the doctrine of **implied powers** under the **elastic clause** in passing a **military conscription act** (draft) when the first flurry of volunteers subsided. The draft was later a cause for discontent. For a fee of $300, a draftee could hire a substitute. Poor Northerners, especially recent Irish immigrants, objected to this discrimination. Severe **anti-draft riots** broke out in New York City in 1863. To protect Northern business and raise war revenue, Congress passed a high tariff in 1861.

Although Lincoln lacked the education and experience of some previous presidents, he dealt effectively with the crisis of the Civil War. One of his biggest problems was a military that was inexperienced at all levels. He went through difficult times with several commanders before finding one who could achieve victory, **Gen. Ulysses S. Grant.**

Lincoln had not committed the Union to a war goal of abolishing slavery. His only goal had been to save the Union. But, by late 1862, with the slaveholding border states held firmly, he issued the famous **Emancipation Proclamation.** The order declared slaves in the states in rebellion to be free.

Although it did not directly abolish slavery, the proclamation did give the Union a "moral cause for victory." The North also enjoyed enormous popular support in Europe. This discouraged Britain's government from giving financial aid to the impoverished Confederacy. Some European politicians had hoped the American "experiment in democracy" would crumble at last. Others hoped for trade advantages in the new, weaker political states that would emerge if the Union dissolved. Foreign actions to help the Confederacy consisted in trading war and food supplies. The Emancipation Proclamation made the war a moral as well as a constitutional struggle and diminished foreign aid to the South.

After four years of bitter fighting, with over 1 million casualties, the prostrate South surrendered in April 1865.

Lincoln And The Constitution

The Constitution States:	Lincoln's Actions:
Congress is given the power to raise and support armies.	Increased the size of the army without Congressional authorization.
No money can be taken from the treasury unless approved by law.	Withdrew $2,000,000 for military purposes without authorization.
The Writ of Habeas Corpus shall not be suspended, except in cases of rebellion or invasion.	Arrested and jailed anti-Unionists giving no reason. No permission was obtained from Congress.
No law shall be made abridging freedom of speech or the press.	Censored some anti-Union newspapers and had editors and publishers arrested.
Accused persons have the right to a speedy trial and impartial jury in the state or district where the alleged act was committed.	Even though U.S. civil courts were operating, he set up military courts to try Confederate sympathizers.

Questions

1   The Southern states were opposed to the election of Lincoln in 1860, because he
   1   proposed immediate emancipation of all slaves.
   2   stepped up federal enforcement of the Fugitive Slave Law.
   3   proposed the 13th Amendment to abolish slavery.
   4   hoped to stop slavery from spreading into new territories.

2   The existence of abolitionists in the South and "Copperheads" in the North during the Civil War indicated that
   1   there was no dissent in either region.
   2   foreign nations played a major role in the war's outcome.
   3   with rigid military discipline, desertion was a minor problem.
   4   not everyone supported the leaders of their section.

3   Which action of Pres. Lincoln was considered unconstitutional?
     1   constant replacement of Union Army commanders.
     2   removing money from the Treasury without Congressional approval.
     3   buying weapons from foreign governments.
     4   choosing Vice-Pres. Andrew Johnson from a slave state.
4   During the Civil War, Congress authorized a draft by using
     1   delegated powers.
     2   reserved powers.
     3   implied powers.
     4   concurrent powers.
5   Restrictions on personal liberties have been most common in the United
     States during
     1   economic recessions.
     2   constitutional debates.
     3   rapid urban growth.
     4   military conflict.
6   Lincoln's main goal from the start of the war was to
     1   abolish slavery throughout the nation.
     2   break the South's dependence on cotton.
     3   preserve the Union.
     4   increase the Federal lands in the west.
7   By suspending the right to a Writ of Habeas Corpus, the government can
     1   arrest individuals and hold them without disclosing the reason.
     2   tax individuals without passing Congressional acts.
     3   station troops in private homes.
     4   compel a person to be a witness against himself.

Essays

1   The ability to compromise is vital for effective operation of American
     government.

     a   Describe THREE instances in which compromise avoided conflict
          after 1820. [12]

     b   How did failure to achieve compromise during the 1850's lead to the
          Civil War? [3]

2   In the first several Presidential elections in the United States, only a few
     Americans were actually able to participate. This began to change in the
     19th century.

     a   Discuss the changes that took place in the electoral process which led
          to an increase in public participation. [7]

     b   Explain why, after these changes, most of the American public was
          still not able to participate in the elective process. [8]

3   Despite an attempt by the authors of the Constitution to find a fair balance between federal power and state power, many Southerners in the first half of the 19th century were still unhappy with this arrangement.

    a   Why were the Southern states dissatisfied with the federal government? [3]

    b   Discuss measures some Southerners threatened to take if disputes with the federal government were not resolved. [6]

    c   Describe some constitutional procedures that could have been taken to resolve these conflicts. [6]

4   Explain how the leadership of Andrew Jackson, Henry Clay, and Abraham Lincoln contributed to the success of the American system of government in the 19th century. [5,5,5]

5   The Constitution attempts to define and limit the power of the three branches of the federal government. Yet, there have been times when one branch tends to exceed these limits. For *each* example below, explain how the branch mentioned went beyond its constitutional limits:

    a   The Supreme Court in the *Dred Scott v. Sanford* decision. [9]

    b   Abraham Lincoln as Commander-in-Chief during Civil War. [6]

Unit Two

Industrialization of the United States

```
1865                    1875                           1885
├─────────────────────────┼───────────────────────────────┤

    • Reconstruction      • Grant Scandals    • Munn v. Illinois   • AF of L founded
        • Johnson's Impeachment                    • Little Big Horn   • Civil Service Act
         • Transcontinental Railroad   • Carnegie Steel Corp.   • Chinese Exclusion Act
```

Cultural Pluralism
Social Darwinism
Laissez-Faire
Urbanization
Gilded Age
Assimilation
Immigration
Reservations
Monopolies
Segregation
Unionism
Populism
Nativism
Socialism

1895   **1905**

- Jim Crow Laws   •Populist Party   • *Plessy v. Ferguson*   •NAACP
  •Sherman Anti-Trust Act   • Pullman Strike   •Spanish-American War
•Interstate Commerce Act   •Wounded Knee

I. The Reconstructed Nation

Reconstruction refers to the period from 1865-1877 when the nation was rebuilding after the Civil War. The two main political tasks became readmitting the Southern States to the Union and granting rights to the newly freed slaves.

A. Reconstruction Plans

President Lincoln started to plan the nation's Reconstruction. However, certain members of Congress did not agree with the President's philosophy. After Lincoln's assassination, conflict deepened between Congress and Lincoln's successor, President Andrew Johnson. Congress then took greater authority in Reconstruction planning.

Lincoln's Plan For Reconstruction

Abraham Lincoln believed that the union had not been broken, therefore the Southern states should not be treated harshly. Under this plan, regained

Enduring Issues **10**

Southern states (those that were taken over by Union troops) could establish new state governments as soon as 10% of those people who voted in 1860 took an oath of loyalty to the Union. High-ranking Confederates would not be allowed to vote.

Radical Republicans in Congress, who believed the Union had been broken and the South should be punished harshly, did not favor this mild plan. Prior to his death, Lincoln approved of a plan drawn up by Secretary of War Edwin Stanton which provided for military authority and provisional governments to be set up in the South. After Lincoln's assassination in mid-1865, Vice-President Andrew Johnson took control of Reconstruction planning.

Johnson's Plan generally followed Lincoln's. In addition, Johnson granted amnesty to most Southerners who took loyalty oaths. Steps for instituting new civilian governments were set up. They included drawing up new state constitutions prohibiting slavery and secession and ratification of the **13th Amendment** which prohibited slavery. Johnson's plan did not work. It was too lenient for the Radical Republicans. The white pre-war leaders regained power in the South. They used the **Black Codes** to block civil rights for the African Americans.

In late 1865, Congress took over Reconstruction. The radical wing of the Republican Party set up its own reconstruction plan involving military occupation.

Congressional Reconstruction

Radical Republicans in Congress had clearly defined goals:
- establish democracy in the South
- ensure voting and civil rights for all, including blacks
- confiscate and redistribute land ("40 acres and a mule")

Not all of these were worked into the final Congressional Reconstruction plan. The Republican-controlled Congress finally passed the **Military Reconstruction Plan of 1867**. Provisions included:

- the U.S. Army would have control until new governments could be established
- former slaves would be guaranteed the right to vote in state elections
- each Southern state had to ratify the **14th Amendment**
- each Southern state had to ratify a Congressionally approved state constitution

Post Civil-War Amendments

Three amendments to the United States Constitution were ratified during the Reconstruction years. Ironically, in each case, ratification would not have occurred without the mandatory approval of the southern states.

The **13th Amendment** (1865) abolished slavery in the United States.

The **14th Amendment** (1868) made blacks citizens by stating: "all persons born or naturalized in the United States...are citizens of the United States..." It prohibited states from abridging citizens' "privileges and immunities," depriving them "due process under the law," or denying "equal protection of the laws."

> Enduring
> Issues
> **4**

This amendment also declared the Confederate debt null and void, excluded former Confederate officials from holding office, and reduced representation proportionally for those states that denied blacks the right to vote. As a result of these clauses in the 14th Amendment, powers in areas such as voting procedures and education, once **reserved** to the states, increasingly came under Federal control. Supreme Court interpretations of this amendment have recently caused federal actions to prevent states from denying individuals their basic civil rights.

The **15th Amendment** (1870) prohibited states from denying the right to vote "on account of race, color, or previous condition of servitude."

Impeachment Of Andrew Johnson

President Johnson and the Republican-controlled Congress did not get along. Relations between the two became strained as Congress enacted provisions designed to silence and restrict the President. One of these was the **Tenure of Office Act** through which the Senate maintained the power to interfere with presidential changes of Cabinet personnel. This act was designed to protect Secretary of War Stanton who sympathized with the Radical Republicans.

When Johnson tried to remove Stanton without Senate approval, the House Judiciary Committee called for his impeachment and trial to remove him from office. In 1868, the House of Representatives (finding enough

Presidential Vetoes		Congressional Overrides
Andrew Johnson: (1865-69)	36	6 (16.6%)
All Presidents: (1789 - 1865)	21	15 (71.1%)

Enduring
Issues
10

evidence to go to trial) indicted Johnson. After a three-month trial in the Senate, the vote for removal from office was one short of the necessary two-thirds.

The acquittal established the precedent that removal from office should only occur in serious situations. Johnson, the only United States President to have been impeached, was allowed to complete the few months left in his term. Years later, the constitutional basis for charges that the Radicals used against Johnson were thrown out by the Supreme Court.

Federal, State, And Individual Relationships

The Reconstruction period saw changes in the way the federal and state governments related to one another. One of the major questions leading to the Civil War, namely states' rights and the ability to secede, was decided in

Enduring
Issues
2

favor of the Union. As a result of the post-war amendments, military occupation, and federal civil rights legislation, there was a growing federal (national) presence in state affairs. Much of the involvement revolved around the individual's right to use the federal government as an intermediary in state-individual disputes. This idea of federal protection of the individual would not be fully accepted and developed until the mid-20th century. The issue of states' rights continues today (modern civil rights movement, highway aid, etc.).

Questions

1   Pres. Johnson could not put his plan for reconstruction into effect because
   1   Congress disagreed with it.
   2   the Supreme Court declared it unconstitutional.
   3   the South threatened to secede if it was implemented.
   4   the plan was considered too expensive.

2   Interpretations of the 14th Amendment by the Supreme Court have
   1   given the states greater control over their reserved powers.
   2   placed heavy restrictions on Congressional powers.
   3   replaced state power with federal authority.
   4   increased Presidential checks on Congressional power.

3   The most accurate definition of Reconstruction is
   1   the period after the Civil War when the South was rebuilding its industrial base.
   2   increased purchasing by the federal government aiding industry.
   3   "picking up the pieces" after the Civil War to reunify the country.
   4   efforts of the South to develop economically according to the North's pattern.

4   Which is the best explanation for the large number of vetoes overridden in the Johnson administration? (refer to the chart below right)
   1   Johnson abandoned checks and balances.
   2   The Supreme Court ordered more than half of the overrides.
   3   Congress was controlled by Johnson's enemies.
   4   Southerners in Congress wanted to re-establish slavery.

	Presidential Vetoes	Congressional Overrides
All Presidents: (1789 - 1865)	36	6 (16.6%)
Andrew Johnson: (1865-69)	21	15 (71.1%)

5   Lincoln's plan for Reconstruction included
   1   laying the blame for the Civil War on the South.
   2   loyalty oaths to the Confederacy.
   3   establishment of new state governments.
   4   execution of high-ranking Confederate officials.
6   In order for a Southern state to regain entry into the Union under Johnson's plan, it had to
   1   renounce the right of secession.
   2   reaffirm the tenets contained in the doctrine of nullification.
   3   refuse to ratify the 13th Amendment.
   4   develop a plan to punish high ranking Confederate officials.
7   By late 1865, Congress took control over Reconstruction planning because
   1   President Johnson had been impeached and subsequently removed from office.
   2   the Radical Republican Congress did not favor the President's lenient policies.
   3   President Johnson had run out of ideas and asked Congress for leadership.
   4   Congress succeeded in vetoing the main policies of President Johnson.
8   Johnson's Plan quickly lost support because
   1   it appeared too lenient for Congressional leaders.
   2   not enough pardons were issued to former Confederate leaders.
   3   the voting rights of former slaves were denied.
   4   personality and power conflicts between the President and Congress were put aside.
9   The main difference between the Congressional Reconstruction Plan and the preceding Presidential plans was
   1   mandatory ratification of a Constitutional amendment.
   2   development of new state constitutions.
   3   role of the military in implementing Reconstruction policy.
   4   prohibiting slavery and granting civil rights to former slaves.
10 The post-Civil War amendments illustrate the
   1   growing power of the federal government to regulate Southern state governments.
   2   continued use of the doctrine of nullification by the South.
   3   federal government's power to insure the political equality of former slaves.
   4   failure of the U.S. Constitution to adjust to changing circumstances.

B. The North

In the post Civil War period, the North became more industrialized with the number of non-agricultural workers and factories increasing dramatically.

Civil War: Economic And Technological Stimuli

Initially, the Civil War hurt businesses in the North and the South as transportation and communication systems were disrupted. By 1862, the Federal government created an enormous market for war connected goods, munitions, ready-made clothing, etc. Vast profits were made. This capital was then used for future investment. Congress passed higher tariff legislation which promoted Northern industries.

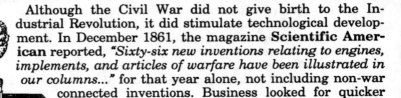

Although the Civil War did not give birth to the Industrial Revolution, it did stimulate technological development. In December 1861, the magazine **Scientific American** reported, *"Sixty-six new inventions relating to engines, implements, and articles of warfare have been illustrated in our columns..."* for that year alone, not including non-war connected inventions. Business looked for quicker ways to mass produce the desired goods. In industry and agriculture, the shortage of labor also contributed to mechanization. Sewing machines, which had been invented before the Civil War, became widely used to produce the massive amounts of clothing needed. Repeating rifles, the steam engine, and the use of iron-clad ship hulls gave rise to new industries and changed the course of warfare. The transcontinental railroad was built from 1862-1869. The gauge of railroad track was standardized, making for quicker transport. The **Bessemer Process** made steel for railroads plentiful, less expensive, and more desirable than softer and weaker iron.

Expanding World Markets

From 1865-1900, the United States enjoyed a favorable balance of trade, exporting more goods than it imported. Markets included Europe, Latin America, and the Far East.

Developing Labor Needs

The skilled and unskilled labor needed to fuel these technological changes were readily available after the Civil War. Immigration, unrestricted for most of the 19th century, provided a constant supply of cheap labor. In 1861, most workers in the United States were involved in agricultural work. By 1900, over 60% of American workers were in non-agricultural jobs.

Industrialization and the spread of the factory system changed workers' lives drastically. Machinery replaced the need for skilled artisans and the workplace shifted from the home to the factory. Within the new factory system, workers' actions

Industrial Era Imports and Exports

Thousands of Dollars

▬▬▬ Exports of U.S. Goods

━━━ Imports of Foreign Goods

1860 '65 '70 '75 '80 '85 '90 '95 1900

were dictated by the work bell and time clock. **Real wages** (amount of goods and services income buys) rose from 1860 to 1890. However, working conditions were less than ideal. Safety precautions were often non-existent. Ten and twelve hour work days and six day work weeks were the rule. Wages were so low that workers were forced to live in tenements and slum conditions. Most children went to work full time before they were 14 years old.

C. The New South

After Radical rule ended, Southern government and politics became dominated by industrialists, merchants, and bankers. The **"New South"** refers to the growing industrialization of the South after the Civil War. However, much of this industrial growth was tied to agricultural products, (e.g., textile mills). Many southern industries were subsidiaries of northern firms and dependent upon capital from northern banks.

Agriculture: Land and Labor

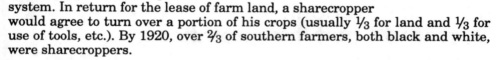

The devastation caused by the Civil War caused a significant change in southern agriculture. The number of property owners remained stable while the number of farms doubled and the acreage per farm decreased. The new agricultural system was one of tenant farming or **sharecropping**. This sharecropping system perpetuated the plantation system. In return for the lease of farm land, a sharecropper would agree to turn over a portion of his crops (usually ⅓ for land and ⅓ for use of tools, etc.). By 1920, over ⅔ of southern farmers, both black and white, were sharecroppers.

Since currency was in short supply in the post-war South, farmers would borrow on their only asset, their expected harvest, agreeing to pay a portion of their crops in return for credit. This is known as the **crop lien system**. High prices for seed, tools, fertilizer, etc. caused the farmers and the South to go deeper and deeper into debt. A single cash crop, cotton, was still the norm. As cotton production increased, cotton prices dropped causing further hardship for farmers.

Status Of Former Slaves

Enduring Issues
8

Most former slaves remained in agricultural occupations as sharecroppers or tenant farmers, the same occupations as before the Civil War. Thus, they experienced **limited economic opportunity**. Those seeking occupation in textile mills and other factory jobs were often refused employment. Although slavery was abolished and the franchise (vote) was granted by new Constitutional amendments, there were many restrictions on blacks' political rights. Southern state governments began instituting procedures to decrease the political power of blacks. **Poll taxes** of one or two dollars were assessed on those wishing to vote.

Poor blacks and whites were unable to pay and therefore could not vote. **Literacy tests** were given. **Grandfather clauses** exempted from the literacy tests whites whose grandfathers had been eligible to vote prior to the Civil War. Socially, segregation continued. Separation of the races had been a long-standing custom in the South. By the 1870's and the 1880's, a number of formal segregation laws were passed. These became known as **Jim Crow laws**, named after an early minstrel show character. Segregation by law or statute is know as **de jure segregation**. Blacks began leaving the South, but not in the tremendous numbers of the great exodus of the World War I era.

Struggle For Political Control

Blacks, exercising their power under the "Civil War Amendments" (13,14,15), elected many black people to public office (including fourteen Congressmen and two United States Senators). A white **backlash** developed. Organized efforts to quiet the black political voice developed. Through intimidation and terrorism, such groups as the **Ku Klux Klan** sought to "keep blacks in their place." Federal legislation was passed to outlaw the activities of the Klan.

Blacks usually supported the Republicans ("the party of emancipation"), but they played a limited role in party politics. The Democratic Party refused membership to blacks. The actions of legislatures and private groups sought to keep blacks disenfranchised. With the end of Reconstruction and the fall of Radical state governments, blacks lost political power. New **"redeemer" governments** (Southerners who took power back from the carpetbaggers) worked with the planter class to insure their own economic, social, and political goals at the expense of blacks.

14th Amendment:
Supreme Court Interpretations

The 14th Amendment guarantees *"equal protection under the laws"* and "due process" of the law to all citizens. In the later 19th century, Supreme Court decisions established the precedent that the amendment protected citizens' rights only against infringement by state governments. The precedents set in these civil rights cases remained in existence until the desegregation decisions in the 1950's and 1960's (see Case Chart on next page).

Enduring Issues 6

Emerging Debate Over Proper Role Of Blacks

During the last quarter of the 19th century, there came from the black community a number of voices addressing the proper role of blacks in society. **Booker T. Washington,** a former slave and self-made man, called for **"realistic accommodation"** and a policy of self-help. In 1881, he founded the **Tuskegee Institute**, a vocational school for blacks.

Washington argued that political equality could only be achieved after economic and property rights were secured. To achieve these, blacks needed to "Dignify and glorify common labor" and promote their own communities. When blacks achieved and proved themselves, their political rights would follow. Whites generally supported this policy of accommodation.

Citizens' Rights Court Decisions

Case	Year	Decision
Slaughterhouse Cases	1873	Decided that the basic rights under the Bill of Rights were not guaranteed by the federal government against state action. State and national citizenship were separate.
U.S. v. Cruikshank	1876	Decided the 14th Amendment guarantees did not cover the actions or misdeeds of private individuals against other individuals.
Civil Rights Cases	1883	Declared unconstitutional the 1875 Civil Rights Act which outlawed segregation. Stated the federal government had no jurisdiction over the behavior of private groups in race relations.
Plessy v. Ferguson	1896	"Separate but equal" doctrine upheld - equal protection requirements met if separate facilities were provided (in this case, railroad cars)
Cumming v. County Board of Education	1899	"Separate but equal" doctrine extended to public education.

The black critics of Washington's accommodation policy included **W.E.B. DuBois**, a New Englander with a Harvard doctorate. He called for a more militant approach to secure equal voting rights and economic opportunities. In 1905, a meeting of supporters near Niagara Falls gave rise to the **Niagara Movement**, a call for increased agitation. According to DuBois, black leadership was to come from the **Talented Tenth**, 10% of the black population, who were highly educated and able.

In 1909, a group of Progressives, both black and white, founded the **National Association for the Advancement of Colored People**. The major focus of the **NAACP** was the protection of civil rights and an end to the disenfranchisement of blacks. DuBois served as its major spokesman. The group appealed mostly to middle class, educated blacks and had little or no contact with rural, sharecropping families. By 1914, the NAACP had over 6000 members joined in 50 branch offices. Despite their differences, both Washington and DuBois agreed that blacks should develop basic middle class values of family and work.

D. The Grant Era

The popular Civil War general, **Ulysses S. Grant**, won his first election in 1868, by a close popular vote. A better warrior than president, his administration became known for political scandals and corruption.

National And Local Political Corruption

During Grant's administration (1869-77), a number of major political scandals became public. In 1869, financial speculators **Jay Gould** and **Jim Fisk** sought to dominate the **gold market** by purchasing all available gold and selling it at higher prices. Through Grant's brother-in-law, they convinced the President that it would be unwise for the Treasury Department to sell any United States gold. Grant agreed to the proposal for a time. When he reversed his position, the price of gold fell so low it caused a financial panic on 24 September 1869, **Black Friday**.

The **Credit Mobilier Scandal** also came to light during Grant's first administration. During the building of the transcontinental railroad, the Union Pacific Railroad had contracted with the Credit Mobilier Company to do the construction. This company swindled over 23 million dollars from the bulk of Union Pacific stockholders. To block a Congressional investigation, stock was distributed at ridiculously low prices to members of Congress and even to Vice-President Colfax.

The **"Salary Grab Act" (1873)** scandal involved Congress' doubling the pay of the President and raising its own salary by 50% for the previous two years. It was later repealed.

The **Whiskey Ring Scandal** involved revenue collectors and liquor distillers cheating the federal government out of tax revenue in St. Louis, Milwaukee, and Chicago.

In the Indian Service Scandal (1876), a House investigation found that Secretary of War William Belknap had accepted bribes in assigning trading posts in Indian Territory.

Corruption occurred even more frequently at the state and local level. One of the most infamous groups was the **Tweed Ring** in New York City. Political boss **William Marcy Tweed** embezzled some 200 million dollars through kickbacks, rent padding, etc. Cartoonist **Thomas Nast**, a German immigrant, gained fame depicting every issue of social or political significance.

One of his cartoons dealing with the corruption of Tweed was responsible for the apprehension and extradition of Tweed from Spain. Nast's barbed comments on political corruption popularized the political cartoon in America.

The "Solid South"

Political alignments became very distinct in the post Civil War South. Although blacks associated with the Republican party, white Southerners became staunchly Democratic, especially after the 1876 election. The **Solid South** refers to the consistent and overwhelming Democratic majorities in elections for almost a century.

Questions

1   The term "redeemer governments" is best defined as
   1   a biased term referring to more conservative Southern governments.
   2   the conversion of thousands of blacks to the Republican party.
   3   carpetbaggers' attempts to institute more democratic Southern governments.
   4   the election of great numbers of Southern Protestants to office.
2   Which did not serve as an obstacle to blacks exercising their right to vote?
   1   literacy tests   3   grandfather clause
   2   the 15th Amendment   4   poll taxes
3   The South began to vote overwhelmingly Democratic after the 1870's because
   1   pardoned Confederates voted against the party of Lincoln.
   2   black voters were being helped by the southern Democrats.
   3   Congress was in the hands of the Democratic Party.
   4   Democrats were free from the political corruption that plagued the Republicans.
4   While racial separation has existed in all areas of the country throughout American history, a predominantly Southern characteristic of segregation has been its
   1   appearance in urban areas.
   2   dependence upon the religious attitudes and beliefs of blacks.
   3   legitimization through state law.
   4   granting of full political equality.
5   Sharecropping is said to have perpetuated the plantation system because the
   1   slaves and sharecroppers were both owned by the landowner.
   2   slaves and sharecroppers were exclusively black.
   3   plantation owners were as wealthy and successful after the Civil War, as before it.
   4   sharecroppers in reality had as little economic independence as the slaves did.
6   The factory worker of the post-Civil War era experienced
   1   adequate safety procedures in the workplace.
   2   increasing real wages.
   3   shortened work days.
   4   appreciation from employers.
7   Which is an accurate statement about Southern agriculture in the late 19th century?
   1   Crop diversification led to large increases in farm income.
   2   A large number of farmers had liens on their crops.
   3   A decline in the world cotton supply caused a rise in prices and profits.
   4   Agricultural profit depended mainly on Southern textile mills.

8   During the years 1861-1866, Northern industry
  1   made vast profits which could be invested back into business.
  2   was hurt by a lack of adequate protective tariff legislation.
  3   was devoting much of its production capacity to overseas trade.
  4   halted new product development due to the fighting of the Civil War.
9   Labor market changes immediately after the Civil War included a greater
  1   reliance on imported raw materials.
  2   demand for equal pay for women.
  3   proportion of the population becoming involved in agriculture than
       before 1860.
  4   demand for cheap immigrant labor.
10   The 14th Amendment protects the individual's rights of
  1   due process and double jeopardy.
  2   equal protection and the right to vote.
  3   equal protection and due process.
  4   the right to vote and due process.
11   During President Grant's administration, he was
  1   able to apply his successful military skills to the presidency.
  2   guilty of poor judgement in his political appointments.
  3   able to stop corruption and scandals in national government.
  4   directly involved in virtually every scandal.

Use the cartoon on the right to answer
the next two questions.

12   The cartoonist is indicating that
  1   large numbers of officials make
       government decision-making
       very difficult.
  2   it is impossible to tell who is
       responsible for taking the
       people's money.
  3   builders are corrupt and should
       not be involved in politics.
  4   political bosses swindled the people of New York City.
13   Thomas Nast's cartoons made the public most aware of
  1   political corruption.
  2   racial segregation.
  3   the violence of the Ku Klux Klan.
  4   unethical business tactics.
14   Opponents of 14th Amendment's guarantees were pleased with the
     decision
  1   in the Civil Rights cases (1883) which prohibited segregation in public
       places.
  2   in *Plessy v. Ferguson* (1896) which allowed de jure racial separation.
  3   in *Cumming v. County Board of Ed.* (1899) which declared the 1875
       Civil Rights Act unconstitutional.
  4   of Congress to deny federal funds to any state which had Jim Crow
       laws.

15 The decision in *Plessy v. Ferguson* (1896) is significant because
  1   it declared the 1875 Civil Rights Act unconstitutional.
  2   it upheld constitutionality of the "separate, but equal" doctrine.
  3   the federal government overturned a state law.
  4   it shows the weakness of the Southern economy 25 years after the Civil War.

16 The goal of the Credit Mobilier Company was to
  1   cheat the government out of millions of dollars of liquor excise revenues.
  2   extend credit to the United States at exorbitantly high interest rates.
  3   secure a monopoly on the supply of gold in the United States.
  4   make millions of dollars by cheating transcontinental railroad stockholders.

17 *"...No race can prosper till it learns that there is as much dignity in tilling a field as in writing a poem. It is at the bottom of life we must begin, and not at the top..."*
This quote can be best attributed to
  1   Booker T. Washington.   3   Jim Crow.
  2   Homer Adolph Plessy.   4   W. E. B. DuBois.

Base your answer to question 18 on the following quote:

"(Black Americans) ...do not expect that the free right to vote, to enjoy civic rights, and to be educated, will come in a moment; they do not expect to see the bias and prejudices of years disappear at the blast of a trumpet; but they are absolutely certain that the way for a people to gain their reasonable rights is not by voluntarily throwing them away and insisting they do not want them..."

18 To achieve racial equality, the author would most likely advocate
  1   the philosophy of Booker T. Washington.
  2   increased agitation for basic political rights.
  3   greater reliance on the policy of accommodation.
  4   a revival of the Ku Klux Klan.

19 Credit Mobilier, Whiskey Ring, Indian Service, and Salary Grab were all indicative of
  1   racial prejudice in Southern politics.
  2   a high level of political corruption.
  3   government interference in the industrial economy.
  4   Grant's personal honesty.

20 Use the statement below to answer question 20:
"From 1850 to 1900 the number of factories in the United States went from 123,000 to 205,000. During this same time, the number of workers increased 10 times."
Which is most clearly supported by these figures?
  1   With the close of the Civil War, the returning soldiers had no jobs to go to other than those in the factories.
  2   As the number of factories increased, the work force increased at the same rate.
  3   An average factory in 1900, employed far fewer workers than an average factory in 1850.
  4   The increase in workers far exceeded the increase in factories.

E. The End Of Reconstruction

By the mid-1870's, Reconstruction was gradually ending, Radical leaders had died or left office, reformers had lost momentum, and others were looking to a new industrial focus.

Disputed Election Of 1876

The Democratic candidate was **Samuel Tilden**, reform governor of New York State. The Republican candidate was **Rutherford B. Hayes**, reform governor of Ohio. Tilden won the popular vote by a slim margin (under 275,000), but he was one electoral vote short of the needed majority. There were a number of disputed electoral votes, primarily in South Carolina, Florida, and Louisiana. The Constitution provided no procedure to decide these votes. Congress appointed a bipartisan (both Republicans and Democrats) electoral commission which decided the election in favor of Hayes.

Some scholars suggest a compromise was worked out between the Republicans and Democrats. Democrats agreed to support Hayes and treat blacks equitably. Republicans agreed to remove federal troops from the South, appoint a Southerner to the Cabinet, and provide federal money for Southern railroads. Other scholars feel that the Democrats realized that they did not have enough support. In 1877, Rutherford B. Hayes became the nation's 19th President.

End Of Military Occupation Of The South (1877-1878)

Although the greatest demobilization of federal troops from the South occurred within one year of the end of the Civil War (from 1 million to 57,000), the final troops were not removed until April of 1877. With their removal, the last Radical Republican state government collapsed signaling a return to conservative, Southern Democratic control.

Restoration Of White Control In The South (1870's And 1880's)

Although the passage of Amendments 14 and 15 and the actions of the Radical governments were designed to minimize the political power of conservative Southern Democrats, white Southerners("redeemers") regained control. The actions of the Ku Klux Klan forced Congress in 1870 and 1871, to pass two **Force Acts** and an **Anti-Klan Law**. These gave law enforcement officials the power to take action against the Klan. Prosecution was rigorous, but conviction was minimal. Nevertheless, the Klan was forced underground.

Congress passed the **Amnesty Act in 1872**, which pardoned most of the remaining Confederates. Eight Southern states were "redeemed" by 1876. Conservative Democratic politicians were in control. Regaining of political control by white Southerners is also referred to as "home rule." Southern attitudes of racial inferiority and discrimination were legitimatized by the passage of **Jim Crow laws** in the 1870's and 1880's. Later to become known as **de jure segregation**, these laws mandated segregation in virtually every situation.

Plessy v. Ferguson (1896)

Enduring
Issues
3

Louisiana passed a Jim Crow law requiring railroads to provide equal but separate accommodations for black and white passengers. As a test case to challenge the constitutionality of this legislation, Homer Adolph Plessy, a mulatto, sat in an all white car. He was arrested and found guilty. The case was eventually appealed to the Supreme Court. The issue involved a Constitutional conflict. *Did a state's reserved rights to pass legislation (10th Amendment) contradict the "equal protection" guarantee of the 14th Amendment?*

The Supreme Court ruled against Plessy calling Louisiana's creation of **"separate but equal accommodations"** a "reasonable use of state power." The actual equality of black and white facilities was never looked at. This judicial precedent remained in effect until the 1954 decision in ***Brown v. the Board of Education of Topeka, Kansas***.

Enduring
Issues
8

F. Impact Of Civil War And Reconstruction Political Alignments

After the Civil War, neither major political party was intensely reform-minded (with the exception of the Radical Republicans). Since the Republican and Democratic parties were composed of a number of special interests, they tended to shy away from specific stands on issues.

Republicans, who won the majority of post-war presidential elections, were supported by Northern industrialists and urban workers, Western farmers, veterans, and the newly enfranchised black voters. The black vote, although made impotent by state and local actions, remained basically Republican until a major realignment occurred during the New Deal of the 1930's.

The Democratic Party's major supporters were from the South and those industrialists and workers who did not favor Republican policies such as high tariffs.

The Nature Of Citizenship

Enduring
Issues
8

According to the **14th Amendment**, all people born or naturalized in the United States are citizens of the United States, and no state may deny them either **due process** or **equal protection of law**. This amendment was initially designed to make the recently freed blacks, citizens. In actuality, the Southern states passed Jim Crow legislation that severely curtailed the civil rights and equality of blacks.

The **15th Amendment** granted the right to vote to citizens regardless of race, color, or previous condition of servitude. However, black and white women were not given the franchise by this amendment. Black voting rights were curtailed further by the use of poll taxes, literacy tests, and grandfather clauses.

Industrial Development Of The North

The Civil War mobilized Northern industries to design, invent, and implement an entire range of new products. In addition, businesses developed new practices of record keeping and distribution to meet the huge demands made on them. The last half of the 19th century signaled a period of tremendous growth for American business.

Federal-State Relationships

Passage of the three post-Civil War amendments and the **1875 Civil Rights** Act gave the national government a possibility of increased control of state affairs.

Enduring
Issues
2

However, several decisions by the Supreme Court in the late 19th century trimmed this control considerably. The Civil Rights Act of 1875 was declared unconstitutional when a narrow interpretation of the 15th Amendment was implemented.

Strides in technology required policies of a national dimension. Developments in communication and transportation made the various geographic areas of the USA more accessible to each other. Now, the mechanisms were in place for the national government to grow increasingly stronger.

Questions

1　Southern state governments were considered "redeemed" when
　　1　Radical state governments finally lost power.
　　2　Southern Republicans gained power from Democrats.
　　3　President Rutherford B. Hayes was elected.
　　4　the KKK was forced underground after the 1871 Anti-Klan Law.
2　Which policy led to home rule by the Southern states?
　　1　the Plessy decision
　　2　removal of all federal Reconstruction troops
　　3　adoption of the 15th Amendment
　　4　passage of voting rights legislation
3　As a result of the Plessy decision, Jim Crow legislation
　　1　increased as it was found to be constitutional.
　　2　was ruled to unconstitutional.
　　3　spread to Northern as well as Southern states.
　　4　was outlawed by civil rights legislation in the 1880's.
4　The Radical program in the South eventually
　　1　died due to a lack of leadership and continued interest.
　　2　succeeded in implementing all of its policies.
　　3　became the program of the Democratic Party by 1875.
　　4　failed miserably with no achievements.
5　Reconstruction officially ended with the
　　1　passage of the 13th Amendment.
　　2　second election of Ulysses S. Grant.
　　3　removal of Federal troops from the South.
　　4　decision in *Plessy v. Ferguson*.

6   Which statement regarding the election of 1876 is true?
   1   The popular vote winner did succeed in finally receiving the electoral vote majority.
   2   The election's outcome continued the post-war presidential dominance of Lincoln's party.
   3   The bipartisan Electoral Commission voted unanimously for the Democratic candidate.
   4   Electoral disputes in three Southern states threw the election into the House of Representatives.

7   The decision in *Plessy v. Ferguson* did not take into account
   1   Adolph Plessy's racial background.
   2   the issue of reserved powers.
   3   the issue of equal protection under the laws.
   4   the actual similarities of black and white railroad cars.

Essays

1   Describe the conflict between the President and Congress over Reconstruction planning. Include in your discussion:

   a   reasons for the conflict;
   b   specific plan(s) of each side;
   c   resolution of the conflict. [5,5,5]

2   For each of the three post-Civil War amendments, explain how they made the United States more democratic. In your explanation, state the provisions of each and one hindrance to achieving this increased democracy. [5,5,5]

3.   The Civil War and its aftermath marked a period of tremendous change for the United States. Describe the economic, political, and/or social effects this period had on:

   a   the North;
   b   the South;
   c   race relations.   [5,5,5]

4   The decisions of the Supreme Court can have a significant impact on public policy in the United States. Trace the Court's 19th century interpretation of the 14th Amendment using at least three specific court cases. Be sure to include a description of the amendment, the issues of the cases, and their outcomes.   [5,5,5]

II. The Rise Of American Business, Industry, And Labor (1865-1920)

A. Technology And Industrialization

The Industrial Revolution changed the way goods were produced. Goods mainly produced in the home were now produced in the factories which utilized machinery, new power sources, and more unskilled than skilled labor. Industrialization first occurred in England then spread to other nations. There are still countries in the world, especially in the "Third World," which have not yet undergone industrialization.

England. England's early industrialization (18th century) was made possible by an agricultural revolution which increased production and used less labor. This freed up workers who gravitated towards cities. The cotton textile industry was the first to be mechanized. Later inventions shifted the workplace from the home to the factory where production increased. This led to a decrease in prices and an increase in the demand for cotton cloth. Much of the cotton for England's textile industry came from the southern United States. Water power eventually gave way to steam power. Better transportation systems developed: roads, canals, and later railroads. Numerous inventions by Europeans and Americans encouraged industrialization in Western Europe and the United States. Wars and a lack of one or more of the factors of production (land, labor, capital, and infrastructure) inhibited rapid industrialization in some countries (France, Italy, and Russia).

Germany. Germany did not become a true industrial power until its unification in the late 1800's under the policies of Otto von Bismark. Once underway, German industry made use of the best technology available. Government policies to create uniform banking and currency regulations, to centralize postal and telegraph services, and to create a high protective tariff and ownership of the railroads encouraged the growth of business. Business was encouraged to develop **cartels**, immense organizations which acted to monopolize industries. By 1900, Germany was rivaling both the United States and Great Britain in world markets.

Japan. As a result of the Meiji Restoration in the 1860's, Japan began a period of modernization. Foreign experts were asked to Japan. Japanese scholars went to Europe and America to study all manner of things, including industry, the military, and educational systems. They copied the best that the Western nations had to offer. By the turn of the century, Japan caught up to the Western industrial states. This caused problems of overpopulation in the cities, leading to increased emigration and shortages of available raw materials. This, in turn, led to Japanese imperialism.

Technological Developments:
Scope Of Development 1750-1860

Developments, such as those below, encouraged industrialization in many nations.

Date	Technology	Inventor
1764	spinning jenny increased thread production	James Hargreaves (Br)
1769	water frame increased thread production	Richard Arkwright (Br)
1769	first modern steam engine	James Watt (Br)
1785	power loom increased cloth production	Edmund Cartwright (Br)
1793	cotton gin	Eli Whitney (USA)
1800	1st battery with a steady stream of electricity	Alessandro Volta (It)
1800	magnetic effects of electric current	Andre Ampere (Fr)
1807	successful application of steamboat	Robert Fulton (USA)
1814	perfected the locomotive engine	George Stephenson (Br)
1839	vulcanization of rubber	Charles Goodyear (USA)
1853	Bessemer steel process	Henry Bessemer (Br) & William Kelly (USA)

Impact On People's Lives:
The English Example

In addition to the development of the factory system and the rise of capitalists, many changes occurred in industrializing nations. Population growth rates increased due to both an increasing birth rate and decreasing death rate. These were due to changes in diet as a result of the agricultural revolution and changes in medicine. In England, a managerial group developed out of the growing middle class, neither factory owners nor workers, which began to exercise increasing economic and later political power.

B. Pre-Civil War Industrial Growth:
Textiles And Iron

One of the most important commercial enterprises in the early development of the English colonies was the iron industry. The valleys of the Appalachian Mountains were a rich source of iron ore. The dense forests of this region provided the fuel needed to smelt the ore. The English colonists provided the skill to fashion it into useful tools.

The competition of these small colonial industries caused the British Parliament to pass a mercantilist **Iron Act** in 1750. The mercantilist system was designed to have colonies compliment the mother country's economy. The Iron Act forbade iron finishing mills in the colonies. Like many other mercantilist regulations, this was ignored. By the Revolution, iron production could be found in every colony.

The iron and steel industry could not develop into a substantial enterprise until increased sources of ore were found, transport made easier, and cheaper, faster production methods were developed. By the mid-1800's these things were beginning to happen. Iron ranges, like the massive **Mesabi**, in the Lake

Superior region were discovered. The Sault St. Marie Canal, connecting Lake Superior and Lake Huron, was completed in 1855.

Early in the 19th century, an Englishman by the name of **William Bessemer** invented a process for iron to be converted to steel. The Bessemer Process was implemented in Pittsburgh factories in the mid-1800's, and spread rapidly. As a result, pig iron production (only 30,000 tons in 1776) was at the 1.1 million ton level by 1864. As production increased, industry developed more machinery to shape and roll the steel, thereby increasing its usefulness.

Textiles. America's textile industry was virtually nonexistent during the colonial times due to a more strictly enforced set of mercantilist regulations. The first textile mill was built in the U.S. in 1790, in Pawtucket, Rhode Island, using plans smuggled out of England by **Samuel Slater**. This technology and the invention of the cotton gin in 1793 heralded the growth of the American textile industry. At first, the needed power came from New England's swift streams and rivers. Early production centered on making thread. Later, steam-powered looms were developed to produce finished cloth.

In 1813, the Boston Manufacturing Company, under Francis Cabot Lowell and Paul Moody, set up a textile factory in Waltham, Massachusetts. It was the first factory to house all the textile operations under one roof. The **Lowell System** also included the large scale employment of young women, who were housed in dormitories. It provided farm girls with a way to earn a marriage dowry. This system hit its peak in the 1830-40 period. Eventually, immigrant labor would supplant native labor, and the Lowell system and the salaries decreased. When the source of southern cotton was lost in the Civil War, the Lowell factory system died out.

C. Business Organizations:

Before the industrial revolution, **proprietorships** (single owner) and **partnerships** (small group of owners) were the most common forms of business organization. These forms were basically for small scale business operations. Nationwide operations demanded a more efficient form which provided wider sources of capital and gave protection to investors. The **corporation** was that form. It allowed for limited sharing of ownership through stock sales. Corporations are chartered by state authority and regulated as legal entities. Therefore, they can own property, lend and borrow money, sue and be sued, and pay taxes.

The Economics Of Scale

National territorial and population increases spurred corporate industrial expansion. Access to foreign markets was made easier, first with the fast clipper ships of the 1830's and then the steamship. Better roads, canals, and developing railroads made widespread distribution of goods possible. Increased profits resulted from large scale production and lowered per item costs. Communication technologies allowed for rapid transfer of ordering information and projection of production quotas.

Mass production, the increase of consumers, and better distribution led to changes in merchandizing. Department stores emerged to replace specialty shops. **John Wanamaker's, R.H. Macy's** and **Marshall Field's** became leading retailers in the nation's major cities. Most transactions were "cash and carry."

Gradually, some businesses began to make limited amounts of credit available to customers, and began delivery services. In 1869, **The Great Atlantic & Pacific Tea Company** applied department store retailing techniques to food. To reach a more rural clientele, companies, such as **Montgomery Ward** and **Sears, Roebuck, & Co.** created mail order merchandizing.

Forms of Business Organization

Form	Advantages	Disadvantages
Proprietorship	• owner close to customers and workers • has total control of management • receives all profits	• owner assumes all risks • limited capital available • one manager's perspective
Partnerships	• more capital can be raised • risks are shared • more management perspective	• profits must be shared • unlimited liability for owners • dissolves if one partner leaves
Corporations	• increased capital through sale of shares (stocks) • losses limited to investment • increased number of managers • ownership transferable • larger growth potential • research facilities possible • risks shared	• state & federally regulated • subject to corporate taxes • management removed from customers & workers

Questions

1 Which had a favorable impact on the development of the steel industry in the United States during the last half of the 19th century?
    1 creation of a gas-burning internal combustion engine
    2 discovery of the Mesabi Range resources
    3 the inventions of James Hargreaves and Richard Arkwright
    4 creation of the Lowell System

2 Industrialization developed first in England because
    1 it was the only country that was politically stable.
    2 it alone had an abundance of critical natural resources.
    3 all the major inventors and industrialists were British.
    4 increased farm productivity freed people to work in factories.

3 Which was an outgrowth of industrialization?
    1 increased urban growth rates
    2 decline in agricultural productivity
    3 decrease in population growth rate
    4 decrease in work related illnesses and health problems

4 America fueled the British Industrial Revolution, in part, because
1 some American raw materials, especially cotton, were central to British manufacturing.
2 American inventors were developing the majority of early machinery.
3 Britain bought the majority of its machinery from the U.S.A.
4 American skilled labor was working in English factories.

5 Which statement about the railroad industry in America is most accurate?
1 The northern transcontinental route was decided upon prior to the outbreak of the Civil War.
2 The railroad network which developed was one of the keys to America's industrial development after the Civil War.
3 Canals and turnpikes proved to be the most popular methods of transportation well into the 1850's.
4 There was not a substantial increase in the track laid during the last half of the 19th century.

6 Which statement is most likely supported by a study of American business growth during the late 19th century?
1 Innovation and invention had little to do with the phenomenal growth of industry after the Civil War.
2 Many of America's businesses were in place prior to the outbreak of the Civil War.
3 As businesses grew, more and more small companies entered and competed successfully with the big businesses.
4 Although the growth was nationwide, the business continued to remain localized.

7 Markets for American goods broadened during the 19th century because
1 local proprietors offered "cash and carry" service.
2 partnerships had limited capital resources.
3 corporations could be taxed as legal individuals.
4 national transportation networks emerged.

8 Which industry was most rapidly developing in the U.S. prior to the Civil War?
1 railroads   3 electric power generation
2 automobile manufacturing   4 oil refining

9 Which statement is an OPINION, rather than a FACT?
1 Most early oil was used to make kerosene as a replacement for whale oil.
2 By 1900 the U.S. emerged as the world's largest steel producer.
3 Even if the Civil War had not happened, the transcontinental railroad would have been built along a Northern route.
4 Development of heavy industry in the United States is directly tied to the increase in coal usage.

10 Which is an advantage of partnerships over proprietorships?
1 There is less capital to worry about in partnerships.
2 Owners know their customers better in partnerships.
3 Partnerships allow for sharing of risks.
4 Proprietorships allow for broader management perspective.

11 Which was an advantage of the corporate form of business organization?
1 single manager making decisions
2 limited legal liability for owners
3 localized range of business
4 limited capital resources

12 Which factor of production was most lacking in Germany's early attempts to industrialize?
   1   land and natural resources   3   eligible work force
   2   unified government   4   capital wealth

13 Which statement is supported by the chart on technological developments? (Use chart on page 71.)
   1   Early innovations and industrial inventions came from all continents.
   2   People from several different nations contributed to the technology necessary to industrialize.
   3   Absence of inventors from nations such as Russia proves there were no inventions of merit being developed there.
   4   Many important early industrial inventions dealt with harnessing traditional sources of power.

14 Proprietorships and partnerships proved to be inadequate for the needs of growing American business because
   1   they maintained too close a relationship with consumers.
   2   they responded quickly to innovations in production and merchandizing.
   3   transportation and communication techniques were inadequate.
   4   their sources of capital were limited.

15 Mail-order companies began to emerge in the late 19th century to
   1   bring mass merchandizing to rural areas.
   2   overcome the lack of urban mass transit.
   3   tap the overseas markets for American goods.
   4   maintain personal contact between proprietors and customers.

16 Development of both the colonial pig iron and the textile industry was
   1   encouraged by the policies of Great Britain.
   2   not affected by Parliamentary restrictions.
   3   regulated by mercantilist rules.
   4   not of great interest to the colonists.

17 Which is a major disadvantage of small business organizations such as partnerships and proprietorships?
   1   Owners have close contact with customers and workers.
   2   Transportation of goods is limited.
   3   Ownership of property is not possible.
   4   There is unlimited risk and total liability.

18 Which contributed to the enormous interest in iron production in America?
   1   the discovery of the Mesabi Range
   2   employment of young girls in the mills
   3   immigrant labor
   4   new mercantilist policies

19 William Bessemer
   1   brought the first plans for a textile mill to the U.S.
   2   discovered the Mesabi Range.
   3   set up the Lowell System in Waltham.
   4   invented a process for converting iron to steel.

20 The Lowell System
   1   created a new method of producing steel.
   2   improved the British mercantilist system.
   3   integrated all the basic operations in one factory.
   4   flourished during the Civil War.

21 A study of the growth of the textile and iron industries in early America indicates
1 the success of the British mercantile system.
2 the negative impact of immigration.
3 a pattern of gradual decline and final collapse.
4 development of industries necessary for American self-sufficiency.

D. Major Areas Of Growth In Business And Industry

Although the major basic industries were developing rapidly before the Civil War, capital accumulated during the war made the Gilded Age one of massive growth and expansion.

Transportation

Mass transportation allowed cities and the nation to grow. Prior to 1870, horses and mules pulled the main modes of urban transit. After 1870, steam (and later electricity) would power trains and street cars to provide commuter transport.

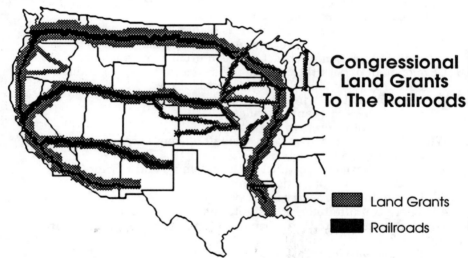

Congressional Land Grants To The Railroads

Land Grants
Railroads

From the 1830's, railroads developed rapidly, and soon supplanted river and road transport. By 1850, there was 9,000 miles of track in the country, mostly in the eastern sector. A northern transcontinental route was being planned when the hostilities of the Civil War intervened. Rail travel was crude until post-Civil War technology refined it. **George Westinghouse's air brakes** and **George Pullman's sleeping cars** were major contributions. On 10 May 1869, at Promontory Point, Utah, the **Central Pacific** and **Union Pacific Railroad Companies** joined the rails of the nation's first transcontinental line. Trackage increased rapidly after that historic meeting. In 1865, there were 35,000 miles of track in the country. By 1890, there were 200,000 miles. By 1900, transcontinental and regional rail networks had created a nationwide market. It caused standardization of time zones (Eastern, Central, Mountain, and Pacific) to accommodate scheduling.

In the 1890's, **Henry Ford**, an electrical engineer in Detroit's Edison Company, spent his spare time developing a gasoline internal combustion engine. In 1903, he opened the **Ford Motor Company** and applied mass production and mass marketing techniques to automobile production. By 1908, his Model T Ford was selling 10,000 cars per year.

Building Materials

New factories and office buildings of huge proportions demanded newer, stronger building materials. Masonry, concrete, and steel soon supplanted wood and stone. America's steel industry had blossomed during the heavy demand years of the Civil War, once localized industries were bought out or consolidated. The largest corporation in the world was formed in 1900, when **J.P. Morgan** bought out the Carnegie Steel Corporation and merged it with others to form **United States Steel Corporation**.

J.P. Morgan

Energy Sources

Coal. Commercial coal mines started in 18th century America, but consumption of coal began to increase as factories turned to steam driven machinery. Steel mills demanded massive amounts for smelting processes. Railroads needed coal for their locomotives. After the Civil War and into the 20th century, coal provided 90% of America's energy needs. Mining became a major industry and the increased demands made on miners made it an extremely hazardous line of work. It is not surprising that major labor disputes of the age centered on this industry.

Oil. The first oil well in America was drilled in 1859 near Titusville, Pennsylvania. An oil boom followed. The major industrial use was not as a fuel at this stage, but as a lubricant for machinery. Pipelines and refineries were built rapidly. Refining oil into kerosene for lighting and heating fuel made the demand for petroleum grow. In 1870, a young man named **John David Rockefeller** organized what would become the major monopoly of the Gilded Age, **The Standard Oil Company of Ohio**. In 1901, at Spindletop, Texas, the richest oil well ever drilled gushed forth, opening rich fields in the southwest in time to start providing petroleum for the automobile revolution.

Electricity. In 1882, **Thomas Alva Edison** started America's first electric power generating station in Washington. However, direct current could not be transmitted over vast distances. Invention and innovation overcame this difficulty. **George Westinghouse** developed alternating current. His electrical transformers made it possible to transport this current over long distances. Eighteen ninety-two saw the creation of the **General Electric Company**. In 1892, the **General Electric Company** was formed. In 1895, an international group of scientists recommended a hydroelectric plant to harness the power of Niagara Falls.

Communications

In the early 19th century, a practical telegraph was made possible by the development of electric storage batteries and improvements to electro-magnets. **Samuel F.B. Morse**, a landscape artist, developed the first **telegraphic sending devices** and a telegraphic signal code which bears his name. Starting in 1843, the federal government's support spread the use of Morse Code rapidly. Eighteen fifty-six saw the formation of The Western Union Telegraph Company. Ten years later, a permanent transatlantic cable linked the communications systems of Europe and America for the first time.

Alexander Graham Bell first transmitted the human voice over wire in 1876. The Bell Telephone Company, created the following year, set up local telephone systems throughout the Northeast. By 1900, the Bell System grew into the **American Telephone and Telegraph Corporation**.

E. Representative Entrepreneurs:
Studies In Concentrated Wealth And Effort

The business leaders of the post-Civil War era have been called both **robber barons** and **captains of industry**, depending on the speaker's point of view. Supporters of the term captains of industry point to the new, highly efficient industries they created. They cite the array of new products and captains' philanthropies as positive accomplishments of these men. Those who call the industrialists robber barons concentrate on the negative actions of the businessmen: exploitation of workers, unscrupulous business practices, and political corruption. In addition to those profiled below, other leaders included **J.P. Morgan** (money trust), **Philip Armour** (meat packing), and **Charles Pillsbury** (flour milling).

Case Studies: Rockefeller, Carnegie, Ford

John D. Rockefeller (Oil). In 1859, John David Rockefeller and his associates built a small refinery in Cleveland, Ohio, and thus began the creation of an oil empire. In 1870, he formed Standard Oil Company of Ohio. Using a variety of business tactics, including price-cutting, railroad rebates, and manipulating the effects of the Depression of 1873, he increased his position in the oil industry. By 1880, Rockefeller had control of nearly all U.S. oil shipping and refining facilities. This control over a limited aspect of one industry is called **horizontal integration**.

The **Standard Oil Trust** was formed in 1882 only to be dissolved ten years later by the Ohio Supreme Court. The trust was replaced by the Standard Oil Company of New Jersey, a holding company. This was dissolved in 1911, by the United States Supreme Court and separated into 34 units. John D. Rockefeller retired in 1897, as the richest man alive with a worth of one billion dollars. He then engaged in philanthropic endeavors, including creation of the Rockefeller Foundation.

John D. Rockefeller

Andrew Carnegie (Steel). Carnegie's story is a classic example of "rags to riches." Andrew Carnegie, a Scottish immigrant, began his career in the railroad business. He later entered the steel business, in which he saw real potential for the post-Civil War period. The company he created secured major aspects of the entire industry, as well as iron ore deposits and steamships to transport ore to steel mills. This control over all aspects of an industry is called **vertical integration**.

Andrew Carnegie

By 1900, Carnegie Steel Company produced over one-half of the nation's steel. In 1901, Wall Street financier J.P. Morgan bought out Carnegie and the **United States Steel Company** was formed. Carnegie retired and spent over 450 million dollars on libraries and other philanthropic works.

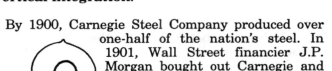

Henry Ford (Automobiles). Henry Ford, a mechanical genius, produced his first car in 1892, and created the Ford Motor Company in 1903. In 1908, he designed the **Model T**, a durable, economical automobile. Using assembly line and mass production techniques, he produced a car that the average American could buy. Like Rockefeller and Carnegie, Ford sought to control the total enterprise from raw materials to distribution of the final product. Although Ford paid high wages, he tolerated no opposition and refused to recognize labor unions.

Horatio Alger
And American Work Ethic

Early America's Calvinist virtues included hard work, an emphasis on self-reliance, and the shunning of idleness, extravagance, and vanity. These Puritan values included emphasis on the lessons of the Bible and thrift. In the late 19th century, these values were compatible with the ideas of laissez-faire economics. Hard workers would get ahead. **Horatio Alger** popularized these ideas in his books. Alger's "rags to riches" stories featured heroes who achieved great wealth through hard work, honesty, and thrift.

Conflict Between Public Good And Private Gain

The industrial leaders commanded vast power and control over resources, production, and distribution. As corporate power grew, critics began to question their business practices and right to control America's resources. As corrupt business practices became more publicized, people looked increasingly to the government to reassert itself to protect the public good.

Questions

1   Gasoline did not become an important fuel source until
    1   the use of the Bessemer Process.
    2   the invention of a gas-powered internal combustion engine.
    3   the development of the railroad industry.
    4   new sources of whale oil were found.
2   America's first major source of energy for industry came from
    1   oil.
    2   gasoline.
    3   natural gas.
    4   coal.
3   The increased use of the telegraph can be attributed to the
    1   inventions of Alexander Graham Bell.
    2   Federal government's backing.
    3   development of the Lowell System.
    4   discovery of the Mesabi Range.
4   In which state did the oil boom first develop?
    1   Texas
    2   Indiana
    3   Pennsylvania
    4   Kansas
5   Which correctly pairs the industrialist with his industry?
    1   Andrew Carnegie - oil
    2   John D. Rockefeller - steel
    3   Philip Armour - steel
    4   Charles Pillsbury - flour
6   Many of the industrialists, whose names became synonymous with the
    Gilded Age, worked to
    1   acquire their businesses horizontally - controlling all the oil
         refineries, or all steel mills.
    2   diversify their interests - owning steel mills and oil refineries, car
         plants, and flour mills.
    3   control their fields vertically - owning many of the businesses used to
         produce a product: refineries, pipelines, distribution center.
    4   amass fortunes with no conscious plan on how to achieve their goals.
7   The biography of which industrialist reads most like a Horatio Alger
    story?
    1   John D. Rockefeller
    2   Andrew Carnegie
    3   Henry Ford
    4   Philip Armour
8   During the latter years of the 19th century, people began to feel that the
    industrialists were
    1   without equal, creating a heaven on earth here in the United States.
    2   out of control, amassing vast fortunes at the expense of the common
         people.
    3   nothing out of the ordinary in the nation at that time.
    4   the saviors of the United States.

Use the information below to answer questions 9 and 10.

SPEAKER A: These men are a pox on America. They have bled it dry for their own personal glory and fortunes. To come out from their domination, something has to be done.

SPEAKER B: Business competition has been destroyed and the consumers have suffered.

SPEAKER C: An American beauty rose is created by sacrificing the smaller buds so that one large, strong one may result.

SPEAKER D: American business is changing and so is America. Both are growing and doing so admirably at this time.

9   Which of the speakers would most likely label the Gilded Age industrialists robber barons?
   1   *A* and *D*   3   *A* and *B*
   2   *A* and *C*   4   *B* and *D*

10 Speaker *A* would most likely support the
   1   continuation of laissez-faire policies.
   2   philanthropic work of Andrew Carnegie.
   3   creation of U.S. Steel Company in 1901.
   4   dissolution of the Standard Oil Trust by the Ohio Supreme Court in 1892.

11 Many of the industrial leaders of the late 19th century
   1   channeled some of their fortunes back into the community through charitable causes.
   2   retired as millionaires who did not engage in any philanthropic work.
   3   were part-time ministers in addition to their roles as industrial leaders.
   4   devoted their energies to improving their workers lives while still in control of their businesses.

12 By tracing the business ventures of John D. Rockefeller, it is accurate to state that
   1   the Federal government supported all of Rockefeller's business practices.
   2   his methods differed significantly from those used by other industrialists.
   3   he used a variety of techniques, many questionable, to achieve his empire.
   4   he supported increased government regulation of business.

13 Henry Ford's Model T was
   1   the first car made in America.
   2   an automobile in the price range of millions of Americans.
   3   affordable only to the wealthy.
   4   hand-crafted and made sparse use of mass production techniques.

14 The industrialists of the late nineteenth century were philosophically opposed to
   1   the ideas of laissez-faire capitalism.
   2   the development of labor unions.
   3   controlling the many components of their businesses.
   4   ridding themselves of business competition.

F. Business And Government Practices

In an effort to deal with America's business expansion and a "roller coaster" business cycle (boom periods, depressions, or panics), business began to develop new methods of organization and combination.

Laissez-faire And Government Support

Laissez-faire implies little or no government regulation of business beyond providing an atmosphere conducive for business development, including maintaining a stable currency, passing protective tariffs, and providing a stable domestic situation. The Federal government, from Alexander Hamilton's plan forward, basically supported and promoted American business. The guarantees of the 14th Amendment were interpreted by the Supreme Court to protect, not only individuals, but also corporate "persons."

> **Enduring Issues**
>
> **12**

Competition And Absorption:
Mergers And Trusts

The last few decades of the 1800's saw business merging and combining to eliminate competition, increase profits, and reduce inefficiency. The mergers were caused in part by the desire of business to secure itself from dramatic swings in the economy. There were several major financial panics in the last half of the 19th century and larger businesses could withstand them better.

- **Pools** were a method of voluntary combination in which a number of similar industries would agree to control output, set prices, and break competition. Agreements were often violated by members.

- **Mergers** created monopolies when industries, usually the strongest in the field, would buy out their rivals.

- **Trusts** were a more common form of combination. Chartered by a state, trusts had a board of directors which held the stock or trust certificates of its members. This allowed for greater control of members' practices.

After 1890, other forms of combination were developed:

- **Interlocking Directorates** occur when one or more persons serve on the board of directors for several corporations.

- **Holding Companies** control one or more companies by holding a controlling number of voting shares in these companies.

Railroad Pooling

Railroad managers in a certain section of the United States would meet to decide what percentage of business each would receive. They then fixed prices, established rebates for large volume customers and engaged in other inequitable practices. These policies were abhorred by most of the farmers who organized politically and demanded government action.

Changing Attitudes On Trusts

Many Americans began to question the tactics of big business. They looked to the government for leadership. The public accused business of destroying competition, the basis free enterprise. In his book, *The Wealth of Nations*

(1776), economist Adam Smith described **market capitalism**. He said competition and the ability to purchase goods and services freely in the market place are the bases of the market system. These economic activities must occur without artificial restrictions placed by government regulation or monopolistic business practices. The simple interaction of supply and demand should determine economic activities.

In the 1870s, farmers of prairie and western states were at the mercy of railroad shippers. These states enacted laws to regulate railroad abuse. The railroad owners quickly challenged these Granger laws. The Supreme Court of the United States initially upheld some **Granger Laws** in 1876 (*Munn v. Illinois*). The Court reasoned that the government could regulate private business when it was in the public interest to do so. *Wabash R.R. v. Illinois* (1886) changed this ruling (see pg. 108). It said states could regulate the railroads only within their state boundaries. *Wabash* said Congress alone could regulate interstate commerce. Farmers and the public turned to Congress for action. In 1887, Congress passed the **Interstate Commerce Act**. It regulated railroad rates and prohibited railroad pools.

> Enduring
> Issues
> **3**

Shortly afterwards, Congress passed the **Sherman Anti-trust Act** (1890). It outlawed monopolies and forbade "combinations in restraint of trade" (trusts, pools, holding companies, etc.).

G. Labor Unionization

In the industrial era, labor organizations developed rapidly. **Craft unions** organized workers by a particular skill and **industrial unions** organized all workers in a particular industry. Although a study of unionism is important to an understanding of American history, only a small percentage of the work force was unionized. By 1900, there were only one million union members from a total work force of 27.6 million.

Efforts At National Labor Unions

As industry grew, owners demanded more of their workers. As management became increasingly distanced from its workers, employees organized to gain recognition and better conditions. They established unions. Workers realized the strength of acting together and engaging in **collective bargaining** (workers uniting to seek common demands instead of doing it individually).

The **Knights of Labor** was organized by **Uriah Stephens** in 1869. It admitted all workers, from skilled to unskilled. Under the leadership of **Terence Powderly** in the 1880's, the Knights urged a number of basic reforms including an eight hour day, no child labor, equal pay for men and women, and establishment of cooperatives. During a strike in Chicago in 1886, a bomb went off and violence erupted. The Knights of Labor were blamed for these incidents, known as the **Haymarket Affair**.

The Knights' strength peaked prior to 1885, when a series of unsuccessful strikes, failure of cooperatives, and the Haymarket Affair turned public opinion against it and lost membership to the American Federation of Labor.

Samuel Gompers founded the **American Federation of Labor (AFL)** in 1881. The AFL emphasized **bread-and-butter unionism**. This means the seeking of better economic and working conditions for its membership, including higher wages and insurance. It did not seek to reform the entire industrial system. Gompers believed workers are concerned with **real wages**, the amount of goods and services that can be purchased by one's wages. The AFL accepted industrial capitalism and sought to improve conditions. They organized along craft lines, accepting only skilled workers. Local units set their own course of action, while the national unit lobbied for legislation, handled public relations, and provided the main organization. Its membership went from 140,000 at its start, to one million members by 1901.

The **International Ladies Garment Workers Union (ILGWU)** is an example of an industrial union. It sought to organize an entire industry and not distinguish among separate crafts within the industry. Eighty percent of the garment workers were women. Efforts were helped by the "Uprising of the 20,000," a general strike called by shirtwaist workers in 1909, and the tragic **Triangle Shirtwaist Co. fire** in New York City in 1911.

The poor conditions in the garment industry were publicized and the union won public support. This primarily female and immigrant union was strong and successful in achieving its goals.

Bread and Butter Unionism concentrated on bettering the economic and working conditions of its membership, as opposed to trying to reform the entire industrial system.

Unions and Education. In general, organized labor insisted on a free and public system of education as a foundation for democracy. In addition, they stressed inclusion of the practical as well as the liberal arts. Compulsory school attendance was another goal. By removing children from the work force, job competition was lessened.

Attitudes Toward Immigrants, Women, Blacks

Immigrants were excluded from many unions, although there were many immigrants involved in various trades. Some unions were openly hostile to women workers. Women were competing for the number of available jobs at lower wages. Some saw women as unfit to work. Blacks were usually excluded from union membership during this time period. They were often employed as **scabs** (strikebreakers). The Knights of Labor's policies included all these minority groups.

Struggle And Conflict

In an effort to secure their demands, unions went on strike. Labor violence sometimes erupted which caused fear in the public and decreased public support for unionism.

Major strikes

Homestead Strike (1892). An AFL affiliated (connected) union, the **Amalgamated Association of Iron and Steel Workers**, went on strike in a refusal to accept pay cuts at Carnegie's Homestead, Pennsylvania plant. Company President **Henry C. Frick** refused to back down and called in **Pinkerton Guards**. Violence erupted and the state militia was called in. The strike collapsed and the union was smashed. Union money was gone, likewise public support. Other steel mills refused to recognize unions in the steel industry until the **United Steelworkers Union** emerged in the 1930's.

Pullman Boycott (1894). George Pullman provided everything for his workers, at cost, of course, but would not negotiate with his workers. In 1894, in response to the Panic of 1893, wages were cut 25-40%, but prices charged for supplies in the company store, rent, etc. were not cut.

The **American Railway Union**, under the leadership of **Eugene V. Debs**, organized a boycott. The boycott spread nationwide and stopped the delivery of the Federal mail. Pullman got a court injunction (stop action order) and Federal troops were called to end the action. Management used provisions from the **Sherman Anti-trust Act** ("no combinations in restraint of trade") to secure the **injunction**. This illustrates the power of the courts to break a strike. Eugene V. Debs was jailed for six months, and the Supreme Court upheld his conviction.

Lawrence Textile Strike (1912). This strike, led by the **Industrial Workers of the World**, was their most notable and successful. A reduction in wages for Lawrence, Massachusetts textile workers and speedups, lead to the strike. The strictly disciplined strike and its songs, pickets, and rallies focused national attention on Lawrence. The American Woolen Company offered terms which met virtually all union demands, including wage increases and overtime pay.

Management's Position

Management's goals are to manage their companies without outside interference, increase productivity and profit with minimal cost, and maintain an open shop (right to hire any workers - union or nonunion).

Powerful Weapons Used On Both Sides

Unions	Employers
• strike	• lockout (refusing to let workers in)
• boycott	• hiring scabs (strikebreakers)
• strike fund - $ for strikers	• injunction (court stop action order)
• picketing	• yellow dog contract - workers agree not to unionize as condition of employment
• publicity	• blacklist

Most labor-management agreements are decided through the process of **collective bargaining** (negotiation). If negotiations break down, mediation or arbitration may be sought. A disinterested third party seeks to work out a solution in **mediation**. The mediator's recommendations are non-binding. In **arbitration**, both parties agree to abide by the decision of a disinterested third party.

Attitude And Role Of Government

Enduring Issues 12

The Federal and state governments passed legislation designed to curb the abuses of big business. Often these same laws, especially the Sherman Anti-Trust Act, were used to curb union activities. The Federal government also used injunctions and Federal troops against unions.

The Radical Fringe

Opponents of capitalism believed that large-scale means of production should cease to be private property, becoming instead the property of the community. Others advocated as little government interference with business as possible.

The **Industrial Workers of the World** (Wobblies) emerged from western mining struggles in 1905. It emphasized worker solidarity and used strike and sabotage. The Wobblies wanted to seize industries without the control of either capitalists or politicians. They emphasized class struggle. Leaders included **Big Bill Haywood, Elizabeth Flynn,** and **Eugene V. Debs.** The IWW rapidly declined in 1917, due in part to negative public reaction to the Russian Revolution.

Middle Class Supporters

The middle class, not only the working class, supported the betterment of working conditions. The **Women's Trade Union,** organized in 1903, was the first broad-based women's union. It lobbied for protective legislation, engaged in educational activities, and advocated women's suffrage and an equal rights amendment. It was dominated by middle class women. Generally non-militant, it dissolved by 1930. The **Consumers' Union** was comprised of groups who sought to support and purchase only those goods produced by factories which had approved conditions.

Questions

1   Business people turned to consolidation because it
    1   was subject to more government regulation.
    2   provided decreased profits for investors.
    3   encouraged business competition.
    4   helped insulate them from the uncertainties of economic cycle.
2   The goal of various types of consolidation was
    1   the creation of a monopoly.
    2   the increase of government regulation.
    3   diversification (to acquire different types) of holdings.
    4   closer relationships with the people business served.
3   A major tactic unions can use in labor disputes is the
    1   blacklist.   3   boycott.
    2   injunction.   4   lockout.
4   What was the main objective of the American labor movement when it first began?
    1   collective bargaining   3   increased fringe benefits
    2   a strong seniority system   4   increased vacation time

5   The *Munn v. Illinois* decision in 1876,
   1   set the precedent upholding laissez-faire government policies.
   2   upheld government regulation of private businesses in the public interest.
   3   ruled railroad pools were constitutional.
   4   signalled a change to less government involvement in economic matters.

6   Trusts replaced pools because
   1   the trust had greater control of member's actions.
   2   pools were ruled to be constitutional.
   3   the public supported trusts more than pools.
   4   pools were only found in the railroad business.

7   The American labor movement
   1   was strongly supported by the government and the public.
   2   developed as a response to industrialization.
   3   concentrated on reforming the capitalistic system.
   4   was dominated by immigrants who formed an important part of the Republican party.

8   Which action did Congress take to control the railroads initially?
   1   *Munn v. Illinois*   3   Interstate Commerce Act
   2   Sherman Anti-trust Act   4   Grange laws

9   Which is a valid statement based on the history of the labor movement in late nineteenth and early twentieth century America?
   1   Majority of workers were unionized.
   2   Primary objective of labor unions was to eliminate class differences.
   3   The Federal Government consistently supported union efforts.
   4   Union organization and tactics differed considerably.

10   By the end of the 19th century, which of these forms of business combination were unlawful?
   1   pools and mergers
   2   interlocking directorates and pools
   3   holding companies and trusts
   4   pools and trusts

11   Which method was used in railroad pooling?
   1   allowing supply and demand to set rates
   2   support of the anti-trust movement
   3   dividing up territory among member railroads
   4   strengthening the Interstate Commerce Act

12   By the end of the l9th century, public reaction towards big business was
   1   growing increasingly more positive.
   2   unconcerned with activities of the trusts.
   3   in favor of current business practices.
   4   increasingly concerned over abusive business tactics.

13   The primary goal of industrial workers in the 1870's was for
   1   more fringe benefits.
   2   higher wages and better working conditions.
   3   a wage and price ceiling.
   4   more say in the company's hiring policies.

14   The Sherman Anti-trust Act of 1890 was
   1   effective and rigidly enforced.
   2   strongly supported by big business.
   3   sometimes used to break up strikes.
   4   ignored totally by government and business.

15 Between 1865 - 1900, labor-management disputes were marked by
 1   a willingness to arbitrate on both sides.
 2   violence on both sides.
 3   public sympathy for strikers.
 4   government mediation.
16 Which is an example of laissez-faire government policy?
 1   the Supreme Court's ruling in *Munn v. Illinois*
 2   the passage of the Sherman Anti-trust Act
 3   Alexander Hamilton's financial plan
 4   the passage of the Grange laws
17 Beyond "bread and butter" unionism, basic reforms suggested by unions include
 1   eight hour work day.   3   less Federal regulation of business.
 2   increased use of child labor.   4   encouraging immigration.
18 The American Federation of Labor is designed on the basis of
 1   craft unionism.   3   industrial organization.
 2   socialism.   4   international workers' unity.
19 In the Granger cases of the 1870's involving railroad regulation, Supreme Court decisions said
 1   racial segregation on transportation facilities is unconstitutional.
 2   the regulation of business is solely a state power.
 3   government can regulate private business in the public interest.
 4   an end to the influence of the Populists was near.
20 AFL President Samuel Gompers said,*"The American worker is primarily interested in his real wages."* Real wages represent
 1   the minimum wages demanded by a union.
 2   the amount of dollars the worker receives weekly.
 3   the amount of dollars the worker receives annually.
 4   the amount of goods and services the worker's dollars will buy.

Essays

1   The industrialists of the late 19th century can be described as robber barons or captains of industry.

 a   Distinguish between these two terms. [3]
 b   Identify TWO industrialists and for each one:
   1) give a brief biographical sketch and
   2) a description of the tactics used to earn these titles. [12]

2   As America industrialized, changes occurred in a number of areas.

   CHANGES
   •   the whereabouts of the workplace
   •   relations between employers and employees
   •   business organizations and combinations
   •   types of businesses developed

   Choose THREE of the areas listed above and for EACH ONE, describe the changes that occurred and discuss one action that was taken by a specific group to deal with this change. [5,5,5]

3   The history of the railroad industry in the United States can be used as a case study to show how big business developed.

    a   Describe how the railroad industry dealt with the problems of size and organization. [5]

    b   Explain the impact of railroad policies on government involvement in economic affairs. Use specific examples. [5]

    c   Discuss the railroads' response. [5]

4   Various methods were used by corporations to control business during the Age of Industrialization

    a   Discuss THREE ways business tried to control competition in the late 19th and early 20th century. [6]

    b   Describe one advantage and one disadvantage of each method in section "a." [4]

    c   Briefly explain the impact of these methods on non-industrial Americans. [5]

5   A number of labor organizations sprang up in the late 19th century to respond to workers' needs and demands in industrial America. Two of these organizations were the Knights of Labor and the American Federation of Labor.

    a   Explain how each of these unions tried to help the worker using different methodology. [6]

    b   Assess the success of each of these unions in achieving their goals. [6]

    c   Identify and describe one other union that developed during this time period. [3]

III. Adjusting Society To Industrialism

The massive changes going on in America during the latter half of the 19th century required major adjustments in American life.

A. Impact Of Industrialization On People

Urbanization, immigration, and the demise of the American frontier left their mark on American life.

Urbanization And The Quality Of Urban Life

American industrial cities grew rapidly. By 1900, New York, Chicago, and Philadelphia each had more than a million inhabitants.

Attractions

Cultural offerings, including libraries, museums, and symphonies were available to the urban public. Urban schools, larger than their rural counterparts, offered a wider range of subjects and had a greater heterogeneous student population. The cities became the manufacturing centers of America, drawn to the vast labor supply and transportation hubs. Therefore, the jobs industrial America had to offer were plentiful in the cities.

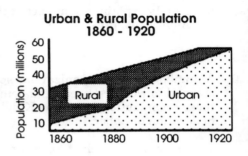

Urban & Rural Population 1860 - 1920

Problems

Despite attractions, cities were riddled with problems, especially for the lower classes. Into the late 1800's, a child born on a farm could expect to live a decade longer than one born in a city. Two of the biggest problems were lack of clean drinking water and a sewage system. Many of the cities were using the same body of water for drinking and disposing of raw sewage. Urban pollution also came from the main mode of transportation, the horse. This and overcrowded living conditions, caused tremendous health problems, including epidemics of tuberculosis and typhus. Acceptance by the 1890's of the "germ theory of disease" slowly brought about the needed reforms. Increased crime rates were also a problem. Gangs, pick-pockets, and worse bothered America's urban dwellers. Since many of America's urban population were immigrants, they were blamed for the crime problem. Police forces became larger and more complex during this period.

Technology

During the last half of the 19th century, America's cities were transformed from "walking cities" to sprawling centers (over 5-6 miles) with suburbs. They also grew in altitude with the rise of **skyscrapers** of five stories or more. Urban expansion came as a result of streetcars and omnibus that were electrified by the 1880's. **Elevated railroads** ("El's") and **underground subway systems** appeared in America before 1900, in Boston and New York City.

Cast iron skyscrapers of up to five stories gave way to steel framed structures which could soar to ten stories or more. Major buildings often housed departments stores such as Macy's and Wanamaker's. Lack of adequate housing, especially for the lower classes, led to the development of tenement houses. It was possible to house up to 4,000 people on one city block (see illustration below). Bridge building technology accelerated the growth of cities. In 1883, the **Brooklyn Bridge** connected Manhattan Island and Long Island. Soon afterwards, Brooklyn and New York merged into Greater New York City (1890).

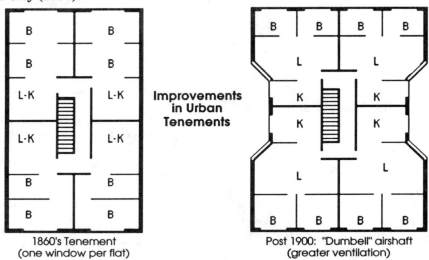

Improvements in Urban Tenements

1860's Tenement
(one window per flat)

Post 1900: "Dumbell" airshaft
(greater ventilation)

The Gilded Age In America (1877-1900)

Author Mark Twain called the era the **Gilded Age**. It was a time of great fortunes, industrialization, urbanization, and new philosophies, but exploitation and corruption made the achievements seem superficial. Rather than a true golden age, Twain and other social critics saw it as only a thin gold coating hiding a coarse and hypocritical society.

Social Darwinism, developed by Englishman **Herbert Spencer** and American **William Graham Sumner**, adapted Darwin's ideas on evolution and survival of the fittest to the industrial experience. According to this philosophy, power and wealth go to those most capable. A **laissez-faire** policy (governmental hands-off) fit perfectly into this idea. People should be completely free to accumulate and dispose of wealth as they see fit. John D. Rockefeller summed it up, *"I believe it is my duty to make money and still more money and to use the money I make for the good of my fellow man according to the dictates of my conscience."*

Some of the wealth of the upper classes was used to help others. **Philanthropy** was a matter of individual choice, although the upper classes believed they had a social responsibility to help those less fortunate than themselves. Following the philosophy that he expounded in his book, ***The Gospel of Wealth***, multi-millionaire **Andrew Carnegie** distributed his vast fortune in various ways, including building public libraries across the United States.

The wealth of the upper classes was apparent in the spending and decorating habits of wealthy Americans. **Conspicuous consumption** called for those who had money to spend it in ways that would be obvious. Large, elaborate homes and furnishings, summer "cottages" in Newport, Rhode Island, and elaborate parties were a part of this.

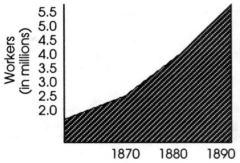

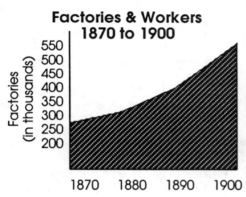

Factories & Workers 1870 to 1900

Work And Workers

Geographic, Economic, And Social Considerations

Working class people and immigrants tended to concentrate in inner-city neighborhoods. This provided ready access to jobs and others of the same socio-economic background.

Political bosses, such as **William Marcy Tweed**, and political machines actively sought the support of these groups by providing jobs and favors in return for votes.

Working Conditions. Division of labor and mechanization made work monotonous. **Sweatshops**, with many people working together in crowded and unsafe conditions for long hours, were common. Unemployment, both seasonal and structural (shut downs for unspecified periods of time) could be disastrous since most workers had no alternatives.

Machinery and practices such as speedups contributed to the hazards of factory work. Death and maiming occurred frequently. Hours were long, averaging ten hours per day - six days a week. Children and women were employed at wages much lower than those for men.

"Wage slavery" refers to the inadequate salaries factory workers were receiving. Real income was decreasing as prices were rising much faster than incomes.

Living Conditions. Many factories, mines, and the like set up company towns where food, housing, and supplies were bought directly from the company, often at inflated prices. In the cities, the working class often lived in tenements. New conveniences, such as the washing machine and telephone, made possible by industrialization, were beyond the reach of working class pocketbooks.

The Working Class Family. The working class standard of living rose for many; however, there was widespread poverty. Entire households often worked to bring in enough money to provide for essentials. Extra money was made by taking in boarders.

Women, Families, And Work

Traditional Roles. The Victorian ideal placed women on a pedestal, making them the "light of the home," protectors of home and hearth, and little beyond that. The reality of women's roles during the Gilded Age depended on class.

Upper-class and middle-class women most fitted the ideal. New labor saving devices liberated middle class women. Lower-class women usually worked just to maintain their existence. Working class women worked in the factories and shops in addition to providing a home life.

Jobs Available. Women, mostly lower class and immigrant, comprised 15% of the American work force in the Gilded Age. Their employment patterns changed dramatically. During the era, traditional female occupations, such as seamstresses, domestics, and other personal service occupations, decreased with the development of new business machines (typewriters, adding machines, and cash registers). Clerical work became increasingly dominated by female employees.

Family Patterns. Most families were **nuclear family units** (mother + father + children), although extended families existed. The average number of children declined to three or four per family. The divorce rate grew during this time. The median age of the United States was twenty-one in 1880. It was a young nation with a young population.

Problems of Child Labor, the Elderly, and Disabled. With most members of the family working, few families could care for elderly or disabled relatives. Birth rates declined. The average number of children per family dropped to three or four. Child labor prevented significant numbers of children from being educated. More and more people looked to the government to provide facilities and care which had been a traditional family role.

Role of Religion in a Pluralistic Society. White Anglo-Saxon Protestants (WASPs) made up the most of the population. The influx of predominantly Catholic and Jewish immigrants in the late 1800's brought a variety of ethnic groups and religious beliefs to the United States. Religious tolerance developed slowly, assisted by the presence of a diversity of beliefs.

The Growing Middle Class

Emerging Standards of Cultural Values. The middle-class benefited from the industrialization of the United States. They enjoyed increased leisure time and an improved standard of living. These contributed to an increase in consumerism. Middle-class salaries (approximately $1,000 yearly) could provide relatively comfortable housing.

Industrialization provided a range of new products for middle class consumers. Enterprising manufacturers found ways of mass-producing imitations of hand-crafted goods designed for the rich. Pressed glass imitated expensive crystal. Silver plate items looked like sterling silver. Advertising in magazines such as *McClure's*, *The Saturday Evening Post*, and *The Ladies' Home Journal* spread practical information about new home products.

Middle-Class Materialism and Morality. The growing middle class provided the purchasing power to fuel American industrial growth. Middle class values mixed certain moral beliefs with materialism. The middle class of the Gilded Age blended Christian charity and strong family loyalties with devotion to laissez-faire capitalism

Leisure Activities. As leisure time increased, so did the number of ways to spend it. Organized sports increased in popularity. They played baseball, croquet, football, basketball, ran track, rowed, swam, and cycled. People participated, but many also watched as spectators. Professional baseball teams first formed in Cincinnati and Pittsburgh. Teams from eight cities from Boston to St. Louis formed the National League in 1876. The railroads brought circuses, musical comedies, and vaudeville performances to small cities and towns.

Art And Literature

Rise of the Popular Press. Joseph Pulitzer's *New York World* and William Randolph Hearst's *New York Journal* popularized newspapers with the techniques of **yellow journalism** or **sensationalism**, exploiting lurid scandals, disasters, and crimes to sell papers. Advertising became a major industry. **Dime novels** (low-priced, adventure paperbacks) were the most widely read print material in the United States. Stories were primarily about the wild west, detectives, or science fiction. **Horatio Alger's** "rags to riches" stories were very popular.

Regional Literature. The lifestyles and flavor of particular geographic areas was captured by certain authors, using local expressions and dialects. Joel Chandler Harris' **Uncle Remus' Stories** romanticized the old South as Hamlin Garland's *Son of the Middle Border* did the Midwest.

The Western writers included **Bret Harte** (*The Luck of Roaring Camp*) and Mark Twain (*Tom Sawyer*, 1876, and *Huckleberry Finn*, 1884). But the realistic and ruthless side of life also emerged in Stephen Crane's *Maggie, Girl of the Streets*, Theodore Drieser's *Sister Carrie - An American Tragedy*, and Jack London's *Call of the Wild*.

Art and Music. Donations by the wealthy opened art museums and symphonies to the public during the Gilded Age. The Metropolitan Museum of Art opened in 1880 in New York City.

Craftsmanship Valued as Art. Industrially produced goods did not mean progress to everyone. Some people rejected ornate, mass produced items. An Arts and Crafts Movement developed. It emphasized quality, simplicity, and hand-craftsmanship. The **Roycroft Movement** began in East Aurora, NY. It manufactured quality designed items and ran a publishing business. Gustav Stickley, a founding member of the Arts and Crafts Movement, crafted simple oak furniture known as Mission Oak. Stickley's sleek, simple designs enjoy popularity even today.

Questions

1 Which statement would provide a correct interpretation of the information in the graph at the right?

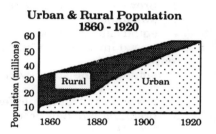

**Urban & Rural Population
1860 - 1920**

  1 During the Gilded Age, the total population of the U.S. decreased significantly.
  2 Urban population growth exhibited a greater increase from 1890-1900 than did rural population growth.
  3 For most of the latter half of the 19th century, America was an urban rather than an agrarian nation.
  4 After the turn of the 20th century, urban population growth leveled off.

Use the statements below to answer questions 2 and 3.

Speaker A: It couldn't be a better place to live. The museums, circuses, and els provide activities and possibilities virtually unknown until this time and are accessible to all.

Speaker B: The conditions in which I and other inhabitants live are disgraceful, no better than animals. Overcrowding, filth, and disease are our constant companions.

Speaker C: These people represent my work force - that is their lot. Iprovide their wages and they provide me with work to produce a profit which I enjoy immeasurably.

Speaker D: It has provided a showplace of new technology. Imagine - the Brooklyn Bridge, Macy's, mass transit! Why, the city has expanded enormously.

2 Which speaker would most likely have engaged in conspicuous consumption?

  1 Speaker *A*   3 Speaker *C*
  2 Speaker *B*   4 Speaker *D*

3 Which speaker would most likely disagree with the ideas of Social Darwinism?

  1 Speaker *A*   3 Speaker *C*
  2 Speaker *B*   4 Speaker *D*

4   Which statement regarding the working class in the Gilded Age is valid?
    1   They tended to concentrate in suburban neighborhoods.
    2   The number of industrial workers decreased as more and more machinery was being used.
    3. Urban political machines actively sought the support of the working class.
    4   Rising wages helped most factory workers to move into the middle class.

5   Adverse conditions met by the working class included
    1   minimum wage legislation.
    2   provision for overtime pay.
    3   sweatshops.
    4   equal salaries for all workers.

6   The social image of the "ideal woman" in the latter half of the 19th century was
    1   similar to the"super-woman" of the 1980's - career woman, wife, mother.
    2   a worker in traditional female jobs such as a seamstress or domestic.
    3   breaking into new occupations such as secretaries, clerical workers, or typists.
    4   in the home - providing a stable and comforting influence in the family structure.

7   At the end of the nineteenth century, America was a nation
    1   with an older population struggling with industrialization.
    2   with a highly sophisticated system of government care for the elderly.
    3   where man and women were on equal footing economically.
    4   where traditional family patterns were changing in the face of industrialization.

8   Middle class America in the late 19th century
    1   could barely afford to buy the new luxuries of the industrial age.
    2   benefited enormously and provided some of the main purchasing power of the age.
    3   exerted little or no effect on the total demand for industrial goods.
    4   did not purchase as much as the working class.

9   Which shows the change in leisure time during the latter half of the 19th century?
    1   The average work day increased by two hours for a total of twelve hours a day.
    2   The popularity of circuses and musical comedies declined.
    3   Few new forms of amusement were created at this time.
    4   Organized sports increaseded both for participants and spectators.

10 Yellow journalism can best be compared to
    1   the regional writing of Mark Twain.
    2   the "rags to riches" writings of Horatio Alger.
    3   the sensationalist tactics of Joseph Pulitzer.
    4   the publications of the Roycroft Press.

B. Immigrant And Changing Patterns

The United States is a "nation of nations." With the exception of Native Americans, everyone in the United States can trace their families back within 400 years to one or several immigrants. In particular, many people living in the U.S.A. can trace their heritage back to those who came through the **Castle Garden** or the **Ellis Island** immigrant processing stations located in New York harbor in the 19th and early 20th centuries.

Early Colonization And "Old Immigration" (1609-1860)

The earlier immigrants to the colonies were primarily from Northern and Western Europe. A popular term for these people was **Old Immigrants**. People who fall into this category arrived prior to 1890 when the frontier was wide open; came from Northern and Western Europe; and supposedly **assimilated** into the existing Anglo-Saxon- dominated culture easily since their customs and traditions were similar.

General Reasons for Immigration:

Political. English, German, and Scots-Irish dissenters (Puritans, etc.) fled oppression and civil war;

Religious. Many European governments had official state religions and persecuted other sects. Examples include: English Puritans, Pilgrims, Catholics, and Quakers; German Pietists, Mennonites, Baptists, and Jews; French Huguenots; Spanish and Portuguese Jews; Scandinavian Catholics, and non-Lutheran Protestants;

Economic. Famines and semi-feudal systems in Europe caused many to flee economic hardship. (Overall, this has been the major reason for immigration.)

Free v. Indentured Status. Not all European immigrants came to the colonies as free and independent citizens. A labor shortage in the New World was met in a number of ways. Those who had means found their own passage to the New World.

Poor people, sometimes petty criminals, especially from the British Isles, who could not pay their passage, entered into a contractual agreement working for four to seven years in return for passage.

Poor parents sometimes sold their children into such contracts. These were known as **indentured servants**. Impoverished Swiss and German immigrants, sometimes called re-demptioners, agreed to have their services sold in the New World to pay for their fare.

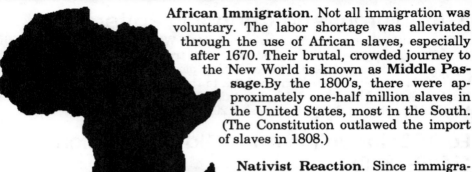

African Immigration. Not all immigration was voluntary. The labor shortage was alleviated through the use of African slaves, especially after 1670. Their brutal, crowded journey to the New World is known as **Middle Passage.** By the 1800's, there were approximately one-half million slaves in the United States, most in the South. (The Constitution outlawed the import of slaves in 1808.)

Nativist Reaction. Since immigration is so prevalent in United States society, the country has had to deal with frequent bouts of anti-immigrant sentiment, or nativist reaction. Prior to the Civil War, the most vocal nativists were some minority parties, especially the **American Party** or "**Know-Nothings**" of the 1840's. They were viciously anti-Catholic and became aroused as large numbers of Catholics, especially Irish and German, began to enter the country. They sought to restrict immigration and office-holding by naturalized citizens. To this day, much nativist reaction is connected to fear of economic competition, because impoverished immigrants often take jobs at low pay to survive.

Enduring Issues 8

Absorption by Conquest and Annexation. As the United States expanded westward, it not only annexed land, but also the people on that land. French-speaking people came with the Louisiana Purchase. Those of Hispanic culture came with territorial acquisitions of Florida, Texas, the Mexican Cession, and the Gadsden Purchase.

Ethnic And Geographic Distribution Circa 1870

- Total Continental U.S. Population - 39,818,440
- Almost even male-female split (slight male edge)
- Almost 5 million non-whites (4.8 million blacks, Indians, Chinese, and very few others)
- 12.3 million people in the Northeast, 13 million in the North Central States, 12.3 million in the South, and approximately 1 million in the West
- Vast majority of Americans (c. 92%) of Northern and Western European ancestry

---

The "New" Immigration 1890-1924

The Impulses Abroad. In the late 1800's, Southern and Eastern Europeans began fleeing high taxes, poor soil, and high land rents. Poles fled the wars and politics that led their country to be divided by foreign powers. Other Eastern Europeans fled harsh imperialist governments. Jews fled religious, economic, and political persecution.

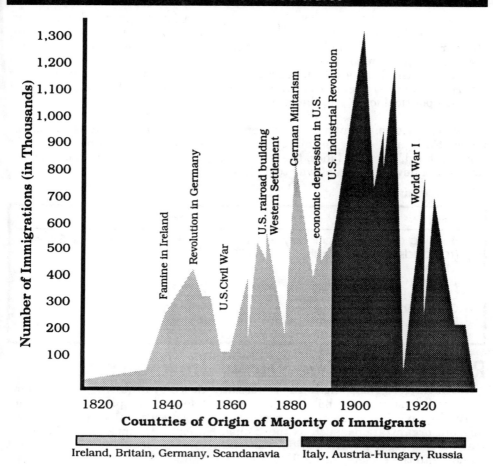

Number of Immigrations (in Thousands)

Countries of Origin of Majority of Immigrants

Ireland, Britain, Germany, Scandanavia   Italy, Austria-Hungary, Russia

Attractions Here. The American Industrial Revolution created a tremendous demand for cheap labor. Settlers were needed to develop the West. Many industries and states advertised in Europe for workers and settlers. New immigrants encouraged family and friends to come.

Urbanization. While most of these peasant peoples dreamed of farms in the interior of America, poverty forced the "new" immigrants of the post Civil War period to settle in cities, especially in the Northeast. They formed ethnic neighborhoods and enclaves which became **ghetto** areas ("Little Italys," "Chinatowns," and "Little Polands").

Americanization Process. Gradually, they learned the ways of their new home. Street life, work in factories, night school for adults, public and private school for children, immigrant newspapers, and ethnic organizations combined to **acculturate** the immigrants.

Impact on Family, Religion, Education, Politics. Many of the "new" immigrants were Catholics and Jews entering a predominantly Protestant country. Initially, many of the immigrants were men that travelled alone. Families were reunited after the men had secured enough money to pay their passages.

Many took advantage of the free public education America offered. (Jews were often denied access to public education in Russia and the Austro-Hungarian Empire.) The influx of immigrants in the cities attracted the attention of the political machines like New York City's **Tammany Hall**. In effect, both the bosses and immigrants benefited from this relationship. In return for favors ranging from finding flats and food to jobs, the immigrant gave his political loyalty to the boss and political party.

Contributions. Immigrant contributions to the United States are enormous. Each and every ethnic group has helped to build America, either through hard, physical labor, the use of special skills or aptitudes, or the discovery of a new or different way to do things.

Examples are:

Field	Groups
• Building of transportation systems (railroads, roads, canals)	Chinese, Irish, Italians, Slavs
• Mining	Welsh, Poles, Slavs
• Textiles/Garment Trades	English, Jews
• Optical Equipment	Germans
• Chemical Industry	French
• Stone masons / sculptors	Italians

Reactions To The "New" Immigration

Assimilation. Adapting to the American culture by acquiring new customs and traditions (sports, holidays, slang, and food) is a process called **acculturation**. This process was accelerated by educational institutions, immigrant organizations, such as the "Polish National Alliance" or the "Sons of Italy," and legal naturalization. **Assimilation** occurs when an immigrant blends into the society. Assimilation is much more difficult to attain than acculturation and seldom happens in the first generation.

Theories Of Americanization

• Homogeneous Culture theory is based on newcomers being changed into English-speaking and -acting Americans.
• Melting Pot theory holds that all immigrants are different, but are transformed (melted) into a new homogeneous, yet ever-changing society.
• Cultural Pluralism theory emphasizes the diversity of the inhabitants of the United States, but recognizes a common center of political and economic institutions, including language. Synonyms include: cultural symphony, cultural mosaic, and "salad bowl."

Nativist Reaction. Reasons for nativist reaction include job competition, belief that immigrants could not be readily assimilated into America, and belief that the "new" immigrants were mentally and physically inferior to the "old." **Stereotyping** (repeated distortion of reality based on ignorance) occurred. Religion also became an issue. After 1890, many groups sought immigration restrictions. Groups, such as the **Ku Klux Klan** and **American**

Protective Association, agitated against Catholic immigration. They argued that if greater Catholic political power continued, the Pope would be dictating American policies. Nativists were also anti-Semitic (against Jews categorically), anti-Asian, and anti-any other minority groups. Agitation by such groups often yielded Congressional legislation which formally restricted the flow of immigration to the U.S.

Governmental Restrictions: Background And Effectiveness

Chinese Exclusion Act (1882): *Background*: West Coast Chinese were regarded as cheap labor, strikebreakers, possessing strange customs and unlikely to assimilate. Many local and state governments passed laws discriminating against them, including segregated schooling. Boycotts of Chinese businesses occurred; violence flared.

Enduring Issues
8

Provisions: Prohibited Chinese immigration for 10 years.
Effect: Drop in immigration caused violence to subside.

Gentlemen's Agreement (1907) *Background*: Nativist fear over jobs resulted in fear of the "Yellow Peril." Violence erupted in the San Francisco area. President Theodore Roosevelt negotiated the Gentlemen's Agreement with Japan.
Provisions: Japan denied passports to Japanese workers intending to go to the United States. San Francisco promised to desegregate its schools.
Effect: Anti-Japanese agitation continued, but Japanese immigration ceased.

Literacy Test Act (1917) *Background*: World War I fueled fear of foreigners and called for immigration restrictions. Previous literacy test bills had been successfully vetoed. This one was not.
Provisions: Immigrants had to pass a literacy test in English or their own language before they could receive a visa to come to the United States.
Effect: Kept very few immigrants out.

Emergency Quota Act (1921) *Background*: As war refugees streamed into the country, Americans upset by the Bolshevik Revolution in Russia and the spread of communism in Europe, feverishly suspected communist infiltration of the United States. There was a belief that revolutionaries were active in the immigrant community. After a series of bombings in 1919, U.S. Attorney General **A. Mitchell Palmer** conducted a series of nationwide raids to round-up suspected communists. Denials of civil liberties occurred.
Provisions: Quotas were set for each country at 3% of the number of each nationality living in the United States in 1910. A general limit set of 350,000 immigrants a year.
Effect: Decreased number of immigrants.

Emergency Quota Act (1924) *Background*: Some people believed the 1921 Act's numbers were too high.
Provisions: Quotas set at 2% of the number of each nationality living in the United States in 1890; prohibited Asian immigration.
Effect: Lowered immigration from Southern and Eastern Europe.

Questions

1   American immigration laws during the period 1890-1924 permitted
    1   an increase in the number of agricultural workers in the United States.
    2   discriminatory practices against Northern Europeans.
    3   large numbers of immigrants to enter the country.
    4   "new immigrants" easy access to the United States.

2   Which immigration policy differs from the others in terms of how it was created?
    1   Gentlemen's Agreement
    2   Emergency Immigration Act of 1921
    3   Chinese Exclusion Act
    4   Emergency Immigration Act of 1924

3   Which statement concerning immigration to the United States is best supported by historical evidence?
    1   The diversity of the immigrant population created a pluralistic society.
    2   The quota laws were designed to prevent discrimination in immigration.
    3   Organized labor generally favored unrestricted immigration.
    4   Industrial growth led to a decreased demand for cheap labor.

4   Which of the following is true about immigrant housing?
    1   Immigrants tended to live in ethnically homogeneous areas.
    2   Acculturation was blocked by poor living conditions.
    3   Segregated ghettoes kept immigrants from participating in political life.
    4   Schools tended to hold back acculturation.

5   For which reason did most early-20th century immigrants to the United States settle in large cities?
    1   Cities provided a wide variety of cultural activities.
    2   Immigrants encountered little prejudice in cities.
    3   Peasant backgrounds made immigrants comfortable in urban environments.
    4   Jobs were available in urban factories.

Deaths and Death Rates for Baxter and Mulberry Streets in NYC in 1888				
	Population		Death Rates	
	5 years +	Under 5	5 Years +	Under 5
Baxter Street	1918	315	13.56	146.02
Mulberry Street	2788	629	15.78	136.70

(Source: Jacob Riis, *How The Other Half Lives*)

6   From the information given in the above chart, which generalization is true?
    1   The death rate for adults and children was the same.
    2   Baxter Street was a more affluent neighborhood than Mulberry Street.
    3   Children under the age of five had a high death rate.
    4   Preventive health care was widely available in the two areas.

7 Which is an example of nativist reaction?
  1 Immigrants settle in ethnic ghetto areas
  2 Passage of the Chinese Exclusion Act
  3 Political bosses helping immigrants in exchange for votes
  4 Government receiving stations for immigrants
8 Which group did not emigrate voluntarily?
  1 blacks in the 18th century
  2 Eastern Europeans in the 20th century
  3 Irish in the 19th century
  4 English in the 17th century
9 An immigrant family arrives in the United States in 1902. Its members
  include mother- age 37, father - age 45, daughter - age 10, son - age 15,
  and grandmother - age 68. Which member would have least likely
  assimilated into American culture?
  1 mother   3 daughter
  2 grandmother   4 father
10 Negative reaction to the immigrants coming to America at the turn of the
  20th century was based on
  1 the feeling that immigrants supplied necessary industrial labor.
  2 the idea that diverse cultures broaden the sense of equality.
  3 a belief that new groups were inferior to earlier settlers.
  4 the political unity of most national groups.

C. The Last Frontier (1850-1890)
The Frontier As Idea And Reality: 1607-Present

A frontier can be defined as the furthermost area of settlement. **Frederick Jackson Turner**, an American historian, presented a paper in 1893, entitled *The Significance of the Frontier in American History*. He argued that the chief influence in shaping the American character was the frontier. His thesis was that the frontier provided: social equality through easy purchase of cheap land; political equality; rise in nationalism; optimistic spirit; independence; and a safety valve for out of work industrial workers.

Land West Of The Mississippi

Under the **Homestead Act** (1862), one hundred and sixty acres of free federal land would be given to any homesteader who would work and live on it for at least five years. Thousands took advantage of this offer.

By 1900, four hundred million acres were settled under this program. Homesteaders and other settlers increased the need for the railroad and for farm machinery.

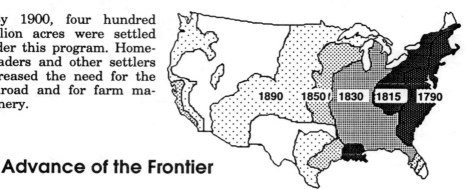

Advance of the Frontier

The Impact Of Industrialization

Food Supply Shipped East. Railroad connections made it possible to ship more and more food eastward. Chicago became a major terminal for cattle shipments and center of America's meat-packing industry. Eastern cities received grain and other foodstuffs from the American heartland.

The Spread of Immigrants. The West lured many immigrants from their homelands and their earliest jobs on the East Coast. Railroad agents often met them in the major eastern cities with offers to move west. In some cases, the agents recruited settlers in Europe. Many Western states opened up immigration bureaus in European countries.

Potential For Investment. There was opportunity in the West. Railroad development, lumbering, and mining employed many people. American and foreign investors earned fortunes. Gold, silver, and less glamorous minerals (copper, lead) attracted hundreds of thousands of people westward. Some ventures prospered, such as Montana's Anaconda Copper Mine. Most fared worse. Cattle ranching also drew thousands of investors, future President Theodore Roosevelt among them. Oil development spread westward, too. The largest oil strike of the era at Spindletop, Texas (1901).

Development of Key Urban Centers. Railroads accelerated the development of urban centers at hubs and along cattle routes. Omaha, Kansas City, Cheyenne, Los Angeles, Portland, and Seattle became bustling transportation terminals and commercial centers. (See railroad map page 76.)

Native-American Peoples: Status Since 1607

Native Americans had close relationships with nature. However, they actively altered and controlled their environment as well. Many Indian tribes engaged in farming. A major way they altered the environment was through the use of fire for communication, scrub removal, and farming practices. They suffered from seasonal scarcity of food supplies. Native-Americans often made full use of supplies. The buffalo provided virtually everything the Plains Indians needed.

Advancing Settlement Pressures

As more and more white settlers came to the New World, problems developed. Native-Americans did not understand European ideas of private ownership or the buying and selling of land.

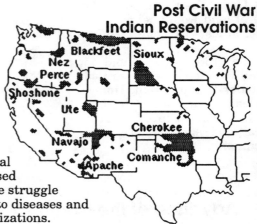

Post Civil War Indian Reservations

They believed in communal or tribal ownership. Cultural differences caused problems. Whites eventually won the struggle with modern technology, immunity to diseases and complex military and political organizations.

Treaties

Prior to the development of the United States, the British tried to successfully solve the problem of hostilities with the Indians by passing the **Proclamation of 1763**. It prohibited colonial settlement west of the Appalachian Mountains, reserving that area for the Indians. It failed. After American independence, many conflicts continued to arise.

United States government relations with the Indians included passage of:

· **The Northwest Ordinance** (1787) governed the area from the Great Lakes, to the Ohio and Mississippi Rivers. This Congressional law said the U.S. government would treat Native Americans in good faith. It would never take without their permission. In reality, it proved meaningless.

· ***Cherokee Nation v. Georgia***. Gold was discovered on the Cherokee reservation in Georgia in 1828. As prospectors moved in, the state of Georgia claimed authority over the federal land and the Cherokee objected. In 1831, they took their case to the Supreme Court. Chief Justice John Marshall ruled that the Cherokee nation was a "dependent state" but that the Court itself had no Constitutional jurisdiction to stop Georgia. He also said that only the Federal government, not the states, had power over Indian nations. Congress took no action.

Enduring Issues
8

· **The Indian Removal Act** (1830) authorized President Jackson to send the U.S. Army to move thousands of Native Americans. Native Americans remember the forced march from the Southeast to areas west of the Mississippi as **The Trail of Tears**. Large numbers died during the episode. Federal agents often bribed Native American leaders to agree to the removal treaties.

Legal Status

Native Americans relocated to the reservations lost their free and independent status. They became wards of the Federal government as if they were legally adopted.

In the **Indian Wars** (1850-1890), the U.S. Army arrayed its advanced technology, weaponry and skills against primitive people. They resulted in a near-genocidal tragedy. Westward migration of the white population increased tremendously with the discovery of gold at **Pike's Peak**, Colorado in 1858. As more and more settlers disrupted the Indian's lifestyle and livelihood, the clashes between the two cultures increased. Plains Indians and federal troops engaged in guerrilla warfare. Although the Indians won some battles, including the defeat of General George Custer by Chief Sitting Bull at Little Big Horn in 1876, they did not win the war in the end. The last battle was a one-sided massacre at **Wounded Knee**, South Dakota in 1896.

Enduring
Issues
8
Legislating Indian Life. By the 1880's, most Indian nations were relocated on reservations, usually on undesirable land. The people became wards of the federal government. In 1881, Helen Hunt Jackson's book, *A Century of Dishonor*, brought attention to the plight of the Indians. In response, Congress passed the Dawes General Allotment Act (1887). It was designed to give each Indian family head a 160-acre farm and American citizenship when they "civilized." It also provided for the selling of "surplus" reservation land. The act did not work. The land was poor and the Indians were unused to farming. Under the act, Native-Americans lost over one-half of their reservation land.

The Cattle Frontier

The Cattle Kingdom. The Spanish introduced cattle ranching to the New World. Eventually, the concept spread to other European settlers. By buying small acreage adjoining public land, the rancher had access to an enormous range for his cattle. This was known as the open range.

Cattle ranching increased rapidly from in the late 19th century. Investors rushed to cash in on its profits. It reached its peak in the late 1880's. Overgrazing, disease, severe winters, and falling prices eventually took their toll, forcing all but a few giant concerns out of business.

Homesteaders and Technology. After the Civil War, homesteaders (farming settlers) arrived in large numbers. The railroad, "the Iron Horse," brought settlers and cut through cattle grazing and buffalo hunting lands. Disputes over land rights occurred frequently between the settlers and the ranchers and between the cattle ranchers and sheep ranchers. The development of barbed wire allowed vast tracts of land to be inexpensively enclosed, cutting down on the amount of open range acreage. Enclosure angered the ranchers, but increased the settlers.

Justice on the Frontier. The frontier towns usually lacked an organized police force to keep order and control their citizens. Violence erupted frequently over land and mining claims. **Vigilante** groups (unauthorized secret citizen groups) were sometimes organized to maintain order. Claiming to represent law and order, they represented mob violence and often threatened the peace and safety of people.

The Farming Frontier

As the heyday of cattle ranching ebbed, farming increased in the western frontier territories.

Nature's Will. The prairie sod encountered by homesteaders and other settlers was difficult to plow and plant. There was little lumber. The tough layer of sod they peeled from the prairie became the primary building material. Homesteaders stacked the sod to build the walls of their primitive houses ("soddies"). For heat, they burned buffalo and cattle manure. Harsh sun, blizzards, drought, flooding, insects, and high winds brought the settlers many problems. The most common phenomena of prairie life was loneliness, especially for the women who were tied to the home.

Effects of Technology. Inventions allowed for successful development of the Great Plains. Windmills provided much needed water. Previously, plains farmers practiced centuries old dry farming techniques. A reliable steel plow was developed to cut through the tough sod. Mechanical reapers allowed for quicker harvesting while utilizing fewer people. In 1862, the **Morrill Land Grant Act** provided for the sale of federal land to fund agricultural colleges and quicken the pace of scientific agricultural development.

Nature's changes had to battled each day on the prairie. Insect plagues, droughts, windstorms and tornadoes made Western farm life difficult and dangerous. Loneliness was a constant problem. Farm families joined to churches and clubs for social contact. In the 1870's, mail order houses such as **Montgomery Ward** and **Sears, Roebuck** arose. They changed the primitive existence of plains farmers. Farm families could enjoy the new manufactured goods of the industrial age without long trips to the cities.

Agriculture's Persistent Problems. The farmers were confronted by a number of persistent problems. High middleman charges and falling prices caused by foreign grain and cattle competition (Canada and Argentina) made the farmers dependent upon market conditions. Railroad pricing policies were charging "what the market would bear." Rates were high on short hauls while fraud and cheating were common. Rebates and price fixing occurred. Preference was given to long-haul shippers and those with large tonnage. The banks were reluctant to grant loans to farmers, and charged high interest rates when they did. Farm debt was usually very high. Because of the distance from the manufacturing centers, the farmers paid dearly for goods, credit, and supplies, while receiving low prices for the fruits of their labor.

Although the American farmers enjoyed a relatively prosperous period during the Civil War years, afterward they complained of low prices for their goods, high industrial prices, high railroad charges, and lack of credit. The farmers began to organize and demand action from the government to counteract these forces.

The Grange Movement. The Grange, formally known as the **National Grange of the Patrons of Husbandry**, founded in 1867, started out as a series of farm clubs. The farmers became politically active as their discontent increased. They elected their own candidates for state and local political office and passed state laws to regulate railroads (**Grange laws**). They also used the idea of **cooperatives**, farmers acting together to purchase major equipment and acting as their own middlemen buying and selling in quantity. Grange cooperatives were not very successful due in part to a lack of organization and training. However, grain elevators (moving and storage of grain) operated by the Grange achieved some success.

> **Enduring Issues 2**

Legal Efforts. Farmers frequently saw the railroads as their biggest problem. From 1875-1900, farm state legislatures tried to regulate the railroads. The railroad companies challenged the state laws and several wound up in the U.S. Supreme Court. The basic issue involved in these cases: *Did the states (government) have the right to regulate a private business for the public's good?*

Some of the major cases are:

- *Munn v. Illinois* (1877). The Supreme Court ruled that states could reg ulate private property engaged in the public interest (the Grange laws were upheld);

- *Wabash, St. Louis, and Pacific R.R. v. Illinois* (1886). The Supreme Court changed its *Munn* ruling. It said that states the railroads within their boundaries (only Congress could regulate interstate commerce);

- *Chicago, Milwaukee and St. Paul R.R. Co. v. Minn.* (1889). The Supreme Court overturned a Minnesota law which denied the right of businessmen to appeal freight rates set by the state government.

Gradually, the Supreme Court introduced the idea that the due process clause of the 5th and 14th Amendments gave the courts the power to review the substance of legislation, for example, the railroad rate legislation.

> **Enduring Issues 12**

National Government Response. The federal government passed the **Interstate Commerce Act** (1887) which stated "all charges ... shall be fair and reasonable." This act created the **Interstate Commerce Commission** (ICC). It regulated the railroads by prohibiting pools, rebates, high rates for short hauls, and rate discrimination. It investigated any alleged violations.

> **Enduring Issues 11**

Populism: A Political Response. The Grange movement declined in power and other "farm" parties appeared. The most significant political party was the **Populist (People's) Party**, established in 1892. Farmers were looking to "raise less corn and more hell." The Populists also sought the support of union members.

The Populist Party Platform

- more government control of the railroads
- graduated income tax
- secret ballot
- direct election of Senators
- 8-hour work day
- government ownership of telephone and telegraph
- restriction of immigration
- free and unlimited coinage of silver at the rate of 16:1

On the silver question, farmers believed that their problems stemmed from the lack of money in circulation. They wanted inflation in order to make their debts worth less. Until 1873, the United States was on a bimetallic standard, both gold and silver used to determine the value of money.

However in 1873, as silver prices rose over the government's price, a law was passed by Congress to stop the issue of silver coins. This upset the farmers who believed money with only a gold backing would become even more scarce. They called it the **Crime of '73**. Hence, they believed the free coinage of silver would increase the amount of money in circulation and end their economic woes.

In the 1892 Presidential election, the Populists made a strong showing, garnering one million votes. They increased their support in the 1894 Congressional elections. The 1896 Presidential election represented the Populist Party's best hope for high national support. The Republicans selected **William McKinley** as their candidate.

The Republicans stood for high tariffs, the gold standard, and no free coinage of silver. The Democrats nominated **William Jennings Bryan** who awed audiences with his anti-Republican/business interest **"Cross of Gold"** speech.

The Democrats advocated free coinage of silver. Bryan won the Populist nomination as well. The candidates campaigned strenuously. The modern presidential campaign can be traced to this election. McKinley won the Northeast, Midwest, California, and Oregon by narrow margins. Bryan won the less populous South and the West by large margins, but nonetheless lost the election in the electoral college. In 1900, the gold standard was formally adopted.

D. Retrospective:
American Society At The Turn Of The Century

As America turned into the 20th century, changes were occurring which would make it a world leader in short order. The American population moved from the rural areas to the nation's new urban centers and from the farms to the factories. According to the census, the frontier, as a recognizable line of western settlement, had disappeared in 1890. As of the 1920 census, over fifty percent of the nation's population lived in cities having more than 2,500 people.

From 1870 to 1910, America's urban population increased by 400%. With the influx of huge waves of immigrants, Americans began to emphasize their own culture. Public schooling, the immigrant press, and immigrant aid societies assisted in the acculturation process.

American business drew on the nation's rich supply of natural resources, the growing labor force, and the wealth of inventions to shape a society and economy which would become a dominant force in the world. During most of the late 1800's, the economic energy conquered the American West and expanded domestic markets. With the close of the frontier, American businessmen looked beyond our borders, first to the Western Hemisphere, and then to the Orient.

Nonetheless, many people believed there were better ways to achieve progress than was currently being done. Major critics of industrialism and exploitation included:

Henry George believed inequality stemmed from a few people cashing in on rising land values as a result of increased demand for land. His proposal to relieve this inequality called for a tax on the rise of land values not attributable to the owner's improvements. All other taxes would be abolished. Simply, it was a single tax to remove undue profits from the sale of land. These ideas were set down in *Progress and Poverty* (1879).

Edward Bellamy advocated a socialist government which owned all the means of production and distribution and set moral laws. As described in *Looking Backward* (1888), unless a fully nationalized state was set up, catastrophe would result.

Henry Demerest Lloyd (1894). In *Wealth Against Commonwealth* (1894), Lloyd criticized the unethical tactics of John D. Rockefeller and all the robber barons. His alternative commonwealth called for a plan similar to Bellamy's.

Questions

1   The basic premise of historian Frederick Jackson Turner's work is
    1   The frontier is one of a number of important factors influencing the development of American society.
    2   The frontier is the single major factor which explains the American character.
    3   American development has been motivated first by our European roots and second by the frontier.
    4   The role of the frontier in American history has been grossly exaggerated.
2   The utopian solutions to the problems of industrialization during the Gilded Age were most similar in the works of
    1   Henry George and Edward Bellamy.
    2   Henry George and Henry Demerest Lloyd.
    3   Edward Bellamy and Henry Demerest Lloyd.
    4   Edward Bellamy and George Westinghouse.
3   "Sod Busters" were
    1   new types of cattle being imported from Mexico.
    2   the McCormick reaper which allowed for quicker harvests.
    3   the swarms of locusts that plagued homesteaders.
    4   the homesteaders settling the Great Plains.

4   The major topographic areas of the United States, from east to west, are
   1   Appalachian Mountains, Mississippi River area, Great Plains, Rocky Mountains.
   2   Appalachian Mountains, Great Plains, Mississippi River area, Rocky Mountains.
   3   Mississippi River area, Appalachian Mountains, Great Plains, Rocky Mountains.
   4   Rocky Mountains, Great Plains, Mississippi River area, Appalachian Mountains.

5   The Homestead Act of 1862
   1   made it possible for settlers to settle areas east of the Mississippi River.
   2   opened up the area west of the Rocky Mountains to settlers.
   3   offered free federal land to those willing to settle and work it for at least five years.
   4   had little effect on the westward expansion of settlement.

6   In the last half of the nineteenth century, the western frontier
   1   was settled slowly since the demand for urban workers was so great.
   2   remained virtually inaccessible to prospective settlers.
   3   was considered too risky for substantial business development.
   4   disappeared rather quickly due to the availability of cheap land.

7   The Indians and settlers came into conflict primarily over differences of
   1   technology of weapons.   3   ownership of land.
   2   use of horses.   4   political organization.

8   A new society in which the government controlled major aspects of the economy was a plan promoted by
   1   Henry Demerest Lloyd.
   2   Edward Bellamy.
   3   Henry George.
   4   John D. Rockefeller.

9   *"Many, if not most, of our Indian wars have had their origin in broken promises and acts of injustice on our part."* The author of this statement would most likely agree that the history of the United States treatment of American Indians was primarily the result of
   1   prejudice toward Indian religions.
   2   the desire for territorial expansion.
   3   a refusal of Indians to negotiate treaties.
   4   opposing economic and political systems.

10   Which statement is accurate regarding open range practices?
   1   Its early use allowed investors quick profits since overhead costs were low.
   2   The federal government's Homestead Act caused cattle ranching to flourish.
   3   It had little appreciable effect on the economic development of the West.
   4   It unified farmers, sheep herders, and ranchers into a powerful political alliance.

11   A major problem facing farmers in the latter half of the nineteenth century was
   1   a lack of arable land.
   2   loss of world markets to foreign competition.
   3   increased government interference in production.
   4   unavailability of modern farm machinery.

12 Which action was supported by the farmers as a way to alleviate their problems?
1   development of cooperatives
2   the open range for cattle grazing
3   the Republicans' gold standard for currency
4   high interest rates on loans

Essays

1   Many changes characterize American life and society during the Gilded Age.

- changes in leisure time
- growth of cities
- expansion of factories
- close of the frontier

Choose THREE of the categories above. For EACH one chosen, describe ONE factor which made it possible and ONE effect it had on American life. (Do not repeat information.) [5,5,5]

2   **Not** everyone benefited from the new technology and expansion that was apparent in the United States at the end of the 19th century.

- Urban dwellers
- Native Americans
- Chinese
- Factory workers
- Great Plains farmers

Choose THREE of the groups above. For EACH one describe how they were negatively affected by industrialization and one method they used to deal with this problem. [5,5,5]

3   Throughout United States history, newcomers to urban areas have tended to live with people who are culturally similar to themselves in areas called ghettos. One sociologist has stated:"... *the ghetto is both beautiful and ugly, full of hope and despair, and a beginning and an end.*"

a   Select ONE group of newcomers to urban areas of the United States in the 19th century and describe to what extend the quotation reflects conditions experienced by that group. [7]

b   Describe how ONE action taken by business has affected the ghetto. [4]

c   Describe how ONE action taken by government has affected the ghetto. [4]

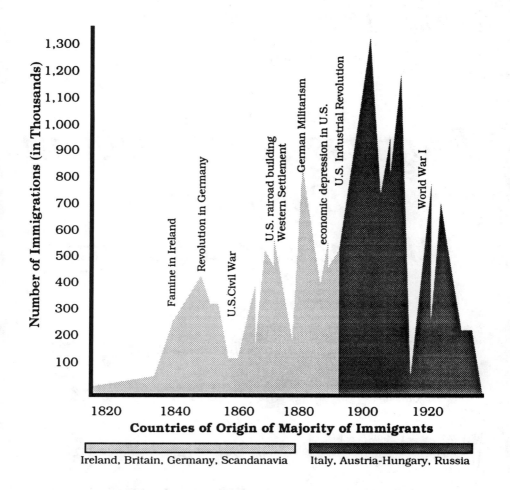

Countries of Origin of Majority of Immigrants

Ireland, Britain, Germany, Scandanavia   Italy, Austria-Hungary, Russia

4   The graph above shows immigration to the United States during the period 1820-1930.

   a   Based on the graph, state TWO generalizations about immigration to the United States. [4]

   b   Describe TWO actions affecting immigration taken by government in the United States and/or by groups of Americans during the time period shown on the graph. Explain why each action was taken and how each affected immigration. [12]

Unit Three

The
Progressive Movement
Reforming
the Industrial Society

1900	1905	1910

- Theodore Roosevelt as President
  - Panama Canal Treaty
- Gentlemen's Agreement

- *Northern Securities Co.v. U.S.*
  - Pure Food & Drug Act
  - Meat Inspection Act

Internationalism
Trust Busting
Progressivism
Disarmament
Consumerism
Conservation
Intervention
Isolationism
Imperialism
Suffragettes
Muckrakers
Diplomacy
Neutrality
Sedition
Reform

1915   **1920**

- Woodrow Wilson as President   • Prohibition   • Red Scare
- Income Tax   • WWI in Europe   • U.S. enters WWI   • Women's Suffrage
- Federal Reserve System   • Versailles Treaty rejected

I. Reform In America
A. The Reform Tradition: A Review

Reform is part of U.S. tradition. Some form of movement to broaden rights or improve life is always present. Reform movements range from expanding rights to changing life patterns. Some focus in very narrow ideals. At other times, movements draw a broad range of causes together.

The American Revolution

The American Revolution resulted in the creation of a democratic republic. Not since ancient times was there a government based on the idea that its power came from the people. Conquest, divine right, or heredity were the bases of medieval governments. The Constitution forbade granting nobility titles. No legalized class structure would create special privileges as in Europe.

Land reform also broadened democracy after the American Revolution. Land ownership determined who could vote. There were two causes of this expansion. First, state governments seized the estates of Loyalists (Tories) who fled after the revolution. States sold their lands to others, increasing the number of landholders (and voters). Second, states abolished **primogeneture** (all inheritance went to the oldest son or brother). Other children became eligible to claim parts of a family's lands. This also increased the land owners (and voters).

The Abolition Movement

In antebellum (pre-Civil War) America, many reform movements appeared. The Abolitionist Movement to abolish slavery became a crusade in the 1830-60's. As seen in Unit One, abolitionist fervor spread rapidly throughout the North. It became a sectional issue and reached a peak as the slavery question became connected to the admission of new states into the union. In the first half of the 19th Century, the issue of states' rights to permit slavery split the nation. It brought on the Civil War. The Abolitionists achieved their goal in 1865, with the passage of the **13th Amendment**, abolishing slavery in the United States completely.

Women's Rights

Enduring Issues 7

During the mid-1800's, women began to agitate collectively for equal rights, including the right to vote. The desire for social, political, and economic equality tied this early Women's Rights Movement and the Abolition Movement together.

In 1848, at Seneca Falls, New York, the first women's rights convention met under the direction of **Lucretia Mott** and **Elizabeth Cady Stanton**. The convention issued the *Declaration of Sentiments* which was modeled after the *Declaration of Independence*.

In matters of economics, legality, education, and politics, women had second class citizenship. The laws gave fathers or other male relatives to control over unmarried women's lives. Husbands had legal superiority over wives. During this time, women seldom had any legal control of their property or even authority over their own children.

Not until the Progressive Era (1900-1920), did **suffragettes** (women crusading for the right to vote) achieve their goal. Wyoming was the first territory and state to grant women suffrage. By 1919, fifteen states allowed the female population the franchise. In 1920, the **19th Amendment** gave all American women the right to vote.

A second women's rights (liberation) movement developed in the 1960's. Economic equity, including **comparable worth** (equal pay for equal work) and a proposed **Equal Rights Constitutional Amendment** rallied women to the liberation movement.

Civil Service
The **spoils system** traces its roots to the Jacksonian Era of the 1830's. Successful politicians gave political jobs to party loyalists. Many unqualified and incompetent persons received government jobs. After the Civil War, the system resulted in widespread corruption in government. In the 1870's, President Hayes and others called a new system of hiring based on **civil service examinations**.

However, Congress did not take action until **President Garfield** was assassinated by a disgruntled office-seeker in 1881. Political bosses and their machines tried to block this reform. The **Pendleton Act** (1883) created a civil service commission which administered the civil service examinations and made appointments based on the scores received. This law provided the basis for the civil service system we have today.

Disadvantaged: Mentally III
As early as the Jacksonian Era, treatment of the mentally ill concerned reformers. Beatings, unsanitary conditions, and unqualified staffs characterized institutions for the mentally ill. In the 1840's, **Dorothea Dix** investigated "insane asylums" in Massachusetts. She publicized the mistreatment of the mentally ill and rallied support for reform. Many states responded with improved facilities, inspections, licensing and training care givers.

B. Pressures For Reform
The changing character of America in the latter 19th and early 20th century caused a number of people to demand reform.

Impact Of Developing Technologies
As industry grew larger, its relations with its workers and consumers grew more impersonal. In an effort to stem this tide, organizations developed such as unions, professional organizations, and social clubs. The increase in leisure time contributed to the growth of these organizations.

Fair Standards

Many groups and individuals became involved in the reform movements to standardize practices within an industry to the benefit of the workers and the betterment of working conditions. With the United States becoming increasingly urbanized and industrialized, more people were directly affected by the poor working conditions than ever before in the nation's history.

Inequities Of Wealth And Poverty

The Gilded Age was an era of vast wealth and grinding poverty. Late in the 19th century, critics of the excessive wealth of the upper classes were appalled at **conspicuous consumption**. This blatant display of wealth caused more people to demand various methods of redistributing wealth.

Rising Power And Influence Of The Middle Class

A well-educated group among the middle class (teachers, lawyers, social workers, doctors, clergy, businessmen) became the core of the Progressive movement. They had both the leisure time to devote to these pursuits, and the moral training that stressed a "Christian duty" to help those less fortunate. Concentrated in urban areas, this new middle class had a sizable impact on the focus of the reform movements.

Mass Communication

Media

Development of mass communication technologies such as the mail, telephone, and telegraph made it possible for reformers to exchange information and coordinate activities. This led to the spread of nationwide organizations, many with reform motivations, including the **American Bar Association** and the **National Consumers League**. Mass production techniques utilized in the publishing and printing industries also helped to mobilize public opinion.

Questions

1   The major reasons for the rise of Progressivism include
    1   the growing middle class indignation and desire for reform.
    2   increasing equality in the distribution of wealth in the U.S.
    3   the desire to return to an agrarian culture.
    4   the responsiveness of business to public demands for safety.
2   Which is the most accurate statement about the history of social reform in the United States?
    1   Reform movements have often declined during times of war.
    2   Most reform movements have sought to overthrow capitalism.
    3   Politicians have played virtually no role in reform movements.
    4   Reform movements have been mainly in the area of religion.

3　At their outset, which two American reform movements were tied together?
　　1　abolition and temperance
　　2　women's suffrage and civil service reform
　　3　care of the elderly and abolition
　　4　women's suffrage and abolition

4　Civil service reform basically called for
　　1　a system modeled after the one used by Andrew Jackson.
　　2　continuation of the spoils system.
　　3　issuance of jobs based on merit rather than political patronage.
　　4　increasing the federal bureaucracy.

5　Generally, reform movements in America have tended to
　　1　seek better conditions for people in urban rather than rural environments.
　　2　broaden the voting base and increasing the standard of living for all.
　　3　concentrate geographically in the Midwest and Western states.
　　4　be a direct result of reform movements in Europe.

6　Which reformer is not correctly paired with his/her reform movement?
　　1　Harriet Tubman - abolition
　　2　Elizabeth Cady Stanton - civil service
　　3　Dorothea Dix - insane asylums
　　4　Lucretia Mott - women's suffrage

7　The abolitionists achieved their goal when which was ratified?
　　1　13th Amendment
　　2　the Pendleton Act
　　3　19th Amendment
　　4　primogeniture

8　As a result of the American Revolution, several reforms were achieved including
　　1　expansion of women's suffrage to reward them for their service during the war.
　　2　expansion of the vote as many received land from the breakup of Loyalist estates.
　　3　creation of a civil service system based exclusively on merit.
　　4　ratification of an amendment prohibiting slavery in colonies.

9　Which is generally characteristic of a nation undergoing the process of industrialization?
　　1　less opportunity for social mobility
　　2　conflicts between modern ideas and traditional ways of life
　　3　shifts in the population from urban to rural areas
　　4　increased reliance on the extended family to supply basic needs

10　Which best explains why the Progressive movement became nationwide?
　　1　A systematic, accessible, and national system of communications was developed.
　　2　There were great disparities between the very rich and the very poor.
　　3　There was a growing middle class.
　　4　The problems were regional in nature.

C. Progress:
Social And Economic Reform

Public outcries against big business tactics came from a number of different voices with a number of different goals. Government at all levels was spurred into action by concerned citizens or the press.

The Muckrakers And Reform

As literacy grew in America, the power of the media grew. Many Progressive reformers worked with journalists who wrote articles exposing the evils of big business. Theodore Roosevelt named these journalists muckrakers because they riled up the public with their exposés.

In the early 1900's, a number of magazines began to feature muckraking articles, the first notable magazine was *McClure's*. Writers included: **Ida Tarbell**, who wrote a series of exposés on the Standard Oil Company; **Lincoln Steffans**, who had a series on **"The Shame of the Cities;"** and others whose works ranged from child labor to corruption in politics.

McClure's
HISTORY of the **STANDARD OIL COMPANY**
IDA TARBELL

Novelists employed muckraking too. Upton Sinclair described the unsanitary conditions in Chicago's meat packing plants in *The Jungle* (1906). Its publication mobilized public demand for government regulation of the industry. **Frank Norris** described the farmers' plight resulting from railroad abuses in *The Octopus* (1901). He showcased the Chicago wheat exchange in *The Pit* (1903). Even earlier, **Jacob Riis'** *How the Other Half Lives* (1890), the first book specifically about urban problems (immigrant slums in NYC), stimulated housing reform.

Legislative Reform

These articles and novels stimulated public demand for government action. The passage of numerous state and Congressional laws is attributable to these writers and the work of other Progressive reformers. Among the most notable are:

• **The Meat Inspection Act** (1906) was the first consumer protection law passed by Congress. It used the interstate commerce clause to subject all meat crossing state lines to strict inspection by federal employees;

• **The Pure Food and Drug Act** (1906) forbade the sale of adulterated goods or those fraudulently labelled. Congressional passage of this law was based on the commerce clause (a delegated power) of the Constitution's Article I.

The Decline Of Literary Exposure

Muckraking journalism faded after the election of 1912. Public weariness with crusades and intense exposés caused the decline. Political reforms led by Theodore Roosevelt, Robert LaFollette, and Woodrow Wilson answered the muckrakers calls for action.

In the long run, the muckrakers reformed journalism itself. Today's investigative reporters follow the muckraking tradition. Investigative reporters triggered protest action on Vietnam (***The Pentagon Papers***), the Watergate Scandal, the Iran-Contra Affair, the S&L Crisis, and Congressional Check Kiting.

Other Areas Of Progressive Concern

Many private individuals and organizations worked for social reform during the Progressive Era as well as writers.

The Settlement Houses

The plight of the urban poor (often immigrants) came to the public's attention in a number of exposés. One of the first was Jacob Riis' *How the Other Half Lives*. Individuals such as **Jane Addams** sought to provide accessible help to those living in urban slums. She created **Hull House** in Chicago (1889) as a social service center. These **settlement houses**, located right in slum neighborhoods, offered adult education classes, job training, clinics, child care, and Americanization classes, among other things. The concept originated in England and spread to urban America, especially the Northeastern cities.

Women's Rights And Efforts For Peace

During the Progressive Era, women were agitating for suffrage and equal rights. **Margaret Sanger**, a nurse working primarily with immigrant expectant mothers on the Lower East Side of NYC, gave up her job in 1912 to promote the use of birth control. Her actions were in violation of existing obscenity statutes and brought her into conflict with the law. She coined the term "birth control."

Many men and women followed **pacifism** (opposition to all war). **Jeannette Rankin** became the first female member of the House of Representatives. As a pacifist, she voted against U.S. entry into World War I. In 1941, she cast the lone dissenting vote against U.S. entry into World War II.

The Search For Racial Justice

The movement for racial equality and equity of treatment was divided over the policies and programs of Booker T. Washington and W.E.B. DuBois. Lynching reached its peak during the Jim Crow era in the South. A number of pieces of anti-lynching legislation were introduced in Congress, but were blocked in the Senate when Southern Senators **filibustered** (endless debate used to postpone a vote). **Marcus Garvey**, founder of the **Universal Negro Improvement Association**, sought to create free and independent nations

Enduring
Issues

8

in Africa. He hoped that American blacks would help to populate these new nations. Although his dreams were not fulfilled, he is regarded as one of the first black nationalists.

Temperance And Prohibition

Originally calling for moderation of the consumption of alcohol, the temperance movement eventually turned to its goal to the prohibition of alcohol. One group, the **Women's Christian Temperance Union** formed in 1876, believed drink was the primary factor in crime, poverty, and vice. **Prohibitionists'** goals were reached when the **18th Amendment** was passed in 1919 banning the sale, manufacture, and distribution of alcohol.

Enduring
Issues
13

Questions

1   The impact of the muckrakers finally decreased because
   1   their activities were eventually outlawed by the national government.
   2   Progressive politicians began instituting some changes.
   3   the cost of printing such journals became prohibitive.
   4   there were very few muckrakers of note.

2   Which term refers to a journalist who exposed social evils in the United States?
   1   carpetbagger
   2   muckraker
   3   robber baron
   4   Anti-Progressive

3   *"According to those who supported the measure, it was a noble experiment. (It led to an amendment.) But it proved impossible to enforce and consequently increased disrespect for the law."* The "noble experiment" described in this passage was
   1   integration of public schools.
   2   prohibition of alcoholic beverages.
   3   passage of child labor legislation.
   4   extension of the vote to women.

4   The programs of the Progressive movement (1900 - 1920)
   1   emphasized the expansion of civil rights for blacks and other minority groups.
   2   were passed by Congress despite strong opposition by the President and other party leaders.
   3   took effect during periods of extended economic depression.
   4   resulted in a greater involvement of the federal government in the daily lives of Americans.

5   Which statement best describes Progressive era support?
   1   Progressive supporters were predominantly from the rural, Western areas.
   2   Progressive support cut across political divisions, but was predominantly middle class.
   3   There are no general characteristics to describe those who advocated Progressivism.
   4   Progressive reformers were predominantly women of all social classes.

6   Publication of *The Jungle* by Upton Sinclair lead to
 1   creation of the Interstate Commerce Commission.
 2   passage of the Meat Inspection Act.
 3   ratification of the 19th Amendment.
 4   increased support for Margaret Sanger's activities.
7   *"Crouched over the (coal) chutes, the boys sit hour after hour, picking out the pieces of slate and other refuse...I once stood in a breaker for half an hour and tried to do the work a twelve-year-old boy was doing day after day, for ten hours at a stretch, for sixty cents a day. The gloom of the breaker appalled me..."*   - John Spargo, 1906
 The author of this passage is most likely a(n)
 1   industrialist.
 2   muckraker.
 3   Populist.
 4   supporter of W.E.B. DuBois.
8   Which reformer is correctly paired with the field he/she is most known for?
 1   Marcus Garvey - urban housing conditions
 2   Jacob Riis - black nationalism
 3   Margaret Sanger - birth control
 4   Jane Addams - temperance

D. Progressivism And Governmental Action
Emerging Progressive Movement: Political Reform
Progressive reform was primarily an urban, middle class movement which influenced many other groups in society.

- **Municipal and State Reform.** Initially, much of the government reform movement was aimed at the municipal and state level, especially cities where the problems of urbanization and industrialization were magnified.

- **Responses to Urban Problems.** In an effort to root out government corruption, reformers sought to make the local governments run more efficiently and more professionally. They called for civil service reform, an end to bossism, and the creation of city commissions and city managers, to name a few reforms.

- **Sudden Growth and Needed Services.** As the urban population grew, inadequacies in various basic services were magnified. Reformers called for government ownership of public utilities, including electricity, gas, telegraph, and telephone, so that these services would be accessible and affordable to the general population.

- **Progressive State Reform.** The reform movement spread to the state level where the reformers looked to the governors for leadership. Goals often differed by regions (West - railroad regulation, South - anti-big-business, North - political corruption and labor conditions).

Wisconsin's Republican-Progressive Gov. **Robert LaFollette** eventually became the state's U.S. Senator. Before he left the governorship, Wisconsin became synonymous with progressive reform including direct primaries, equitable taxes, and regulation of railroads. One way reform was achieved hinged on the activities of commissioners who reported directly to the governor. They used a scientific approach to collect data and make reports.

After the Spanish-American War of 1898, Teddy Roosevelt was elected Governor of New York State. He championed social legislation including improving conditions in urban tenements and taxing public utility corporations.

Following the lead of the Midwestern states and New York in the East, Massachusetts limited women's working hours to 60 per week. Twelve years later in 1912, Massachusetts created a commission empowered to recommend minimum wages for women and expose employers who did not comply.

State Reforms

Initiative -	process where voters can suggest new laws and amendments
Referendum -	people allowed to vote directly on legislation
Recall -	process where voters can remove officials from office before their term is up
Secret Ballot -	voters could make their choices in privacy

States began using their **police powers** to regulate the health and safety of their citizens. Reforms undertaken using these powers included: factory inspections, insurance to cover job accidents, minimum employment age, maximum hours for child labor (usually 8-10 hours per day), limit on hours for women, and old age pensions.

National Reforms:
Theodore Roosevelt And The Square Deal

Roosevelt's campaign theme demanded that business and government give consumers a **Square Deal**. His policies also became known as the **New Nationalism**. The dynamic president indicated trusts were necessary evils and part of American life, therefore controls were needed to curb the more flagrant monopolistic tendencies.

The Stewardship Theory of the Presidency. Roosevelt saw the presidency as providing the leadership to give Americans that "Square Deal." He felt the president controlled and wielded power in the best interests of the people. The public good must be the overriding concern of the holder of the executive office.

Legislation In The Square Deal

Programs pushed through Congress during Roosevelt's tenure as chief executive included:

- The **Commerce Department** (1903) was created to collect information necessary to enforce existing anti-trust legislation;

- **Elkins Act** (1903) expanded powers of the Interstate Commerce Commission and made rebates illegal;

- **Pure Food and Drug Act** and **Meat Inspection Act** (1906);

- **Hepburn Act** (1906) strengthened the Elkins Act and gave the ICC power to reduce objectionable railroad rates subject to court approval (It also allowed the ICC to regulate interstate commerce as done by oil pipelines, railroad terminals, sleeping car companies, bridges, etc.).

"Trust Busting"

Due in large part to the energetic activities of the Commerce Department, Theodore Roosevelt took action against over forty American trusts. As a result, Roosevelt was often referred to as a "trust buster." In 1904, in the ***Northern Securities Co. v. U.S.***, the Supreme Court ordered the breakup of one of Wall Street titan J.P. Morgan's railroad monopolies in the Pacific Northwest. In 1911, the Supreme Court ordered the dissolution of the Standard Oil Company of New Jersey, declaring it represented an "unreasonable restraint of trade." Under the High Court's **"rule of reason,"** trusts were not automatically condemned. Instead, their actions had to be analyzed as to their effects on trade in general.

> Enduring Issues
> **12**

Labor Mediation

In 1902, anthracite coal miners went on strike demanding higher pay, shorter working hours, and union recognition. The strike began to affect Americans when the colder weather approached. **President Theodore Roosevelt** took action by calling union leaders and mine owners to Washington. When discussions broke down, he threatened to use troops to get the mines producing again. The operators finally agreed to binding arbitration. The union saw some of their demands met, including half the wage increase sought. Public support for Roosevelt increased dramatically as a result of his mediation.

Teddy Roosevelt

Conservation

A tradition of natural abundance and waste caused Americans to become aware of the dangers of environmental deterioration belatedly.

Roosevelt's Concern For The Environment

In 1907 Roosevelt said, *"We are prone to think of the resources of this country as inexhaustible; this is not so."* He used his presidential powers to add 150 million acres to national forests and preserves belonging to all. He sought a well conceived plan for resource management.

Federal Legislation And Projects

Going back to 1891, Congress authorized the President to remove United States owned timber land from sale. Roosevelt used these provisions enthusiastically.

Newlands Act (1902) used money from the sale of western lands for irrigation and created the National Forest Service;

| Enduring Issues 1 | Antiquities Act (1906) provided that sites of historic and/or scientific interest be placed under national protection and control, including the Grand Canyon and Niagara Falls; |

Inland Waterways Act (1907) planned control and improvement of river systems.

Gifford Pinchot And John Muir

New Yorker **Gifford Pinchot** was a conservationist and later the nation's chief forester. He was instrumental in calling the National Conservation Congress in 1908. He played a large role in the national conservation movement of this time. **John Muir**, a naturalist, was instrumental in bringing the Yosemite area into the National Park System in 1891.

1895 N.Y. Constitution And Adirondack Preserve

A New York State law was passed in 1885 establishing the **New York State Forest Preserve** which includes the Adirondack and Catskill Mountains. This area has 2.75 million acres, almost as much land as the national park lands east of the Mississippi River. The 1895 NYS Constitution designated these lands as "**forever wild**," designed to prevent misuse of land and keep it as a source of water, timber, and recreation area. This "forever wild" designation is a matter of much controversy today.

Working Conditions

In the 1890's, many states used their police powers to regulate and improve working conditions for laborers. Not all agreed with these reforms. Two Supreme Court decisions illustrate the battle for judicial acceptance of legislative reform:

Lochner v. New York (1905) involved a progressive New York State law limiting bakers' hours to 10 a day, 6 days a week to ensure the health of the bakers and protect consumers. Lochner, a bakery owner, was found guilty of violating this law and appealed to the Supreme Court. In a split decision, the law was found unconstitutional. The Court's reasoning held that the law violated due process guarantees of 14th Amendment infringing on workers' rights to work more than 10 hours a day. Justice Oliver Wendell Holmes wrote a classic dissenting opinion on this case.

| Enduring Issues 13 | In _Muller v. Oregon_ (1908), an Oregon laundry owner was found guilty of violating an Oregon law limiting women workers to 10 hours work a day. He appealed the decision to the Supreme Court. The lawyer for Oregon, later Justice Louis |

Brandeis, entered a **Brandeis Brief**. Instead of long citations of judicial precedents, Brandeis' argument focused on a wealth of scientific data and statistics to show this occupation was unhealthy.

Woodrow Wilson

Oregon won the case and two important precedents were set: non-legal data could be used and admitted as evidence, and certain circumstances justified the use of a state's police powers.

Woodrow Wilson And The New Freedom

In 1912, Woodrow Wilson became the first Democrat to be elected president in 20 years. He was a relative newcomer politically, but a true progressive reformer. Under the banner of **New Freedom**, he viewed trusts as fundamentally evil entities and sought to break them and restore free competition in the marketplace.

Progressivism At Its Zenith: The Election Of 1912

The 1912 Presidential election featured three candidates, all with reform credentials. One reason to account for Wilson's electoral victory is the split within the powerful Republican Party. Theodore Roosevelt, unimpressed with the policies of his successor William Howard Taft, entered the race seeking the Republican nomination. Factionalism at the convention caused him and his liberal Republican supporters to form the Progressive Party (also known as the Bull Moose Party). Conservative Republicans supported the incumbent, Taft. Wilson won a slim plurality, but an overwhelming electoral majority.

Underwood Tariff And Graduated Income Tax

Over Congressional opposition, Wilson secured the passage of the Underwood Tariff and a federal income tax. Many people saw international competition as a result of lowered tariffs as another way to combat trusts. The **Underwood Tariff** reduced duties on imported goods to approximately 26% of the product's value.

The Populist-inspired **income tax** was finally achieved by Progressive reformers. A **progressive income tax** (one in which tax rate increased as the amount of income increased) took the tax burden off those who could least afford to pay it - the lower classes. Previous revenue tariffs were said to be **regressive** (placing an unfair tax burden on those who could not afford to pay it).

> Enduring
> Issues
> **13**

The ratification of the **16th Amendment** in 1913 gave Congress the authority to tax personal and corporate income. The **Revenue Act (1913)** placed a 1% tax on incomes over $3,000 and surcharges on those over $20,000. The bulk of Americans did not pay any tax.

Clayton Anti-trust Act And Federal Trade Commission

In an effort to curb trust activities, the Clayton Anti-trust Act was passed and the Federal Trade Commission created. The **Clayton Act (1914)** was designed to strengthen the earlier Sherman Anti-trust Act.

The new act specified the abuses considered monopolistic, including rebates, certain interlocking directorates, and exclusive sales contracts. It exempted labor unions and agricultural cooperatives, but hostile court decisions rendered this exemption meaningless. It was helped by the creation of the **Federal Trade Commission** in 1913, which could investigate monopolistic practices and "kill a monopoly in the seed." It could issue **cease-and-desist orders** when monopolistic tactics were found. Unfair practices included: mis-branding and adulterating products; spying and bribery; and misleading advertising. Hostile Supreme Court decisions hurt its effectiveness.

Enduring Issues 12

The Federal Reserve System

Reform in the banking system was designed to wrest power away from controlling eastern banks. People believed that financial instability was caused by banking policies, especially their reluctance to lend money.

The **Federal Reserve System**, established by Congress in 1913, under the Federal Reserve Act, set up a **government controlled banking system** designed to allow for an **elastic currency** (one which could expand or contract as the economy required). It is a three-tiered system: (1) At the top is the Board of Governors. Members are appointed by the President to supervise and regulate the activities of the system, or **"The Fed."** (2) Twelve regional banks, which act as "banks' banks" hold reserves and lend money to (3) member banks (all nationally-chartered banks and other banks who wish to join the system).

Enduring Issues 7

The Women's Suffrage Movement

Suffrage for women was finally achieved in 1920, with the ratification of the 19th Amendment which prohibited denial of voting rights to anyone because of their sex.

World War I And Its Effects On Domestic Reform

Domestic reform programs may be crippled by wartime priorities. By 1916, the Progressive movement had run its course. Concern over the growing conflict in Europe and the eventuality of American participation required coordination of the government and cooperation by all involved, not conflict between various groups. The enemy was now "over there." Government regulations were dropped or relaxed to stimulate war production.

Questions

1   Which third party played an important role in the election of 1912?
    1   Republican
    2   Populist
    3   Bull Moose
    4   Suffragettes
2   The Clayton Act strengthened the Sherman Anti-trust Act by
    1   providing a specific listing of unfair practices.
    2   making restrictions apply to unions and cooperatives.
    3   prohibiting the use of adulterated products.
    4   eliminating the Interstate Commerce Commission.

Base the answer to questions 3 and 4 on the chart below:

```
$0 - 3,000  - 0%
3,001 - 20,000 - 1%
20,001 - 30,000 - 2%
```

3   A tax based on the chart above is called a
   1   regressive tax.   3   tariff.
   2   progressive tax.   4   poll tax.

4   The authority for the United States Congress to pass such a tax was based on
   1   an amendment and a law.
   2   a Congressional statute.
   3   an amendment.
   4   voluntary approval of the states.

5   The Federal Reserve Board has great control over the United States economy because it has the power to
   1   regulate the money supply.
   2   increase and decrease income taxes.
   3   determine the Federal debt ceiling.
   4   determine the value of the dollar abroad.

6   The Progressive movement of the early 20th century represented an attempt to
   1   repeal the antitrust laws.
   2   protect the rights of racial minorities.
   3   destroy the capitalistic system of the United States.
   4   deal with the problems created by industrialization.

7   Wilson's New Freedom differed from Roosevelt's New Nationalism in that
   1   Wilson tried to help the monopolies deal with increasing government restriction.
   2   Roosevelt's policies accepted the continued existence of monopolies.
   3   Wilson's program is not considered part of the Progressive Era.
   4   Roosevelt attempted to completely eradicate business monopolies.

8   Which would be considered an unfair business practice by the Federal Trade Commission?
   1   lowering prices due to competition.
   2   opening up a branch store.
   3   misleading advertising.
   4   raising prices due to rising costs.

9   Progressive reforms prompted the passage of a number of amendments to the Constitution including
   1   income tax and direct election of United States Senators.
   2   protective tariffs and the Federal Reserve System.
   3   anti-trust prosecution and workers compensation.
   4   prohibition of alcohol and creation of the Interstate Commerce Commission.

10   Which statement regarding the end of the Progressive reform movement is correct?
   1   All reforms sought by Progressive reformers were enacted.
   2   Preparation for a wartime economy took attention away from reform.
   3   Power of the trusts overwhelmed democratic government.
   4   There was no leadership in the White House.

11 Theodore Roosevelt's attitude toward government control of business was
    1   only state governments had the authority to control business.
    2   a strict policy of laissez-faire should be followed.
    3   business at this point was uncontrollable.
    4   federal government should eliminate bad business practices.

12 Which statement is true of Progressivism at the state level?
    1   Many of its ideas grew out of the reform philosophy at the local level.
    2   Most Progressives were from minority groups.
    3   It achieved few of its goals at the state level.
    4   Progressive governors proved weak and ineffectual at instituting
        change.

13 Which statement is not accurate regarding local and state Progressive
    reform?
    1   It included such measures as referendum and recall which put more
        power in the hands of the voters.
    2   It had virtually no impact on national politics since the issues were
        regional rather than national.
    3   It provided a training ground for reformers and politicians who later
        expanded their goals.
    4   It led to the institution of reform measures, especially in the urban
        areas.

14 Which statement does not apply to the conservation movement during the
    Progressive era?
    1   All conservation measures were instituted by the national
        government.
    2   The State of New York was among the first states to protect its land.
    3   Theodore Roosevelt's personal interest was important to the federal
        government's interest in conservation.
    4   The withdrawal of public lands from sale and the creation of the
        Forest Service were keystones in national conservation.

15 Who is most likely the author of the following quotation? "We do not wish
    to destroy corporations, but we do wish to make them sub-serve the public
    good."
    1   Woodrow Wilson
    2   Gifford Pinchot
    3   Theodore Roosevelt
    4   John D. Rockefeller

Essays

1   The reforms of the Progressive Era were enacted by local, state, and
    national authorities. Their impact is still felt today since many reforms
    were incorporated into the United States Constitution. There are four
    Progressive Era amendments in the Constitution. For THREE of these
    amendments:

    a   State the provision of the amendments.

    b   Describe the conditions that lead to the amendment's inclusion.

    c   Explain why these were considered to be major reforms. [5,5,5]

2   Reform movements have affected different aspects of United States society. Some of these aspects are:

- public education
- equal opportunity
- family life
- participation in government
- working conditions
- public welfare

Choose THREE aspects of United States society listed above. For EACH aspect chosen, describe a reform in the Progressive Era which affected that aspect of life and discuss the conditions which the reform movement was attempting to change. [5,5,5]

3   There were several Supreme Court decisions of note during the Progressive era.

- *Northern Securities v. United States, 1904*
- *Lochner v. New York, 1905*
- *Muller v. Oregon, 1908*
- *Standard Oil Co. v. United States, 1911*

Choose THREE of the cases above and for EACH one chosen, describe the issues in the case, the Supreme Court's decision and the significance on American life. [5,5,5]

4   Reformers during the Progressive Era were from a number of different political parties, classes, and occupations. Prove this statement by describing THREE specific individuals involved in this reform movement. Briefly explain why all of them can be considered to be part of the Progressive Era. [5,5,5]

II. America Reaching Out

A. Industrial - Colonial Connection

During the second half of the 19th century, expansion of American industry propelled the United States to look beyond its borders for markets and raw materials. The resulting American colonial empire, though not as large as those of European powers, was geographically far flung and ethnically diverse. While many Americans supported expansionist policies, concern was voiced over the growing global involvement of the United States.

Economic Imperialism

United States Industrial Productivity. American industry experienced tremendous growth in the decades after the Civil War. Americans with surplus capital looked beyond North America for new places to invest. They looked overseas for new markets and new sources of raw materials. The "close" of the frontier in 1890, indicated to many that it was time to expand abroad. Pursuing these policies, government and business leaders hoped to strengthen America's position as a leading industrial nation.

Development of Commercial and Naval Power. Between 1870 and 1900, the value of American agricultural and industrial exports more than tripled. The ever increasing output of factories and farms could not be consumed within the nation. American merchant and naval fleets were strengthened and modernized to give the nation a greater role in international commerce.

Captain Alfred Mahan authored several books in the period which attempted to show that throughout history, nations with sea power dominated the world. Mahan urged that it was time for Americans to "look outward" for naval bases, markets, and raw materials. Modernization of the U.S. Navy was already underway. By 1900, the U.S. Navy was ranked third in the world.

Technological Advances spurred some of the growing interest in international affairs. The increased speed of steamships made trade more profitable, and the need for "coaling stations" forced Americans to take an interest in Pacific Islands.

Trans-oceanic telegraph cables brought the hemispheres closer together. Continued industrial growth required new sources of raw materials and improved military weapons made conquest easier.

Cultural Paternalism:
European Imperialism And Missionary Impulse

Led by Britain and France, European nations rushed to gain control of colonies in the second half of the 19th century. Nearly all of Africa, India, and Indo-China came under the domination of Europe. The Europeans attempted to justify their conquests by claiming it was the **"White Man's Burden"** to bring the benefits of western civilization to less developed regions.

Early in the 19th century, Christian missionaries ventured into various parts of Asia and the Pacific to find Christian converts. Hawaii was of particular interest to New England Congregationalists. By the close of the 19th century, many Americans came to believe that it was the "divine mission" of the United States to spread the benefits of democracy, liberty, and Christianity to the less civilized. A number of authors, including the **Rev. Josiah Strong**, popularized the belief that it was the duty of Americans to "uplift" the less fortunate. Such popular ideas made it easier for Americans to accept an imperialistic role for the United States.

The Tariff Controversy:
Free Trade v. Protectionism

One of the more hotly debated political issues of the 19th century was the tariff. **Protectionists**, usually Republicans and their business backers, argued that high tariffs protected the wages and jobs of workers as well as the profits of capitalists. **Free Trade** supporters advocated lower tariffs. They were often Democrats and claimed that high rates raised the price of manufactured goods for consumers, benefited only a few, and interfered with America's ability to sell goods overseas. The tariff rose and fell depending on the party in power.

Throughout American history, high protective tariffs have been used as an expression of economic nationalism. The high rates have not always helped the economy, because the benefits of foreign trade were lost. But lower tariffs, while promoting trade, have combined with other economic factors to cause trade deficits and loss of American jobs.

> Enduring
> Issues
> **12**

In the 20th century, the government has resorted more frequently to the use of "quotas" rather than high tariffs in an effort to control foreign imports. The **General Agreement on Tariffs and Trade** (GATT), signed in 1967, reduced the tariffs in the major industrial nations by as much as fifty percent. Large U.S. trade deficits have piled up in the 1980's, and protectionist voices arose once again (see Unit Six).

Questions

1 A nation will often restrict its importation of foreign products to
   1 protect domestic jobs.
   2 reduce prices on domestically produced goods.
   3 limit the flow of inferior quality products.
   4 widen the variety of products available to consumers.

2   In the late 19th century, many of the leading industrial nations began a policy of imperialistic expansion because of
1   a desire to gain control of strategic locations in preparation for World War I.
2   the need for new capital funds that colonies could provide.
3   a desire to obtain supplies of raw materials and expand markets for trade.
4   the need for a place to put surplus population.

3   In the United States, which group benefited most from the establishment of overseas colonies during the late 19th century?
1   factory workers
2   investors and manufacturers
3   members of the armed forces
4   farmers

4   The "close of the frontier" around 1890, caused Americans to
1   rush to settle the little available land left in the west.
2   begin considering the exploration of space.
3   develop strategies to restrain population growth.
4   consider overseas expansion.

5   The conquest of colonial areas was made easier in the second half of the 19th century because
1   most native populations were willing to be ruled by Europe.
2   the native populations were usually Christian.
3   new weapons and technology made conquests easier.
4   European Christianity easily assimilated native religions.

6   Which statement best reflects the attitude of British, German, and French leaders toward Africa and Asia during the 19th century?
1   We should not become involved with people who are different from us.
2   These lands are sources of raw materials and markets for our products.
3   There are many advantages to sharing and learning from other cultures.
4   The political power and wealth of these areas are threats to our position in the world.

7   Demands for "protectionism" in 1980's are largely a result of
1   inferior products
2   trade deficits
3   human rights violations
4   cultural paternalism

8   "We must bring the benefits of Western civilization and Christianity to the less fortunate." This idea has been used to justify
1   imperialism
2   socialism
3   nationalism
4   feudalism

B. An Emerging Global Involvement

The Civil War, Reconstruction, and internal growth limited American interest in foreign affairs for much of the 19th century. While Americans prospered from the benefits of foreign trade, efforts at expansion were often ridiculed (Alaska - 1867). However, the last decades of the century saw a change as public support increased for overseas adventures.

Manifest Destiny And Expansion To The Pacific

In the first part of the 19th century, Americans made their way across the continent spurred on by the belief in **Manifest Destiny**, that America had a "divine mission" to conquer the entire continent. The annexation of Texas, settlement of the Oregon dispute, and the spoils of the Mexican War brought the Americans to the Pacific by 1850. The new west coast ports increased interest in Far Eastern trade.

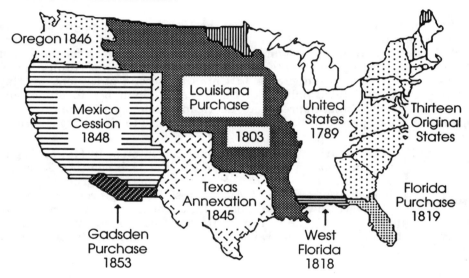

Japanese Contacts (1857-1900). Japan had isolated itself in the mid 17th century, having little to do with western civilization. Disputes over American whaling rights and interest in trade led to a visit in 1853, by **Commodore Matthew Perry**. Perry was able to persuade the Japanese to open several ports to American commerce, which was soon followed by European powers making similar demands. The Japanese were impressed by modern technology and military power of the westerners. By 1900, Japan had a modern government, a thriving textile industry, and rapidly growing heavy industries. Japan also modernized its military and began its own era of imperialism.

The China Trade: Chinese Interest Since Colonial Times. Despite a distance of over 12,000 miles, American east coast merchants carried on a profitable trade with China from the 1780's. The opening of additional ports following Britain's victory in the Opium War in the mid 1800's, the speed of American clipper ships, and the addition of the Pacific ports contributed to an increase in the China trade prior to the Civil War.

While Americans were interested primarily in trade and missionary activity, imperialist nations annexed territory and established economic control (spheres of influence) over large parts of China toward the end of the 19th century. While not wanting territory, the United States was fearful of losing trading privileges, and began to play a role in Asian politics.

Pacific Overtures

The United States and China: **The Boxer Rebellion.** Foreign nations exerted increasing control over the domestic affairs of China. In 1900, a group of patriotic Chinese, the Boxers, went on a violent rampage killing foreigners and destroying property. After several months, an international military force, which included U.S. troops, ended the rebellion, and an indemnity was assessed on the Chinese government. (The United States eventually gave much of its share back to China).

The Open Door Policy. At the end of the 19th century, foreign spheres of influence and possible annexations threatened U.S. trade in China. Secretary of State **John Hay** issued a statement which became known as the **Open Door Policy.** It sought to create an atmosphere of equal opportunity for all in trade, investments, and profits in China. A second statement by Hay ordered the imperialistic nations of Europe and Japan not to annex any Chinese territory. China appreciated American efforts on its behalf, but the Open Door Policy proved difficult for the United States to effectively enforce.

Enduring Issues 9

Acquisition of Hawaii. American interest in Hawaii began with missionary activities early in the 19th century. As sugar growers also flocked to the islands, Americans gradually dominated affairs. In 1893, American settlers engineered a successful overthrow of the Queen Liliuokalani. The new rulers requested annexation by the United States, but President Cleveland determined that most native Hawaiians opposed annexation, and the matter was dropped.

Five years later, fighting, in the Philippines during the Spanish American War, convinced some that Hawaii was needed to send supplies and men across the Pacific. President McKinley and Congress quickly approved the annexation of Hawaii in 1898. In addition to agricultural benefits, Hawaii also provided the American military with the important Pearl Harbor naval base.

Niihau

Kauai

Oahu

Molokai

Lanai

Kahoolawe

Maui

Hawaiian Islands

Hawaii

Naval Base: Samoa. The Samoan Islands in the South Pacific served as a coaling station for the United States beginning in 1872. Britain and Germany also showed interest in the islands. After much diplomatic haggling, the United States and Germany each annexed part of Samoa, with Britain receiving other considerations.

"Hesitant Colonialism"
The Spanish American War
The Spanish American War in 1898 had a number of causes:

- harsh treatment of Cubans by Spanish rulers
- desire by investors to continue a profitable agricultural trade
- yellow journalism, false and exaggerated stories published by American newspapers
- explosion of the battleship Maine incorrectly blamed on the Spanish. With the American public clamoring for war, President McKinley and Congress gave approval for American military intervention on behalf of the Cuban rebels. The American victory was achieved in less than four months, though serious deficiencies in the nation's military preparedness were exposed. Poor planning, rotten food, and unsanitary conditions killed many more than combat. The United States extended its control over several new areas, but some Americans felt uneasy about having colonies.

Influence Of The Monroe Doctrine (1823-1898)
In 1823, President Monroe stated that the European nations would be prohibited from any further colonization in the Western Hemisphere, and that the U.S. would stay out of European affairs. It was to the political and economic benefit of America for the newly independent nations of Latin America to be weak and detached from Europe. Realistically, the United States was not powerful enough to enforce the doctrine, but no one challenged it for forty years. An attempt by France to control Mexico during the Civil War (the Maxmillian Affair), was condemned by the United States and eventually abandoned by the French. Latin American nations initially welcomed the Monroe Doctrine, but increased American meddling in their internal affairs began causing resentment. Beginning in the 1890's, recurrent American intervention led to frequent friction and increased distrust.

United States Empire
The fruits of the Spanish-American War gave America a small, but widely spread empire. United States overseas expansion coincided with a renewal of European imperialism.

Dealings With Cuba
- **Teller Resolution:** In 1898, Congress promised not to annex Cuba.
- **Platt Amendment:** In 1901, modified independence was granted. Political, economic, and military concessions were given to the U.S.
- **Franklin Roosevelt's Administration** gave the Cuban people total independence in 1934.

Puerto Rico Made A U.S. Commonwealth
- **Foraker Act** (1900) granted territorial status to Puerto Rico, with limited self-government.
- **Jones Act** (1917) extended American citizenship to residents.
- **Commonwealth Status** (1952). Residents were permitted to elect their own legislature and governor, but were not represented in Congress

nor in the Electoral College. It was also stipulated that Puerto Rico could become a state if the Puerto Rican people desired and had U.S. Congressional approval.

Philippines

Located over 7,000 miles from the U.S. mainland, the Philippines presented greater difficulties. A number of Americans claimed the islands were too far away, too hard to defend, and populated by an alien race. A bloody revolt lasting three years followed the American annexation. During U.S. control of the islands, sanitation programs, economic development, literacy, and democratic ideas were all put in place. Filipinos continued to ask for independence, and the **Tydings-McDuffie Act** freed the islands in 1946.

Territorial expansion prior to the 1890's consisted mostly of sparsely inhabited areas contiguous to the North American continent. It was fully expected that these areas would eventually achieve statehood. Acquisitions after 1890, however were far from the mainland and populated by foreign peoples, with little possibility of statehood. A Constitutional question arose: Are the people in these new areas protected by the U.S. Constitution? (Does the Constitution follow the flag?) In the **Insular Cases** (1901), the Supreme Court decided that areas not likely to become states (unincorporated areas) were under the authority of Congress. While certain civil liberties were guaranteed by the Constitution, most Constitutional protections, such as citizenship, voting, and representation could be legislated by Congress.

Latin American Affairs

United States influence and intervention in the domestic affairs of many Latin American nations grew tremendously in the decade following the Spanish-American War. In creating an "American Lake" in the Caribbean, the United States was meeting the strategic and economic demands of the nation. Many Latin American nations harbored increasing resentment toward U.S. meddling in their internal affairs.

West Indian Protectorate ("The Big Stick")

President Theodore Roosevelt believed it was important for the U.S. to make a strong show of force, to wave a "Big Stick" in foreign affairs. This policy would keep Europeans out of the Western Hemisphere, and bring the Latin American nations in line with American wishes.

During Roosevelt's administration, the "Big Stick" was used in Cuba to end a rebellion, and in the Dominican Republic and Venezuela to collect debts. Though many Latin American nations were poorly governed, they nonetheless resented the "Big Stick" policies, and similar interventions by later Presidents.

Enduring
Issues
9

Panama Canal: Acquisition And Construction

In the 1850's, American settlement of California aroused interest in a Central American canal connecting the Atlantic and Pacific. The water route from New York to California was 13,000 miles, but would be cut in half with a canal. The French company that built the Suez Canal tried in Panama, but failed. With the addition of territories in the Caribbean and the Far East, a canal became a vital strategic and commercial necessity.

The United States paid the French company 40 million dollars for the land rights in Panama, and negotiated a treaty with Columbia, which controlled Panama at the time. When the Columbian Senate refused to ratify the treaty, U.S. naval ships helped stage a revolt in Panama, leading to Panamanian independence. A treaty was then finalized with Panama, with Roosevelt boasting of "having taken the canal." After ten years of construction, the two oceans were joined in 1914.

As part of the agreement, the United States took title to a ten mile wide strip of land and paid Panama annual rent for its use. A small, affluent American community resided in the Canal Zone, in contrast to the poverty of most Panamanians. Growing resentment to the U.S. ownership surfaced as riots erupted in 1964. After years of negotiations, a 1977 treaty provided for the gradual return of the area to Panama. (see Panama Canal Treaties)

Monroe Doctrine Update

The original intent of the Monroe Doctrine (1823) was to prevent the reappearance of European colonialism in the Western Hemisphere. By the 1890's, it was being interpreted to extend American political and economic influence over Latin America.

British refusal to submit a boundary dispute between Venezuela and British Guiana to arbitration led to American intervention in 1895. Secretary of State **Richard Olney** warned Britain to reconsider, as he claimed that the *"U.S. is practically sovereign on the continent."* Hostilities were averted when Britain agreed to arbitration of the disputed area.

President Theodore Roosevelt went further, stating that in cases of "chronic wrongdoing," the United States can use "international police power" in Latin America. This became known as the **Roosevelt Corollary to the Monroe Doctrine**. It was applied in 1905 to the Dominican Republic when it was unable to repay debts to European nations. To keep Europe out of the Americas, the U.S. took over the economy of the Dominican Republic and supervised the debt repayment. A similar method was used by the United States in a similar instance in Haiti.

Many Latin Americans grew increasingly suspicious of the "help" and "protection" given to them by the United States. One Latin American official issued the **Drago Doctrine**, condemning both the use of force to collect debts and the interference of the United States. Few American leaders considered the wishes of Latin American nations; however, Presidents involved the U.S. militarily, politically, and economically well into the 1920's.

Taft And Dollar Diplomacy

President Taft expanded America's "international police power" in Latin America. Nicaragua, Haiti, and the Dominican Republic were all occupied by U.S. military forces in order to protect American investments and loans. This "Dollar Diplomacy" was supported by American business, but met with considerable protest in the Latin American nations.

President Wilson And The Mexican Revolution

A revolution against Mexican dictator Porfiro Diaz in 1910, initiated nearly a decade of civil war in that country. American businessmen watched with concern as the government changed hands several times, and threatened to end foreign investment.

President Wilson applied a policy of "Watchful Waiting," resisting calls for American military intervention, but also refusing to recognize a Mexican government with questionable authority. This worked for a time, but when rival Mexican leader Pancho Villa crossed the border and killed American citizens in 1916, U.S. troops led by General John Pershing pursued him into Mexico. Order was finally restored to Mexico after 1917, but Villa was never captured.

Questions

1   Japanese policy of isolation ended in 1853-1854, because Japan
    1   needed more territory as an outlet for its surplus population.
    2   needed European markets for its manufactured goods.
    3   became involved in a war with China.
    4   was pressured by United States naval power to open its ports.

2   An immediate outcome of Perry's visit to Japan in the mid 19th century was that Japan
    1   increased exports of its agricultural surpluses.
    2   recognized its need for Western technology.
    3   needed a market for its many industrial products.
    4   desired to send some of its population to settle in the Western nations.

3   As Western trade with China expanded during the 19th century, U.S. policy was to
    1   establish and maintain a colony in East Asia.
    2   partake in the international division of Chinese territory.
    3   increase and strengthen trading privileges.
    4   encourage Chinese emigration.

4   The major goal of the United States' Open Door Policy was to
    1   aid the Chinese in the fight against Communism.
    2   prevent Japan from invading China.
    3   weaken the Chinese Emperor.
    4   protect United States trading rights in China.

5   A major reason for proclamation of the Monroe Doctrine was the desire to
    1   force Latin American nations to cut their tariffs on United States exports.
    2   prevent Spain from regaining its former colonies in the Western Hemisphere.
    3   weaken French influence in the Louisiana Territory.
    4   free Cuba from Spanish rule.

6   *"In our infancy we bordered upon the Atlantic only; our youth carried our boundary to the Gulf of Mexico; today, maturity sees us upon the Pacific. Whether they will it or not, Americans must now begin to look outward."*
    This late 19th century quotation best reflects a United States policy of
    1   imperialism   3   isolationism
    2   militarism   4   neutrality

7   At the end of the 19th century, a major objective of United States foreign policy was
    1   continental expansion.
    2   breakup of the British Empire.
    3   development of an overseas empire.
    4   incorporation into the European balance of power.

8 Which reflects a foreign policy of Presidents Monroe and Theodore Roosevelt?
1 Close economic ties with Asia must be maintained.
2 Non-involvement in world affairs is the wisest policy for the U.S.
3 U.S. influence in Latin America must be accepted by other nations.
4 The U.S. should help in the settlement of internal European disputes.
9 The most important reason for the construction of the Panama Canal was the need to
1 increase the security of the United States.
2 spread the United States way of life to less developed nations.
3 encourage the economic development of Central America.
4 prevent European colonization of Latin America.
10 During the early part of the 20th century, the basic goal of United States policy toward the nations of Latin America was to
1 spread democratic ideas throughout the area.
2 provide the United States with more territory.
3 support United States economic and political interests.
4 form military alliances to counteract the growing power of European nations.
11 In 1898, in a cable sent to Cuba to the artist Frederic Remington, newspaper publisher William Randolph Hearst was quoted as saying, *"You furnish the pictures and I'll furnish the war."* This reflects the
1 control of the press over military strategy.
2 power of one individual to influence public taste in the arts.
3 influential role of the press in generating public sentiment concerning an issue.
4 need for government censorship of the press during war time.
12 The Dollar Diplomacy of the Taft administration resulted in
1 the forming of military alliances to fight Communism.
2 increased animosity between the U.S. and Latin America.
3 huge investment in the U.S. by Latin American nations.
4 military takeover of most of the Latin American republics.

C. Restraint And Involvement: 1914-1920

In contrast to Latin America and the Pacific, the United States avoided involvement in European political affairs. America prospered from European trade and became a refuge for millions of immigrants, but abstained from the "entangling alliances" as George Washington had counseled in his Farewell Address. Although Wilson struggled to preserve neutrality at the beginning of World War I, as a major world power, the United States would eventually be drawn into the conflict.

European Background To World War I

Nationalistic Rivalries. European nations had formed several alliances in order to maintain a balance of power on the continent. Germany, Austria-Hungary, and Turkey formed the **Triple Alliance** (Central Powers), while France, Great Britain, and Russia comprised the **Triple Entente** (Allied Powers). Each was pledged to help the other members of the alliance in event of war. An intense atmosphere of nationalism in Europe convinced people to support their government, regardless of the consequences.

A tremendous build-up of military forces and weapons took place in the early part of the century. New weapons, such as submarines, tanks, poison gas, artillery, machine guns, and airplanes made warfare much more deadly and expensive. Some ethnic groups, especially in the Balkans and central Europe, sought freedom from Germany, Austria-Hungary, and Russia.

Colonialism and the Spread of War. The rush to colonize Africa and Asia led to numerous disputes among the European nations over matters such as boundaries and trade. Germany and Italy, having few colonies, wished to create colonial empires of their own. With large military forces available and national pride very strong, Europe was a "powder keg." It erupted when a Serbian patriot assassinated the Austrian Archduke Franz Ferdinand in 1914. Austria retaliated against Serbia, and within a week, the promises made within each alliance brought all the major powers of Europe into the conflict.

Importance of Control of Sea Routes: At the start of hostilities, Britain attempted to choke off Germany by blockading the European coasts. To retaliate, Germany used submarine warfare against enemy shipping in the Atlantic. This threatened the shipping rights of neutral nations. Traditional rules of warfare, which required enemy ships to identify themselves before sinking a merchant ship, were impossible for the submarine, which needed to remain underwater to be effective.

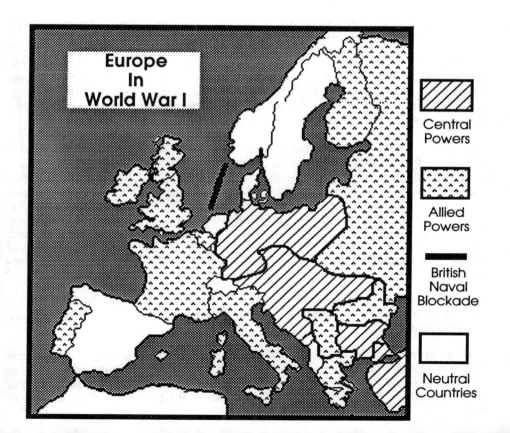

Europe
In
World War I

Central Powers

Allied Powers

British Naval Blockade

Neutral Countries

This **unrestricted submarine warfare** killed many innocent people. The most deadly attack occurring against the **Lusitania**, when over 1,000 lives were lost. Germany, though widely condemned, defended her actions as the only way to break the British blockade.

United States Involvement

Efforts at Neutrality and "Preparedness." Upon the outbreak of hostilities in Europe (1914), President Wilson issued a **Proclamation of Neutrality**, but most citizens favored the Allied Powers: Britain, France, Russia, and Italy.

America's Anglo heritage, belief in democracy, trade, and investment with the Allies all influenced the nation's thinking. Though both sides violated American rights on the seas, unrestricted submarine warfare of the Germans was much more deadly and costly to the United States. While official government policy was neutrality, Germany complained of America's aid to the Allies, especially shipments of arms and extension of credit.

The American military was unprepared to wage war. It was understaffed and short of supplies. A few farsighted Americans urged the establishment of officer training camps, but Congress reacted slowly. In 1916, a slight increase was authorized in manpower and equipment, but the United States was still far behind its European counterparts.

Causes of United States Entry into the War. For over two years, the American government maintained neutrality, and Wilson campaigned for re-election in 1916, as the candidate "who kept us out of war." Events of early 1917, would drag the United States into war, however. Hostility had been building toward Germany for several years.

| Enduring Issues 9 |

The **Zimmerman Note** angered Americans when British intelligence announced a plot by minor German diplomats to persuade Mexico to declare war against the United States. In 1916, Wilson demanded an end to Germany's random sinking of merchant ships. The German government agreed to halt these attacks when they issued the **Sussex Pledge**. A few months later, Germany renewed unrestricted submarine warfare, and sank four American merchant ships. Wilson, no longer able to ignore the outward acts of aggression, asked Congress for a declaration of war. On 6 April 1917, Congress overwhelmingly approved.

By 1917, the European war was a stalemate. With brutal but indecisive battles being fought desperately in the trenches of France, the Allies were starting to run out of men.

When Russia withdrew from the war early in 1918, Germany shifted thousands of troops to the Western Front severely pressing Britain and France. It took over six months for American troops to be trained and to reach Europe. But, by 1918, the United States had a substantial fighting force on European soil.

Under the command of **General John Pershing**, the **American Expeditionary Force** helped to stop the German advances at **Chateau-Thierry** and **Belleau Wood**. Near the end of the War, American troops suffered heavy casualties leading the Allied counteroffensive at **Argonne Forest**. Germany surrendered as the Allies neared the German border in November 1918.

United States Reaction to the Russian Revolution. As the Russian Revolution developed in 1917, many Americans were not sorry to see an end to the autocratic rule of the Czar. But, the sudden withdrawl of Russia from the war and its takeover by the Marxists (Bolsheviks) presented new problems. American forces accompanied Allied forces to Siberia and other parts of Russia to prevent a German capture of Russian arms and to keep an eye on imperialistic Japan. The United States also tried to keep the communist Bolsheviks from gaining control of any military supplies. Fighting between the rival White and Red groups in Russia continued for several years after the War. The United States give limited but ultimately unsuccessful aid to the anti-communist White Armies.

Questions

1   Just prior to World War I, the nations of Europe believed that the balance of power could best be maintained by
   1   a system of alliances.
   2   an international court.
   3   increases in tariff barriers.
   4   open agreements, openly arrived at.
2   Which resulted from late 19th century European nationalism?
   1   economic unification of Europe
   2   creation of strong international peace-keeping organizations
   3   development of new European colonies in the Western Hemisphere
   4   intensified rivalry and conflict among European nations
3   At the outbreak of World War I, the U.S. government favored a policy of
   1   remaining neutral.
   2   entering the war on the side of the Allies.
   3   invading Europe in order to acquire territory.
   4   settling conflict through an international peace organization.
4   The Triple Alliance and the Triple Entente represented a foreign policy technique designed to
   1   collectively deter the power of rival groups of nations.
   2   prevent runaway arms races among member nations.
   3   contain the spread of worldwide communism.
   4   encourage self determination for colonial people.
5   The Zimmerman Note gave the United States reason to
   1   continue its policy of neutrality.
   2   consider war against Russia.
   3   consider war against Germany.
   4   extend credit to the German government.
6   Although the President is responsible for foreign policy, Wilson had to ask Congress
   1   for a Proclamation of Neutrality.
   2   to sever relations with Germany.
   3   to condemn the sinking of the Lusitania.
   4   for a declaration of war against Germany.

D. Wartime Constitutional Issues

Opposition to American involvement has developed in varying degrees during every war which the United States has entered. World War I was no exception. A small but vocal group of Americans protested. The government instituted a tremendous propaganda campaign aimed largely at denouncing the Germans and uniting the American public. In the interest of national security, certain limits had to be placed on civil liberties. This resulted in the arrest of a number of individuals causing some ardent supporters of the war effort to criticize the government for placing restrictions on basic Constitutional freedoms.

I WANT YOU
FOR U. S. ARMY
NEAREST RECRUITING STATION

War Opposition And Patriotism: The Draft Issue

When war was declared, not everyone believed that Americans should be forced to "make the world safe for democracy." Mention of a draft evoked bitter memories of Civil War riots, and visions of German militarism. The urgent need for men convinced Congress to pass the **Selective Service Acts**, which required registration of all men between the ages of 18 and 45. By the end of the war, nearly 5 million served in the military, 3 million of whom were draftees.

Espionage And Sedition Acts

To prevent obstruction of the war effort, Congress passed the **Espionage Act** in 1917 and the **Sedition Act** in 1918. The Espionage Act attempted to halt acts of disloyalty and closed the mails to publications that printed such material. The Sedition Act stipulated jail terms for those who disrupted the government's war effort, and prohibited the use of disloyal language. A number of patriotic Americans who supported the war were critical of these measures, citing them as unconstitutional restrictions on civil liberties.

Enduring Issues 4

Eugene Debs, "Big Bill" Haywood, And Emma Goldman

Socialists, communists, and anarchists were under close surveillance during the War. Socialist-Labor Party leader **Eugene Debs** spoke out against the "capitalist war" and was convicted under the Espionage Act. The **Industrial Workers of the World** (IWW) organized a number of strikes in important industries during the War, delaying government production schedules. IWW leader **William "Big Bill" Haywood**, and over 100 other "Wobblies," received jail sentences of up to 20 years for hindering the war effort. **Emma Goldman**, an anarchist from Russia, opposed militarism and the use of force. She received a two year jail sentence for speaking out against the draft, and was later deported to Russia.

Schenck v. United States (1919): Clear And Present Danger

Charles Schenck, a leading Socialist, printed and distributed pamphlets that discouraged young men from registering for the draft. This obstruction of the war effort violated the Espionage Act, and Schenck was convicted and jailed. He appealed his conviction, claiming his 1st Amendment right to freedom of the press had been violated. His appeal was accepted by the Supreme Court. A unanimous Court ruled against Schenck, pointing out that his actions were a "**clear and present danger**" to the security of the American people in wartime. This "clear and present danger" rule set a **judicial precedent** that has often been used to determine the constitutionality of measures which restrict free speech and press.

Enduring
Issues
4

Red Scare - 1918-1919

The 1917 Bolshevik Revolution in Russia and communist triumphs in the following years was of concern to many Americans. Some believed that the Bolsheviks' next move would be in the United States, and many blamed the small Communist and Socialist Parties for a number of disruptive strikes. Several unexplained explosions between 1919-1921, were also blamed on these two groups.

In order to stem the "red tide," several actions of questionable constitutionality were put into effect. Over 5,000 revolutionaries, socialists, and communists were searched and detained without warrants. Some states passed "criminal syndicalism" laws, which made it unlawful to advocate violent change. While the threat of a communist takeover in America was remote, the hysteria of the Red Scare made the possibility seemed real.

E. Search For Peace And Arms Control: 1914-1930

President Wilson hoped to negotiate a fair and just peace, but power rivalries among the European nations frustrated attempts to implement many of his moral ideas. Ultimately, Wilson failed to get any treaty approved in the United States. Several political blunders, illness, and stubbornness resulted in Senate defeat of the Treaty of Versailles.

Though disappointed with the results of World War I, the United States continued to have a limited involvement in international matters, especially measures to promote peace and arms control. The nation could have played a much larger role in foreign affairs between 1920-1940, but choose instead to turn away.

The Peace Movement

A number of women's organizations opposed war in general and American entrance into the League of Nations in particular. Representative Jeannette Rankin voted against the declaration of war against Germany, and organized the **American Women Opposed to the League of Nations**. The **Women's International League for Peace and Freedom** opposed the League of Nations because it still permitted war in certain cases. They also protested the use of income tax monies for military purposes.

Wilson's Aims: The 14 Points

Early in 1918, President Wilson announced America's war aims and proposed a plan for world peace: **The 14 Points.** The plan included the following provisions:

- An end to secret diplomacy;
- Freedom of the Seas;
- Free and Open Trade;
- Reduction of Armaments;
- Consideration for native populations in colonial areas;
- Self determination for subject nationalities of Europe, including Poland, Czechoslovakia, and Alsace-Lorraine;
- A general association of nations to protect the political independence and territorial integrity of all nations.

The idealistic 14 Points were distributed to all nations. The Central Powers, especially Germany, were hopeful for them becoming the basis for a just peace. The proposals met with objections from some of the Allied Powers, who hoped to gain some strategic and economic benefits from the spoils of the War. These conflicting goals proved fatal for Wilson's plan.

Versailles Treaty: Wilson's Role

Amid some objections at home, President Wilson personally represented the United States at the Versailles Peace Conference. Especially critical were Senate Republicans, with whom the Democratic Wilson barely consulted dur-

Europe After World War I

ing the negotiations. This was a fatal blunder. The Republicans controlled the Senate which would have to ratify any treaty the President signed.

President Wilson (U.S.), **David Lloyd George** (Britain), **Georges Clemenceau** (France), and **Vittorio Orlando** (Italy) dominated the Versailles Conference. Wilson soon discovered that secret treaties had been made at the start of the war, parcelling out territory to the victors. Wilson decided compromise was the only solution, even if some of his 14 Points had to be shelved. After several months at Versailles, a treaty was completed.

Wilson's most important goal, the creation of a League of Nations, was included in the Treaty, as well as self determination for several European nationalities. However, the President was unable to secure the adoption of his other points. The European powers demanded huge reparations from Germany, German disarmament, and in France's case, German territory. Colonial areas were put under League of Nations mandate, but still dominated by Europe.

Historians generally agree that Wilson did the best he could under the circumstances, at least in softening some of the Allies' more extreme demands. Fifteen years later, the vengeful treaty would come back to haunt the European powers as Hitler used the Germans' resentment to build his Third Reich.

League Of Nations:
Henry Cabot Lodge And U.S. Senate Rejections

Despite its drawbacks, Wilson urged Senate ratification of the Treaty of Versailles in 1919. Republicans, led by **Henry Cabot Lodge** of Massachusetts had regained control of the Senate in the 1918 Congressional elections. They were especially opposed to American entrance into the League of Nations, which would require the U.S. to support the European members against acts of aggression. Opponents to the Treaty also feared loss of sovereignty and the possibility of entangling alliances.

Enduring Issues
10

Lodge and other Republicans were willing to support the Treaty with "reservations." These would protect the United States and give Congress the final say on military commitments to Europe. Wilson refused to compromise with the Senators. Instead, he embarked on a nationwide tour to gain public support for the treaty.

Halfway through the tour, the exhausted Wilson suffered a stroke and remained in seclusion for many months.

Several votes were eventually taken on the treaty, but political fighting led to rejection both times. The Republicans refused to approve the treaty as presented by President Wilson. Wilson directed the Democrats in the Senate to vote down any version of the treaty which included the Lodge group's reservations.

Historians have blamed both the power-hungry Senate and Wilson's stubbornness as reasons for the failure to ratify the treaty. Separate peace agreements were finally made with Germany and other Central Powers in the 1920's.

Washington Naval Disarmament Conference

To attain naval defense, the United States embarked on a shipbuilding program during World War I. The cost of this effort was a burden to American taxpayers and complaints increased after the War ended. Growing demands for disarmament led to a meeting of the United States, Great Britain, Japan, France, and Italy in 1921. This **Washington Conference** established ratios which limited the number of capital ships that each nation could possess (see chart at right). While no limits were placed on smaller ships, Japan continued to demand parity with America and Britain on larger ships.

Reparation And War Debts

The United States as a World Banker. As a result of the tremendous amount loaned by the United States during World War I, the nation changed from a debtor to a creditor nation. That is, foreign nations owed money to the United States. The United States government had loaned the Allies over 10 billion dollars, and expected repayment after the War.

With high tariffs restricting trade during the 1920's, the foreign governments found it impossible to raise the money. The United States extended payment time and lowered interest rates, but much of the debt was still outstanding by 1930. Europe claimed that they should not have to repay the debt since the U.S. did not experience physical destruction during the war, and suffered fewer casualties.

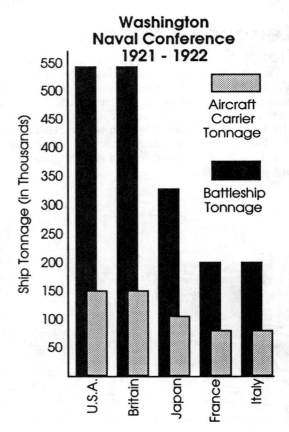

Washington Naval Conference 1921 - 1922

In addition, the Allies pointed to Germany, who repaid little of its war reparations bill of nearly 33 billion dollars. The American government still demanded payment in full, and eventually denied further loans to those still in arrears. No further payments were made, however, and the issue was eventually dropped in the face of the Great Depression.

Kellogg-Briand Pact (1928). In an idealistic attempt to prevent war, the United States and France negotiated the Kellogg-Briand Pact in 1928. The agreement, eventually signed by over 60 nations, outlawed war and required settlement of disputes by peaceful methods. But, it also permitted the use of military force in the case of self defense. Since war would have to be used to prevent war, the agreement had little practical value.

The World Court. In an effort to settle international disputes, the League of Nations helped establish an independent World Court in 1920. It was suggested by Presidents Harding and Coolidge that the United States become a member, but the Senate once again feared foreign entanglements. An attempt to join in 1926, was rejected by the Court when the Senate added several "reservations" to United States membership. Franklin Roosevelt tried again in the 1930's, but to no avail. The Senate reflected the deepening isolationist sentiments of the American public, which began at the conclusion of World War I and continued through the 1930's.

Questions

1   Restrictions of constitutional guarantees during wartime most often involve
   1   free speech and press.
   3   the right to bear arms.
   2   the quartering of soldiers.
   4   excessive bail.

2   The fact that people opposed the draft during World War I indicated that
   1   German agents had infiltrated the government.
   2   the American army was of adequate strength.
   3   some Americans opposed mandatory military service.
   4   France was not supplying her share of troops in the war.

3   By implementation of the 14 Points, President Wilson hoped to
   1   weaken Germany so it could never fight another war.
   2   divide the territory of the Central Powers among the Allies.
   3   formulate a peace which would help prevent further war.
   4   set up democratic governments throughout Europe.

4   The Washington Naval Conference (1921-1922), was an attempt at
   1   disarmament.   3   collective security.
   2   imperialism.   4   mercantilism.

5   In the case of Schenck v. United States, the Supreme Court ruled that an individual's
   1   opposition to the draft during wartime must be tolerated.
   2   rights can be compromised if there is a clear and present danger to society.
   3   opposition to the draft is permitted by the Constitutional guarantee of free speech.
   4   right to due process of law does not apply to the military.

6   The "Red Scare" in the U.S. was indirectly a result of a communist revolution in
   1   Germany   3   Russia
   2   France   4   China

7   Convictions of Debs, Goldman, and Haywood during World War I indicated that
   1   presidential power was increasing too rapidly.
   2   civil liberties are not always protected.
   3   most Americans supported withdrawal of the United States from the war.
   4   the policy of isolation was still favored by a majority of American people.

8   The Senate rejected U.S. membership in the League of Nations after World War I mainly because Senate opponents
   1   feared that membership would infringe upon national sovereignty.
   2   believed that membership would block U.S. participation in military alliances.
   3   did not want to give financial aid to an international organization.
   4   were more concerned about the economic problems of the Great Depression.

9   Which statement about the League of Nations is an opinion?
   1   Senator Lodge was a leader in the fight to keep the U. S. out of the League.
   2   President Wilson traveled widely to gather support for U.S. entry into the League.
   3   The Senate's rejection of the Versailles Treaty also blocked entry into the League.
   4   Wilson's unwillingness to compromise kept the U.S. from joining the League.

10   Europe was unable to repay her war debts to the U.S. in part because
   1   communist governments had nationalized all industry.
   2   high tariffs prevented European countries from earning needed cash.
   3   the Versailles Treaty allowed payment only to members of the League of Nations.
   4   most of the money was used to industrialize colonial areas.

11   Wilson should probably have worked more closely with the Senate during peace negotiations because
   1   all treaties must be approved by a 2/3 vote of the Senate.
   2   Wilson needed Senate support to run for another term in 1920.
   3   the Senate was controlled by his own political party.
   4   the Senate was responsible for the war debts of the Allies.

12   During the period between World War I and World War II, which general theme was more dominant in U.S. foreign policy?
   1   overseas expansion
   3   militarism
   2   internationalism
   4   isolationism

13   Which of Wilson's 14 Points was eventually included in the Treaty of Versailles?
   1   freedom of the seas
   2   heavy war reparations for Germany
   3   an end to secret diplomacy
   4   a general association of nations

14 The Kellogg-Briand Pact was doomed from the start because
1 the major nations of the world refused to sign.
2 to prevent aggression, it permitted war.
3 none of the major powers was strong enough to defend it.
4 the United States refused to join another entangling alliance.

15 Wilson's leadership was weakened in the last year of his administration because he
1 was an ineffective Commander-in-Chief.
2 was elected in 1916 without a majority of the popular vote.
3 became seriously ill during a speaking tour.
4 directed the Attorney General to round up radicals.

Essays

1 The United States acquired a colonial empire at the start of the 20th century for a number of reasons:

   • economic / commercial
   • military / strategic
   • humanitarian

For each reason listed above, describe a specific instance when the United States used that reason to justify an imperialistic action. (Use a different area for each reason) [5,5,5]

2 a State the original purpose of the Monroe Doctrine. [7]
  b Show how this original purpose was altered by the United States at the beginning of the 20th century. [8]

3 The twenty years following World War I was a cautious period for the United States in the area of foreign policy.

  a Describe the reasons for U.S. rejection of the Treaty of Versailles. [3]
  b Discuss another example besides the Treaty which showed a retreat to isolationism during this period. [3]
  c Show two examples of U.S. involvement in world affairs between 1920-1940, despite isolationist tendencies. [9]

4 Describe the effect of the following economic policies had on the United States:

  a Protective tariffs [5]
  b Dollar Diplomacy [5]
  c Extension of credit to World War I Allies [5]

Unit Four

At Home and Abroad:
Prosperity, Depression, and War
1917 - 1940

Relief - Recovery - Reform
Keynesian Economics
Pump - Priming
Business Cycle
Unemployment

Laissez - Faire
Trickle - Down
Pragmatism
Contraction
Depression

Recession
Charisma
Socialism
Coalition
Demand

1920	1925	1930

- Harding scandals   • Sacco-Vanzetti trial   • Stock Market Crash
   • National Origins Act   • "Talkies"   • Hawley-Smoot Tariff
• Business Boom   • *Babbitt*   • *The Great Gatsby*   • Lindburgh flies Atlantic

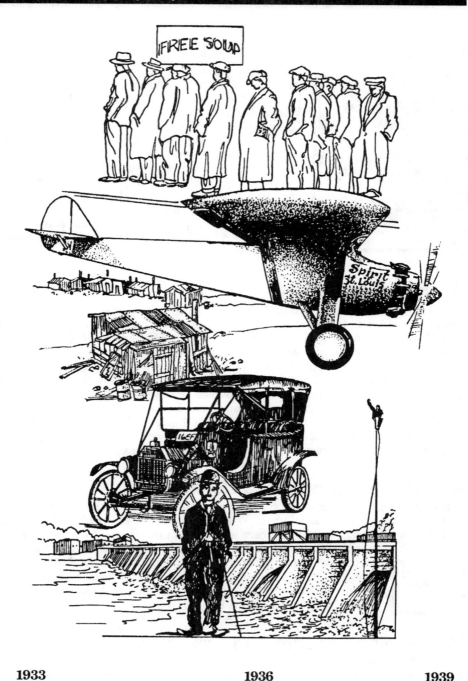

1933   1936   1939

· FDR Elected   · "The Hundred Days"   · Court Packing

· Great Depression   · NRA   · WPA   · National Labor Relations Act

· Bonus Army   · FDIC   · CCC   · AAA   · Social Security   · *Grapes of Wrath*

I. War Economy And Prosperity

1917 to 1929

In the years between the two World Wars, America rode a roller coaster of economic highs and lows. Part of this was due to the devastation of World War I, but a good deal of the instability was the result of human blunder and ignorance. The worldwide actions and inactions of governments, business leaders, and private individuals contributed to the massive economic collapse that came in the 1930's. Out of that sorry state of human misery there arose the dictatorships that would plunge the world into a second world war. Unit Four shows the complex economic interdependence of public and private institutions which shaped these events.

A. War Economy

In April of 1917, a reluctant President Woodrow Wilson went before Congress to ask for a declaration of war against the **Central Powers**. The moment he had dreaded had come, and as Commander-in-Chief, he would now have to recruit, train, and send an **American Expeditionary Force (AEF)** to Europe. Congress granted him enormous emergency powers to mobilize the economy to support not only the AEF, but our allies as well. In doing so, Congress moved the U.S. temporarily toward a **command economy**. In this type of economic structure, a governmental authority plans and makes the basic economic decisions for the public. The basic U.S. system is **a market economy**. The aggregate decisions of consumers and businesses give the economy its general direction with minimal governmental interference.

Government Boards And Controls

The government began to command substantial sectors of the economy under these wartime measures. Wilson created a **Council of National Defense** made up of cabinet officers and civilian advisors which established a number of agencies to organize economic forces of the home front. To run them, he also recruited experienced public servants, such as **Herbert Hoover** (Food Administration), and private businessmen, such as Wall Street financier **Bernard Baruch** (War Industries Board).

Enduring
Issues
12

Mobilization Of Labor And Armed Forces

Organized labor was represented on the Council of National Defense in the person of AFL President **Samuel Gompers**. He worked with Wilson to rally labor to a no-strike pledge and set up a **War Labor Board** to mediate disputes and grievances. Some of the labor force was siphoned into the military. Nearly half of all who served in the armed forces were volunteers, but Congress also passed the **Selective Service Act** which drafted nearly three million men by the end of the war.

Government Operation: Railroads, Communication...

Although arteries of transportation like railroads and the shipping industries were virtually commandeered by the government, they were operated efficiently and were managed profitably. Official government communication was managed by a **Committee on Public Information** under Wilson advisor **George Creel**. Creel launched a massive propaganda campaign featuring anti-German news releases, posters, and slogans.

> Enduring
> Issues
> **1**

Revenue Sources And Financial Management

To pay for all of this, Congress raised taxes and authorized bond drives. The chart below indicates the extent of the government's management of the American economy during World War I.

U.S. Government Command During WW I

Federal Agencies	Economic Sectors Managed
War Industries Board	Allocated raw materials; Supervised war production
War Labor Board	Mediated labor disputes to prevent strikes
Shipping Board	Built transports for men and materials
Railroad Administration	Controlled and unified R.R. operations
Fuel Administration	Increased production of coal, gas, and oil; Eliminated waste
Food Administration	Increased farm output; Public campaigns to conserve supplies
Raising Funds For The War Effort	Increased income and excise taxes; "liberty Bond" and "Victory Bond" Drives

War's Impact On Gender Roles And On Blacks

Volunteer enlistment and the draft combined to create a labor shortage. This increased the already large number of blacks leaving the segregated South and migrating into Northern industrial cities. The accelerated pace of wartime industrial production easily absorbed nearly half a million blacks. The increasing flow northward continued into the next decade.

Women would also fill some of the gaps working in factories doing many jobs previously reserved for men. Many married women were also forced into the labor market because of the lack of income when their husbands and fathers were drafted for military service.

Reconversion And "Normalcy" 1918-1920

As the war ended, the government began to **demobilize**, dropping its demand for war material. This caused a general **economic contraction** (decline), leading to production cuts, plant closings, layoffs, and widespread unemployment.

Freed from the restrictions of "wartime no-strike pledges," labor unions began a long series of bitter and sometimes violent strikes. However, the massive growth of industry during the war, along with the vast profits made, allowed most of the larger firms to manage through the conversion. Seeking to pull their lives back together, civilian workers and returning servicemen cashed in war bonds and began spending their savings on homes, autos, and other consumer goods. This new consumer demand gradually pulled the economy out of the post-war conversion depression.

In 1920, presidential candidate **Warren G. Harding** captured this mood when he accidentally coined a phrase indicating that a public weary of war, depression, and reform crusades now wanted a return to "normalcy."

Questions

1 In general, the major economic problems of the 1917-40 period were caused by the
   1   devastation of European countries during World War I.
   2   high military expenditures for U.S. armed forces in the 1920's.
   3   expense of implementing the Progressive Era consumer protection laws.
   4   dictatorial way government managed the economy during WW I.

2 In which type of economy is the primary decision-making power placed in the hands of government planners?
   1   free enterprise   3   command
   2   market   4   underdeveloped

3 What caused the 1919 - 1921 economic contraction?
   1   an increase in minority groups in the labor force
   2   investment of war profits by businesses
   3   people cashing in war bonds
   4   a decrease in government spending

4 During the war, railroads were
   1   forced to operate at huge losses.
   2   plagued by frequent strikes.
   3   run by government agencies.
   4   replaced by the trucking industry.

5 The chart on page 157 characterizes the U.S. economy during WW I as
   1   laissez-faire   3   command
   2   market   4   underdeveloped

6 During World War I, financier Bernard Baruch, labor leader Samuel Gompers, and public administrator Herbert Hoover
   1   managed the transportation systems of the nation.
   2   increased taxes and raised funds for the government.
   3   helped to mobilize the American economy.
   4   assisted Wilson in readjusting the economy after the war.

7   Employment in war industries had some positive influence on the status of women and black Americans, because they were
    1   allowed to join unions for the first time.
    2   given pay equal to that of white males.
    3   performing well in management positions.
    4   filling large gaps in the labor force.

8   Money to finance war expenditures came from
    1   selling liberty bonds.
    2   rationing of scarce goods.
    3   building and selling ships.
    4   increasing tariffs.

9   During the war, the government's Public Information Committee
    1   settled strikes peacefully.
    2   preserved the civil rights of dissenters.
    3   ran propaganda campaigns.
    4   staged rallies to sell war bonds.

B. The Twenties:
Business Boom Or False Prosperity?

Americans entered the 1920's disillusioned with world politics and wanting to put the experience of recent years behind them. They responded to the kind of sentiment Harding expressed with his "normalcy" phrase.

There was an intense desire to achieve the **American Dream**, to seek personal satisfaction, material wealth, and to lead a trouble-free life. In such a mood, Americans were receptive to the unleashing of market forces by business which would characterize the wild, wonderful, but structurally uneven prosperity of the twenties.

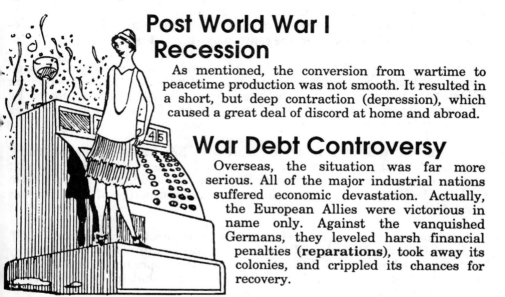

Post World War I Recession

As mentioned, the conversion from wartime to peacetime production was not smooth. It resulted in a short, but deep contraction (depression), which caused a great deal of discord at home and abroad.

War Debt Controversy

Overseas, the situation was far more serious. All of the major industrial nations suffered economic devastation. Actually, the European Allies were victorious in name only. Against the vanquished Germans, they leveled harsh financial penalties (**reparations**), took away its colonies, and crippled its chances for recovery.

The long years of war had savagely drained national treasuries. Both sides had very large debts owed chiefly to the United States. Their only recourse was to levy increased taxes on already broken economies making recovery a longer, and more painful experience.

Avarice And Scandal: Teapot Dome

At home, Americans did their best to forget the war and the problems in Europe. In an atmosphere which seemed to be a reaction to Progressivism and Wilsonian idealism, most wanted to forget political affairs altogether and to enjoy the promise of American prosperity.

Harding's *normalcy* shifted political leadership toward Congress, and without a watchful press and public, special interest groups easily got their way. The good-natured President unwittingly allowed unscrupulous individuals to take advantage of the public's mood of apathy. The result was a number of unsavory scandals involving the **Ohio Gang**, associates to whom Harding generously gave jobs. As the scandals emerged, during a trip to Alaska, Harding died of complications resulting from an embolism.

The most famous scandal was the **Teapot Dome Affair**, in which Secretary of the Interior **Albert Fall** was convicted of accepting bribes to lease government oil reserves in California and Wyoming to private companies. In other scandals, the Attorney General was tried on conspiracy charges, the Director of the Veterans Bureau was convicted of mishandling funds for hospital supplies, and the Custodian of Alien Property was found guilty of fraud.

Coolidge Prosperity

After the brief **post-war contraction** (1919-21), American business began to take advantage of new production and distribution ideas developed during the war to focus on the consumer market. Business improved on **assembly-line patterns** set up earlier in the century by **Henry Ford**.

Electricity, more available as a result of expanded war production, changed factory production and working hours. **Mass advertising** campaigns became widespread. Industry adopted the scientific analysis theories developed by efficiency expert **Frederick Winslow Taylor**. Corporations sometimes streamlined their operations by questionable mergers.

Government, returning to a pre-Progressive Era **laissez-faire attitude**, tended to "look the other way" when it should have been bringing **anti-trust suits** against many of these mergers. Both Harding and his successor, Calvin Coolidge, believed firmly that the leadership and prosperity of America was best left in the hands of the businessman.

Principal regulatory agencies (**Interstate Commerce Commission [ICC]**, **Federal Reserve Board**, and **Federal Trade Commission**) were run by bureaucrats who reflected this attitude. Even the Supreme Court adopted a more lenient attitude toward business, announcing that it would apply the "rule of reason" in anti-trust prosecutions.

Problems On The Farm

Agriculture did not follow the pattern of prosperity. During the war, farmers greatly expanded production to feed our allies. They continued to feed millions through the post war international relief effort headed by **Herbert Hoover**. However, by the early 1920's, European recovery had cut back this profitable demand.

American farmers, hoping to pay off machinery purchased during the war, continued to produce more. As world demand for their produce declined, even technology began to work against them. Refrigeration and transportation improvements, which allowed larger farmers to compete in far off markets, ran smaller local farmers out of business. To fight back against high U.S. tariffs, many nations **reciprocated** with high tariffs of their own, diminishing the chances of U.S. farmers to sell their surplus overseas.

The Mellon Tax Reductions, Tariff Manipulations, And Reciprocation

While adopting a laissez-faire attitude toward mergers, the government stimulated business through its tax policies. It encouraged investment by reducing corporate taxes. It also stimulated consumer spending by reducing personal income taxes. This stimulation policy was mainly the idea of millionaire financier **Andrew Mellon**, Secretary of the Treasury for both Harding and Coolidge.

Mellon also pressured Congress to pass the enormously high **protective tariffs** (Fordney-McCumber [1922] and **Hawley-Smoot** [1930] acts). These aimed at shielding American manufacturing from recovering European competition. This protectionism backfired when the Europeans and Japanese **reciprocated** with their own high tariff **duties** against American goods.

Speculative Boom In Stocks

Throughout most of the 1920's, Americans were optimistic about the material changes in their society and personal lives. Although the increase in wealth was far less dramatic than commonly believed, the optimism led many to blindly risk their life savings in stocks and real estate.

Brokers on **Wall Street** enjoyed a heyday. They called it the "**Big Bull Market**" as stock and **security** prices rose rapidly. Many borrowed money just to buy stocks on "**margin**" (paying on installment plans with high interest rates). Riding this wave of giddy optimism, many unscrupulous characters drew unsuspecting people into deceptive schemes. It was a shaky, hollow economy which grew more unstable as the decade continued.

Questions

1   In the election of 1920, Warren Harding's idea of a "return to normalcy" appealed to the voters' mood because they wanted
   1   a new reform movement in politics.
   2   an end to frequent government scandals.
   3   to pursue the "American Dream."
   4   to play an influential new role in world affairs.

2   European economic recovery after WW I, was difficult because
   1   American forces withdrew too quickly.
   2   enormous war debts had to be repaid.
   3   the U.S. Senate did not ratify the peace treaty.
   4   emergency food supplies were mismanaged.

3   Rapid government demobilization after wars usually causes
   1   public disillusion.   3   economic expansion.
   2   a "bull" market.   4   economic contraction.

4   Harding's administration was hurt by
   1   unscrupulous behavior by officials.
   2   the president's unpopularity.
   3   over-regulation of business.
   4   women's suffrage.

5   The guiding principle during the Coolidge prosperity of the middle 1920's was
   1   progressive reform.
   2   strict commercial regulation.
   3   tariff reciprocation.
   4   laissez-faire.

6   Which aided business growth in the early and middle 1920's?
   1   technological advancement, mergers, and efficiency
   2   progressive legislation by Congress
   3   government anti-trust prosecutions
   4   generous wage agreements with labor

7   Farm problems of the 1920's were caused by
   1   scandals in government farm aid programs.
   2   high food prices.
   3   slow recovery by European farmers.
   4   overproduction and declining demand.

8   Secretary of the Treasury Mellon's tax policies
   1   favored big business.
   2   aided European economic recovery.
   3   were opposed by the Supreme Court.
   4   improved farm production.

9   The widespread stock speculation in the 1920's, revealed that
   1   the government strictly enforced financial regulations.
   2   efficiency studies improved industrial production.
   3   farming income declined.
   4   overconfidence made investors reckless.

10 Reciprocation by Europe and Japan to high U.S. tariff policies resulted in
   1   lower prices on imported goods.
   2   higher wages for most American workers.
   3   cutting down American exports.
   4   increased consumption by the middle class.

C. Consumerism And Clash Of Culture

The Twenties was an age of bewildering contrasts. New inventions were changing daily life rapidly. Personal beliefs and long-held traditions were being questioned. The mood was a combination of strange uneasiness and giddy optimism. It produced an underlying social tension which manifested itself in a variety of ways.

Consumerism

The economy became focused on the middle class consumer, and nothing was more symbolic of this new consumer society than the automobile. Wartime demand had forced many custom-built auto manufacturers to adopt Ford's mass-production techniques, which they continued into the 1920's. To assure a market, manufacturers and banks popularized credit buying on the **installment plan**, borrowing for a car and making small payments with interest.

Registration of autos tripled, and middle class life-styles changed dramatically. As road construction and tourism increased, many Americans saw in the auto a chance to have their families live away from the noise, congestion, and fast pace of the cities. The auto allowed people to commute to work and live a more peaceful life in the open spaces of **suburbia**. A real estate boom began in the middle 1920's. Like the stock market, however, the speculative nature of this real estate boom became a staging ground for dishonest schemes in which many lost vast sums of hard earned money.

A better life-style for the middle class meant more leisure time, and a host of technical advancements led to the entertainment business becoming a major part of the American economy. No longer was entertainment centered in the vaudeville theatres of the big cities. The film industry could take movies into every town and by decade's end, the "silents" would give way to **"Talkies."** Commercial radio shows could aggressively promote sponsors' products in nearly everyone's parlor.

Educational advances allowed major changes in publishing. Readership of newspapers and older popular magazines, such as *The Saturday Evening Post*, and *Colliers*, multiplied. Many new periodicals including *Time, Newsweek, Reader's Digest, Life, The New Yorker*, and others began and flourished during the inter-war period.

Constitutional And Legal Issues

During World War I, **propaganda** and fear had made Americans more suspicious of subversive activities. Intolerance against German sympathizers grew and spread to any groups that reflected foreign influences (immigrants, Catholics, Jews, blacks, radicals). The fear and emotionalism did not subside in the economic and political turmoil of 1918-1920. In such an atmosphere of emotional stress, individual rights are often trampled.

Enduring Issues 4

As the war drew to a close, nearly 3,600 strikes broke out nationwide, as workers sought to hold on to the wage and hour gains they'd made. This disruptive situation was made worse by a wave of fear generated by radical labor groups. They spoke about the U.S. workers following the lead of the **Bolsheviks** who had just taken power in Russia. Strike-plagued employers sought public sympathy by condemning all strikes as revolutionary. In the spring of 1919, radicals were blamed for a series of nationwide terrorist bombings aimed at public officials. During this "**Red Scare**," Wilson's Attorney General, **A. Mitchell Palmer**, sanctioned a series of Justice Department raids against the headquarters of radical groups in 33 cities. In these "**Palmer Raids**," over 3,000 people were denied **due process** rights, such as habeas corpus, reasonable bail, defense lawyers, and jury trials. Over 550 aliens among them were eventually deported.

Denial of due process and anti-immigrant sentiment were also issues in the celebrated **Sacco-Vanzetti trial**. The two Italian immigrants, avowed anarchists, were arrested by Massachusetts officials and tried for robbery and murder on weak, circumstantial evidence. By the time they were electrocuted in 1927, the case and its appeals had come to symbolize the atmosphere of repression in the country.

Enduring Issues 8

Anti-foreign feeling, or **xenophobia**, was also at the heart of the unusual resurgence of the **Ku Klux Klan** in the twenties. The new version of the Klan (its predecessor had been outlawed in the South during Reconstruction), attracted thousands of Americans throughout the nation to its racist, anti-foreign teachings. It was influential in pressuring Congress to pass a series of restrictive immigration acts. The tense years after World War I saw a renewal of the massive waves of immigrants and anti-immigrant sentiment grew. Congress passed the **National Origins Act** in 1929, which limited immigration with a prejudicial set of **quotas** aimed at southern and eastern Europeans and Asians (see page 101).

Repression of ideas became an issue in the celebrated **Scopes Monkey Trial** in 1925, in which **William Jennings Bryan** battled for fundamentalist groups trying to stop the teaching of evolution in Tennessee schools.

The deep social divisions in the nation in the 1920's were also illustrated by passage of the **18th Amendment** to the Constitution, **Prohibition**. Long desired by reformers, it cut the nation's alcohol consumption, but it also caused a substantial rise in crime.

Prohibition aimed at regulating moral behavior. In the rapidly changing society of the 1920's, it failed. There was no **consensus** (general agreement) on what proper moral behavior was. Prohibition was repealed by the **21st Amendment** in 1933.

Enduring Issues 13

Shifting Cultural Values

In the 1920's, American culture was being rapidly transformed by technology and science. The genteel traditions of a rural society were falling away as those of a new, fast-paced urban society took hold.

A younger generation, disillusioned by the bloody experience of war in Europe, seemed to be openly rejecting the past and embracing the new life-style which placed material pleasure and personal wealth above patriotism or service to others. The rise of the entertainment industry, the growth of night clubs, and the faster pace of **Jazz** music and dances, like the **Charleston**, give some indication of a changing pace of life.

By 1920, a powerful combination of factors had begun to break down earlier **Victorian ideas** about the status of women. Broader educational opportunity for women had gradually taken hold in the industrial era. During the war, women had put that education to use in playing new, vital economic roles. The **19th Amendment**, women's suffrage, had given them a new political status. This combination of changes in economic and political status created a feeling of **female emancipation**. It showed itself in new fashions: short skirts, slacks, and shorts. It also showed itself in the break-down of old social restrictions: disappearance of chaperones, increasing participation in sports, and **co-ed** schools.

This re-evaluation of the role of women would raise moral questions. It would cause a more open discussion of sexual behavior, which often shocked and embarrassed the older generation. It would change thinking about marriage, and divorce rates would rise in the 1920's.

The 1920's produced literature that reflected the unsettled mood of the times. Among the works portraying disillusion and frustration are those of novelists **F. Scott Fitzgerald** (*The Beautiful and the Damned, The Great Gatsby*), **Ernest Hemingway** (*The Sun Also Rises*), and Sinclair Lewis (*Main Street, Babbitt*), and poets and playwrights such as **T. S. Elliott** (*The Waste Land*) and **Eugene O'Neill** (*Emperor Jones*).

In the opening decades of the 20th century, many African-Americans moved north, escaping the Jim Crow system of the South. The freedom of the Jazz Age also saw a new cultural consciousness among them as they expressed their hopes and frustrations in the arts. **Langston Hughes'** and **Gene Toomer's** novels, along with the poetry of **Claude McKay** and **Countee Cullen**, and the music of **Duke Ellington, Louis Armstrong**, and **Bessie Smith** became the center of a movement known as the **Harlem Renaissance**.

Questions

1 Which invention had the greatest socio-economic change on American life?
   1   the phonograph   3   refrigeration
   2   cinematography   4   the automobile

2 Prohibition was a political attempt to
   1   regulate morality.   3   fight organized crime.
   2   limit due process rights. 4   regulate a particular industry.

3 Writers of the 1920's,
   1   glorified technological achievement.
   2   questioned the materialism of the age.
   3   encouraged a return to traditional values.
   4   focused on patriotic themes.

4 The "Red Scare" of 1919-1920, led to
   1   repression of civil liberties.   3   a move to the suburbs.
   2   a new military buildup.   4   more socialist legislation.

5 The Ku Klux Klan enjoyed wide popularity because of
   1   America's new leadership role in world affairs.
   2   intellectual disillusionment with society.
   3   reaction to rapid change and mass immigration.
   4   a need to protect civil liberties.

6 Women in the 1920's,
   1   returned to pre-World War I social status.
   2   lost political and economic power.
   3   were brought into important government positions.
   4   assumed new social roles.

7 The National Origins Act of 1929,
   1   set up prejudicial quotas.
   2   encouraged the flow of immigrants.
   3   aided World War I refugees.
   4   abolished the practice of xenophobia.

8 The Sacco-Vanzetti trial symbolized
   1   the materialism of modern life.
   2   the failure of prohibition.
   3   women's emancipation.
   4   denial of due process.

9 Which episode demonstrates a clash between traditional beliefs and new scientific influences?
   1   the Red Scare   3   the Prohibition issue
   2   the Scopes trial   4   the Sacco-Vanzetti case

10 Read the quote from humorist Will Rogers on life in the 1920's:

"No nation in the history of the world was ever sitting as pretty. If we want anything, all we have to do is go buy it on credit. So that leaves us without any problems whatsoever, except perhaps some day to have to pay for them."

— Will Rogers, (*Claremore, OK*: The Will Rogers Company, 1969)

Of which aspect of the 1920's economy is Rogers being critical?

   1   high tariffs   3   laissez-faire
   2   installment plans   4   overspeculation

II. The Great Depression

A. Onset Of The Depression

To those groups that did well during the 1920's, the technological and social advancements seemed to make it a golden age. In 1928, **Herbert Hoover,** who would become Calvin Coolidge's successor, said, *"We in America are nearer to the final triumph over poverty than ever before in the history of any land."* **Gross National Product** (GNP), the sum total of all goods and services produced in the nation in a given period, had shot up 50% in the decade and the "American Dream" seemed to have become a reality.

Weaknesses In The Economy

It is natural to have ups and downs in a **market economy,** especially one as large as that of the United States. Demand for goods and services, savings, investments, and employment can never be perfectly in line in a system that allows freedom of choice. A combination of hundreds of factors cause the economy to soar at times and decline in others. The illustration at the right is a graphic representation of this **cycle of demand,** or what some economists call the "**business cycle.**"

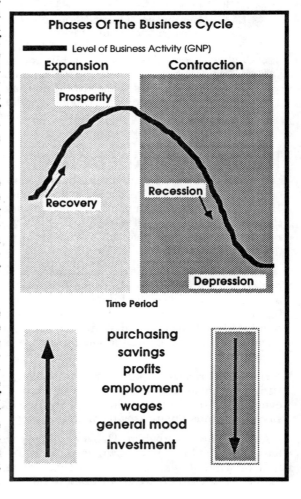

Industrialization had made most Americans aware of the cycle, but there was something very different about the collapse of 1929-32. It was much worse than ever before. Economists list many reasons for this:

1) During the Twenties, the wealth was flowing into the hands of only 5-10% of the population. American manufacturers were **overproducing** massive amounts of goods. As the years went by, the number of people who could afford to buy goods actually declined. The number of those who could consider themselves **middle class** stagnated. Wages had not kept pace with the GNP.

Farmers, miners, and textile workers' incomes were declining from the mid-1920's. The number of poor Americans grew rapidly after 1925. Consumer purchasing began to level off.

> **Enduring Issues 12**

2) Government saw some of the signs, but the Harding-Coolidge-Hoover administrations were locked into a laissez-faire philosophy. They steadfastly refused to "tamper" with income taxes and interest rates or make use of the regulatory power that government had acquired in the Progressive Era.

3) To make matters worse, after the stock market crash, businessmen's fear pressured Congress into raising tariffs even higher with the **Hawley-Smoot Act** (1930). It sealed off American markets from other nations, and they reciprocated by raising their own tariffs against the United States. Without U.S. dollars circulating, buying American goods and paying debts to U.S. bankers became impossible. World trade dried up, and other national economies collapsed.

The Stock Market Crash

Businesses showed enormous profits, and people rushed to buy shares in the "Bull Market." In the fall of 1929, little more than a year after Hoover had made his optimistic pronouncement, business declines caused public confidence to falter. Edgy stockholders began to sell shares rapidly. Margin loans were called in by brokers. Many could not pay. The wave of selling turned into a panic. The economy collapsed so rapidly and completely that it left the nation and the world in a state of shocked disbelief.

The Hoover Response

Herbert Hoover was an accomplished businessman and one of the most talented public administrators ever to be elected to the White House (1929-1933). After less than a year in office, his administration had to struggle with the worst economic catastrophe in history. He believed the market could repair itself, but he also felt government could help to battle the spiraling depression.

This belief was not shared by others who surrounded him. Although he supported some spending to relieve suffering, he would not unbalance the budget and destroy business confidence. He refused to centralize power, because he felt it would take power from state and local governments and destroy individual freedom. He held White House conferences with business leaders to encourage increased production and wage stability, but little came of these meetings.

Hoover increased expenditures on public works projects. He put a **moratorium** (suspension) on war debt payments by European nations to the U.S. and even set up the **Reconstruction Finance Corporation** (RFC) which helped save numerous businesses from bankruptcy.

As the Thirties opened, Hoover's efforts were too restrained and the economy continued to spiral downward. In 1932, the Gross National Product was half of what it was in 1929. In those same years, more than 5,000 banks closed. Wages and prices continued to fall, and employment plummeted.

Labor Force and Unemployment, 1929 - 1941

(Numbers in Millions)

Year	Labor Force	Number Unemployed	Percent Unemployed
1929	49.2	1.6	3.2
1930	49.8	4.3	8.7
1931	50.4	8.0	15.9
1932	51.0	12.1	23.6
1933	51.6	12.8	24.9
1934	52.2	11.3	21.7
1935	52.9	10.6	20.1
1936	53.4	9.0	16.9
1937	54.0	7.7	14.3
1938	54.6	10.4	19.0
1939	55.2	9.5	17.2
1940	55.6	8.1	14.6
1941	55.9	5.6	9.9

Source:
U.S. Dept. of Commerce: Historical Statistics of the U.S.

Americans were bewildered and shocked by the collapse. At first, most people did not expect government to act. However, by 1932, people were clearly expecting more decisive leadership. In June of that year, destitute veterans sought a bonus promised to them by Congress. From all over the nation this **"Bonus Army"** descended on Washington for mass marches. When the bonus bill failed, a nervous Hoover allowed Army Chief of Staff **General Douglas MacArthur** to lead U.S. Army troops in dispersing the veterans with bayonets and tear gas, setting fire to their camps.

The public was outraged. That summer, farmers tried to organize a general strike to withhold their produce to drive prices up, but it collapsed in disillusion. It was an election year, desperation was growing, and the people began to see Hoover's leadership as timid and frightened. He was soundly defeated at the polls in November.

B. FDR And The New Deal: Relief, Recovery, And Reform

In Hoover's place, the nation elected Democrat **Franklin Delano Roosevelt** in a massive **landslide** vote. It seems strange they would turn to this **patrician** (upper class) New Yorker, born to wealth, and not at all like the self-made Hoover. Raised on the family's beautiful estate in Hyde Park, N.Y., Roosevelt's wealthy parents sent him to upper-class schools. After a brief private law practice, he entered New York state politics. He was not a social reformer, but he was attracted to the Progressive Movement because of his concern for human suffering.

He had enthusiastically supported the progressive Woodrow Wilson in 1912, and was named Assistant Secretary of the Navy as a reward. In 1920, he ran for vice-president on the Democratic ticket with **James M. Cox.** They were soundly defeated by Harding.

A year later, Roosevelt was tragically paralyzed with polio and never regained the use of his legs. In 1928, he narrowly succeeded in winning election as Governor of New York. His willingness to help people cope with the Depression helped him not only win reelection in 1930, but put him in a position to easily gain the Democratic nomination for president in 1932.

He was a vigorous campaigner, exuding confidence with his *"Happy Days Are Here Again"* theme song. He was an inspiring orator:

"I pledge you, I pledge myself, to a new deal for the American people." He criticized Hoover's lack of action, but he was vague about his own programs.

Two Philosophies of Government Stimulation

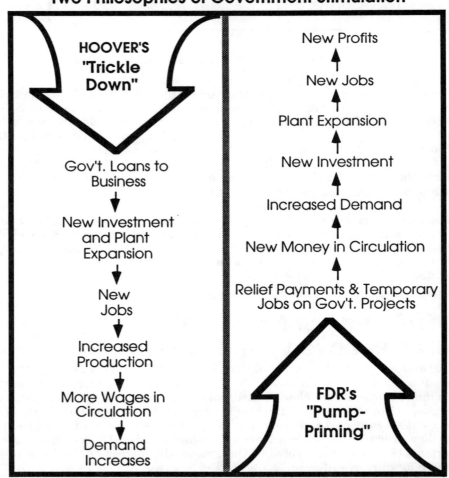

HOOVER'S "Trickle Down"

Gov't. Loans to Business
↓
New Investment and Plant Expansion
↓
New Jobs
↓
Increased Production
↓
More Wages in Circulation
↓
Demand Increases

New Profits
↑
New Jobs
↑
Plant Expansion
↑
New Investment
↑
Increased Demand
↑
New Money in Circulation
↑
Relief Payments & Temporary Jobs on Gov't. Projects

FDR's "Pump-Priming"

The New Deal Philosophy

Actually, FDR had only a few programs in mind, but he did represent a different philosophy of government's role in the economy. Hoover and the Republicans followed a **trickle-down theory**: that, if government legislated so that big corporations and the well-to-do had their wealth protected, their investments would expand the economy and make life better for everyone.

FDR and his advisors felt that government should use a **prime-pumping**, working from the bottom up. It should take actions that would make the consuming public secure and optimistic. Their spending would then generate business for the wealthy and keep the economy growing.

Roosevelt felt that in an economic contraction, government must first take **relief** actions to stabilize the economy, then **recovery** actions to stimulate it. From his earlier experiences in the Progressive Movement, Roosevelt felt that the system needed basic changes (**reform**) to keep it functioning. Later, this idea would become part of a more complex formal theory in British economist **John Maynard Keynes'** *General Theory on Employment, Interest, and Money,* which would challenge the classical approach to market economics and advocate an activist role for government.

FDR As Govenor Of New York

As the new governor of New York, FDR inherited a state which had gone through much social reform under his predecessor, **Al Smith**. Smith was the 1928 Democratic Presidential candidate against Herbert Hoover. In less than a year, Roosevelt was faced with helping his state deal with the Great Depression. New York was hard hit with unemployment.

With the federal government reluctant to aid the states, Governor Roosevelt had to take the initiative. With the NYS Legislature's cautious approval, he set up the **Temporary Emergency Relief Agency (TERA)**. He chose a young social worker, **Harry Hopkins**, to be its head. Later, Hopkins became a central figure of the New Deal.

Many of those who later became cabinet officers and White House advisors (**Louis Howe, Henry Morganthau, Frances Perkins**) were with FDR in Albany. This influential group laid the groundwork for what became the New Deal. They guided many measures through the state legislature that called national attention to the state and its governor: **work-relief** on public building projects; **minimum wage** and **maximum hour** laws; **old-age insurance, unemployment relief; increased school aid;** a **gas tax** to finance road construction; and **regulation of banking** and **public utilities**.

Eleanor Roosevelt strongly influenced FDR's return to public life after he was stricken with polio. She played a vital role in these New York years. She campaigned hard and often made public appearances when it was impossible for her husband. Touring the state, she saw suffering and returned to Albany to press Franklin for action. Her sympathy for disadvantaged youth, women, and minorities was enormously influential.

To alleviate unemployment, Governor Roosevelt had his Public Works Commissioner, **Robert Moses**, construct 5,000 new acres of parks, 33 miles of parkways, and two new subway lines. In New York City alone, Moses directed the completion of the Triborough Bridge complex, two new subway lines, and a new airport (later to be named in honor of Mayor LaGuardia).

In 1932, the same year that the dynamic FDR won election to the White House, New York City elected a new and equally energetic mayor, "The Little Flower," **Fiorello LaGuardia**. This son of Italian-Jewish immigrants led an astonishing career as an Ellis Island interpreter, diplomat, criminal prosecutor, WW I combat pilot, and maverick Republican congressman. He was one of the greatest reformers in the city's history. He recruited a tough Police Commissioner, **Lewis Valentine**, and a special prosecutor, **Thomas E. Dewey**, to fight crime and corruption.

Despite the fact that LaGuardia and FDR were of different parties, they worked well together. With one billion dollars in federal aid, he put the nearly bankrupt city back on its feet. The activist mayor began the first major **publicly-funded housing project** in the nation. LaGuardia was also instrumental in arranging **federal guarantees** for the Metropolitan Life Insurance Company to build the largest privately-funded housing project in the nation, **Parkchester**.

The New Deal Administration: "The Brains Trust"

Roosevelt carried the momentum and high powered personnel from New York to Washington in March of 1933. Howe remained at his side as a personal advisor. Morganthau and Perkins became cabinet members. **Raymond Moley** and **Rexford G. Tugwell** headed a brilliant group of personal advisors nicknamed **"The Brains Trust."** They were dynamic, pragmatic thinkers, ready to try new ideas to aggressively attack the problems of the depression. Perhaps the most famous of these was **Harry Hopkins**, a midwestern social worker, who headed up the work-relief programs. Later, Hopkins was FDR's chief foreign policy advisor and trouble-shooter during World War II.

Enduring Issues 1

Relief Of Human Suffering

Once in the White House, FDR focused on **relief, recovery,** and **reform** to get the national economy functioning. In the first three months of his administration, nicknamed **"The Hundred Days,"** he and his staff rushed a mass of "3R's" legislation through Congress. The breathtaking scope and pace of "The Hundred Days" raised public confidence. Under **relief,** immediate measures had to be taken to stop the downward trend of the economy.

The nation's banking system was on the verge of total collapse. On 6March1933, Roosevelt closed all the nation's banks, declared a "Bank Holiday," and called Congress into special session. The **Emergency Banking Act** was passed. Treasury officials, under Secretary **Henry Morganthau,** examined banks and let solvent ones reopen.

The New Deal's 3 R's

President and Advisors
(Suggest Legislation)

↓

Congress
(Legislates Programs)

Relief	Recovery	Reform
Immediate Action to Halt the Economy's Deterioration	"Pump - Priming" Temporary Programs to Restart the Flow of Consumer Demand	Permanent Programs to Avoid Situations Causing Contractions and Insurance for Citizens Against Economic Disasters
Bank Holiday	Agricultural Adjustment	Securities & Exchange Commission
Emergency Banking Act	National Industrial Recovery Act	Federal Deposit Insurance Corporation
Federal Emergency Relief Act	Home Owners Loan Corp.	Social Security Administration
Civil Works Administration	Works Progress Administration	National Labor Relations Board

Congress rushed through his **Federal Emergency Relief Act** (FERA) to give direct aid to the poor and starving in the country.

A **Civil Works Administration** (CWA, 1933-34) was created to ease unemployment. Under Relief Administrator **Harry Hopkins**, the CWA created over 3 million work-relief jobs repairing roads, parks, and public buildings. Criticized as wasteful, the CWA was dropped and replaced by the better planned **Works Projects Administration** (WPA) in 1935. Between 1935 and 1941, the WPA employed 8 million workers and spent $13,000,000 on highway, park, post office, and school construction. Another measure was the **Civilian Conservation Corps** (1933-1942). The CCC enrolled over 2.5 million unemployed young men in a military-like organization doing **reforestation** and flood-control work.

Economic Recovery

Relief measures helped people survive, but were insufficient to move the economy upward. **Recovery** meant short-term programs to generate demand in the marketplace to encourage the natural flow of supply and demand.

Stimulation Measures (pump-priming) were passed to start industry and agriculture moving again. To create production incentives, the **National Industrial Recovery Act** (NIRA) and **Agricultural Adjustment Act** (AAA) were created.

The NIRA was a complex scheme involving voluntary industrial codes on production quotas, price agreements, and wage guarantees. It was mobilized by the **National Recovery Administration** (NRA) in a vast patriotic campaign with rallies, parades, and its own **"Blue Eagle"** symbol.

Enduring Issues **12**	The AAA was a similarly complex program to aid destitute farmers and to manage agricultural production and prices. Legal challenges eventually ended in both of these programs being declared unconstitutional.

To stimulate the construction industry, the government created the **Home Owners Loan Corporation** (HOLC) which set up the **Federal Housing Administration** to guarantee mortgages and spur home purchasing. It also made money available so people could refinance mortgages, giving more stability to the banking industry.

Search For Effective Reform

Amid the whirlwind of New Deal legislation, Roosevelt also led Congress to seek permanent reform of the economic system. These changes made life more secure and helped avoid many of the situations that had caused the Great Depression:

Enduring Issues **1**	• The most far-reaching reform created a financial security program for individuals. It was based on earlier Progressive Era ideas and on the examples already adopted by many European nations. Under the **Social Security Act** (1935), a system of in-

surance was created to assist people in coping with the loss of income due to old-age, unemployment, and physical handicaps. FDR called it "the cornerstone" of his administration.

Adapted from a political cartoon which appeared in 1933, in the Salt Lake (Utah) Tribune, the above is typical of reactions to the speed of Congressional action during the New Deal.

- The financial structure of the nation was significantly altered in several ways:

> The **Glass-Steagle Banking Act** created the **Federal Deposit Insurance Corporation** (FDIC) to insure depositors against bank failures, but it also required banks to undergo frequent examinations of their operations.
>
> The **Federal Reserve Bank** was given more power to oversee banking in general.
>
> A **Securities and Exchange Commission** (SEC) was created to watch over the stock market.

- Basic rights of working people were also established. Reasonable working hours, basic conditions of safety, and a federal minimum wage were established under the **Fair Labor Standards Act** (1937). Workers' rights to organize and to negotiate with employers (**collective bargaining**) were established under the **Wagner Act (National Labor Relations Act of 1935)**.

Popular Response

There were mixed reactions to the whirlwind of activity in Washington. To a considerable extent, the New Deal spirit of reform took hold in the country.

In labor, **John L. Lewis,** leader of the United Mine Workers, had tried for years to gain acceptance for his union in the powerful **American Federation of Labor.** The "A.F. of L." took the position that it was an organization of **skilled tradesmen** and rejected the idea of affiliating with broad-based **industry-wide unions.** After a dispute with the A.F. of L., Lewis formed his own national organization of unions, the **Congress of Industrial Organizations.** The two organizations then began a long and fierce competition for membership which finally ended in their merging into the **A.F.L.-C.I.O.** in 1955.

Like the LaGuardia administration in New York City, most state and local governments responded well to the offers of New Deal aid. Some conservative Democrats in the South opposed Federal interference, and many rural Republican communities of the North and Mid-West refused to participate in what they called "FDR's creeping socialism."

In the middle of the New Deal, conservative businessmen formed the **American Liberty League** to raise funds for conservative candidates. It was the main backing for Kansas Governor **Alf Landon,** the Republican Party's Presidential candidate in 1936.

Controversial Aspects Of The New Deal

The United States is a democracy. Although the American public was generally supportive of the New Deal, no true democracy could go through such alterations of policy without public discussion and opposition. Although Congress was generally in agreement with the president's programs, checks and balances were operating all through the New Deal years.

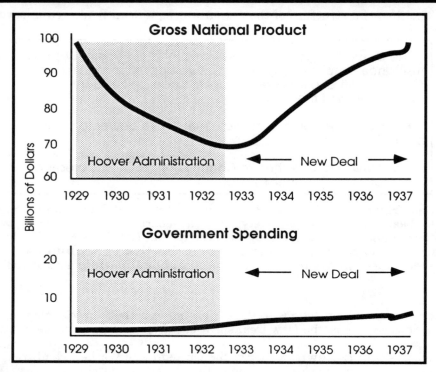

Critics attacked:

• *the growth in federal spending to finance the New Deal*

Opponents spoke out against the unbalanced government budget. Because raising taxes would have a negative effect on consumer spending and investment, increasing revenues to balance the budget was difficult. **Tariff barriers** were lowered to increase trade opportunities. With government income low, Treasury Secretary Morganthau felt the only recourse was for the government to use **deficit spending** (government borrowing heavily to finance its operations). Many considered this concept to be poor economic management.

• *the growth of the Federal agencies and their staffs*

This unleashed an outcry against **big government**. Opponents pointed out that taxes would have to go up to maintain such a large operation. Worse, they said, more people and offices meant a complex and inefficient **"bureaucracy"** would run the country.

• *the liberal stretching of legislative and executive power*

Opponents of many of the hastily devised New Deal programs immediately launched legal challenges. By 1935, the Court was declaring key laws unconstitutional. The Court said that Congress had stretched its power over interstate commerce too far and struck down the AAA in *United States v. Butler,* and the NIRA in *Schechter Poultry Corp. v. United States.* The Court also ruled that New Deal laws on pensions, bankruptcy, and the minimum wage were questionable.

Riding high on a landslide re-election in 1936, FDR tried to have Congress change the composition of the Supreme Court to make it friendlier to his programs. At the height of his popularity, checks and balances handed him his most devastating political defeat. His **"Court Packing Plan,"** would enable him to name additional federal judges for those over 70 years old who refused retirement. The plan received nationwide criticism and was soundly defeated by Congress.

> **Enduring Issues**
> **3**

Another action widely denounced was Roosevelt's decision to run for a third term in 1940. This broke a precedent set 150 years before by George Washington. Even though there was no limit on the number of Presidential terms in the Constitution, it had been a tradition. Many were deeply disturbed to see it broken, and felt that it undermined the basic constitutional principle of **limited power**. (In 1951, the **22nd Amendment** to the United States Constitution was adopted to limit presidents to two terms.)

The Human Factor

The New Deal had numerous effects on the American people. Some helped to ease the pain and suffering of the Depression, some did not:

• *Roosevelt as a masterful communicator.* Undoubtedly, one of the things that helped the New Deal was Roosevelt's own personality. The optimistic and dynamic FDR was able to project a positive attitude toward life in his frequent press conferences, in the short clips people saw weekly in theater newsreels, and most of all, in his radio addresses. The latter became known as **"Fireside Chats,"** because he talked in a direct, almost personal tone to the radio listener.

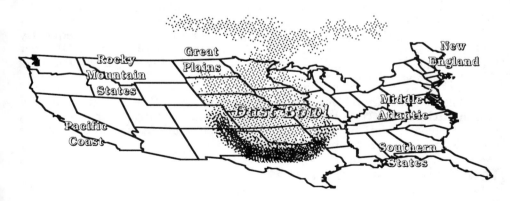

• *The Dust Bowl.* One of the most tragic human stories of the Depression Era occurred in the midwestern states. Farmers in general were suffering financially long before the collapse of 1929, but in 1932, nature turned tragically against them. A devastating drought that would last more than four years in some areas hit the midsection of the nation from Texas and Oklahoma to the Dakotas. In the area which became nicknamed **"The Dust Bowl,"** winds picked up the parched soil, and destitute farmers watched helplessly as it blew their fortunes away.

A million or more "**Oakies**" and "**Arkies**" packed up their families and possessions and sought work in the agricultural regions of the West Coast but were often to find rejection in western towns fearing their economic competition. **John Steinbeck** wrote sympathetically about the tragedy in his classic novel, *The Grapes of Wrath.*

> **Enduring Issues 7**

• *The New Deal and Women.* Despite the new status women had achieved during the 1920's, they were to suffer the same discrimination as blacks when the Depression struck. Women were brought into FDR's administration. Secretary of Labor **Frances Perkins** became the first female cabinet officer, and women were also appointed to judgeships and foreign service posts. Mrs. Roosevelt used her considerable influence with the president, and her syndicated daily news column, *My Day,* to press for more equal treatment for women under New Deal programs.

• *The New Deal and Minorities.* The record of the New Deal in helping **minority groups** is not inspiring. Although the problems plagued all Americans during the Depression, black wage earners and farmers were particularly hard-hit. Already suffering from discrimination in housing and jobs, they disproportionately felt the economic collapse in increased layoffs, foreclosures and evictions. In 1932, they made up nearly 20% of the unemployed. Politically, they backed Roosevelt, but the Democratic leadership was cautious on racial matters.

> **Enduring Issues 8**

• *Segregation* was still strong in the North and South. Blacks were not given equal treatment in the administration of New Deal programs. Since Southern legislators held key positions in Congress, and the success of the New Deal was largely in their hands, FDR was reluctant to challenge their power with reforms for blacks. The Works Projects Administration (WPA) did have nondiscrimination clauses in its hiring regulations, but still by 1935, three times as many blacks were on relief as whites. **Eleanor Roosevelt** became a strong voice for equal treatment of minorities and met frequently with black leaders including, **A. Philip Randolph**, **Ralph Bunche**, **Robert Weaver**, and **Mary McLeod Bethune**, who was a director of the National Youth Administration.

• *Native Americans* did little better than blacks. The 1934 **Indian Reorganization Act** (Wheeler Act) gave them greater control over their lands, and improved educational opportunities for their youth. A special bureau was also created for reservation work under the CCC.

The Culture Of The Depression

The New Deal made a significant cultural contribution to American life. Reaching out to help people, programs were designed to assist creative artists. Under **Harry Hopkins**, the WPA created theater and art projects. Artists worked on building murals and illustrations for federal publications, and dramatists and choreographers created new works which were performed throughout the nation under the **Federal Theater Project**. The WPA also supervised oral history projects, helping to preserve regional folklore. The New Deal also created a dramatic photographic record of rural life in the 1930's through the artistry of **Dorothea Lange** and **Walker Evans**.

Entertainment in the 1930's reflected a desire for **escapism**. Radio and Hollywood films catered to this desire, both experiencing a golden age. Escapism is very evident if one pictures Americans flocking to the cinema to watch **Fred Astair** and **Ginger Rogers** in formal wear dancing their cares away, or **Judy Garland** flying over the rainbow in the *Wizard of Oz*. At home, they escaped with the comedy of **George Burns and Gracie Allen**, the music of **Bing Crosby**, melodramas, such as *Lights Out* and *Suspense*, or the many soap operas that filled the airwaves.

Political Extremism

Not everyone was bent on escaping reality in the troubled 1930's. There were many groups that would gain popularity by trying to radically change the American system. As a movement, American **communism** had suffered greatly in the 1920's, after the "Red Scare," but it drew new attention in the dark days of the depression and party members gained influence in several large industrial unions. Communism was especially attractive to **intellectuals**. However, the intense loyalty of leaders **William Z. Foster** and **Earl Browder** to international policies directed by the U.S.S.R. and constant talk of radical revolution alienated many from the communist movement.

The **Socialist Party** also gained a larger following, and its leader, **Norman Thomas**, constantly criticized Roosevelt as being too timid about government acts to help the working class. **Fascist** groups also emerged, admiring the type of system that seemed to be working in Italy and Germany.

Home grown radical movements also arose. **Dr. Charles Townsend** attracted thousands to an **Old Folks' Crusade**. He pressed for a $200 a month pension system. Townsend clubs helped to organize support for the **Social Security Act**, although they saw it as too limited.

From Louisiana came the socialistic **"Share Our Wealth"** program launched by its powerful Senator, **Huey Long**. Long was a hero to some, a **demagogue** and potential dictator to others. He wanted to limit individual wealth, guarantee everyone a home, a minimum $2,500 income, a free college education, and a pension by taxing the rich. He began to criticize the New Deal for being too cautious. By 1935, "Share Our Wealth" clubs were forming nationally and Long was preparing to launch a challenge to Roosevelt for the 1936 Democratic nomination. The movement declined after Long was assassinated on the steps of the state capital in Baton Rouge.

A third powerful critic of the Roosevelt administration was **Father Charles E. Coughlin**. The Michigan "Radio Priest" had gained popularity in the early Depression. He used his devotional radio broadcasts to denounce the Hoover administration's lack of social conscience. Coughlin advocated a mixture of socialist and populist causes and denounced modern capitalism. At first, he endorsed the New Deal, but later, when FDR ignored his schemes, Coughlin denounced the New Deal as communistic. He created a lobby called the **National Union for Social Justice**. In 1936, he transformed it into the **Union Party** and attracted former supporters of Huey Long's movement. The Union Party did not do well at the polls in 1938 and gradually deteriorated. Coughlin continued to be a Roosevelt critic, but his movement became more and more radically right-wing and lost many followers.

The New Deal In Perspective

By 1938, the New Deal was losing momentum. At that point, the economy was inching upward, and attention was focusing more on foreign problems. Historians still argue about whether the New Deal was a success. Supporters feel the New Deal:

- preserved the free enterprise system by remodeling its weakest parts.

- forged a new connection between the individual and government.

- established the role of government as stimulator of economy.

FDR

Questions

1   A major reason for the collapse of the American economy after 1929, was
  1   the failure of the prohibition experiment.
  2   over-regulation of banking by the Federal Reserve.
  3   restriction of the free flow of immigration.
  4   wage levels did not keep pace with economic growth.

2   The tariff policies of the U.S. government in the 1920's led to
  1   increased profits for farmers.
  2   a decrease in world trade.
  3   overexpansion of European industry.
  4   over-speculation in the stock market.

3   Economic thinking which dominated the Republican administrations of the 1920's, rested on creating prosperity by
  1   implementing programs favorable to business investment.
  2   stimulation of military spending.
  3   setting production incentives for agriculture.
  4   expanding the lower class' consumption capacity.

4   As the Great Depression deepened, President Hoover
  1   refused to launch programs to aid the needy.
  2   adopted a limited program to aid business investment.
  3   pressed Congress to lower tariffs.
  4   demanded European nations pay their war debts.

5   Because of the "Bonus Army" episode in 1932, President Hoover
  1   began to try new approaches to the economic crisis.
  2   increased military spending to stimulate the economy.
  3   suspended war debt payments for European nations.
  4   lost public confidence.

6   In the campaign of 1932, Franklin Delano Roosevelt
  1   had no previous experience in dealing with the Depression.
  2   supported the "trickle-down theory."
  3   made only vague promises about fighting the Depression.
  4   denounced Hoover's struggle to keep the budget balanced.

7   Immediately after taking office, FDR
1   closed the banks.
2   ordered pensions for the aged.
3   raised the minimum wage.
4   expanded minority rights.
8   FDR tried to have the federal court system revised because
1   the justices needed a better retirement plan.
2   he felt life terms were undemocratic.
3   the courts were falling behind in their work.
4   the courts were dismantling his New Deal programs.
9   During the "Hundred Days" in 1933, Congress
1   passed many work-relief programs.
2   blocked FDR's New Deal.
3   fought the President to preserve laissez-faire.
4   eliminated the unemployment problem.
10 The Wagner Act symbolized reform because it
1   created a national old-age pension system.
2   focused on reclaiming the "Dust Bowl."
3   established collective bargaining rights.
4   provided for unemployment insurance.
11 Social Security symbolized reform, because it established
1   insurance of bank deposits.
2   pensions and unemployment insurance.
3   a federal minimum wage.
4   guaranteed employment for the jobless.
12 One characteristic New Dealers shared with Roosevelt was their
1   pragmatic approach to problems.
2   belief in command economies.
3   socialistic philosophy.
4   escapist attitude.
13 Which concept reflects the New Deal approach to social responsibility?
1   Interaction between buyer and seller is all the consumer protection
    necessary.
2   The federal government's power over the economy should be limited.
3   Moderation of the effects of the business cycle is a Federal govern-
    ment function.
4   Government policies should be approved by the boards of directors of
    the major corporations.
14 Two important New Deal measures that were declared unconstitutional
    were the
1   Civilian Conservation Corps and the Works Progress Administration.
2   National Industrial Recovery Act and the Agricultural Adjustment
    Act.
3   Fair Labor Standards Act and the National Labor Relations Act.
4   Social Security Act and the Home Owners Loan Corporation.
15 The WPA embodied both the relief and recovery ideas of the New Deal,
    because it
1   hired the unemployed and stimulated purchasing.
2   promoted the creative arts.
3   restored public buildings.
4   set production quotas for industry.

Labor Force and Unemployment
1929 - 1941
(Numbers in Millions)

Year	Labor Force	Number Unemployed	Percent Unemployed
1929	49.2	1.6	3.2
1930	49.8	4.3	8.7
1931	50.4	8.0	15.9
1932	51.0	12.1	23.6
1933	51.6	12.8	24.9
1934	52.2	11.3	21.7
1935	52.9	10.6	20.1
1936	53.4	9.0	16.9
1937	54.0	7.7	14.3
1938	54.6	10.4	19.0
1939	55.2	9.5	17.2
1940	55.6	8.1	14.6
1941	55.9	5.6	9.9

Source: U.S. Dept. of Commerce:
Historical Statistics of the U.S.

16 Which generalization can be validly drawn from the chart above?
   1 The New Deal restored employment to its 1929 level.
   2 Industrial production improved after 1933.
   3 New Deal legislation improved working conditions.
   4 Employment levels generally improved in the New Deal era.

17 A key advisor to FDR on relief programs was
   1 Douglas MacArthur.
   2 Al Smith.
   3 Andrew Mellon.
   4 Harry Hopkins.

18 Fr. Charles Coughlin, Dr. Charles Townsend, and Sen. Huey Long were leaders of
   1 the Roosevelt coalition.
   2 the Ohio Gang.
   3 anti-Roosevelt groups.
   4 the Brains Trust.

19 The radio and film industries blossomed in the 1930's, because they
   1 offered jobs to the unemployed.
   2 provided an escape from dismal reality.
   3 were considered luxuries for the rich.
   4 received many government subsidies.

20 The New Deal reflected the idea that the United States government should
   1 regulate and reform the economy.
   2 restrict its actions to foreign affairs and defense.
   3 own and operate vital industries.
   4 reduce the scope of the welfare system.

Essays

1 Most significant policy changes in history have both positive and negative effects. Listed below are some economic changes that occurred during the New Deal Era:

- A government old-age pension system
- A Federal minimum wage
- Government insurance of bank deposits
- Government-owned electric power projects
- Guaranteed collective bargaining for unions
- Price guarantees for farmers
- Price, wage, production quota agreements among businesses sponsored and monitored by government

Choose THREE changes in the economy listed above. For EACH one chosen, identify one group that would be affected positively and one group that would be affected negatively by that change. Discuss how each group would be affected economically by that change. [5,5,5]

2 In his book, *The Big Change*, historian Frederick Lewis Allen indicates, "the New Deal permanently altered the nature of the American economy." Below are several of the new economic roles he says that government acquired:

- Protector of the underdog
- Stimulator of Employment
- Umpire of the marketplace
- Friend of Labor
- Manager of the Economy

Choose THREE of the above governmental economic roles. For EACH role, discuss TWO specific actions taken during the New Deal and explain how they changed the nation's economic structure. [5,5,5]

3 Franklin D. Roosevelt and his advisors had a different concept of the relationship of government and the individual than did Herbert Hoover and those who staffed his administration.

a Explain the differences between the philosophies of government in the two administrations. [6]

b Explain the general approach EACH administration used to alleviate the economic problems of the Great Depression. [6]

c The Reagan administration has used "supply side economics" to deal with the economic problems of the 1980's (see Unit Six). It is quite similar to the Hoover administration's approach. Why do you think it has worked in the 1980's, where it failed in the 1930's? [3]

Unit Five

The United States

in an Age of Global Crisis:
Responsibility and Cooperation

1930	1935		1940
• Nazis Come to Power	• US recognizes USSR	• Axis Pact	• WW II in Europe
• Good Neighbor Policy		• US Neutrality Acts	• Destroyers -for- Bases

Clear and Present Danger
Storm - Cellar Isolation
Command Economy
Nuclear Deterrent
Loyality Program
Totalitarianism
Appeasement
Iron Curtain
Containment
Superpower
Aggression
Holocaust
Cold War
Genocide
Summit

	1945			1950

- US enters WW II
- Atlantic Charter
- Lend-Lease
- rationing
- D-Day
- Yalta
- Hiroshima
- WWII ends
- Fair Deal
- Marshall Plan
- Berlin Airlift
- McCarthy Era
- NATO

I. Peace In Peril: 1933-1950

A. Isolation And Neutrality

Precedents For Neutrality 1790-1917: Post-WW I Diplomacy

The Great Depression did not just upset personal lives and national economies. A very delicate structure of peace, set up at Versailles in 1919 and world conferences in the 1920's, was also destroyed by the collapse. The peace depended on the smooth operation of the major nations' economies. The chaos, bitterness, and disillusion of the depression years became fertile ground for extremists and radical movements.

By 1929, only a few nations had physically recovered from the devastation of World War I. Germany, saddled with an enormous war debt and forced to pay war reparations to Britain and France, resorted to churning out worthless currency. The staggering German economy was finally shattered in the chaotic period that followed the American collapse in 1929. **Adolph Hitler** and the **National Socialists (Nazi)** came to power in 1933.

Adolph Hitler

Nearly a decade earlier, Italy had turned to a **fascist** structure which concentrated economic power in state-directed arrangements under **Benito Mussolini**. Hopes for a lasting peace structure were dashed as nations pursued their self-interest in the Great Depression years.

After the Senate's rejection of President Wilson's pleas for the Versailles Treaty and the League of Nations in 1919, U.S. foreign policy had followed a zig-zag course. The Harding, Coolidge, and Hoover administrations made gestures toward international cooperation (see page 150) but refused to commit any military power to peace-keeping. This remoteness was also reflected in anti-immigration policies, stubborn international economic dealings and exorbitantly high tariff policies (see page 161).

> *"It is our true policy to steer clear of permanent alliances with any portion of the foreign world."*
>
> *George Washington, Farewell Address, 1796*

Many Americans felt comfortable with **isolationism**. Its proponents cited the 18th and 19th century traditions of neutrality. Isolationists quoted **Washington's Farewell Address** of 1796. The first President had warned against foreign alliances. From the early struggles of Presidents Adams, Jefferson, and Madison to keep us out of the Napoleonic Wars of the early 19th Century, to Wilson's attempts to keep us neutral throughout most of World War I, the advice of Washington had been a cornerstone of American policy.

Isolationists also cited the **Monroe Doctrine** (1823) which, while warning Europe to cease colonization of the Western Hemisphere, also indicated our resolve to stay out of European affairs.

In the 1930's, the isolationists argued that this neutral tradition was the safest path for America. To them, the imperialism of McKinley (1898), the world power vision of Teddy Roosevelt, and the internationalism of Woodrow Wilson were only brief deviations from the proper path of American policy.

Adding fuel to this oversimplified view was the fact that the two oceans still afforded reasonable protection for us. (The true potential of the air age was not yet evident in the 1930's.) The emotional disillusion still present from the post-World War I days and its elaboration in the popular literature of the era, was a potent force for isolationist sympathies. Japan's aggression in Manchuria in 1931, and similar moves by Italy and Germany in the mid-1930's, added strength to the isolationists' position.

The truth was that America had always played a much more active role in world affairs than the isolationists believed. 19th century involvement over territorial expansion and trading rights had brought us into conflict with the Barbary States, Spain, France, Britain, Mexico, Germany, and even Tzarist Russia. Late 19th century industrial growth and tipping the balance in World War I, had placed the U.S. among the world's great powers, and no amount of wishful thinking about the past could change these facts.

Franklin D. Roosevelt understood the potency of the isolationist movement, but he was a product of 20th century America, a Progressive of the Wilsonian school. He shared the Progressives' belief that America's rise to power had given it a major role to play in world affairs. He believed in seeking peaceful, economic solutions to problems and was troubled when militarism once again reared its ugly head in Europe and Asia. Roosevelt and his Secretary of State, **Cordell Hull**, sought to aid American trade in world markets by a free trade policy. They refused to be bound by any agreements at the **London International Economic Conference** (1933), arranged by Herbert Hoover before he left office. They pressed Congress for the **Reciprocity Act** (1934) giving the President power to negotiate tariff rates with individual nations and gave government aid to American companies seeking favorable trade conditions abroad.

| Enduring Issues **9** |

These initiatives led to two major diplomatic changes in the early days of the New Deal: the **Good Neighbor Policy** and the **diplomatic recognition of the U.S.S.R.** The Good Neighbor policy involved Secretary Hull's pledge at the Pan American Union's **Montevideo Conference** in 1933 to end the long history of U.S. **interventionism** in the internal affairs of Latin American nations. This was followed by FDR's effective use of the **Reciprocity Act** which doubled the trade between the U.S. and Latin America by 1935. Less successful was a similar policy toward the U.S.S.R.

Over many protests, FDR recognized the Soviet regime in Russia in 1933, and sent **William Bullitt** to Moscow as our first ambassador to the U.S.S.R. However, Soviet leader **Joseph Stalin** was more interested in negotiating a defense treaty against the rising threat of Japan than talking about trade, and the initiative failed.

Geneva Disarmament Conference Of 1932-34

Despite the growing isolationist sentiments and the problems at home, the Hoover administration had been enthusiastic about a major disarmament conference in Geneva in 1932-34. He believed that arms manufacturing did not produce real wealth needed for reestablishing a healthy world economy. The Conference was doomed to failure especially

Joseph Stalin

since the French were becoming more wary of a rehabilitated arms industry in Germany. While it met off and on for the next two years, and Roosevelt continued support after replacing Hoover as President, the Conference made no headway. French fears remained the chief stumbling block, especially after Hitler began to rearm Germany.

The Nye Committee

Isolationism gained even more popularity as a result of the **Nye Committee report** in 1935. North Dakota Senator **Gerald Nye** headed the controversial "merchants of death investigation" into rumors that U.S. bankers and manufacturers, seeking war profits in 1915-17, from the British and French, had effectively undermined President Wilson's neutrality position.

Storm Cellar Diplomacy

Act	Provisions
Neutrality Act of 1935	When the President proclaimed that a foreign war existed, no arms could be sold or transported on American ships to the nations involved. No Americans could travel on the ships of warring nations.
Neutrality Act of 1936	When the President proclaimed that a foreign war existed, no loans could be made to the warring nations.
Neutrality Act of 1937	No Americans could travel on ships of warring nations. All provisions of the above Neutrality Acts apply to civil wars.
Neutrality Act of 1939	Nations fighting aggression were allowed to buy war material from U. S. manufacturers on a "cash and carry" basis. President could proclaim "danger zones" and forbid U. S. ships to enter the danger areas.

This was a major reason why the U.S. had been drawn into World War I. While the Nye Committee found many financial arrangements had existed, it found no evidence to connect them to government policies. However, the isolationist press ignored the lack of evidence and helped many Americans jump to the conclusion that the arms business had pushed America into war in 1917. The resulting outcry helped pave the way for Congress to pass the **Neutrality Act of 1935.**

Neutrality Acts 1935-37

Enduring Issues 9

Tension began to mount during 1933, when Japan violated its pledge (**Nine-Power Treaty of 1922**) to keep trade with China open. Japan left the League of Nations when that body censured its aggression in Manchuria. Isolationist sentiments ran even higher in 1935, when Mussolini announced Italy's plan to conquer Ethiopia. Congress responded by passing the **Neutrality Act of 1935**. In an attempt to avoid the kinds of things that had led us into World War I, the sale or shipment of arms to **belligerent nations** (countries at war) was forbidden. The following year, Congress forbid private loans to belligerents in the **Neutrality Act of 1936**. Roosevelt was against these restrictions, because his foreign policy was centered on spurring economic recovery in the Great Depression, and he viewed the arms trade as vital.

Spanish Civil War

A year later, Congress again altered the neutrality legislation due to the outbreak of a civil war in Spain which had become a republic in 1931. During the summer of 1936, it was torn by a savage civil war which became a focus of international attention. The Spanish Republic's forces were attacked by a right-wing, conservative coalition of army officers backed by Catholic Church leaders. Mussolini and Hitler, now joined in the **Axis** alliance, gave significant aid to this group, led by "El Caudillo," **Francisco Franco**. The weaker, socialist-leaning Republican forces were receiving aid from the Soviet Union, but fell in 1939. The fascist Franco proclaimed Spain neutral in World War II, but remained sympathetic to Hitler.

There were many calls for the U.S. to assist one of the two warring sides in the Spanish Civil War. Fear of the conflict erupting into another major war led Congress to extend its earlier trade restrictions to include civil wars. In the **Neutrality Act of 1937**, FDR was able to gain some flexibility. Congress added a "**cash and carry**" amendment to allow belligerents to buy **nonmilitary** goods in America if they made immediate payment and transported them in their own ships.

FDR's "Quarantine" Speech Of 1937

In July 1937, Japan, trying to expand its **Manchurian** territory, again attacked **China**. Roosevelt sensed that Americans wished to send aid, but the Neutrality Acts stood in his way. Japan's control of the Pacific made "cash and carry" too risky for the Chinese. Early in October, he made his famous "**quarantine**" speech indicating that aggression must be stopped by peace-loving nations. Isolationists loudly denounced him, but it appeared that the public was beginning to change its mind as they watched aggression mount in the world.

Enduring Issues 9

The League of Nations unsuccessfully tried to use Roosevelt's "quarantine" idea to get members to collectively cut off trade with aggressor nations, but no one wished to sacrifice their economic welfare for peace. At that same point, a severe recession threatened to push the slowly recovering economy back to its pre-1933 level. The economic slump, mounting aggression, and the League's failure to act allowed the President to convince Congress to agree to an increase in defense spending for naval and air power.

Questions

1   In coming to power in Germany, Hitler was aided by the
   1   zig-zag course of U.S. diplomacy.
   2   failure of welfare programs by the German government.
   3   anti-immigration policies of the U.S.
   4   economic chaos of the worldwide depression.

2   American foreign policies between the two world wars reflected
   1   both isolationism and internationalism.
   2   strong faith in the League of Nations.
   3   consistent promotion of free trade.
   4   aggressive military action.

3   A basic argument used by isolationists is that the tradition of U.S. neutrality stems from
   1   Lincoln's "Emancipation Proclamation."
   2   Washington's "Farewell Address."
   3   Teddy Roosevelt's "Big Stick Policy."
   4   Wilson's "New Freedom."

4   In 1933, Secretary of State Cordell Hull implemented FDR's "Good Neighbor Policy" toward Latin America. The basis of the policy was
   1   more trade and less intervention.
   2   military protection for weak countries.
   3   diplomatic recognition for dictatorships.
   4   increased arms sales to military regimes.

5   The Nye Committee's report in 1935, aroused U.S. public opinion about
   1   Secretary Hull's new policies toward Latin America.
   2   mishandling food supplies to war-torn nations.
   3   financial connections of business and foreign governments in WW I.
   4   Roosevelt's diplomatic recognition of the U.S.S.R.

6   "Storm Cellar Diplomacy" is a term indicating U.S. that foreign policy in the late 1930's,
   1   abandoned the Monroe Doctrine.
   2   sanctioned arms sales to belligerents.
   3   continued to raise high tariffs to protect home industry.
   4   attempted to avoid involvement in foreign wars.

7   The Spanish Civil War in the 1930's,
   1   strengthened the cause of communism.
   2   was boycotted by fascist governments.
   3   caused Congress to tighten neutrality legislation.
   4   brought in the idea of "cash and carry" for belligerents.

8   Franklin Roosevelt made his "quarantine" speech in 1937, because
   1   Congressional neutrality acts prevented him from aiding China.
   2   he wished to enter the League of Nations.
   3   the U. S. could not trade with Japan.
   4   Japanese trade was hurting U.S. business recovery.

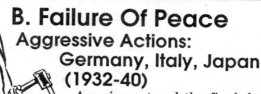

B. Failure Of Peace
Aggressive Actions:
Germany, Italy, Japan (1932-40)

America entered the final days before the outbreak of World War II with an isolationist policy reinforced by neutrality legislation restricting President Roosevelt's diplomatic capabilities. The President's hands were tied by Congressional limitations and Britain and France were not ready for the speed with which the pattern of aggression was growing.

Japan's 1937 push south into China from its Manchurian territory seemed to unleash a rapid unfolding of events. Mussolini simultaneously achieved success in Ethiopia. In 1938, Hitler moved into Austria and threatened the **Sudetenland** region of Czechoslovakia.

Appeasement: Munich Conference (1938)

No major nation in Europe was prepared to face the combined war machines of Nazi Germany and Fascist Italy. To try to resolve the Czech problem, a fateful **summit** meeting was convened at Munich, Germany, on 29 September 1938. France and Britain agreed to let Hitler take the Sudetenland in exchange for a pledge to cease further aggressive claims by Germany and Italy. Britain's Prime Minister **Neville Chamberlain** claimed the world had purchased "peace with honor" at Munich.

Roosevelt reluctantly denoted his approval but indicated to his Cabinet that such an **appeasement** of the Axis dictators was shameful. He was aware of the Germans' diplomatic activities in Latin America which were undercutting his "Good Neighbor" policy. With the time bought at Munich, Roosevelt worked intensely to cement friendly relations in Latin America.

The appeasement at Munich did not buy much time. In 1938, German troops occupied Czechoslovakia. France and Britain were negotiating with the Soviet Union in an effort to balance the geographic power of anti-Axis forces. By this, they hoped to deter Hitler's ambitions. However, Stalin was suspicious of the anti-communist policies of the western democracies. In a shocking diplomatic move in late August 1939, the U.S.S.R. announced a mutual non-aggression treaty with Germany.

German Attack On Poland - WW II Begins

The 1939 pact created a strange alliance between the fascist government of Germany and the communist government of the Soviet Union. This alliance took pressure off Germany's eastern borders and gave Hitler and Stalin the opportunity to advance into the long-coveted nation of Poland. Hitler demanded a return of German territory given to Poland after World War I.

Prelude To World War II

Act	Response	Result
1931 Japan invades North Manchuria	League of Nations reprimand; U.S. issues Stimson Doctrine, refuses to recognize Japanese claim to territory	Japan quits League of Nations, annexes Chinese conquests
1935 Italy invades Ethiopia	U.S. passes Neutrality Act, no arms sales to belligerents, League of Nations reprimand	Italy conquers and annexes part of Ethiopia
1936 Germany invades Rhineland region	No response	Germans build fortifications along Rhine River borders in violation of Versailles Treaty
1936 Germany & Italy back Franco in Spanish Civil War	U.S. broadens neutrality acts to include arms trade ban for civil war belligerents	Franco victorious, becomes "silent partner" for Axis alliance
1937 Japan invades China	FDR calls for "quarantine" of aggressor nations. League of Nations fails with trade embargo against Japan.	Japan conquers and occupies most of N.E. China
1938 Germany invades Austria	No response	Germany proclaims "Anschluss" - unification of Germany & Austria
1938 Germany claims Czech territory	Britain & France appease Hitler, allow Germans to take over the area at Munich Conference	Germany annexes Sudetenland region
1939 Italy invades Albania	No response	Italy conquers and occupies Albania
1939 Germany and U.S.S.R. invade Poland	Britain and France declare war; U.S. modifies neutrality acts to allow "cash and carry."	World War II begins

On 1 September 1939, a mere nine days after the Nazi-Soviet pact, Hitler launched his **blitzkrieg** (lightning war). Bound by treaty to defend Poland, Britain and France declared war two days later. World War II had begun in Europe. While France and Britain began to mobilize, the massive German technological war machine rolled through Poland and conquered the country in three weeks.

Swiftly, the Soviets took a share of eastern Poland, began annexing the tiny Baltic nations of Estonia, Latvia, and Lithuania, and then launched their own lightning invasion of Finland which fell in only four months.

The winter of 1939-40 was misleadingly calm in Europe, allowing talk of intervention by America to die down and isolationists to regain strength. A frustrated Roosevelt, wishing to aid victims of aggression, reluctantly invoked the Neutrality Acts.

Enduring Issues 1

Unexpectedly, Hitler launched a blitzkrieg against Denmark and Norway in April of 1940. Then in May, German forces rolled through the Netherlands and Belgium, conquering both before the month ended.

The Battle of France opened on 5 June, and Italy attacked from the south on 10 June. Paris fell to the Germans on 14 June. A **Free French** government under General **Charles DeGaulle**, fled to exile in Britain. On 22 June, Field Marshall **Henri Pétain** surrendered. In a matter three months, all of Western Europe, except Great Britain had fallen to the Nazi war machine.

Gradual U.S. Involvement

The speed and success of the Axis offensive jolted America into action. Roosevelt set up a task force to arrange for the defense of the western hemisphere. Plans were approved by the **Pan-American Union**, and a **Joint Defense Board** was set up with **Canada**.

Congress raised taxes and the debt limit to allow for more military purchasing. Congress authorized absorbing National Guard units into the U.S. armed forces, and the nation's **first peacetime draft**. Fear of spy activities led Congress to pass the **Smith Act** to monitor alien activities. The act also made it illegal to advocate or teach the forceful overthrow of lawful government in the United States.

Enduring Issues 9

The Neutrality Acts hampered Roosevelt's efforts to help Britain which was standing alone and under a relentless series of German air attacks. In September of 1940, knowing public opinion had changed, FDR took a landmark step. By extending his power as Commander-in-Chief, he took fifty World War I navy ships and gave them to Britain in exchange for the use of naval base sites in Canada, Bermuda, and the Caribbean (**Destroyers-for-Bases Deal**).

Roosevelt's worst fears came in that same month when Japan announced it had joined the Axis alliance. He angered the Japanese by authorizing an **embargo** (stoppage) of iron and steel shipments outside the Western Hemisphere (except Britain).

In January of 1941, at his precedent-breaking third inaugural, FDR delivered his famous **Four Freedoms Speech** (freedom of speech, worship, freedom from want, and fear), framing what would become America's war aims. In that speech, he also called for a **Lend-Lease Act** by Congress, to allow the U.S. to lend and transfer arms and war supplies to Britain and other victims of aggression.

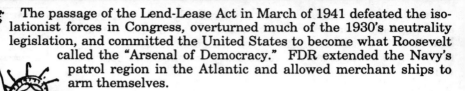

The passage of the Lend-Lease Act in March of 1941 defeated the isolationist forces in Congress, overturned much of the 1930's neutrality legislation, and committed the United States to become what Roosevelt called the "Arsenal of Democracy." FDR extended the Navy's patrol region in the Atlantic and allowed merchant ships to arm themselves.

In June, while still pounding Britain from the air, Hitler turned on his ally, Stalin, launching an all-out blitzkrieg against the U.S.S.R. Within a few months, Roosevelt extended Lend-Lease to the U.S.S.R.

America's commitment to the survival of Britain took another step in the summer of 1941. Roosevelt and Prime Minister **Winston Churchill** met off the Canadian coast and drew up an informal set of anti-Axis war aims. Known as the **Atlantic Charter**, this document was eventually signed by 15 nations including the U.S.S.R. In 1945, it became the basis for the **United Nations Charter**.

Questions

1   Public support for Congressional neutrality legislation began to change after
    1   the Munich Conference.
    2   Italy conquered Ethiopia.
    3   Franco was victorious in Spain.
    4   France fell to Hitler.

2   The pattern of response to the acts of Germany, Italy, and Japan in the "Prelude to World War II" (see chart on page 192) shows
    1   quarantining aggressors was the only effective way to stop them.
    2   lack of strong response can encourage aggressors.
    3   the U.S. was the only nation to stand up to the aggressors.
    4   forceful counteractions deterred continued aggression.

3   One lesson of the 1938 Munich Conference is that appeasement
    1   is sometimes a very effective diplomatic strategy.
    2   promotes neutrality.
    3   counterbalances aggression.
    4   encouraged more aggression.

4   The Lend - Lease Act
    1   nearly threw us into another depression.
    2   raised high protective tariff walls.
    3   set up the defense plan for the Western Hemisphere.
    4   effectively ended Congressional neutrality.

5   The Destroyers-for-Bases Deal between Roosevelt and Churchill shows that
    1   a President can bypass Legislative restraints in foreign policy.
    2   the U.S. focused on problems in the Pacific.
    3   Americans were nervous about espionage.
    4   the American boycott of trade with Japan was working.

6   Before we actually declared war, FDR stated our war aims in
    1   the New Deal and the Geneva Convention.
    2   the Quarantine Speech and the Good Neighbor Policy.
    3   the Atlantic Charter and the Four Freedoms Speech.
    4   the Farewell Address and the Versailles Treaty.
7   President Roosevelt rallied Americans to help Britain and the U.S.S.R. against the Axis nations by stating we must
    1   "make the world safe for democracy."
    2   "remain neutral no matter how costly."
    3   "remember that we have nothing to fear but fear itself."
    4   "become the great arsenal of democracy."

C. The United States In World War II
Pearl Harbor

Japanese-American relations were also reaching a crisis stage. In 1940, Japan was again seeking oil and rare metals in the Southeast Asia region (Indo-China), where the fallen France had been the chief colonial power. Secretary of State Hull issued a steady stream of warnings to the Japanese.

Just a few months before Hitler turned the full force of his war machine against the U.S.S.R., Stalin was able to convince Japan to sign a non-aggression pact. The Soviet-Japanese tensions in Asia were eased and Stalin could focus attention on defending his European borders. With no powerful enemies in Asia, the pact also allowed Japan to confidently begin conquest of the mineral-rich area of Indo-China. In July 1941, Japan attacked Thailand and the nearly defenseless French colonies. Diplomatic protests were issued by Hull, and FDR embargoed nearly all trade with Japan.

In the late fall of 1941, aggressive militarists under **General Tojo** took power in Japan. They planned a sneak attack against several U.S. naval installations to devastate America. The majority of American seagoing power in the Pacific was located at the **Pearl Harbor** naval base in Hawaii, assumed to be far out of range for the Japanese. The main concern was for the forces in the **Philippines**, which was still a U.S. possession.

The Japanese struck Pearl Harbor on **7 December 1941**. The U.S. was totally unprepared. Scholars now agree this was due to the Americans' poor intelligence and communications. With over 5,000 casualties, it was probably the most costly defeat in American history. Six major battleships and many lesser vessels were rendered useless. It left Japan nearly invincible in East Asia and the Pacific. Congress declared war on Japan the next day.

Within a week Japan's Axis partners, Germany and Italy, declared war on the United States. All the internal debates about isolationism were put to rest. The posturing about staying out of Europe's problems had proven useless. America now had to face the reality of World War II.

The War In Europe

Hitler had not been told by his Japanese allies of their plan to attack the U.S. He was angered because he had not yet disposed of Britain, and his attack on the U.S.S.R. was slowly unraveling. In declaring war in mid-December, he hoped the U.S. would focus on Japan in the Pacific and Lend-Lease to Europe would slow down.

With public opinion united behind him, Roosevelt became an extremely powerful commander-in-chief and set America's overall strategic goals. His strategy was the opposite of what Hitler had guessed. The American commanders were to temporarily "hold the line" in the Pacific and focus attention on the European theater of the war.

To assure this strategy, FDR's brilliant Chief of Staff, **Gen. George C. Marshall**, sent his most talented assistant, **Gen. Dwight D. Eisenhower**, to Europe as Allied Commander. Taking the war to Germany's homeland, he ordered bombing attacks by the Royal Air Force and U.S. Army Air Corps on strategic production centers.

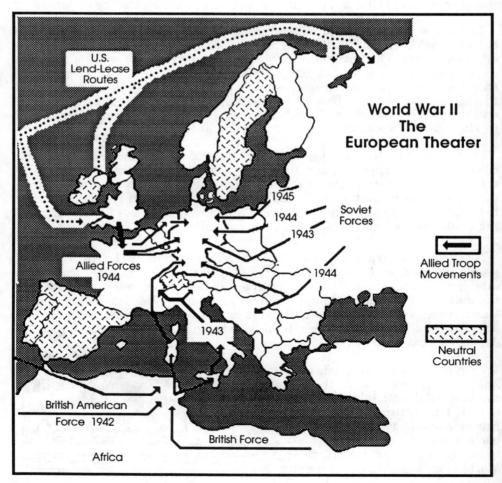

U.S. Lend-Lease Routes

**World War II
The
European Theater**

1945
1944
1943

Soviet Forces

1944

Allied Forces 1944

Allied Troop Movements

1943

Neutral Countries

British American Force 1942

British Force

Africa

Marshall then turned his attention to North Africa where British forces, under **General Bernard L. Montgomery**, had begun to turn the tide. At El Alamein in Egypt, Montgomery defeated the Germans' legendary "Desert Fox," **General Erwin Rommel**. In November 1942, Eisenhower's forces landed in North Africa, and his field commander, **General George Patton**, pushed eastward toward Montgomery, bottling the Germans up at Tunis. Victory in North Africa in May 1943, gave the Allies access to the Mediterranean and a southern staging point for invading Europe. At the same time, the Soviets halted the Axis invasion of their homeland after a brutal six months siege of **Stalingrad**.

With the Allied momentum building, Sicily was invaded in July 1943, followed by the Italian mainland in September. Mussolini fled Rome and the Italians surrendered on 8 September 1943. However, the German forces in Italy fought on, and it was not until June 1944, that the Allies were able to inch their way to Rome.

Eisenhower, now Supreme Allied Commander in Europe, launched **Operation Overlord**, the largest **amphibious** invasion in history. On 6 June 1944, nearly 200,000 troops, 600 ships, and 11,000 planes attacked the beaches of **Normandy**, France. Its success meant a second European front was now open. The German resistance was ferocious. By the end of that summer, Montgomery's British invasion force liberated the Netherlands and Belgium. A combined Free French, American, and Canadian army, under **General Omar Bradley**, liberated Paris at about the same time.

Hitler was now caught between the Soviets driving from the east and the combined Allied force moving rapidly from the west. In July, some of his general staff attempted to assassinate him. Shaken, he tried to stem the tide by ordering the new **V-2 rockets** launched at Britain in massive incendiary raids. Nearly overcome by Allied air power and with Allied forces already in Germany, Hitler made a last, desperate attempt to protect his homeland. In December, he threw ground forces against a weak section of the Allied line in Belgium. In the **Battle of the Bulge** (Dec.'44 - Jan.'45), the French-Anglo-American-Canadian forces were thrown back. However, a massive drive toward Germany from Poland by the Soviets, and another from Holland by the British forced the Germans to retreat. The Allies regained their momentum. With Berlin under attack, Hitler committed suicide on 30 April 1945. German **Field Marshall Alfred Jodl** agreed to **unconditional surrender** on 8 May 1945.

The War In The Pacific

In 1943, Roosevelt allowed his military advisors to turn their attention to the Pacific theater. By that time, Pacific Commander **General Douglas MacArthur** had evacuated the Philippines, the British and Americans had retreated to Australia, and the Japanese had overrun most of Southeast Asia and Indonesia (Dutch East Indies). The Japanese advance was stopped by tough Navy and Marine resistance in mid- 1942, at the battles of the Coral Sea and Midway. A successful Allied attack on Guadalcanal just north of Australia threw the Japanese into a defensive position. A murderous "island-hopping" offensive through the Pacific was authorized.

Furthest extent of Japanese conquest (1942)

The Pacific Theater - World War II

Intense cooperation between MacArthur and **Admiral Chester Nimitz** allowed the Americans to move simultaneously in the south and central Pacific. Wake and Guam were recaptured by mid-1944. This put the Americans in position to increase the devastating carrier air strikes on Japan itself. The drive toward the Japanese Islands grew more bloody and costly. **Iwo Jima** (18,000 Allied casualties) and **Okinawa** (45,000 Allied casualties) were taken in early 1945.

Enduring Issues 9

Tragically, FDR died of a cerebral hemorrhage on 12 April 1945. Vice-President **Harry S Truman** became the nation's Commander-in-Chief. Shortly thereafter, the Germans surrendered. Truman focused his attention on the bloodbath in the Pacific. It was felt that the Japanese would not accept **unconditional surrender**, but would fight to the last. Truman increased air attacks on Japan, hoping for surrender. The President then received word that an **atomic weapon** had been successfully developed by **J. Robert Oppenheimer** and a team of scientists working on the **Manhattan Project** in the New Mexico desert. After much agonizing, the President decided he could end the war quickly and end the bloodletting in the Pacific by authorizing the use of the bomb. On 6 August 1945, the first atomic bomb was dropped on **Hiroshima**, but there was no reply from the Japanese.

On 9 August a second bomb was dropped on the Japanese naval base of **Nagasaki**. The following day, Japanese Premier **Suzuki** offered to surrender, if the **Emperor Hirohito** was allowed to keep his throne. The Allies accepted the Japanese surrender on 14 August 1945. America had over a million casualties in World War II (nearly 325,000 dead and 700,000 wounded).

The Human Dimensions Of War

America's phenomenal three and one-half year drive to overthrow the Axis was fought equally hard on the **home front**. Roosevelt harnessed the entire economic capacity of the nation to the war effort. He created a number of wartime agencies to manage the home front. Industry was somewhat slow to respond to war needs in 1942, reluctant to give up profits from a booming consumer market.

Roosevelt persuaded industry to patriotically donate the services of their top managers. "Dollar-a-year-men," like Sears-Roebuck's **Donald Nelson**, ran the **War Production Board** which supervised military production, tripling the nation's GNP by 1945. Federal spending jumped from 20 billion dollars in 1941 to almost seventy five billion dollars in 1945. The **War Labor Board** handled labor disputes and kept the country relatively strike-free.

Enduring Issues
12

The **War Manpower Commission** was able to coordinate the draft of nearly 14 million men into the armed forces while at the same time keeping a steady flow of trained workers moving into the nation's factories.

The **Office of Price Administration** kept the inflation-prone economy working on a fair basis as consumer goods became scarce due to military production demands. The OPA imposed **price ceilings** and supervised the **rationing program** so that people would be able to get a fair share of goods in short supply. This program called for much self-sacrificing on the part of the public. The people responded when government "We Do Our Part" poster programs urged those on the home front to support those doing the fighting.

As in World War I, the role of women in the economy expanded. As men were drafted for military service, seventeen million women entered the work force. Many worked in non-traditional jobs. Patriotic posters, animated film shorts, and even a pop song glorified a new American heroine, *"Rosie the Riveter."* Women also joined newly created corps of the Army, Navy, Marines, and Coast Guard relieving men of non-combatant duties.

The war would cost the American people more than 300 billion dollars. To finance it, Congress not only raised and expanded the income tax system, but also changed the method of collection to require employers to **withhold** taxes from workers' paychecks. Major **war bond drives** were launched in workplaces and a movie-going public saw filmed appeals to buy bonds at every picture show.

Many famous entertainers such as Kate Smith, Frank Sinatra, Bob Hope, and Bing Crosby volunteered to tour the country staging **bond rallies** in major cities. The War Bonds purchased accounted for nearly two-thirds of government war revenues.

Personal Diplomacy

In 1943, Roosevelt said he was switching hats from "Dr. New Deal" to "Dr. Win-the-War." Actually, the coming of the European war in 1939 had led Roosevelt to change his leadership role. Especially after Lend-Lease, the problems of the Great Depression began to subside as employment increased in defense industries. In 1942, Roosevelt let the CCC and WPA fade as the **War Manpower Commission** and the **Selective Service Act** became operative. Some New Deal reforms on working hours and corporate price agreements had to be put aside in order to boost industrial productivity.

As the dangers in Europe and Asia mounted, the President became more involved in foreign affairs and less in domestic issues. As **Chief Diplomat** and **Commander-in-Chief**, he had to meet personally with Allied leaders. With diplomatic groundwork laid by advisor Harry Hopkins, FDR travelled long distances to Africa and Asia to confer with Britain's Prime Minister **Winston Churchill**, the U.S.S.R.'s Premier **Joseph Stalin**, Free France's General **Charles DeGaulle**, and China's Generalissimo **Chiang Kai-shek**. The Allied leaders gathered at **summit meetings**, usually involving the "Big Three" (U.S., Britain, & Soviet Union), in Casablanca, Cairo, Teheran, and Yalta. Just after being elected to his **fourth term** as President, FDR was within a month of his death when he journeyed to the Soviet Union in February 1945.

| Enduring |
| Issues |
| **9** |

At the **Yalta Conference**, in the southern U.S.S.R., FDR met with Stalin and Churchill to plan for the final stage of the war and shape the peace that would come thereafter. Roosevelt has been criticized for making too many concessions to Stalin in Eastern Europe, but the Soviets had been invaded from the west in both world wars and were deeply concerned about their security. By the Yalta Conference, the Soviets had already conquered most of Eastern Europe. Roosevelt and Churchill felt they had made great headway getting a reluctant Stalin to agree to have free elections in Soviet-conquered territories, to help establish the new **United Nations** peace organization, and to join the war against Japan as soon as he could.

In July 1945, a final wartime summit took place at **Potsdam**, Germany. Truman met with Churchill and Stalin to make agreements on the peacetime treatment of Germany and on the location of Polish borders. Truman came away from the meeting very pessimistic about dealing with Stalin in the future. From World War II on, **summit meetings** and **personal diplomacy** became an important and burdensome responsibility for Presidents in the modern era.

U.S. Military Occupations

Despite all these Allied meetings, the war ended without a general peace treaty. The failure to construct such a general agreement paved the way for the tensions and suspicions that resulted in a **Cold War** between the Soviet Union and the western democracies. Germany was placed under **military occupation** by the Allies. It was split into an eastern zone with Berlin as its capital, and administered by the U.S.S.R., and a western zone with Bonn as its capital, and jointly administered by Britain, France, and the United States. Isolated inside the Soviet zone, Berlin later became the scene of much post-war tension (see map on page 211).

Treatment of Japan was different. The U.S. tried about 4,000 Japanese officials for "war crimes," executing only General Tojo and a several other leaders. The Americans occupied and rapidly reconstructed the nation. Pacific commander General **Douglas MacArthur** was appointed military governor and created a democratic constitution adopted in 1947. In 1951, the former Allied nations, with the exception of the Soviet Union, signed a formal peace treaty with Japan.

World War II: Impact On Minorities

The war created numerous problems for minority groups at home and abroad. A panic broke out on the west coast of the United States after Pearl Harbor. Anti-Japanese feelings ran high. Fear of sabotage and espionage caused many unfounded charges to be leveled at Japanese aliens and American citizens of Japanese ancestry (**Nisei**). Japanese-Americans were most densely settled in California.

In the early spring of 1942, on the advice of his Western Defense Commander, FDR issued an order to the FBI to round up 100,000 Japanese-Americans, most of them citizens, and ship them to relocation centers in Utah and other Southwestern states, where they remained for the duration of the war. Americans of Italian and German descent were not treated in similar fashion. This apparently racially-motivated denial of **due-process rights** was eventually challenged in the Supreme Court. In the case of *Korematsu v. U.S.* (1944), the court upheld the government's actions under the "clear and present danger" rule based on the World War I *Schenck* decision. Later appeals in the 1950's and 1960's, were won by the Nisei and partial compensation was made by the government for their suffering.

Filmed footage of the Allied liberation of Hitler's concentration camps in Germany, Poland, and Eastern Europe brought home the shocking reality of what racism can truly mean. There was knowledge of Nazi atrocities against minorities early in the 1930's, but the world was shocked beyond belief by the documentation of the **genocidal** extermination of six million Jews in the Nazi death camps at **Auschwitz, Belzec,** and **Treblinka**.

"**The Holocaust**" could not be brushed aside in dealing with the captured enemy leaders.

More barbaric Nazi practices were revealed at the "war crime" trials conducted by the Allies at Nuremberg in 1945. Twenty-two major Nazi leaders were placed on trial for violations of the basic rules of war and inhumane treatment of political prisoners. Half of the accused were sentenced to death, half received prison terms.

Black Americans also suffered from racial policies during the war. Many migrated north to take advantage of government non-discrimination clauses in hiring defense plant workers. However, such mass migrations caused race riots to break out in Los Angeles, Mobile, New York, and Detroit. In the military, black servicemen were still assigned to segregated units, but more saw combat than in World War I.

Demobilization
Inflation And Strikes

Truman was a strong-willed man, but many people in his party doubted whether he could fill the shoes of the departed Roosevelt. Some felt that he and his advisors were overreacting to the Soviet moves in Europe, and he was incapable of conducting a   sound foreign policy. Congress was not as enthusiastic as it had been in the New Deal days about the liberal reforms that Truman wanted on civil rights, housing, Social Security, and labor conditions. Nonetheless, they followed his recommendations and created an **Atomic Energy Commission** to supervise military use of nuclear energy and research its future applications.

The President also convinced Congress to pass the **Maximum Employment Act of 1946**, which incorporated the **Keynsian** concept of a permanent government role in keeping the economy stable and growing. Wages were not keeping up with inflation. Labor reacted to the problem. The United Mine Workers Strike so hurt the economy that Truman had to threaten to use the army to keep coal production up. He again threatened to use the army to end a national railroad strike.

| Enduring Issues 12 |

In mid-1945, war-weary Americans clamored for a speedy demobilization. Truman, new to foreign policy-making, was suspicious of Soviet moves in Eastern Europe. He wanted a very gradual dismantling of United States power and was criticized by Congress and the public for dragging the process out. The aid Truman began sending overseas to reconstruct war-devastated areas served as an economic stimulus at home, as did continued military spending to provide for the occupation forces.

As consumer production gradually increased, the administration ended rationing. The public's cashing of war bonds stimulated the economy even more. The Truman administration fought with Congress, trying to keep wartime **price controls** while attempting to balance supply with consumer demand to avoid the classic pattern of inflation and post-war recession. Recession was avoided, but inflation increased enormously as people willingly paid high prices for autos and appliances they hadn't been able to purchase during the war.

The "G.I. Bill"

In 1944, as the fortunes of war began to change, Roosevelt had been far-sighted enough to anticipate the domestic problems that would occur as the war moved toward its conclusion. To ease the economic dislocations of converting from wartime to peacetime, he had the War Production Board planning to let some industries increase their consumer production while cutting back on military output. As a gesture of gratitude to those who had done the fighting, he managed to have Congress pass the **Servicemen's Readjustment Act**, commonly called the "**G.I. Bill of Rights**." It provided for physical and vocational rehabilitation of wounded veterans, granted one year's unemployment compensation, and allowed for low cost business and housing loans. It also provided funds for veterans to continue their college and vocational educations. The act helped to ease the impact on the economy of demobilizing thousands of servicemen by avoiding massive unemployment. In the long run, it created a better educated work force and stimulated construction on university campuses.

Partisan Problems

Truman's ability, growing inflation, and the slow demobilization became issues in the 1946 Congressional elections. The Republicans regained control of Congress for the first time in sixteen years. The new 80th Congress was more conservative than in the New Deal days, and Truman's liberal positions on civil rights pushed many southern Senators and Congressmen toward a **coalition** with the Republicans. The business-oriented Republicans handed him a bitter defeat when they overrode his veto of the anti-union **Taft-Hartley Act** in 1947. It outlawed **closed-shops**, permitted **government intervention in strikes**, and cancelled many of the collective bargaining gains made under the **National Labor Relations Act** of 1935. Truman was running into a stone wall of opposition on domestic issues, but he was able to reorganize the military. Congress did pass the administration's **National Security Act of 1947** which consolidated all military affairs under the **Department of Defense**, coordinated the military command under a **Joint Chiefs of Staff**, and formed the **Central Intelligence Agency (CIA)**. His aggressive foreign policy of **containment** (see Truman Doctrine below) also began to earn him popularity. Stalin was breaking the Yalta and Potsdam agreements in Eastern Europe and Iran. Truman's tough diplomatic stance was unexpected.

The 1948 Election

Perhaps this personal characteristic of scrappy toughness helped Truman win an uphill battle in the election of 1948. It is considered one of the greatest "come-from-behind victories" in the history of Presidential elections. The Democrats nominated him rather unenthusiastically, and the southern wing of the

Enduring Issues **11**

party, opposed to his civil rights position, walked out of the convention. They formed their own **States' Rights Party**, nicknamed the **Dixiecrats**, and nominated Governor **Strom Thurmond** of South Carolina as their standard-bearer. A small, **left-leaning** group of Democrats also bolted the party in protest to Truman's anti-Soviet policies and nominated former Vice President **Henry A. Wallace** to run on a new **Progressive Party** ticket.

With the Democrats badly split, the Republicans could sense victory. They renominated their 1944 candidate, Governor **Thomas E. Dewey** of New York. The overconfident Dewey ran a slow-paced, lackluster campaign. Truman threw himself into an enthusiastic campaign. Crisscrossing the country by train, he emphasized his down-to-earth style and the lack of cooperation from what he called a "Do-nothing 80th Congress." He upset Dewey by a mere 2 million popular votes on election day 1948. He had managed to attract a strong black vote, the labor vote, moderate liberals, and those who agreed with his tough containment policies. He restored the Democrats' control of Congress.

The Fair Deal

With a slightly friendlier Congress, Truman was able to get more of his **"Fair Deal"** domestic program passed. A new Federal Housing Act, a revised Fair Labor Standards Act with an increased minimum wage, major expansion of Social Security, and federal assistance for city slum clearance programs were passed in his term. The Republican-Southern Democrat coalition still handed him defeats on programs to aid education and the small farmer, health insurance for the elderly, and enforcement of civil rights. As Chief Executive, he appointed a national **Harry S Truman** **Civil Rights Commission** in 1947, issued executive orders to end segregation in the the armed forces and in federal jobs, and had the Justice Department challenge segregation in federal housing projects. Truman was able to show strong leadership in domestic affairs.

Questions

1   The Japanese attack was a devastating blow to America because
    1   Japan had always been a trusted ally.
    2   the U.S.S.R. refused to come to our aid.
    3   it destroyed a large segment of our Pacific fleet.
    4   it showed Lend-Lease had been a mistake.

2   The basic war strategy adopted by FDR was
    1   to keep supplying Britain with Lend-Lease while we focused on Japan.
    2   elimination of Hitler first, then focus on Japan.
    3   an all-out effort in both Europe and the Pacific.
    4   to rebuild the Pacific fleet before entering the war.

3   The Allies' first victories against the Axis came
    1   with the invasion of Sicily.
    2   after crossing the English Channel.
    3   in North Africa.
    4   at the Yalta Conference.

4   Gen. Dwight Eisenhower's major contribution to the war effort was
    1   placing priority on strategic use of nuclear weapons.
    2   stressing that the European War must be won on the sea.
    3   as a brilliant armored cavalry commander.
    4   managing to co-ordinate various Allied forces and commanders.

5   Germany's last major offensive was fought at
    1   the Battle of the Bulge.   3   Stalingrad.
    2   El Alamein.   4   Normandy.
6   The first success of the Allies in the Pacific came in late 1942, when they attacked
    1   Guadalcanal.   3   Iwo Jima.
    2   the Philippines.   4   Hiroshima.
7   The war in the Pacific involved a difficult
    1   co-ordination of British, French, and American forces.
    2   intense rivalry between the British and American navies.
    3   island-hopping strategy.
    4   conquest of mainland China.
8   To meet the demands of World War II, Roosevelt had to virtually convert the U.S. economy system to one based on
    1   command.   3   tradition.
    2   laissez-faire.   4   free enterprise.
9   The Manhattan Project
    1   changed the nature of modern warfare.
    2   netted numerous Axis spies in the U.S.
    3   coordinated wartime industries.
    4   generated much revenue to finance the war.
10   Truman's decision to use the atomic bomb turned on his desire to
    1   demonstrate U.S. power to Churchill.
    2   force Hitler to surrender.
    3   halt wartime inflation of the economy.
    4   reduce the loss of American lives in the Pacific.
11   Which became the most powerful wartime economic agency?
    1   Manhattan Project
    2   Federal Reserve System
    3   War Production Board
    4   Selective Service System
12   Women made their most significant contribution to war effort by
    1   administering the rationing program.
    2   serving in combat units.
    3   filling industrial jobs.
    4   acting as diplomatic couriers.
13   Which of the following programs had to be abandoned as we entered the war?
    1   bond rallies   3   Good Neighbor Policy
    2   Lend-Lease   4   New Deal
14   An economic idea begun in WW II that is still with us today is
    1   rationing of consumer goods.
    2   "dollar-a-year men."
    3   the withholding tax system.
    4   Lend-Lease.
15   In upholding the internment of U.S. citizens of Japanese ancestry (*Korematsu v. U.S.* 1944), the Supreme Court used the rule set in the *Schenck* decision (1919) that individual rights may be suspended when
    1   there is a danger to the society.
    2   the economy is in a state of depression.
    3   the doctrine of habeas corpus is used.
    4   state and national governments are in conflict.

16 The "Big Three" negotiating at Yalta
  1   shaped the post-war world.
  2   decided how Germany would be divided.
  3   ended the use of personal diplomacy by world leaders.
  4   resulted in the decision to drop the atomic bomb.

17 At Potsdam in 1945, Truman realized
  1   Churchill would no longer support the U.S. military actions.
  2   Stalin would be difficult to deal with in the post-war world.
  3   the Western allies would have to move out of Berlin.
  4   Germany would not accept unconditional surrender.

18 The Cold War emerged after World War II partly because the
  1   League of Nations collapsed.
  2   U.S.S.R. refused to use its nuclear weapons.
  3   Allies failed to agree on a peace settlement.
  4   American economy went into a post-war depression.

19 The Servicemen's Readjustment Act (1944) actually helped
  1   end segregation in the U.S. armed forces.
  2   increase the number of men being drafted.
  3   prevent mistreatment of Axis war prisoners.
  4   convert the economy to peacetime.

20 President Truman slowed the process of demobilization to
  1   reorganize the armed forces.
  2   stabilize the economy and monitor Soviet behavior.
  3   slow down rapidly falling prices.
  4   delay the production of nuclear weapons.

21 President Truman almost lost the 1948 election because of his
  1   veto of the Taft-Hartley Act.   2   pro-civil rights policies.
  3   weak foreign policy.   4   decision to drop the atomic bomb.

22 The Taft-Hartley Act was aimed at
  1   curbing the power of labor unions.
  2   helping World War II veterans readjust to peacetime.
  3   limiting the number of Presidential terms.
  4   increasing Social Security benefits.

23 Truman was unable to get many of his legislative proposals passed because he
  1   retained wartime price controls too long.
  2   had no background in legislative matters.
  3   was opposed by a coalition of conservatives and segregationists.
  4   condemned Keynsian economic theories as wasteful.

24 Republican Presidential candidate Thomas E. Dewey lost the 1948 election because
  1   Republicans wanted friendlier relations with the Soviet Union.
  2   his advisors underestimated Truman's popular support.
  3   the Democrats were solidly united behind Truman.
  4   he supported segregation in the South.

25 The National Security Act of 1947
  1   made Truman unpopular with minorities.
  2   was a concession to the U.S.S.R.
  3   was based on Keynsian theories.
  4   reorganized the armed forces.

II. Peace With Problems: 1945-1955

A. International Peace Efforts

Despite the friction between the Allies at the war's end and the failure to achieve a general peace agreement, significant efforts were made to achieve some structure of peace.

Formation Of The United Nations

In the 1930's, Woodrow Wilson's great dream of a **League of Nations** to preserve the peace after World War I had failed. Nations had refused to sacrifice their sovereignty for the sake of stabilizing world order. At the end of World War II, Franklin Roosevelt attempted to renew Wilson's dream by devoting his last diplomatic efforts to a new structure, the **United Nations**. He knew the organization could only stand with the cooperation of the United States and the Soviet Union. At Teheran and Yalta, he bargained intensely with Stalin to make the U.N. a reality.

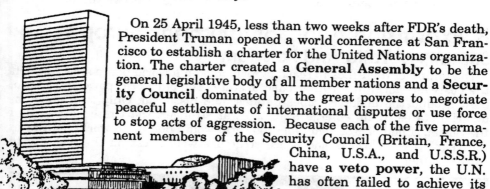

On 25 April 1945, less than two weeks after FDR's death, President Truman opened a world conference at San Francisco to establish a charter for the United Nations organization. The charter created a **General Assembly** to be the general legislative body of all member nations and a **Security Council** dominated by the great powers to negotiate peaceful settlements of international disputes or use force to stop acts of aggression. Because each of the five permanent members of the Security Council (Britain, France, China, U.S.A., and U.S.S.R.) have a **veto power**, the U.N. has often failed to achieve its original goal in settling east-west controversies.

Although it has not lived up to initial expectations, the U.N. has achieved three major goals in the years since its inception:

- world problems have been rapidly brought to public attention and openly debated

- significant humanitarian actions have been coordinated under its health and economic cultural aid programs in underdeveloped regions

- trusteeship programs have transformed former colonies into independent nations

Universal Declaration Of Human Rights

Always a fighter for justice, **Eleanor Roosevelt** accepted an appointment as head the of the new U.N.'s commission on human rights in 1946. She worked diligently to design a basic statement of the rights all human beings should enjoy. In 1948, the United Nations adopted the *Universal Declaration of Human Rights* authored by her committee. It sums up the ideals to which all freedom-loving people have long aspired: that all individuals should be able to live their lives in peace and dignity, free from the oppression of political forces and discrimination. This simple, yet profound document has since become a statement of goals for the establishment and monitoring of justice and human dignity throughout the world.

Enduring Issues 8

Displaced Persons

The war destroyed lives in many ways. Most survivors in war-torn areas began to reconstruct their lives with privately or-ganized relief efforts. However, many in Europe were uprooted and could not return to their homes in Soviet-dominated nations. These **"displaced persons"** looked to the U.S. as a land tradi-tionally open to the world's troubled peoples. The restrictive immigration acts of the 1920's, barred large numbers of refugees especially from Eastern Eu-ropean origins from moving to the United States. Plagued with problems of demobilization and economic readjustment, Congress moved slowly to aid such people. In 1948, amendments permitted the President to make emer-gency adjustments in the admission quotas, allowing an additional 200,000 carefully-screened persons to enter the country in the next two years.

B. Expansion And Containment: Europe
Summitry: Yalta And Potsdam

The failure of the Allies to reach agreements on a world peace structure left the post-war world in a rather chaotic state. The old world power structure, built around the major European states, had dissolved. Only two major in-dustrial states would emerge from the war stronger: the United States and the Soviet Union. These two "superpowers" would dominate world politics in the years that followed. The peace structure would rest on their ability to work together.

At summit meetings, Stalin had made it clear to Roosevelt and later to Truman that the Soviet Union would try to maximize its security and protect its extensive borders by setting up friendly governments in the areas that its armies had liberated. At Yalta, Churchill and Roosevelt had understood this to mean conducting free elections in these countries after a brief period of military occupation. To Stalin, it meant something else. In 1945 and 1946, Soviet officials administering the occupied nations moved quickly to insure these states would have communist-oriented governments. American and British diplomats protested that the Soviets were not living up to the spirit of the Yalta agreements. The Soviets ignored the protests.

At the Potsdam summit conference, Churchill and Truman brought up the question of free elections in Poland, but Stalin brushed it aside. The Soviets had already begun a plan to have a bloc of communist satellite nations become a buffer between themselves and the West. American policy-makers began to see an inevitable **polarization** of world affairs (the world divided into two armed camps around the superpowers: the Soviets and their allies on one extreme, and the western democracies on the other). They saw the U.S. in store for a long, drawn out "cold war" for the survival of its way of life.

Winston Churchill And The Iron Curtain

In the year that followed the war's end, Congress and the American people had characteristically focused on the problems of returning to peacetime. They were aware of the difficult situation with the U.S.S.R. but had a certain confidence that we could work things out with our former allies. Within the Truman administration, especially among veteran State Department officials, such as Undersecretary **Dean Acheson**, and diplomats experienced in dealing with the U.S.S.R., such as **Averill Harriman** and **George F. Kennan**, the mood was more ominous.

Truman's own optimism about the Soviets was severely shaken at Potsdam. In February of 1946, when the Soviets refused to end their occupation of **Iran**, British oil interests appealed for help. When the U.S.S.R. ignored the American and British complaints in the U.N., Secretary of State Byrnes issued a threat of American force. The Soviets withdrew, but it convinced Truman that the U.S.S.R. was going to mount a real challenge to world peace.

The following month, former British Prime Minister Winston Churchill delivered an address in Missouri. Churchill had become a modern-day folk hero in America, and his **Iron Curtain** speech shocked the public and drew attention to the suspicious behavior of the U.S.S.R. Support for Truman's tough stance began to grow.

> _From Stettin on the Baltic, to Trieste on the Adriatic, an Iron Curtain has decended across the continent._
>
> _Winston Churchill_
> _March 1946_

Truman Doctrine: Greece And Turkey

A year after the Iranian incident, the Soviets again attempted to influence events on their southern border. A weak Turkish government was put under pressure by the U.S.S.R. to agree to negotiate control over the Straits of the Dardenelles, leading to the Soviet's Black Sea ports. The U.S. and British sent stern notes and the Soviets again backed off. A stronger Soviet effort was aimed at helping communist rebels overthrow Turkey's neighbor, Greece. The British had been nearly bankrupted at the end of the war and indicated to Truman that they could not hold out any more.

Truman was advised by Acheson to make a strong showing of American commitment in the Mediterranean. The President went before the Republican Congress and boldly stated that it was America's obligation to see that dem-

ocratic nations would not be abandoned to communistic aggression. This idea gradually came to be known as the **Truman Doctrine**. The memory of the impotence of the democracies at Munich when Hitler was appeased was still fresh in most people's minds.

Congress responded positively to Truman's request, and the first principle of America's new **containment policy** was born: America would give military aid and training to nations resisting communist takeovers. Not only did Congress allocate the 400 million dollars that Truman had requested to aid Greece and Turkey, but it would eventually add an additional 200 million dollars by 1950.

Marshall Plan

A second great principle of the containment policy was set in place at the urging of Truman's key policy advisors: economic aid to stabilize tottering regimes in western Europe. On 5 June 1947, former Army Chief of Staff General George C. Marshall, then serving Truman as Secretary of State (1947-1949), unveiled a dramatic program for saving the economies of European nations. The **European Recovery Act**, later become known as the **Marshall Plan**. The Secretary proposed that the European economy could be stabilized by joint efforts of the European states and grants-in-aid from the U.S. Again, a reluctant Congress had to be prodded by Truman.

The communist overthrow of a moderate government in Czechoslovakia brought home the seriousness of the situation in Europe and Congress agreed to fund the Marshall Plan for 12 billion dollars. In the long run, the plan stimulated both the western European economies and our own, and it was undoubtedly a major factor in helping to avoid another 1930's style depression.

The Marshall Plan also paved the way for a number of projects which caused the Western European nations to begin to cooperate among themselves. In 1952, French Foreign Minister **Robert Schuman** organized France, West Germany, Belgium, and the Netherlands into a **European Coal and Steel Community**, to administer tariffs, prices, and supply vital industrial resources. On this base was built the **European Economic Community**, or "**Common Market**," in 1957. It began to break down tariff barriers and coordinate trade in Western Europe.

The Common Market has also created a political assembly whose delegates debate problems of mutual concern. Known as the **European Parliament**, it is modeled after the "Council of Europe," an idea sponsored by Winston Churchill after World War II. It is a general advisory body and has few legislative authority or enforcement powers.

Berlin Blockade And Airlift

Friction grew between the United States and the U.S.S.R. as the Truman Doctrine and the Marshall Plan became reality. To strengthen Western Europe, the United States, Britain, and France had earlier agreed to merge the administration of their zones, into a single **Federal Republic of Germany**. The U.S.S.R. was bent on keeping Germany weak and would not agree to creating a new nation. The Soviets retaliated by making it more and more difficult for the other Allies to administer their half of Berlin deep inside East Germany.

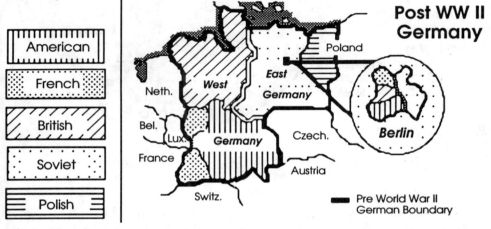

At the end of the war it was agreed that the German capital would be divided into four zones, but no provision had been made for guaranteeing land and water access to the city through the surrounding Soviet Zone.

On 24 June 1948, Truman saw some of his worst suspicions about the Soviets proven. They blockaded all road, railroad, and canal routes to Berlin in an effort to get the other occupying nations to leave. Truman could use force or fly over the blockade. He chose the latter. An elaborate **Berlin Airlift**, called "Operation Vittles," was devised. For 300 days, the U.S. and Royal Air Forces kept half of the city alive with round-the-clock air shipments of nearly 12,000 tons of essential goods each day. Stalin, embarrassed by the show of moral strength, lifted the roadblocks in May of 1949.

Formation Of The Nato Alliance

Nearly four years of difficulties with the Soviets in Germany plus the pattern of their domination of Eastern European nations convinced Truman that a major break with American tradition had to take place. The containment of communism and Soviet aggression could not take place merely by economic and emergency military measures.

Military Containment

The NATO Alliance
(1949)

Other Multi-lateral Alliances:

OAS (1947):
20 nations of
Latin America

ANZUS (1951):
Australia,
New Zealand

SEATO (1954):
Britain, France,
Thailand, Pakistan,
and Philippines

China

U.S.S.R.

Canada

Europe

U.S.A.

Atlantic

Bi-lateral Agreements:
In the late 1940's and early 1950's,
the U.S. entered agreements with Taiwan,
Japan, South Korea, and the Philippines.

In its weakened state, western Europe could not withstand a military move on the part of the Red Army. America would have to enter into a permanent defense alliance for the first time since the French Alliance of 1778. Secretary of State **Dean Acheson** (1949-1953) carefully laid the groundwork with Congress and the European allies. The **North Atlantic Treaty Organization (NATO)** united ten nations of Western Europe with Canada and the United States. Any attack on one member is considered an attack on all under the concept of **collective security.**

U.S. And The Third World

Truman also recognized that the U.S. role in containing communism could not focus solely on Europe. As the old European colonial empires began to break up, new underdeveloped nations were being formed in the "Third World." Communist activities seemed to be sparking trouble in these new countries.

In Truman's January 1949 inauguration speech, he made a proposal, now called the **Point Four Program,** in which technological assistance would be given to new and struggling nations to build their economic bases so that they could resist communist insurgency. Out of this proposal came a flow of billions of American dollars for foreign aid to underdeveloped nations which continues to this day.

By 1949, the essential elements of the containment policy were in place: global economic and military aid to help others resist communist aggression. It became:

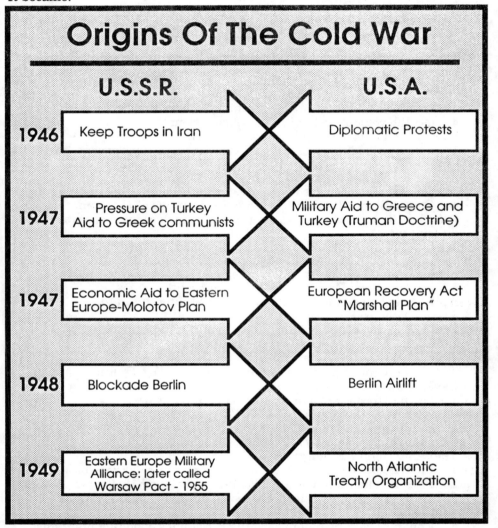

Origins Of The Cold War

	U.S.S.R.	U.S.A.
1946	Keep Troops in Iran	Diplomatic Protests
1947	Pressure on Turkey Aid to Greek communists	Military Aid to Greece and Turkey (Truman Doctrine)
1947	Economic Aid to Eastern Europe-Molotov Plan	European Recovery Act "Marshall Plan"
1948	Blockade Berlin	Berlin Airlift
1949	Eastern Europe Military Alliance: later called Warsaw Pact - 1955	North Atlantic Treaty Organization

Questions

1 The United Nations was to be an improvement over the League of Nations, because it created a Security Council of major powers to
   1 manage world trade.
   2 assist former colonies in becoming full-fledged nations.
   3 monitor violations of human rights.
   4 solve international disputes.

2 Soviet support for communist insurgency movements in Greece and Turkey led to the
   1 Truman Doctrine.   3 Yalta summit.
   2 Fair Deal.   4 Berlin Blockade.

3 The United Nations' most impressive achievements have been in the area of
  1 easing the tensions of the cold war.
  2 helping underdeveloped nations.
  3 prosecuting human rights violations.
  4 controlling the nuclear arms race.

4 The original intent of the U.N.'s Security Council has not been achieved because the great powers tend to
  1 be out-voted by neutral Third World nations.
  2 use summit meetings to settle their differences independently.
  3 favor economic matters over military ones.
  4 use the veto to block effective police actions.

5 Polarization means that after World War II,
  1 nations allied themselves with one of the two superpowers.
  2 there was intense competition for the last remaining unsettled regions.
  3 world tensions focused on the issue of freedom for Poland.
  4 Churchill and Truman took opposite positions at Potsdam.

6 President Truman's desire to aid the war's displaced persons was made difficult by
  1 Soviet vetoes in the U.N. Security Council.
  2 the restrictive immigration policies of the United States.
  3 opposition of senators from segregated states.
  4 the Universal Declaration of Human Rights.

7 At the Potsdam summit, Premier Joseph Stalin refused to
  1 enter the war against Japan.
  2 join with the Allies in the "Iron Curtain" Program.
  3 discuss the end of Soviet occupation in Poland.
  4 share nuclear secrets with Britain.

8 The Soviet Union's post-war actions outside of Eastern Europe prompted the Truman administration to
  1 begin to formulate a new American foreign policy.
  2 return the U.S. to its traditional neutrality.
  3 continue Lend-Lease aid to the U.S.S.R.
  4 share our nuclear secrets with the Soviets.

9 The term "cold war" indicates
  1 international disputes over mineral rights in polar regions.
  2 intense competition and confrontations between the "superpowers."
  3 "superpower" hostilities were cooled down by United Nations' mediation.
  4 Congress became cool toward the President's spending programs.

10 The new foreign policy adopted by the Truman administration rested on the idea of "containment." This means
  1 patient negotiating with one's opponents.
  2 isolating oneself from world events.
  3 taking actions to restrain the influence of one's enemy.
  4 restraining the civil rights of troublesome minority groups.

11 By the Truman Doctrine the U.S. pledged
  1 military assistance in fighting communist aggression.
  2 economic aid to repair war damage in Europe.
  3 rapid demobilization of the U.S. armed forces.
  4 to give independence to its overseas colonies.

12 In the Marshall Plan, the U.S. pledged
    1   military assistance to fighting communist aggression.
    2   economic aid to repair war damage in Europe.
    3   rapid demobilization of the U.S. armed forces.
    4   to give independence to its overseas colonies.
13 One result of the Marshall Plan was that the
    1   expense caused the American economy to go into recession.
    2   Soviet Union became indebted to the United States.
    3   power of the U.N. was increased.
    4   European nations increased cooperation among themselves.
14 Which episode best illustrates the cold war tensions of the late 1940's?
    1   An Allied airlift in answer to the Soviet blockade of Berlin.
    2   U. S. bombing of Hiroshima and Nagasaki.
    3   Congress overriding Truman's veto of the Taft-Hartley Act.
    4   Tensions over the approval of the U.N.'s Declaration of Human Rights.
15 N.A.T.O. was a momentous step for the United States, because it
    1   recognized the president's new role as Commander-in-Chief.
    2   was formulated by Secretary of State Dean Acheson.
    3   expanded the Marshall Plan to the "Third World."
    4   was our first peacetime military alliance since the American Revolution.

C. Containment In Asia

The United States And Japan

The general behavior of the Soviet Union in Asia and communist insurgents in China in the post war period led State Department officials to help rebuild Japan in much more rapid fashion than originally planned. The U.S. had been supporting the Chinese **Nationalists** under **Chiang Kai-shek** with the hope that the country could be rebuilt into the stabilizing power in East Asia. Difficulties in settling differences between Chiang and the communists under **Mao Zedong** caused Secretary of State **Acheson** to convince Truman to shift attention to rebuilding Japan.

Japan had been stripped of its wartime territorial gains and its military power, but harsh reparations were not levied by the Allies. The democratic constitution **Gen. MacArthur** created allowed only a small defensive military. The U.S. provided protection on a large scale. A bilateral (two-sided) defense agreement in 1949, eventually reduced the U.S. occupation forces, but allowed the U.S. to maintain bases on Japanese soil. This meant that Japan could devote its resources to peacetime production. U.S. aid was stepped up, paralleling the Marshall Plan in Europe, and a campaign began to convince American business to invest in Japanese industrial growth.

As a result, the U.S. helped create a formidable capitalist democracy with strong trade links to the American market. As economic recovery was accelerated, an independent Japanese government took over the reins of power in 1949 just as Chiang's forces were losing their final battle and the communists completed their takeover in China.

The United States And China

Between 1945 and 1949, over two billion dollars was sent to aid Chiang Kai-shek's Nationalist Chinese forces to resist the communist rebels, but gross mismanagement and corruption plagued the Nationalists. The struggle between Chiang's government and Mao's rebels had been going on all during the years of Japanese occupation. Some of the U.S. aid money and supplies for Chiang's armies had been traded off by his own officers to the communists. After the war, the U.S. had attempted to resolve the Chinese civil war through diplomatic mediation. Truman even sent retired Secretary of State George Marshall, but Marshall concluded Chiang had lost the peoples' support. During the long struggle, Chiang's Nationalists began to be associated with the powerful landed aristocratic class, while the communists moved to help the peasants. In the end, the Nationalists defeated themselves. Mao proclaimed victory and established the new **Peoples' Republic of China** on 1 October 1949. The U.S. broke diplomatic relations with China, and the two countries would not speak again for nearly a quarter of a century.

U.S.S.R. Tests An A-Bomb (1949)

The loss of China to the communists was an even more bitter pill to swallow since President Truman had announced only a month earlier that the U.S.S.R. had tested its first nuclear weapon. The American monopoly on atomic weapons was over, and the Cold War power structure had changed. These two events, coming in such rapid succession, were viewed as considerable setbacks for the Truman administration's containment policies. The Republicans, again hoping for victory in the 1950 Congressional elections, loudly criticized the Democrats for allowing such strategic blunders. Acheson came under assault for inept diplomacy, some even charged the State Department was riddled with communists who had "sold out" China.

"Hot War" In Asia: The Korean Conflict

A new side of the Cold War in Asia emerged in the late spring of 1950. On the morning of 25 June, North Korea, a Soviet satellite, attacked U.S. backed South Korea, and the Cold War turned "hot." Korea, long dominated by the Japanese, had been divided into two occupation zones after Japan's surrender in 1945. The Allies had intended reunification, but the post war tensions between the U.S. and the U.S.S.R. prevented it. The U.N. was asked to study the question in 1947.

In the south, the U.S. set up a democratic constitution. A U.N. supervised election was held, and the **Republic of Korea** emerged in 1948. Late in that same year, the U.S. withdrew its occupation forces at the request of the U.N. The U.S.S.R. quickly set up the People's Republic of Korea in the northern half of the peninsula. Skirmishes began between the two countries across the 38th Parallel border. Truman sent financial aid to help the South Koreans.

When the June 1950 invasion occurred, the U.S. requested the **U.N. Security Council** to take action against the aggression by North Korea. With the Soviet Union boycotting the Security Council and unable to veto the Korean resolution, the U.N. voted to assist South Korea.

The Korean Conflict

U.S.S.R.

China

Yellow Sea

38th Parallel

Farthest U.N. advance Nov. 1950

Sea of Japan

Final armistice line August 1953

MacArthur's Inchon landing Sept. 1950

Farthest North Korean advance Sept. 1950

Truman acted quickly. Terming it a "police action," he ignored Congress and ordered U.S. troops, joined by small contingents of other U.N. members, into Korea.

Truman placed General MacArthur in command. The speed of North Korea's attack nearly pushed the U.N. and South Korean troops off the peninsula. In September, MacArthur ordered a surprise attack with a brilliant and amphibious landing behind the North Koreans at Inchon. The North Koreans were thrown on the defensive and retreated behind the 38thparallel. The goal of restoring the border had been achieved.

Truman then took an unexpected step. He authorized MacArthur to enter North Korea, provided the Soviets or Chinese didn't enter the war. Nervous about United Nations and United States presence near its border, China invaded North Korea in November and pushed MacArthur's forces back to the 38th parallel.

Enduring Issues

9

MacArthur began criticizing Truman and the Joint Chiefs of Staff for restraining him from launching a massive counterattack against the Chinese. In one of the most controversial moves of his Presidency, Truman relieved MacArthur of command. A cease-fire was declared and a round of negotiations began that lasted two years. An armistice was signed on 27 July 1953, restoring the border. The war ended in a stalemate that continues to this day.

D. Cold War At Home

The post war period was a stormy time domestically. Not only were there economic ups and downs, but adjusting to the new role of the U.S. as the worldwide anti-communist defender of democracy was not easy for Americans. The actions of the Soviet Union in Europe and Asia and the vigor of the Truman administration's response caused many to grow fearful. In Washington, politicians in both parties were indicating that communist subversion was widespread.

Truman And Government Loyalty Checks

The anti-communist concern caused Truman to form a **Loyalty Review Board** which investigated thousands of federal employees, some of whom were dismissed or resigned. The country began to show signs of paranoia. Notarized **loyalty oaths** began being required of public and private employees under pain of dismissal.

The Smith Act And Congressional Investigations

In 1947, the House authorized its **Committee on Un-American Activities** to investigate the rampant charges of left-wing activities in the government. The Committee launched its investigation of the American Communist Party by leveling contempt charges against leaders who refused to testify. In the summer of 1948, the Justice Department successfully prosecuted eleven of these leaders for violation of the **Smith Act** of 1940, which made illegal

Enduring Issues 5

the teaching or advocating of the forceful overthrow of the U.S. government. The communist leaders appealed, claiming the act violated their **1st Amendment** right of free speech. In the *Dennis v. U.S.* decision in 1951, the Supreme Court upheld the Smith Act and opened the door for many more prosecutions of Communist Party members in the early 1950's.

Enduring Issues 3

Years later, the Supreme Court indicated that the Smith Act had actually gone too far. In *Yates v. U.S.* (1957), the Court ruled that speaking, studying, or teaching about theories of forcible overthrow of the government were not the same as participating in an actual conspiracy. In the same year, in *Watkins v. U.S.*, the Court held that witnesses summoned before Congressional committees must be properly informed of the nature of the questions to be put to them and care must be taken to preserve their Constitutional rights.

A full-blown **anti-Red crusade** began as the Committee on Unamerican Activities held hearings all over the country. Refusal to answer questions that might incriminate oneself is a basic right protected by **5th Amendment**. "Taking the Fifth" cast enough doubt on some witnesses, especially in Hollywood, to cause them to be "blacklisted" and lose their jobs. California Congressman **Richard Nixon** achieved national attention as a member of the committee, and was able to gain a U.S. Senate seat as a result.

The Alger Hiss Case

In mid-1948, sensational spy cases began to unfold. The Committee on Un-American Activities investigated **Alger Hiss**, who had been a State Department official in the Roosevelt years. Whittaker Chambers, an admitted communist, had openly accused Hiss of passing classified government documents to Soviet officials in the 1930's. Hiss, head of the prestigious Carnegie Endowment for Peace, vigorously denied the charges before the committee. He was later charged with perjury and convicted in a series of sensational trials.

Enduring Issues 5

The House Committee on Un-American Activities eventually sponsored legislation designed to stop subversive activities. In 1950, Congress passed the **McCarran Internal Security Act** which essentially allowed the President to arrest and detain persons suspected of any affiliations with groups which might *"...contribute to the establishment ... of totalitarian dictatorships in the United States."*

President Truman vetoed the bill, saying it would undermine the basic civil liberties of Americans. Congress easily overrode the veto. At the same time, Truman continued to expand the activities of his own Loyalty Review Board.

The furor caused by the Committee hearings also caused the FBI to broaden its espionage investigations. One of these resulted in the famous **Rosenberg Case.** Ethel and Julius Rosenberg were arrested and accused of having arranged to pass U.S. atomic secrets to the Soviet Union during World War II. On 5 April 1951, they were found guilty of treason and were sentenced to death. Appeals continued for two years, but they were finally electrocuted in June 1953. Much doubt still remains about the evidence presented at their trial. Like the case of Sacco and Vanzetti in the Red Scare of the 1920's, there has been speculation the Rosenbergs may have been victims of a fear-ridden social environment.

McCarthyism

Enduring Issues
5

The U.S. Senate was not silent in this growing atmosphere of mistrust. Wisconsin Republican **Joseph R. McCarthy** began to make a series of shocking accusations about communist influence on high government officials which included General Marshall, Dean Acheson, and Democratic Presidential candidate Adlai Stevenson. As chairman of the Senate Committee on Government Operations, McCarthy led his own anti-communist investigations, making brash charges and ignoring the civil rights of those he subpoenaed to testify. He never unearthed any conspiracy or any communists in government, but he came to symbolize the great anti-communist crusade of the early 1950's. His fellow Republicans had enjoyed his attacks on the Truman administration but began to change their minds when he began attacking officials of the Eisenhower administration.

Loyalty And Dissent: The Oppenheimer Case

Even as eminent a person as **Dr. J. Robert Oppenheimer,** who had developed the first atomic bomb, was placed under the "security risk" category by the Eisenhower administration. Oppenheimer had quit his government job in 1949, in opposition to the development of the more powerful hydrogen bomb. In 1954, he was working at Princeton, but was still a consultant to the Atomic Energy Commission. Eisenhower, trying to show he was better at cleaning out security risks than the Democrats, directed Oppenheimer's security clearance be cut. He protested, but the AEC gave weak excuses. Years later, Oppenheimer was exonerated.

"McCarthyism" finally met its match when the Senator pledged to get the communists out of the U.S. Army. Millions of Americans watched the televised hearings. The Senator was shown to be reckless and irresponsible. His unpopularity became an embarrassment. The U.S. Senate officially **censured** him in 1954.

By 1955, Americans were becoming accustomed to the tensions of Cold War, the Korean Conflict was over, and McCarthy was silenced. The hysteria over internal security subsided and the public's attention was drawn to other matters.

Questions

1 After World War II, the U.S. moved to strengthen Japan as an economic power in Asia
   1 as a logical extension of Manifest Destiny.
   2 after the disastrous attack on Pearl Harbor.
   3 to balance the threat of the Axis alliance.
   4 once it appeared Mao would control China.

2 The series of multilateral and bilateral defense agreements set up after 1949 showed that the U.S. desired to
   1 surround the communist nations militarily.
   2 send aid to underdeveloped nations.
   3 protect its borders.
   4 isolate itself.

3 Chiang Kai-shek's forces lost the 1949 Chinese civil war because
   1 U.S. diplomats misjudged the Communists' strength.
   2 massive military reinforcements were sent in by the U.S.S.R.
   3 Nationalist leaders were disorganized and sometimes corrupt.
   4 the U.S. refused to become involved in China's internal politics.

4 The Korean conflict in 1950 signified the first time
   1 American and Soviet troops fought each other directly.
   2 a world peace organization used force against aggressors.
   3 a president was impeached for unauthorized use of military.
   4 U.S. troops had fought in Asia.

5 During the Korean conflict, President Truman relieved General MacArthur of command, because the General
   1 refused to use American troops in a U.N. action.
   2 publicly criticized the President's orders.
   3 ordered U.N. forces to fight Chinese troops.
   4 negotiated a cease-fire with the Soviet commander.

6 In the late 40's and early 50's, Americans became increasingly
   1 isolationist in their world views.
   2 confident in the idea of nuclear disarmament.
   3 fearful of communist activities inside the country.
   4 opposed to joining the United Nations.

7 The Smith Act forbid
   1 employers to require employees to take loyalty oaths.
   2 witnesses at Congressional hearings to use 5th Amendment protections.
   3 organizing of communist groups inside United States territory.
   4 teaching or advocating forceful overthrow of the government.

8 Senator Joseph McCarthy's activities were criticized because they
   1 often violated individual's constitutional rights.
   2 attempted to discredit the Democratic Party at election time.
   3 focused narrowly on the U.S. State Department.
   4 provoked the communist attack on South Korea.

9 President Truman's containment policy rested on military aid against communist subversion, economic rebuilding of war-torn nations, formal alliances, and
   1 obtaining civil rights for minorities.
   2 re-institution of tariff protection for American businesses.
   3 liberalizing U.S. immigration policies.
   4 aid to developing Third World nations.

10 The House Committee on Un-American Activities
  1   restricted U.S. immigration by imposing nationality quotas.
  2   ordered the execution of convicted Soviet spies.
  3   investigated communist activities.
  4   brought impeachment charges against the President.

Essays

1   The pattern of U.S. foreign policy in the years before World War II is a strange blend of isolationism and internationalism.

    a   Explain why U.S. policy has traditionally been isolationist. [3]

    b   Choose TWO of the following and explain why each reflects the uncertainty of U.S. foreign policy in the 1930's. [6,6]
  - London Economic Conference of 1933
  - Japanese Aggression in Manchuria
  - Spanish Civil War
  - Good Neighbor Policy
  - Neutrality Acts of 1935-'36-'37
  - Recognition of the U.S.S.R.

2   Policy-makers do not always control events, sometimes the reverse is true. Choose THREE of the following events. For EACH event, explain why it drew us closer to entry into World War II and whether the event helped or hindered American foreign policy goals. [5,5,5]
  - The Fall of France
  - The Destroyers-for-Bases Deal
  - Hitler's Attack on Stalin
  - The Lend-Lease Act
  - Japan's Attack on the Hawaiian Islands
  - The Atlantic Charter

3   Choose THREE of the following and explain the relation of each to Truman's containment policy. [5,5,5]
  - The Yalta and Potsdam Conferences
  - The Berlin Blockade
  - Communist Revolts in Greece and Turkey
  - The Point Four Program
  - The NATO Alliance
  - The Marshall Plan

4   In times of tension, it is often difficult to strike a balance between preserving the rights of the individual and the security of the society as a whole. Discuss the relationship of this statement to any THREE of the following. [5,5,5]
  - The Nisei internment during World War II
  - Truman's Loyalty Review Board in the late 1940's
  - The House Committee on Un-American Activities hearings in the late 1940's
  - The Army - McCarthy Hearings
  - The Oppenheimer Controversy

Unit Six

A World in Uncertain Times

1950 - 1985

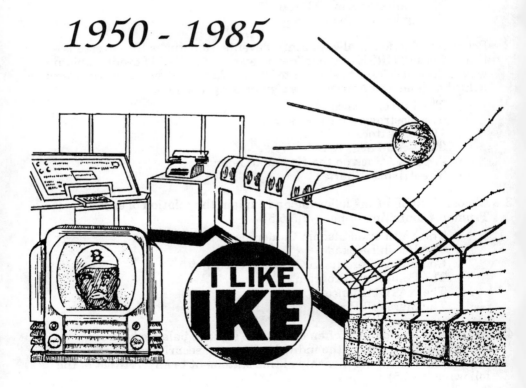

1960	1965	1970

- Brinksmanship   • Berlin Wall   • Civil Rights Revolution   • Moon Landing
- Little Rock   • Sputnik   • War on Poverty   • Vietnam Escalation
- *Brown v Bd. of Ed.*   • Cuban Missile Crisis   • *Miranda v. Arizona*

Racism
Abortion
Terrorism
Affluence
Third World
Desegregation
McCarthyism
Accommodation
Draft Amnesty
Fundamentalism
Environmentalism
Electronic Media
Consumer Revolution
Women's Liberation
Immigration Reform
Civil Rights Movement
Supply - Side Economics

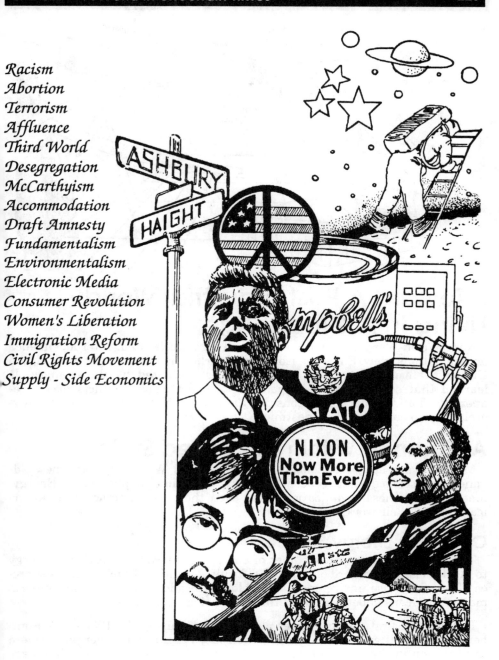

1975	1980	1990	2000

- Vietnam Withdrawal   · Iranian Hostages   · "New Federalism"   · Persian Gulf
- Watergate   · *Roe v. Wade*   · SALT   · Reaganomics   · U.S.S.R.
    · Detente   · Arab Oil Crisis   · ERA   · Deficits   · Tax Reform   Collapse

I. Toward A Post-industrial World: Living In A Global Age

After World War II, the pace of global change accelerated. Interdependence among nations grew. Since the isolation of earlier times no longer worked, the United States tried to meet the challenges presented by the changes. It learned that seeking global cooperation was not easy. Conflicts arose frequently. The U.S. learned to consider the basic desire of all nations for sovereignty and control of their destinies.

A. Change Within The United States

Modern wars spur technological growth. World War II sparked new advances in science that generated many peacetime applications. Energy, materials, business organizations, and even the basic approach that Americans had to their work, changed rapidly.

Changing Energy Sources

The U.S. is the largest consumer of energy in the world. Supplying energy to meet a rising standard of living is difficult. Traditional fuels used as sources of energy cause environmental problems. In addition, petroleum imports make Americans dependent upon the whims of other nations.

In 1957, the first nuclear power plant opened. During the 1960's, the number of new facilities mushroomed. By the 1990, 112 nuclear power plants were in operation in the U.S. One quarter of the world's nuclear power plants are in the U.S. Nuclear plants generate nearly 20% of the nation's electricity.

Supporters of nuclear energy praise the cleanliness and efficiency of nuclear power over conventional oil or coal generators. Initial construction of nuclear reactors is expensive. However, long-term operational costs are lower than fossil fuel plants. Nuclear power plant construction peaked in the 1970's. Twenty-six opened in 1973. Since then, demand for electricity has slowed.

Also, inflation and safety considerations have driven construction costs to over $4 billion per plant. America also became more energy conscious after several Arab oil boycotts in the 1970's.

Many critics question the safety of nuclear reactors. Plant breakdowns sometimes resulted in the leakage of small amounts of radiation. Many plants lack a safe, permanent place to dispose of deadly nuclear waste. A 1979 nuclear accident at the **Three Mile Island Reactor** near Harrisburg, Pennsylvania heightened awareness of the dangers. Existing plants will continue to operate into the 21st century. The future of nuclear generated energy depends the success of researchers to perfect fusion techniques, a more desirable approach.

Changing Materials

Stronger and lighter materials affect every aspect of modern life. New **plastics** can withstand changes in weather, are lighter than metals, and retain strength for many years. Plastics have widespread applications in the construction industry. Automobiles and airplanes use **lighter metals** and **alloys** to reduce weight and fuel consumption. The medical and communications industries now use **fiber optics**. This process sends light through minute fiber rods. Scientists are also making rapid progress in **superconductivity**. This process will revolutionize sending electricity over long distances.

Changing Technology

In the past decade, computers became a part of everyday life in America. The first mass-produced computers manufactured after World War II were huge, bulky machines with vacuum tubes. These were slow machines with limited capacity. They filled entire rooms.

By the 1960's, **transistors** increased speed and decreased computers size. In the 1980's, **silicon chips** enabled microcomputers to do millions of operations per second.

In business and industry, computers speed communication, accounting, inventories, and banking. Computers help factories automate operations. In government, computers increased the efficiency of law enforcement and tax collection. Military strategy and pinpoint bombing techniques depend on a wide range of computer guidance systems. On-board computers do millions of split second calculations needed for space exploration. In health and medicine, computers aid in diagnoses and monitor complex equipment.

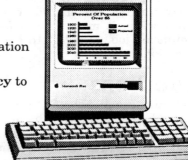

The computer age has also meant:

- **fewer "blue-collar" jobs** when automation and robotics replace human labor

- **increased need for computer literacy** to qualify for jobs in nearly all fields

- **reduced individual privacy** due to governments' and private data collecting organizations' greater capacity to access information on individuals.

Changing Corporate Structures

After World War II, many corporations internationalized their operations. Today, **multinational corporations** are common in manufacturing, mining, banking, and petroleum production. Advantages to large scale operations include: access to raw materials, cheap labor, and international markets. Because they operate in many countries, multinationals can avoid the restrictions imposed by individual governments. Smaller corporations doing business within one nation do not have this advantage.

Supporters of multinationals point out that these corporations provide economic development beyond the capacity of national governments. They also create jobs and teach new technologies in developing nations. Critics of multinationals fear corporations will interfere in the domestic affairs of nations. They also say **LDCs** (less developed nations) will become dominated by multinationals. American critics denounce multinationals shifting operations overseas for cheaper labor. The activities of multinational corporations operating in the Republic of South Africa caused international controversy during the 1980's. Foreign businesses operating in South Africa strengthened the economic power of a government dedicated to apartheid.

Corporate mergers also changed the structure of American business. Firms that used to sell a single product merged with others into giant **conglomerates**. A typical merged-management conglomerate includes operation in diverse fields: manufacturing, transportation, entertainment, travel, communications, and food processing. Some mergers combined two competing firms in the same product line (provided they did not violate the trust laws). This gave conglomerates staggering market power.

Changing Nature Of Employment

When the Constitution was written, over 90% of the American population was **agrarian** (made living by farming). The technologies developed in the 19th century shifted the economy to industry. Since World War II, however, many older industries have closed or moved. Foreign competition and automation resulted in huge drops in the steel and textile industries, mining, and other "blue collar" jobs.

Growth in today's economy results in employment in service industries. These industries create jobs in health care, retailing, education, finance, food service, and recreation. Economists cite the decline in manufacturing jobs as a new stage of economic development (**post-industrialism**). For the American worker, it means more frequent occupation changes in mid-life, and diminished job security. In addition, many jobs will require more technical education.

Questions

1 Which is a global effect of the growth of technology?
   1 Economic activity became dependent on domestic natural resources.
   2 International cooperation broke down.
   3 Cultural isolation diminished.
   4 Nationalism prevented progress.

2   The labor force in the United States since the end of World War II
    experienced the largest growth in the percentage of
    1   blue collar workers.   3   agricultural jobs.
    2   unskilled workers.   4   technical and service jobs.
3   Which is a fact about nuclear reactors?
    1   They are the safest method of power generation.
    2   Orders for nuclear reactors reached a peak in the mid-1970's.
    3   Inflation caused the decline in building nuclear reactors.
    4   Solar power generators replaced most nuclear reactors.
4   Which development would most likely help reverse the trend that has
    occurred since 1976 in the building of nuclear reactors?
    1 Activation of pipelines to the oil reserves in Alaska.
    2 A worldwide agreement on the limitation of nuclear arms.
    3 Perfection of superconductors.
    4 Development of the process of nuclear fusion.
5   One negative result of the increasing use of computers is the
    1   jeopardizing of the right of privacy.
    2   rising cost of living.
    3   decreasing of the individual's leisure time.
    4   increasing property tax rates.
6   Isolationism as a foreign policy is more difficult to achieve in the 20th
    century than in prior times because
    1   the world's population has declined.
    2   there are more sovereign nations.
    3   modern technology makes nations interdependent.
    4   officials can ignore public opinion on major issues
7   What is an advantage of living in an age of computers?
    1   employees need less training.
    2   individuals have greater job security
    3   it is possible to process quickly large amounts of data
    4   lower unemployment rates for the uneducated.
8   The growth of multinational corporations and the international exchange
    of information shows increasing
    1   disillusion with communist governments.
    2   prosperity in most developing countries.
    3   trends of isolation in national foreign policies.
    4   interdependence among nations.
9   In 1900, about 31% of the American population lived on farms. In 1980,
    about 3% lived on farms. This change is directly related to
    1   the government providing transportation and communications
        improvements.
    2   the decline in domestic consumption of agricultural products.
    3   cheap agricultural imports becoming available.
    4   agricultural productivity sharply increasing.
10 "Technology has increased to the point where most work which has been
    done by people having less that a high school diploma can now be done
    more cheaply by machines."
    The author of this statement is trying to point out that
    1   the cost of education is a wasteful use of tax dollars.
    2   people no longer need a high school education to operate simple
        machines.
    3   the need for blue-collar workers will expand soon.
    4   it will be increasingly difficult for high school drop outs to find jobs.

B. Change In Global Conditions

In the industrial nations of North America, Western Europe, and East Asia, modern farming techniques enable small numbers of farmers to produce enough food for the entire population. The opposite is true of the LDCs of Asia, Latin America, and Africa. Although most people in LDCs are farmers, starvation is common. Most farms operate on subsistence levels. Cash crops for export (cotton, tobacco) seriously cut the amount of acreage devoted to food production.

Agriculture:
Traditional Patterns And The Green Revolution

Many LDCs have yet to take advantage of the Green Revolution. Intense scientific effort developed new technology, machinery, and fertilization. Improved strains of food staples, such as disease-resistant wheat, increased production and protein intake in industrialized nations. Some LDCs, such as China and India, show progress in adopting Green Revolution methods. Other LDCs, such as those in Saharan Africa, experience difficulties for a number of reasons:

- resistance to changes in traditional lifestyle

- unpredictable weather patterns, poor soil, and erosion

- illiteracy

- lack of governmental cooperation

- inadequate infrastructures

Manufacturing:
Developed Nations v. LDCs

Since World War II, the older industrial nations (Britain, France, and the U.S.) saw declines in heavy industries (steel, autos). After the War, U.S. aid helped rebuild devastated nations in Western Europe and Asia. This gave them a more technologically advanced industrial base. Japan, South Korea, Taiwan, and Hong Kong now produce products which compete with those of the U.S. Developed nations are also the homes of multinational corporations which control much of the world's business.

World War II upset the prewar global colonial structure of Western European nations. Independence movements swept through Asia and Africa in the 1950's and 1960's. With the change came the "Revolution of Rising Expectations." It created a hope that LDCs could imitate the higher standards of living of Western nations. Developed nations shared technology and gave loans to former colonies. Some of the multinationals provided technical training and investment capital. Unstable governments, unskilled labor, and lack of capital hindered progress. Rapid population growth often offset industrial gains. In some cases, skilled workers emigrated from their homelands seeking higher wages in developed nations.

Projected World Population

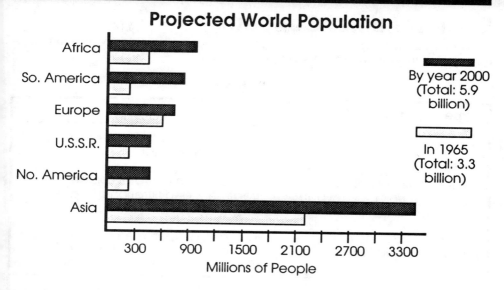

By year 2000
(Total: 5.9
billion)

In 1965
(Total: 3.3
billion)

Millions of People

World Population Growth: Hunger And Control

In recent times, population growth declined in most industrialized nations. Changing social values caused much of the decrease. The growing importance of careers for women and later marriages limit child-bearing years. In most developed nations, people voluntarily reduced family size. The expense of raising children is a major reason for this.

The reverse is true for most of LDCs. After World War II, advances in medicine and science reduced infant mortality. Medical advancements increased longevity. Birthrates remain high in LDCs. In many countries, the population doubles every thirty years. Reasons for high birthrates in LDCs include:

- children are workers in traditional agricultural societies

- marriage at a young age

- religious traditions and importance of male heirs

- illiteracy

Poor living conditions and food shortages result from population explosions. Inadequate transportation and lack of communication (especially in Africa), make the problems worse.

In the 1970's, India and China undertook massive public education campaigns to convince couples to limit child bearing. They have not met with much success.

Environmental Concern

Every human pays a significant price for technological advancement. Industrial wastes pollute the environment.

Pollution

Type	Cause	Solution
Air	Factories and Automobiles	Burn cleaner fuels; Install pollution control equipment
Water	Factory discharges, municipal sewage wasteplants	Conservation of water sources; Treatment and filtration of water
Land	Garbage dumps Buried toxic waste	Recycling paper, metals, and glass; Clean up landfills and toxic waste dumps; seek safer storage areas

In environmental matters, the actions of one nation can affect many. Trying to clean up the environment often takes international cooperation. Some examples of international problems include:

- **Acid Rain** from the effluent of U.S. factories, which hurt both Canadian wildlife and farms

- **Chemical Dumping** in rivers that flow through several European nations

- **Nuclear testing** over oceans that cause widespread radiation fallout

- **Lethal pesticide** residues carried by air currents

- **Ozone depletion** caused by the release of the chemical compound CFC (used in refrigeration) into the upper atmosphere

The misuse of natural resources and destruction of the land concerns environmentalists. In developed nations, industrial and urban growth results in more roads, shopping centers, and housing. This reduces farm acreage and forests. The danger of flooding increases. **Strip mining** (tearing up large chunks of land for valuable resources) ruins the ecological balance. Both of these situations are now starting to occur in LDCs.

Over-grazing and poor soil management are turning large areas into deserts. Nations eager for industrialization do not place very high priorities on environmental protection. The expense is too high. Meeting consumer demand and protecting nature conflict as goals. Governments find it difficult to do both. They have to make too many agonizing tradeoffs.

Changing Power Relationships

For centuries, the struggle for global leadership took place among the nations of Europe. Shifting alliances constantly changed the European balance of power. In modern times, the main players were England and France. Spain, Germany, Italy, and Russia had varying influences.

World War II changed the international power structure. The United States and the former Soviet Union became **superpowers**. An East v. West power struggle emerged. The nations of Eastern Europe and China allied with the Soviets, and the nations of Western Europe and Japan allied with the U.S. This **bipolar division** left out most LDCs. As Western European colonial empires broke up, new nations emerged from independence movements in Africa and Asia. The East-West power structure remained in place until the Soviet Union dissolved in 1991.

Nearly all the LDCs are in the Southern Hemisphere. Most industrial nations are in the Northern Hemisphere. This is significant. The LDCs of the South have most of the raw materials needed by the developed North. Some of the "have not" nations use their economic power to pressure the industrial North. The West suffered economic distress when OPEC boycotts reduced oil supplies in the 1970's.

the "Have" Nations

the "Have Not" Nations

Questions

1   A major problem for most developing nations is
   1   a lack of natural resources.
   2   competition from neighboring nations.
   3   government ownership of industry.
   4   a lack of investment capital and managerial skills.

2   Which factor is likely to lead to interdependence among nations?
   1   limited availability of natural resources
   2   the natural desire of people to help each other
   3   the spread of democratic ideals
   4   emerging unity among religions

3   In the 18th century, some predicted that the world's population would soon outdistance its food supplies. This has not happened because
   1   since the late 1700's, worldwide birthrates have declined.
   2   agricultural productivity has increased.
   3   as the population grew, more people entered farming.
   4   natural catastrophes helped keep the world's population from growing.

4   "Major conflicts of the future will be along a North-South axis instead of the East - West axis." This statement assumes that major divisions in the world will exist between the
   1   geographically larger and smaller nations.
   2   socialist and capitalist nations.
   3   colonial powers and their former colonies.
   4   more developed vs. less developed nations.

5   Which is the major reason why families in highly industrialized nations are smaller today than in the past?
   1   Modern religious beliefs prescribe smaller families.
   2   Many governments offer financial incentives for smaller families.
   3   Families need fewer children as producers.
   4   Agricultural production will not support large families.

6   The "Revolution of Rising Expectations" refers to the
   1   growth of the wealthy class in many developing nations.
   2   rapid conversion of agricultural land to industrial land.
   3   desire of developing nations to improve living standards.
   4   support of guerrilla warfare in developing nations by the superpowers.

7   Which occurs when health care measures improve in a developing country while other conditions remain the same?
   1   People abandon birth control measures.
   2   Infant mortality increases.
   3   Distribution of jobs becomes more even.
   4   Life expectancy increases.

8   A cause of population growth in developing nations is
   1   strengthened military power.   3   improved health standards.
   2   traditional farming methods.   4   new political structures.

9   Which situation in developing nations tends to hinder efforts to raise living standards?
   1   continued high rates of population growth
   2   existence of widespread disease and starvation
   3   inability of scientists to increase staple crop yields
   4   reluctance of leaders in developing nations to adopt new technology

Base your answer to questions 10 and 11 on the statements below and on your knowledge of social studies.

Speaker A: Increased contact among nations and peoples is characteristic of our times. A single decision by OPEC or a multinational corporation can send ripples of change throughout our global society.

Speaker B: If the last 500,000 years were divided into lifetimes of years, there would be 800 such lifetimes. Humans spend the first 650 of these in caves, and the most important changes have occurred only during the final lifetime.

Speaker C: If we are to survive, all passengers on our Spaceship Earth must participate in efforts to solve the issues that threaten mankind: poverty, resource depletion, pollution, violence, and war.

Speaker D: We must understand that no single culture's view of the world is universally accepted. Other people have different value systems and ways of thinking and acting. They will not see the world as we do.

10 Speakers *A* and *C* express the concept of
   1   self determination.
   2   conservation.
   3   nationalism.
   4   interdependence.

11 Which statement best summarizes the main idea expressed by Speaker *B*?
   1   Humans have always had to deal with many changes during their lifetime.
   2   The rate of change has increased greatly in the 20th century.
   3   Throughout history there has always been great resistance to change.
   4   Conditions in the modern world are better than in any prior era.

II. Containment And Consensus: 1945-1960

A. Eisenhower Foreign Policies

The rebuilding of Europe and Asia after World War II revealed a lack of cooperation between the great powers. Soviet-American disputes over Germany, Eastern Europe, the Middle East, and Korea caused bitter and lasting divisions. The decade of the 1950's saw a continuation of the U.S.–U.S.S.R. rivalries. The Eastern and Western Blocs became firmly entrenched. Each side attempted to strengthen its influence among the developing nations.

Under **President Dwight David Eisenhower**, the U.S. attempted to maintain world peace while continuing the campaign to check the spread of communism, especially in Asia. The proliferation of nuclear weapons and the introduction of long-range missiles gave international conflicts the potency of global annihilation.

Eisenhower

End Of The Korean Conflict

The conflict in Korea had turned into a stalemate. The Panmunjom peace talks had bogged down on the questions of repatriation of prisoners of war. A personal visit by Eisenhower fulfilled a campaign pledge, but it failed to end the deadlock. An armistice was finally signed in July of 1953, leaving the nation divided at the 38th Parallel. The U.S. claimed victory in its attempt to contain communist expansion.

The Diplomacy Of John Foster Dulles

President Eisenhower appointed career diplomat **John Foster Dulles** as his Secretary of State. Dulles had held many State Department posts in his long career and had been a delegate to the United Nations. He was a staunch opponent of communism and believed that the U.S. had to make forceful moves to prevent Soviet advances. Dulles pledged that the tragic result of appeasing Hitler at Munich was not to be repeated in the West's dealings with the Soviet bloc. War could be avoided only if America was constantly ready to deploy deterrent force. This policy of being on the brink (edge) of war earned Dulles' diplomacy the name "brinkmanship." Dulles hoped that the threat of **massive retaliation** would discourage the Soviets from risking a direct confrontation with the West.

Indirect communist aid to insurgents in Asia continued. The poor, weak nations of Southeast Asia were prime targets. The possibility of the nations falling to communism one after another became known as the **domino theory**. Dulles sought to form a NATO-like organization to strengthen resistance in Asia. In 1954, the **Southeast Asia Treaty Organization** (SEATO) was formed. Unfortunately, it lacked the unity and power of the older European alliance and was unsuccessful.

H-Bomb & Atoms For Peace

Any advantage the U.S. had as sole owner of the atomic bomb was short-lived. By 1949, the U.S.S.R. had exploded its first nuclear device, followed by Britain and France. India and China joined these ranks in the 1960's. Pakistan and Israel acquired the bomb in the 1970's.

In the early 1950's, both superpowers exploded devices known as **hydrogen bombs**, which were hundreds of times more powerful than those dropped in 1945.

The possibility of nuclear annihilation became increasingly real. The failure of the **Baruch Plan** in the late 1940's showed the difficulty of nuclear diplomacy. The Soviets balked at establishing international inspection teams to verify continued compliance with disarmament agreements.

In 1953, President Eisenhower hoped to increase the peaceful benefits of atomic energy by proposing the **Atoms for Peace** program. Under this international agreement, nations would share knowledge and materials in order to advance peaceful applications of nuclear power. The U.N. approved the plan, which has done much to aid in international study, but it did little to curb the arms race.

Summits And U-2's

Khrushchev

A prolonged power struggle took place in the Kremlin after the death of Soviet dictator Joseph Stalin in March of 1953. **Nikita Khrushchev** emerged as the new First Secretary of the Communist Party. Some changes were made to the diplomatic image of the U.S.S.R., but an actual shift in the Soviet policy did not take place. The leaders of the **"Big Four"** (U.S., U.S.S.R., Britain, and France) met at a summit in Geneva in 1955. Little progress was made on major issues, such as the reduction of nuclear arms and the reunification of Germany.

Khrushchev was the guest of Eisenhower in a two-week tour of the U.S. in 1959. No specific agreements were reached, but a **Spirit of Camp David**, and a pledge to meet at a summit the following year, gave the world some hope that Soviet-American relations were improving.

However, the Paris summit in May of 1960, was a disaster. Two weeks before the meeting, a U-2 reconnaissance plane of the U.S. Central Intelligence Agency (CIA) was shot down 1,000 miles inside the borders of the U.S.S.R. At first, American officials denied the spy charges. An embarrassed Eisenhower was later forced to acknowledge the blunder when the Soviets produced the pilot alive and well for a public propaganda trial. An outraged Khrushchev used the incident to demand an apology from Eisenhower. When none was forthcoming, Khrushchev cancelled the Paris summit before any meetings actually took place.

China Policy: Taiwan, Quemoy, And Matsu

Throughout the 1950's, the United States continued its refusal to recognize Mao Zedong's communist regime on mainland China. It held that Chiang Kai-shek's Nationalist government in exile on Taiwan was the legitimate government of China. Under Eisenhower, the U.S. signed a mutual defense agreement with Taiwan, forcing Mao to postpone launching an invasion from the mainland.

Chiang Kai-shek

The Nationalists also held a few small islands in the Formosa Strait just off the Chinese coast. With U.S. naval help, they managed to fend off an attempt by the communists to take two of them (Quemoy and Matsu) in 1958.

Mao Zedong

At the same time, the U.S. managed to discourage the Nationalists from launching their own invasion of the mainland. The U.S. wished to protect Taiwan, but not to become involved in an all-out Asian war. Mao's forces greatly outnumbered the Nationalists and could easily overrun them.

Middle East: Aswan And Suez

With Britain and France greatly weakened after World War II, independence movements sprang up throughout their colonial empires. In Egypt, **Colonel Gamal Abdul Nasser** seized power in 1954. He promised modernization of Egypt, linking his success to the Aswan Dam irrigation and

Abdul Nasser

hydroelectric project on the Nile. Coolness by the British and Americans led Nasser to begin flirting with the U.S.S.R. for financial aid. Nasser's actions caused the Americans to withdraw. Nasser then seized the Suez Canal in July of 1956. Britain and France, fearing an interruption in their vital oil supply lines from the Middle East, invaded the Suez area. They were joined by Israel, which wanted to stop guerrilla attacks from Egypt. The U.S., fearing Soviet entry into the quarrel, opposed any military action and voted for a cease-fire resolution in the United Nations. The Anglo-French-Israeli force was withdrawn and replaced with a U.N. peace-keeping force. The Soviets later agreed to an aid package for Nasser to build the Aswan Dam.

Polish And Hungarian Revolution

One reason for the U.S. decision not to support the Anglo-French Suez invasion was that it condemned a similar action by the U.S.S.R. when it sent its forces into Hungary to suppress an internal revolt. Soviet-dominated leaders in Poland had recently granted more rights to individuals, inspiring protests in neighboring Hungary. Students and workers took to the streets demanding freedom. Khrushchev brutally crushed the revolt by sending Soviet tanks into Budapest. Thousands were killed or deported to work-camps in the U.S.S.R. The U.S. voiced its outrage with Moscow and suspended its immigration restrictions to allow Hungarian refugees to seek asylum.

Eisenhower Doctrine: Lebanon Intervention

Enduring Issues
9

In reaction to a widening role of the U.S.S.R. in the Middle East, President Eisenhower followed the precedent of the Truman Doctrine in Europe. He requested Congressional funds to aid in fighting communist aggression. Under the **Eisenhower Doctrine**, any Middle Eastern nation that suspected a communist takeover could apply for U.S. assistance. When Lebanon was threatened with a revolution in 1958, it asked for U.S. aid. Eisenhower dispatched a force of U.S. Marines. The Soviets protested, but the situation was brought under control, and the Marines were withdrawn. The U.S. indicated its dedication to the containment policy, but the Soviets were still able to spread their influence in the region.

Sputnik: The Space Race

By the end of 1957, the Soviet Union had orbited two unmanned space satellites (Sputnik I and II). The U.S. rocket program had not received much priority from the government, and most Americans were shocked that Soviet technology was superior to ours. In addition to the loss in prestige, there was concern that the Soviet's rockets now gave them intercontinental ballistic missile capability to launch nuclear warheads directly at the U.S.

In a flurry of activity, the United States launched its first satellite and Congress funded the **National Defense Education Act** to help states upgrade school courses in science and mathematics. The rivalry in space occupied the attention of the American public for the next decade.

Questions

1   Which was a direct result of the Korean War?
    1   Annexation of Korea by Nationalist China
    2   Continuation of a divided Korea
    3   The return of militarism to Japan
    4   U.S. return to traditional isolationism
2   Nasser's Suez Canal seizure provoked a military response from
    1   the United States.   3   Saudi Arabia.
    2   the Soviet Union.   4   Britain and France.
3   The Eisenhower Doctrine was designed to halt communist expansion in
    1   The Middle East.   3   Southeast Asia.
    2   Eastern Europe.   4   Taiwan.

4   SEATO was established to prevent
    1   anti-colonial revolts against Britain and France in Asia.
    2   tariff wars between former colonies.
    3   nuclear confrontations among developing nations.
    4   communist insurgency in Southeast Asia.

5   Which was a major cause of tension in Europe in the decade following World War II?
    1   The formation of Soviet-dominated governments in Eastern Europe.
    2   The failure of non-communist nations to support the U.N.
    3   An increase in the U.S. combat troops stationed in Europe.
    4   A trade boycott of Western Europe by the U.S.

6   A policy of "massive retaliation" meant that the U.S. would have to
    1   keep large detachments of ground forces in Europe.
    2   discuss disarmament with the U.S.S.R.
    3   constantly upgrade its nuclear capability.
    4   maintain a favorable balance of trade.

7   Tensions between the U.S. and the U.S.S.R. have arisen most often due to policy differences in the area of
    1   maintaining a strong national defense.
    2   influencing the internal affairs of other nations.
    3   exploring space.
    4   advancing scientific research.

8   During the "Cold War" of the 1950's, U.S. foreign policy was characterized by
    1   a policy of neutrality.
    2   increasing trade with Eastern Europe.
    3   numerous compromise agreements with communist nations.
    4   moves to protect others from communist aggression.

9   The results of the 1956 Hungarian Uprising indicated that the Soviet Union
    1   encouraged open opposition.
    2   would submit domestic disputes in its satellites for U.N. arbitration.
    3   would not permit dissent in Eastern European satellite nations.
    4   was open to alternative government plans in Eastern Europe.

10 Secretary of State Dulles believed that the United States needed to take a strong posture in opposing communist expansion, because
    1   appeasing aggressor nations prior to World War II had tragic results.
    2   Soviet nuclear superiority after World War II had to be overcome.
    3   most Western European nations were strongly pro-communist.
    4   communism was already successful in most Latin American nations.

B. Domestic Politics And Constitutional Issues: The Eisenhower Peace

World War II hero Gen. Dwight David Eisenhower easily defeated Illinois Governor **Adlai E. Stevenson** for the Presidency in both 1952 and 1956. The Republicans rejoiced in putting their first candidate in the White House since Herbert Hoover. In the 1952 election, they also won control of both houses of Congress. The Democrats regained control of Congress in the 1954 elections, but Eisenhower's moderate approach led to a broad cooperation between the White House and Capital Hill during his two terms.

Returning The U.S. To A Peacetime Economy

As the Korean War ended, Eisenhower hoped to stimulate the economy by lifting government wage and price controls. Government defense and foreign aid spending renewed inflation during the rest of the 1950's, but was offset by the steady growth of the economy. Eisenhower managed to balance the budget in three of his eight years, but high tax rates continued. As recovery from World War II took hold in Europe, demand for U.S. agricultural products lessened, and profits began to decline. Inflation was not bothersome to most expanding sectors of the economy, but it ate up the little profits farmers were making.

> Enduring
> Issues
> **12**

Eisenhower instituted a more flexible system of farm-price supports, hoping to reduce farmers' dependence on government subsidies and reduce over-production. A federal **Soil Bank Plan** paid farmers to take land out of production and convert it to pasture or forest. These plans did not solve the farm problem. Surpluses mounted and many farmers lost money.

Offshore Oil

While continuing many New Deal reforms, Eisenhower favored a reduced federal role in several areas, especially electric power generation and offshore oil drilling rights. States and private industries profited from these policies. Florida, Louisiana, Texas, and California had large deposits of oil and natural gas off their coasts. The **Submerged Lands Act** (1953) gave states drilling rights up to 10.5 miles off their shorelines. Opposition from environmentalists was largely ignored.

> Enduring
> Issues
> **2**

Public And Private Power

In order to bring cheap electricity to large sections of the country, the New Deal and Fair Deal expanded federal power projects in the South and West. Eisenhower wanted federal projects cut back to allow private companies to expand. His program met with strong opposition when he backed private companies rights in the region serviced by the **Tennessee Valley Authority**. He did manage to get private power producers' rights to open nuclear power facilities.

> Enduring
> Issues
> **12**

Labor Unrest

In the years that followed World War II, labor unions experienced much success at the bargaining table. Attracting more members, unions received regular cost-of-living raises, expanded pension benefits, and health insurance. In 1947, the Republican Congress had attempted to control the power of organized labor by passing the **Taft-Hartley Labor Management Relations Act** over President Truman's veto (see page 203). Despite its growth and influence, labor was not able to get the Taft-Hartley Act repealed during the Eisenhower era.

In 1955, the nation's two giant labor organizations merged. The American Federation of Labor and the Congress of Industrial Organizations, rivals from the days of the Great Depression, formed the **AFL-CIO**. George Meany became the first president of the 15 million member organization.

Corruption plagued many major unions in the 1950's. Congress launched intense investigations against racketeering in the **International Longshoremen's Association** and the **International Brotherhood of Teamsters**. Out of these investigations came the **Landrum-Griffin Labor Management Reporting and Disclosure Act** (1957). It required unions to publish financial statements, hold regular elections, use secret ballots, end secondary boycotts, and forbid communists and convicted felons from holding union office.

The Teamsters continued to have problems. They were ejected from the AFL-CIO in the 1960's. In 1967, their long-time president, **James R. Hoffa**, was sent to prison. He mysteriously disappeared after his release in 1972, and was never heard from again. Hoffa's disappearance triggered a long internal struggle and clean up. The Teamsters union was readmitted to the AFL-CIO in 1987.

A generally prosperous economy and moderate inflation resulted in fewer major strikes during the Eisenhower years. The most serious strike was one by the steelworkers in 1959. After 116 days, Eisenhower invoked the 80-day **injunction** (suspension) provided in Taft-Hartley. The strike was settled in 1960, with the workers securing most of their original demands.

Enduring Issues 3

The Warren Court

In 1953, the governor of California, **Earl Warren**, was appointed Chief Justice of the Supreme Court by President Eisenhower. For the next fifteen years, the "**Warren Court**" followed a policy of **judicial activism**. This meant that decisions of the Court not only provided interpretations of the Constitution, but initiated broad changes in American life. Issues of equality and fairness were being dealt with by Congress, but very slowly. There were many critics who claimed the Court was actually performing legislative tasks, and taking power away from the individual. Most notable decisions were:

Warren Court Judicial Activism

Decision	Significance
Brown v. Board of Ed. of Topeka (1954)	Racial segregation of schools violates the 14th Amendment.
Baker v. Carr (1962)	"One person, one vote" rule ordered states to set up Congressional Districts on equal basis.
Engel v. Vitale (1962)	State laws requiring prayers in schools violated the 1st Amendment.
Gideon v. Wainwright (1963)	State laws denying felony suspects legal counsel violate the 6th Amendment.
Miranda v. Arizona (1966)	Authorities must inform accused persons of their "due process" rights under the 5th and 6th Amendments.

Civil Rights

Enduring Issues 6

After the Civil War, the **13th, 14th,** and **15th Amendments** freed former slaves, made them equal citizens, and gave them suffrage. As Reconstruction ended, southern state leaders found legal ways to avoid equal treatment for blacks. **Jim Crow Laws** established **de jure segregation** throughout the South. In 1896, in a narrow vote, the U.S. Supreme Court upheld the southern contention that racial separation was legal as long as the facilities for both races were equal (***Plessy v. Ferguson***). The net result was that de jure segregation was considered constitutional. It quickly evolved that transportation, education, dining, and entertainment facilities were always separate, but rarely were they equal.

Jackie Robinson: The Color Line Breached

Condemnations of Nazi racial policies and efforts of blacks in segregated units of the U.S. armed forces in World War II raised consciousness of inequality. African Americans were making progress in educational achievement and gains in political power in northern cities. They no longer wanted to be treated as second class citizens. Segregation in the military was ended by President Truman in the late 1940's. At the same time, **Jackie Robinson** became the first African American player in major league baseball. Despite prejudice from opposing teams and fans, Robinson's dazzling play helped win the National League championship for Brooklyn and Rookie of the Year honors.

Brown v. Board Of Education Of Topeka, Kansas (1954)

Enduring Issues 6

Black leaders had long been challenging segregation laws in the south. Efforts by the Truman and Eisenhower administrations to end racial segregation had been blunted by southern senators' use of the filibuster. The Supreme Court was not subject to the same political pressures as the other two branches. After World War II, in a series of civil cases brought by the **National Association for the Advancement of Colored People (NAACP)**, the Court began applying the 14th Amendment's *"equal protection of the laws"* phrase against various state segregation laws. In 1954, the Court issued its decision in ***Brown v. the Board of Education of Topeka***, which reversed the doctrine of "separate but equal" put forth in the 1896 Plessy case. At the time of *Brown*, racially segregated schools were the norm in nearly 20 states. In *Brown*, the Court used a procedure called "obiter dictum" to "speak beyond" the Topeka situation and announced that racial segregation of schools was inherently wrong and must cease throughout the nation.

The decision had little immediate effect. Outraged Southern Governors and Senators claimed that education was a reserved power of the states, and the Supreme Court had no jurisdiction in the matter. In some states, militia and state police kept blacks from registering, while angry mobs threatened violence.

Enduring Issues 2

Civil Rights Movement
Beginnings For African Americans

The Montgomery Movement: The ruling against separate schools prompted blacks to demand an end to segregation in all aspects of life. Many African American leaders recognized that court challenges would move slowly against Southern politicians' resistance. They began to take new avenues toward change. In 1955, Rosa Parks, a black seamstress refused to give up her seat to a white on a Montgomery, Alabama bus. Her arrest led to a year-long boycott of city buses organized by a young Baptist minister by the name of **Martin Luther King, Jr.** King rose to national prominence during the incident. The boycott ended in an agreement by the city and the bus company to desegregate the transportation facilities. The Supreme Court later declared such segregation unconstitutional.

Martin Luther
King Jr.

The Little Rock Crisis: Eisenhower was not a strong advocate of increasing Federal power over the states. In 1957, he did take decisive action in civil rights. In Little Rock, Arkansas, Governor **Orville Faubus** was defying federal court orders to admit black students to Central High School. At one point, the governor had Arkansas units of the National Guard fix bayonets to keep a handful of students out of the school. Eisenhower could not let such flagrant abuse of federal power go unanswered. On national TV, he ordered the Arkansas National Guard demobilized and sent regular U.S. Army troops to escort the students into the school.

Non-violent, Direct Action: African Americans began an intense campaign to overcome the injustice of segregation in all public facilities. In 1960, they began to illegally but peacefully sit at segregated lunch counters in restaurants throughout the south. Another group, called **Freedom Riders**, rode buses to try to desegregate the bus terminals. Their tactics were called *non-violent, direct action*. They were often arrested and filled the local jails under the glare of national television cameras. The sometimes brutal tactics of Southern officials in dealing with these "agitators" caused public interest and empathy to grow.

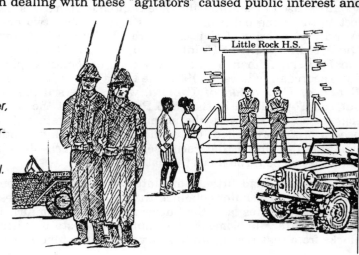

By order of President Eisenhower, U.S. Army troops escort African American students into Little Rock Central High School.

Little Rock H.S.

Civil Rights Legislation: In 1957, Congress overcame the Southern filibusters and passed its first Civil Rights Act since the Civil War days. The 1957 law created a Civil Rights Commission to investigate and prosecute injustices. It was also authorized to secure voting rights for blacks in the South. Another Civil Rights Act in 1960, furthered voting rights but relief was slow and painful, and the full force of the federal government was not put behind enforcement of these laws.

Enduring Issues
6

Questions

1 President Eisenhower's actions in the areas of offshore oil and electric power indicated a desire to
   1   increase the power of the Federal government.
   2   increase the power of the Presidency.
   3   reduce the role of the Federal government.
   4   consult with the Supreme Court before making decisions.

2 The main purpose of the Taft-Hartley Act was to
   1   prevent Federal government intervention in labor disputes.
   2   modify the power of labor unions.
   3   prohibit strikes by public employees.
   4   encourage employers to hire non-union workers.

3 Which description best characterizes the decisions of the Warren Court?
   1   Activist, with a loose construction of the Constitution.
   2   Cautious, with a strict construction of the Constitution.
   3   Traditional, with actions to guard the powers of the states.
   4   Conservative, seeking to maintain the status quo on civil rights.

4 The issue of offshore oil was a major concern to
   1   civil rights activists.   3   environmentalists.
   2   labor leaders.   4   segregationists.

5 Which practice in public education was declared illegal in the 1954 *Brown* decision?
   1   recitation of prayers   3   corporal punishment
   2   locker searches   4   racial segregation

6 The Supreme Court's decision in ***Brown v. Bd. of Ed. of Topeka*** was based on the constitutional principle of
   1   free speech.   3   equal protection of the law.
   2   right of assembly.   4   voting rights.

7 Sit-ins by blacks during the 1950's and early 1960's, were designed to
   1   increase voter participation in Presidential elections.
   2   promote black-owned businesses in Northern cities.
   3   end white domination of the military.
   4   end the racial segregation in the South.

8 The career of Jackie Robinson was significant, because he was
   1   a leader of the Montgomery Bus Boycott.
   2   responsible for the *Brown* decision.
   3   the first African American to play major league baseball.
   4   the first African American Senator from a Southern state.

9 The use of Federal troops at Little Rock in 1957 indicated that
   1   blacks were unwilling to attend all-white schools.
   2   states were refusing to comply with Federal court orders.
   3   there was concern over interference by foreign governments.
   4   there was no Constitutional base for Eisenhower's actions.

C. People: Prosperity And Conservatism

The 1950's was a time of prosperity. The post war international stress, Korea, and McCarthyism left most Americans desirous of a stable environment. The Eisenhower domestic policies were conservative by nature, and most people welcomed a lessening of government reform efforts after nearly three decades of upheaval.

Postwar Consumption

The demands for consumer goods boomed during the postwar period. Savings from higher wartime wages gave many Americans cash to spend. Nearly 50 million autos were sold between 1950 and 1960, with most families owning a car by the end of the decade. The federal interstate highway system, which began in 1956, made automobile travel faster and easier. Demand was great, allowing European manufacturers recovering from World War II, to profitably export to the United States. Germany's **Volkswagen "Beetle"** became enormously popular. However, the number of American auto makers declined. Old names, such as Studebaker and Packard disappeared as mergers and reorganizations narrowed the field to the **"Big Three"** (Ford, General Motors, and Chrysler).

While invented in the 1920's, television was not ready for mass production until after the war. Postwar prosperity enabled the majority of American families to obtain the rather costly black–and–white receivers by the middle 1950's. A wide variety of sports, news programs, and game shows were developed for television. Old Hollywood movies were popular, and many of the comedy and dramatic shows from radio were able to retain audiences for their sponsors by jumping to the video medium. Critics began to assail TV almost immediately for the violence on popular western and detective shows.

New Educational Opportunities

Colleges and universities were flooded with eager young people in search of the higher education needed to qualify for engineering and administrative jobs in expanding American corporations. The **G.I. Bill** aided returning World WarII and Korean War veterans with generous education allowances. College enrollments would continue to expand through the 1970's, with some state institutions enrolling as many as 25,000 or more students.

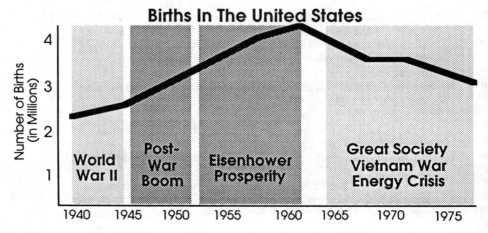

Births In The United States

The Baby Boom

Returning veterans and postwar economic expansion also resulted in a fifteen year surge in the American birth rate. This "baby boom" created a demand for more schools and teachers. By the end of the 1950's, the economy began catering to the increasing number of young people. New forms of dress, entertainment, and music ("Rock 'n' Roll") began to have a definite youth orientation.

Migration And Immigration

New Immigration Patterns

Enduring Issues
8

Prior to 1965, the National Origins system passed in the 1920's, gave preferential quotas to immigrants of "old" ethnic groups from northern and western Europe (see pages 101 and 164). The **Immigration Act of 1965** abolished the National Origins Quota System altogether. It created a limit for the Eastern and Western Hemispheres and based admission on a first-come, first-served basis. It gave preference to relatives of American citizens and those with needed job skills. Immigration patterns changed as groups fleeing political turmoil in Asia and Latin America began to dominate the ranks of newcomers. Economic instability in these areas have kept their numbers highest in the last twenty years.

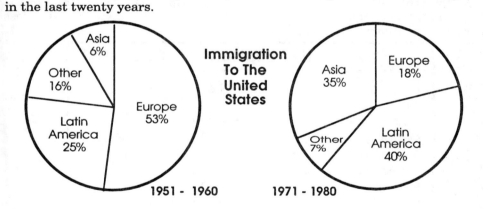

Immigration To The United States

1951 - 1960   1971 - 1980

Suburbs

Americans have always moved in search of a better life. Relatively few new homes were built during the Great Depression and World War II, despite a growth in population. The post war demand made prices skyrocket. Government officials retained wartime rent control rules. (New York City still maintains rent controls.) The 1950's saw millions of new, affordable homes springing up in suburbs for young families. Shortages of housing and crowding conditions in the cities made commuting from the suburban areas seem more reasonable. Young families flocked to the suburbs in the 1950's. The **G.I. Bill** aided veterans in securing mortgages and gave even more incentive to construction. The **Levittown Developments** in New York and Pennsylvania are examples. Thousands of mass-produced single-family houses were constructed at affordable prices. With employment and shopping at a distance, a second automobile often became a necessity. The mass exodus to the suburbs caused a secondary boom in the construction of shopping centers, roads, water supply, and sewage system construction.

Cities

The exodus of young middle class families had a devastating economic effect on urban areas. Poorer, unskilled groups from agricultural regions, where jobs were declining, were moving into the cities. Elderly people on fixed incomes held on to their rent-controlled apartments. War refugees gravitated toward the lower paying job opportunities in city factories as new immigrants had always done. Nor could minority group victims of prejudicial hiring practices and overcrowded slum conditions break the poverty lines.

The result was that cities began to see a declining tax base which made it more difficult for municipalities to meet the need for public housing. Private developers were reluctant to risk capital in urban housing. They preferred the suburbs or building office complexes for major corporations in downtown areas. Businesses began to leave the cities, too. They fell victims to rising city tax rates and the decline in city services. Many followed the more skilled middle class workers into the suburban regions. As businesses left, the resulting unemployment caused conditions of urban decay to spiral downward, bringing many older cities in the Northeast and Mid-West (dubbed "**The Rust Belt**" by the mass media) to the brink of bankruptcy by the 1960's.

As the table below shows, some cities did prosper. The "**Sun Belt**" in the South and West attracted people with warmer climates, new jobs, and less crowded conditions.

City	1980 Population	Since 1950
New York	7,071,639	-820,000
Chicago	3,005,072	-615,000
Philadelphia	1,688,210	-383,000
Detroit	1,595,138	-646,000
Baltimore	786,000	-163,000
Los Angles	2,966,850	+996,000
Houston	1,595,138	+999,000
Dallas	904,078	+470,000
San Diego	875,538	+541,000
Phoenix	789,000	+683,000

Questions

1 Which was a major characteristic of United States population patterns between 1950 and 1980?
   1 Decline in the number of college enrollments.
   2 Decline in the number of Asian immigrants.
   3 Migration to the Sun Belt.
   4 Increasing number of European immigrants.
2 Colleges experienced growth after World War II because
   1 the G.I. Bill provided tuition assistance to returning veterans.
   2 there was an influx of foreign students.
   3 federal loans were made available for all students.
   4 state colleges were converted to Federal universities.

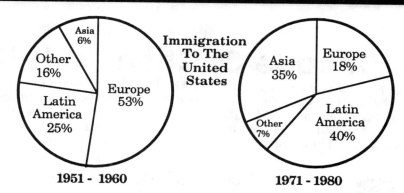

Immigration To The United States

1951 - 1960   1971 - 1980

3   Which is a valid conclusion based on the immigration graphs above?
   1   Immigration doubled between 1960 and 1980.
   2   Immigrants' countries of origin have changed greatly.
   3   Illegal immigration has declined significantly.
   4   The U.S. had become less ethnically diverse.

4   Which has been a major result of the movement of people from the cities to the suburbs in the 1950's and 1960's?
   1   Urban crime rates have declined.
   2   The need for federal urban assistance funds has declined.
   3   Tax revenues have increased as urban property values rose.
   4   The proportion of low income families in urban areas has risen.

5   During which year did the "Baby Boom" peak?
   1   1950   3   1960
   2   1955   4   1965

6   In the 20th century United States, which factor contributed most to the development of suburban life?
   1   the improvement of transportation systems
   2   a decrease in per capita income
   3   an increase in the number of women employed in industry
   4   the demand for agricultural produce by the middle class

7   The boom in American auto sales in the 1950's and 1960's resulted in
   1   an expansion in the number of manufacturers.
   2   government control of the auto industry.
   3   decreased competition from foreign manufacturers.
   4   dominance of the market by Ford, Chrysler, and General Motors.

8   Cities that lost the most population in the last 30 years are primarily located in the
   1   South.   3   Northeast.
   2   Northwest.   4   Southeast.

9   Which combination of factors caused the urban problems in the past generation?
   1   housing shortages, suburban exodus, increasing tax base
   2   high crime, declining services, inadequate transportation
   3   increasing unemployment, poor waste disposal, rising welfare costs
   4   increased immigration, school dropouts, decline of organized religions

III. Decade Of Change: 1960's

The general peace and prosperity of the Eisenhower years disintegrated as the 1960's progressed. Television brought the Vietnam War and urban riots into living rooms and divided public opinion as it had not been since the Civil War. By the end of the decade, the nation went sour on social reform programs that had held great promise when the 60's had dawned.

A. The Kennedy Years

In the very close Presidential campaign of 1960, Democratic Senator **John F. Kennedy** of Massachusetts defeated Eisenhower's Vice-President, Richard M. Nixon. Kennedy was young, rich, and the first Catholic candidate since Al Smith in 1928. Southern Protestant votes were retained because Kennedy's running mate, Senate Majority Leader Lyndon B. Johnson of Texas, helped "balance the ticket."

The "New Frontier" Program

John F. Kennedy

The youth-oriented Kennedy promised to lead a new generation Americans to a "New Frontier" with energetic proposals for the space program, civil rights, urban renewal, social welfare, and a new image in foreign policy.

Domestic Policy Stalls In Congress

To achieve his ambitions, Kennedy convinced the Democratic Congress to pass legislation which lowered tariffs, increased the minimum wage and Social Security benefits, and helped the beleaguered cities. Most

Enduring Issues 10

of his suggestions ran into opposition from conservative Republicans and Southern Democrats opposed to expanding federal influence, especially in civil rights. Federal aid to education, subsidized medical care for the poor and elderly, tax cuts, and civil rights reforms met with defeat, often through the use of Senate filibusters. Many of these programs did eventually become law, but not until after the young President's tragic assassination in 1963.

Civil Rights

The *equal protection of the law*, guaranteed in the 14th Amendment, was painfully slow to materialize in the South. Racially prejudiced Americans worked to oppose attempts at integration and equality, while civil rights organizations, old and new, began a new phase of the crusade for justice.

In the decade that followed ***Brown v. Board of Education of Topeka***, few Southern schools had actually carried out the Supreme Court's order to integrate *"with all deliberate speed."* In 1962, **James Meredith** attempted to become the first African American student to register at the University of Mississippi. The scene was a replay of the violent Little Rock Crisis of 1958.

Once again, the governor personally barred Meredith's entry. A riot broke out and two persons were killed before Kennedy sent in federal troops to enforce the Constitution. With the help of federal marshals, Meredith was finally enrolled.

The city of Birmingham, Alabama was most adamant in its refusal to integrate. The **Rev. Martin Luther King, Jr.** led a series of non-violent marches to protest the stubbornness of city officials.

> Enduring
> Issues
> **8**

Millions watched on television as police turned fire hoses, tear gas, and attack dogs on the marchers. While under arrest for leading the peaceful marches, Dr. King wrote his famous _Letter From a Birmingham Jail_. In it, he equated the non-violent struggle of blacks in America with the struggle of early Christians and the Indian independence movement of Mohandus Gandhi. To the opponents of the civil disobedience movement King said,

"We will match your capacity to inflict suffering with our capacity to endure suffering...We will not hate you, but we cannot obey your unjust laws..."

Dr. King indicated that African Americans had waited more than a hundred years to see the promise of freedom. He criticized the political system which excluded blacks from the law-making process, and he called on all Americans to join the fight for justice and equality.

Violence continued in the South while Kennedy's efforts in Washington stalled in Congress. In the spring of 1963, NAACP leader **Medgar Evers** was assassinated in Mississippi. In August, over 200,000 people marched on Washington and heard Dr. King's _I Have a Dream_ speech and sang the battle hymn of the movement, _"We Shall Overcome..."_

Even as Dr. King spoke, the non-violent movement was beginning to wear thin. In September, in an ugly answer to the March on Washington, four young black children were tragically killed as a church was bombed in Birmingham. The level of frustration among younger civil rights activists was rising. Dr. King began to lose his control on the civil rights movement.

Action In Foreign Policies
Cuban Problems

The unsettled history of U.S.-Latin American relations had not improved greatly in the period after World War II. Suspicion of U.S. actions still remained despite the efforts made by FDR with the **Good Neighbor Policy** and Truman with the **Organization of American States**. U.S. business interests still tended to support military Latin American regimes which harshly maintained economic stability. These regimes resisted reform and often used foreign aid funds for their own purposes.

One such regime, that of Cuban dictator Fulgencio Batista, was overthrown by a small group of rebels led by **Fidel Castro** in 1958. Hopes for a new type of democracy ended shortly afterward, when Castro condemned the U.S. and announced that his would be a Marxist state, allied with the Soviet Union.

This was a serious blow to the policy of containment. Eisenhower broke off relations with Cuba and gave tacit approval to a CIA plot to train and assist Cuban refugees in launching a counterrevolution. When Kennedy took over the White House, he allowed the CIA to go forward with the plan.

In April 1961, two thousand Cuban exiles landed at the **Bay of Pigs** in Cuba. An air strike by CIA-trained Cuban fighter pilots, to be launched from Guatemala, never materialized, nor did a planned revolt inside Cuba. The invaders were captured on the beach, and Castro and Khrushchev openly denounced the United States. An embarrassed Kennedy Administration took responsibility for the failure but refused to apologize.

| Enduring Issues 9 |

In the fall of 1962, U-2 reconnaissance planes provided pictures of what the U.S. government had feared most about the Cuban-Soviet alliance. Missile bases with nuclear capacity were being constructed 90 miles from U.S. territory. After verification, Kennedy invoked the Monroe Doctrine and publicly condemned the Soviet intrusion in the Western Hemisphere. He ordered the U.S.S.R. to remove the missiles immediately, claiming them a threat to the security of the entire Hemisphere. A naval blockade was ordered to prevent Soviet ships from delivering any additional nuclear missiles or related supplies. The show of force caused Khrushchev to back down and remove the missiles under U.S. observation in exchange for an American pledge not to launch any further invasions of Cuba. Khrushchev's misjudgment of Kennedy's resolve was a costly personal blunder. Within a few months, the Soviet Politburo would force him to resign as Premier and First Secretary.

The Kennedy administration moved to stem the tide of communism in Latin America by offering a generous aid program called the **Alliance for Progress**. This ten-year program poured over 20 billion dollars into Latin American republics for housing, schools, hospitals, and factories. In return, the governments were to have initiated political reforms to achieve greater economic opportunity for the masses, but few were truly effective.

Peace Corps

President Kennedy also created a unique way for Americans to volunteer to personally help people in the underdeveloped nations, the Peace Corps. Response was great. In the past quarter of a century, many thousands have used their skills to help others develop agricultural, educational, and medical facilities in Third World countries.

The Race To The Moon

After the success of Sputnik, Americans were eager to match the Soviet accomplishments. In 1961, Kennedy proposed the goal of landing a man on the moon by the end of the decade. In 1962, John Glenn became the first American to orbit the Earth. Two-man Gemini flights brought space-walks and more technological achievements as the Americans slowly moved ahead of the Soviets in the space race.

The Berlin Wall

In the spring of 1961, Kennedy travelled to Vienna to meet Khrushchev at a summit which did little to ease tensions between the superpowers. The U.S.S.R. continued to demand that the western democracies leave the city of Berlin inside the communist state of East Germany (see map page 211). Thousands of people were escaping to freedom through West Berlin annually. Khrushchev ordered the East German government to seal off the flow of refugees by building a 25 mile long wall between the two sectors of the city. Thousands were cut off from relatives and jobs by this action.

Berlin remained a divided city until November of 1989, when a vast movement for democratic reform swept through Eastern Europe. In East Germany the reforms resulted in the ruling communist group's resignation and a new government allowing Berlin Wall to be dismantled. In 1991, the two halves of Germany reunited into a single democratic nation.

The Nuclear Arms Race

Continued atmospheric testing of nuclear weapons threatened to poison the environment with radiation, but the superpowers could not agree on methods of limitation and verification.

After years of negotiation, a **Nuclear Test-Ban Treaty** was signed by the U.S., U.S.S.R. and 100 other nations in 1963, although France and China refused to agree. The agreement prohibited testing of nuclear weapons in the atmosphere, under-water, or in outer space. (Another agreement in 1967, prohibited testing on the moon.) However, underground testing and stockpiling of warheads still continued. In addition, the U.S. and U.S.S.R. also agreed to establish a direct telephone line (the **"hot line"**) between Moscow and Washington to be used to prevent accidental nuclear conflict.

Assassination In Dallas

On November 22, 1963, while in a motorcade through Dallas, Texas, President Kennedy was shot and killed by **Lee Harvey Oswald**. Vice-President Lyndon Baines Johnson was immediately sworn in as the nation's leader.

Oswald himself was shot and killed two days later by **Jack Ruby**, a Dallas bar owner. President Johnson appointed Chief Justice Earl Warren to head an investigation to determine if the shootings were part of a conspiracy.

The **Warren Commission** concluded that both Oswald and Ruby had acted alone, but many doubts and suspicions about the tragedy linger to this day.

John F. Kennedy
1917 - 1963
(died in office)

Questions

1 President Kennedy met opposition in the Senate regarding his
   1 plan to place a man on the moon.
   2 establishing a "hot line" to Moscow.
   3 civil rights program.
   4 approval of the Bay of Pigs Invasion.
2 The movements led by Martin Luther King, Jr. and Mohandus Gandhi of India were similar because both
   1 supported attempts to overthrow the established national government.
   2 used civil disobedience to bring about social change.
   3 appealed primarily to the upper classes for support.
   4 resulted in their leaders being elected to national office.
3 Several Southern states attempted to prevent blacks from attending all-white schools, claiming that
   1 the Constitution does not say anything about equal rights for the races.
   2 management of public education is a power reserved to the states.
   3 the black students were actually residents of other regions of the country.
   4 the President should not enforce the Supreme Court's orders.
4 Which statement best expresses the concept of civil disobedience?
   1 Legislators have the right to make any law citizens demand, and loyal citizens must obey such laws.
   2 Federal laws are an unfair burden to the average citizen.
   3 Consciously and publicly breaking a law one holds to be unjust and accepting punishment is an honorable act.
   4 Violence is acceptable means to undo unjust legislation.
5 The New Frontier can best be described as Kennedy's attempt to
   1 drive the Soviets out of East Berlin.
   2 compete with the Soviets in the nuclear arms race.
   3 increase the pace of reform in American society.
   4 aid the nations of South America.

6 The Good Neighbor Policy and the Alliance for Progress were efforts to
  1   contain communism in underdeveloped nations.
  2   get Americans to volunteer as to help Third World nations.
  3   create a better climate of relations with Latin America.
  4   use force to overthrow dictators.
7 The Peace Corps has been successful because it
  1   improved the image of the U.S. in underdeveloped nations.
  2   drove communists from Eastern Europe.
  3   brought about a negotiated settlement to the Arab-Israeli disputes.
  4   set the groundwork for a Nuclear Test Ban Treaty.
8 The Cuban Missile Crisis ended when
  1   the Soviet leaders decided to remove the weapons.
  2   the U.S. sponsored a successful invasion by anti-Castro rebels.
  3   NATO forces threatened to invade Cuba.
  4   no proof could be offered by the U.S. of the presence of Soviet missiles.
9 The first nuclear test ban treaty prohibited testing of weapons
  1   in the atmosphere.
  3   in neutral countries.
  2   underground.
  4   by any member of the U.N.
10 The Berlin Wall was constructed to
  1   contain the spread of communism in Europe.
  2   stop East Germans from escaping to the West.
  3   defend East Germany in case of a NATO invasion.
  4   be a symbol of America's pledge to defend West Berlin.

B. Lyndon Johnson And Great Society

Lyndon B. Johnson had over 20 years of experience in Congress before becoming President. After filling a little over a year of the slain Kennedy's term, he easily won election in his own right in 1964. Johnson polled more than 60% of the popular vote against conservative Republican candidate **Senator Barry Goldwater** of Arizona. The Democrats also increased their already substantial margin of seats in Congress that year.

Johnson had come to Washington during the New Deal and believed in the concept of social reform. With his legislative skill, LBJ capitalized on the desire to honor the fallen Kennedy. Johnson was able to achieve victory for stalled New Frontier programs and use the momentum to work out his own Great Society program.

Johnson envisioned this **Great Society** as one in which poverty, illiteracy, hunger, and racial injustice would be eliminated, while all Americans would enjoy freedom, equality, and prosperity. Implementation of his program would expand the role of the federal government in everyday life, but it would also strain the national budget.

Lyndon B. Johnson

Great Society Programs

Johnson, helped by the legislative skill of his new Vice-president, former Senate leader **Hubert Humphrey**, was able to guide many legislative measures through Congress which had previously been rejected.

Enduring Issues 12

The War On Poverty

Despite the prosperity of the post-World War II years, an estimated 35 million Americans lived below the poverty line in 1960. The highest concentration of poverty existed in Appalachia, on Indian reservations, inner cities, and in the rural areas of the South. Johnson proclaimed a *"War on Poverty"* and established the **Office of Economic Opportunity** (OEO) to attack the problems. OEO directed the **Volunteers in Service to America** (VISTA) program, which was touted as a "domestic Peace Corps," in which Americans volunteered to use their skills to help people in poverty regions. OEO also administered the **Job Corps**, which trained school dropouts and unemployed youth, and **Project Head Start**, which helped prepare young children from disadvantaged families for a more productive early childhood education. By 1969, the number of Americans living below the poverty level had been reduced to 22.5 million. Experts still argue whether this was due to the efforts of the Great Society or the general rise in incomes due to the booming economy.

Medicare

During the 1940's, President Truman's proposal for helping the poor and elderly meet medical expenses was turned down by conservatives and the medical profession fearing governmental control. In 1965, President Johnson secured passage of the **Medicare** and **Medicaid** bills. The former helps defray doctor and hospital expenses for senior citizens. The latter helps states pay similar costs for the economically disadvantaged through their welfare systems. Critics of the programs complain of the increasing costs burdening the government and the opportunity for fraud in the system. Medicare costs rose dramatically from 3 billion dollars per year in the 1970's to over 60 billion dollars in the 1990's. Part of the increase is due to the addition of catastrophic illness insurance coverage. However, experts feel that medical industry costs also soared out of control in recent years.

Enduring Issues 2

Aid To Education

Federal involvement in education became a controversial subject during the Johnson administration. While the need was great and the quality of education varied from state to state, the states were reluctant to give up any reserved power in this area. The **Elementary and Secondary Education Act of 1965** provided more than 1billion dollars in Federal funding for schools with disadvantaged students. Subsequent programs provided money for efforts to improve nutrition and health conditions. Colleges also received grants and loans for enrollment of educationally disadvantaged students.

Enduring Issues 1

Environmental Improvement

The Great Society also launched programs to deal with air and water pollution, as well as toxic waste and sanitary garbage disposal. The **Wilderness Act** helped preserve the national forests. The **Highway**

Beautification Act sought removal of billboards and junkyards. The Water Quality Control Act provided funds for community waste disposal treatment plants. The **Clean Air Act** of 1970 ordered auto manufacturers to equip cars with pollution control devices to curb auto exhaust. The actions did clean up the environment in many communities, as well as opening many Americans' eyes to the extent of the environmental problems.

Congress also gave permission for the Johnson administration to form two new cabinet-level departments: **Housing and Urban Development (HUD)**, and the **Department of Transportation (DOT)**.

While the Great Society programs helped millions, the problems addressed did not go away. Its scope was enormous, and so was its cost. The unpopularity of Johnson's foreign policies soon undercut support for his domestic reforms. Subsequent presidents were reluctant to undertake the kind of commitment of resources involved in these programs.

Moon Landing

President Kennedy's earlier pledge to place U.S. astronauts on the Moon was achieved on 20 July 1969. The tragic deaths of three astronauts in a 1967 launch delayed the program schedule, but one year later, an Apollo spacecraft orbited the Moon. The following summer, **Apollo 11** astronauts **Neil Armstrong** and **Buzz Aldrin** finally set foot on the lunar surface.

While contributing greatly to scientific, medical, and technical knowledge, as well as launching the age of satellite communication, the space program was again criticized by those who thought it too costly. Declining public interest and budgetary restraints in the 1970's forced Congress to scale down the space program.

First Man to Set Foot on the Moon: July 20, 1969

Continued Demands For Equality: The Civil Rights Movement

The movement for racial equality, begun in earnest after the Supreme Court's landmark decision in *Brown v. Board of Education of Topeka, Kansas* (1954), continued in the Johnson years. World events focused even more attention on racial problems in America, as leaders of African nations struggled successfully to win freedom from European colonial powers. Never tightly organized, the Civil Rights Movement in the United States encompassed a growing variety of organizations. While they all sought social justice and political equality, many differed as to their specific notion of what those ideals meant and what means would be employed to achieve such goals.

NAACP

The **National Association for the Advancement of Colored People** (NAACP) is the oldest and largest civil rights organization. Founded by W.E.B. DuBois and others in 1909, the NAACP has used legislative pressures and legal challenges to actively protest racial injustice. The NAACP was the driving force behind the monumental victory in the *Brown* decision.

Urban League

Another traditional organization following the pattern of the NAACP is the **Urban League**. Founded in 1910, it worked mainly to assist blacks migrating to Northern cities from the rural South. It has fought constantly to improve urban living conditions and taken a leading role in seeking fair treatment of minorities in industry.

SCLC

The **Southern Christian Leadership Conference (SCLC)** was formed by Dr. Martin Luther King, Jr. and other ministers after the Montgomery Bus Boycott. SCLC attempted to make churches the focal point of the civil rights movement and attempted to use non-violent, direct action techniques to confront injustice through marches and public demonstrations of civil disobedience.

SNCC

The **Student Non-violent Coordinating Committee (SNCC)** was formed in 1960 by college students arranging the sit-in demonstrations at segregated restaurants in the South. A widely used, non-violent, and passive resistance tactic, the sit-in, spread rapidly as a protest technique. SNCC's leaders became increasingly militant as frustration with the violent white racist resistance mounted in the middle 1960's.

SNCC leader **Stokley Carmichael** began to openly question the tactics of Dr. King and older civil rights leaders. Carmichael's raised fist and calls for militant **"Black Power"** alienated some political figures as well as some general popular support of the movement among liberals.

CORE

The **Congress of Racial Equality (CORE)** was organized in 1942, to promote peaceful means of calling the public's attention to racial discrimination. CORE organized the Freedom Riders of 1961, which staged demonstrations in segregated buses, terminals, and waiting rooms in the South.

Black Muslims

The **Black Muslims**, a fast-growing group of followers of the Islamic faith in the mid-1960's, held that true equality was nearly impossible under the U.S. political system. They began a movement for a separate black state within the U.S. The popular **Minister Malcolm X** became the foremost spokesman for the group, until he was assassinated by a rival Muslim faction in 1965. Malcolm was beginning to advocate more active accommodation with U.S. society rather than separatism, an approach of the 70's and 80's.

Black Panthers

The **Black Panthers** were the most radical of the groups of the 1960's. They espoused revolution by the black population and armed take-over of the country. Because they sought to actualize these doctrines by accumulating weapons and often using them to incite violence, they were under constant surveillance by the F.B.I., and their leaders were forced to go underground. Considered too violent and radical, they failed to gain much serious support from the black community.

Civil Unrest
The Kerner Commission Report

Although many whites supported the goals of equality, others harbored continuing prejudice. Some feared a change in traditional life patterns, while others feared economic competition. After a decade of crusading for reform, the Civil Rights Movement could point to some progress. Yet, large numbers of blacks continued to live in poverty in the rural South and in the urban ghettoes all over the U.S. Efforts to improve their status were hampered by limited educational opportunities and continuing discrimination in employment.

In the **"Long, Hot Summers"** from 1965 to 1967, riots broke out in many American cities. The most serious disturbances occurred in Los Angeles, Detroit, and Newark, N.J. In these cities, over 100 persons died, thousands of people were arrested, and millions of dollars in property was destroyed.

President Johnson appointed a special commission, headed by Illinois Governor **Otto Kerner**, to investigate the riots and seek solutions. The **Kerner Commission** reported that "white racism" had caused the riots. The deep-seated prejudice in some sectors of the nation was often the cause of blacks being denied equal opportunity. The report also concluded that America was still far from overcoming segregation and inequality. It suggested more job training, improved schools, increased assistance for the needy, and wider construction of low income housing. How all this was to be accomplished, and how it would be paid for, was not treated in the report.

Shocking Assassinations

To a nation in which vocal protest and tense civil confrontations were more and more frequently followed by episodes of violence, a series of brutal murders of key leaders intensified the shock and bewilderment of the late 1960's.

In April of 1968, Dr. Martin Luther King, Jr. was in Memphis to show support for striking sanitation workers. He was shot and killed by an escaped convict, **James Earl Ray**. In 1983, the U.S. Congress honored the memory of the slain civil rights leader by declaring Dr. King's birthday a national day of commemoration.

In June of the same year, President Kennedy's brother, Senator **Robert F. Kennedy** of New York was himself shot and killed by assassin **Sirhan Sirhan**, an Arab sympathizer unhappy with the Presidential candidate's statements in support of Israel.

Investigations of both slayings concluded the assassins were both acting alone and not part of any organized conspiracy. Nonetheless, Americans were shocked by the increasing violence around them.

Legislative Impact Of The Civil Rights Movement

The persistent effort of the Civil Rights Movement gradually influenced the legislative and executive branches of the federal government to take actions to insure a greater degree of justice and equality in America. It was the Supreme Court, however, that led the way. *Brown v. the Board of Education of Topeka* (1954) was a landmark decision, for it ignited a social revolution which is still with us to this day. The decision stated that segregated schools violated the true spirit of the 14th Amendment. The decision triggered a decade of marches, sit-ins, freedom rides, boycotts, and demonstrations which helped partially achieve the goal of equality.

> Enduring
> Issues
> **3**

The actions of the Civil Rights Movement in the Eisenhower years were directed at **de jure segregation**, or racial segregation by law. As the movement progressed into the 1960's, it became evident that racial discrimination in neighborhoods throughout the country had established **de facto segregation**. All black and all white neighborhoods were served by local schools which were, in fact, racially segregated schools.

A Federal Court decision in 1971 approved busing of students to schools in different parts of communities to achieve racial balance. The technique was successful in some cities, but triggered violent confrontations in others. It also increased the rate of "white flight" as more and more white middle class families fled the cities for the less turbulent suburbs.

To the basis of the civil rights legislation of the Eisenhower years, the Johnson administration saw Congress respond with four new actions to achieve equality. The **Civil Rights Act of 1964** attached stiff criminal penalties for discrimination in voting and employment, ended segregation in most public facilities, and withheld federal funds from school districts and communities practicing discrimination.

> Enduring
> Issues
> **6**

The **Civil Rights Act of 1968** banned discrimination in rental units and real estate transactions and gave broader federal protection to civil rights workers.

In 1963, only 335 out of 15,000 black citizens in Selma, Alabama could legally meet the state requirements for voting. Civil rights demonstrations met with harassment by local officials. A historic march from Selma to Montgomery was marred by violence, but it brought the problem to the attention of the nation. President Johnson called on Congress to pass the **Voting Rights Act of 1965**. The act suspended literacy tests in counties where more than half the population could not vote, provided federal help to register new voters, and began action to end state use of poll taxes.

A second **Voting Rights Act of 1970** ended all literacy tests and established 30-day residency requirements. As a result of these two acts, a majority of African American citizens were registered to vote by the mid-1970's, and the number of black officeholders increased dramatically. Additional legislation in 1975, required bilingual ballots in certain districts, and in 1982, Federal protection was continued in areas of the country which had a history of discrimination toward minority voters.

In 1964, Congress proposed and the states ratified the U.S. Constitution's **24th Amendment**, which prohibited the **poll tax** in Federal elections. Shortly thereafter, the Supreme Court decided that all use of poll taxes was unconstitutional because, once again, under the **14th Amendment**, poll taxes denied citizens equal protection of the law.

In its decisions concerning civil rights, the U.S. Supreme Court has moved and shaped public policy when the other two branches of government were at a standstill. *Brown v. the Board of Education of Topeka* ordered an end to racial segregation in the schools. *Swan v. the Board of Education of Charlotte-Mecklenburg* declared busing a valid desegregation technique in 1971. In the Truman administration, the High Court had made rulings which broke ground on discrimination in real estate. In 1962, *Baker v. Carr* applied the 14th Amendment to bring about equally sized election districts.

| Enduring Issues |
| 13 |

The perceptions of the nation were beginning to change as a results of the civil rights struggle. In an effort to end discriminatory practices, some corporations and educational institutions began **affirmative action programs**. These programs set aside a certain percentage of positions for blacks and other minorities. Whites who were denied jobs or school admission, because of these programs, complained of "reverse discrimination."

In *Bakke v. the Regents of the University of California* (1978), the Supreme Court ruled that while the use of such affirmative action quotas was constitutional, they must be administered in such a way that the rights of others are not violated.

Demands For Equality: Women

As the Civil Rights Movement focused the nation's attention on the subject of racial inequality, other groups also renewed their struggles for equality. Throughout the history of western civilization, women had traditionally been afforded an inferior status. In the American experience, women had been denied political and legal rights. (See Unit Three for a discussion of the early Women's Rights struggle.)

In 1961, President Kennedy set up a **Committee on the Status of Women** which concluded that legislative and judicial reform was needed to end discriminatory legal practices, allow equal job opportunities, and establish equal pay for equal work. It also recommended increased child care facilities and greater involvement of women in the political process.

Enduring Issues 7	In 1963, Congress passed the **Equal Pay Act** which provided that men and women doing the same job be paid equally. Incorporated into the **Civil Rights Act of 1964** was **Title VII**, which prohibited discrimination against women in employment and job promotions.

The **National Organization of Women** (NOW) was founded in 1966, by Betty Friedan, author of the 1963 work, *The Feminine Mystique*. The book made a singular contribution to raising women's consciousness of their inferior status in American society. N.O.W. is usually perceived as representing middle class women and pursues change through legislative and judicial channels. N.O.W. has also become politically active, supporting or opposing certain candidates and spearheading campaigns for the Equal rights amendment and on the abortion issue.

In the **Higher Education Act (Title IX)**, passed by Congress in 1972, colleges were forbidden to discriminate against women. By 1980, all public and most private colleges were co-educational.

Key Women's Issues

Since the turn of the century, the percentage of women in the work force has increased dramatically. In 1900, 17% of the work force was women; in 1980, they made up 43% of the work force. Women continue to dominate clerical positions, domestic work, and service jobs in hospitals and restaurants. At the same time, the number of women in professional, managerial, and supervisory positions has increased.

Women today are more apt to put off marriage and child rearing until later in life, seeking to develop their careers. Women's groups also seek more publicly funded day-care facilities for children of mothers who wish to continue careers while raising a family. It is also a more frequent occurrence today that many women must work to help meet basic family expenses.

To guarantee equality with men in all circumstances nationwide, many women's groups wanted an **Equal Rights Amendment (ERA)** to the U.S. Constitution. The proposed amendment stated, *"Equality of rights under the law shall not be denied or abridged by the United States or any state on account of sex."*

In 1972, ERA won quick approval in Congress, but failed by 3 states to gain the approval of the ¾ of the states necessary for it to be included in the Constitution. Some opponents feared laws which protect women would be nullified

VOTES FOR WOMEN

and that women would be drafted into the military in wartime. Also, the general terminology of the amendment produced fear that it would be too susceptible to court interpretations.

In *Roe v. Wade* (1973). the U.S. Supreme Court invalidated all state laws which prohibited abortion in this decision. Many women's groups saw it as a victory for women's rights, proclaiming that they now had **"freedom of choice."** Others saw abortion as murder and formed **"Right to Life"** movements, with the goal of getting the Court to reverse its decision or prohibiting abortion with a new constitutional amendment. While unsuccessful on either of the latter approaches, Right to Life groups have succeeded in halting the use of federal Medicaid funds for abortions.

Statistics indicate that women earn considerably less than men. Women's groups claim that much of the inequality is due to the fact that women are paid less even when jobs are similar in nature. Some states have passed "equal-pay-for-equal-work" laws, which mandate the same pay scale for jobs requiring similar skills. Critics of this idea cite an increased economic burden on businesses and the subjective way in which different jobs are equated. In a 1981 court decision, it was ruled that women could sue for equal pay, even if the work was not identical.

Wanted

Cleaning Woman	Sanitary Engineer
$5 per hour	$10 per hour

While women have made tremendous advances in the workplace, many still find roadblocks when trying to gain positions in management. Although sexual harassment is illegal, it continues as a problem, especially for those breaking into jobs traditionally held by males.

Enduring
Issues
6

Demands For Equality: American Indian Movement And Other Protests

Native American Indians have been one of the most impoverished groups of Americans in modern America. Long subject to the confusing and inept policies of the Federal Department of the Interior's **Bureau of Indian Affairs** (BIA), Native Americans have been plagued by high unemployment, poor health, and little education.

In 1968, the **American Indian Movement** (AIM) was organized by Indians demanding equal rights and greater government concern for the problems of Native Americans. AIM soon became a militant organization, using direct and often violent actions to achieve their goals. While not the only Indian rights organization, AIM was to be the most visible.

Near the end of 1969, several Indian rights groups occupied the empty Federal prison on **Alcatraz** Island in San Francisco Bay. They remained there for over a year, demanding Federal authorities return the island to them as its original owners. Government efforts at compromise, such as making the property a Native-American museum, failed. Federal marshals removed the remaining demonstrators in 1971. News of the occupation of Alcatraz spurred Native Americans to attempt similar tactics elsewhere to raise the public's consciousness of their problems.

In **The Long March** of 1972, over 500 Native-Americans marched across the country to protest government policies in Washington, D.C. Organized by AIM, it was called the "Trail of Broken Treaties." The demonstrators occupied the Bureau of Indian Affairs building, doing over 2 million dollars in damage. After the incident, federal officials agreed to pay more attention to problems.

Enduring Issues 8

In 1973, the town of **Wounded Knee** was the site of the last massacre of Indians by Federal troops during the 19th Century. Early in 1973, members of AIM occupied the town. They demanded that the Federal government honor past treaties and reform the BIA. The government agreed to consider some of the demands, but not before confrontations with Federal marshals left several dead and injured.

Tribes in Canada and the U.S. joined to form the International Treaty Council to create a more favorable image of Native-Americans and seek justice in their treatment by national governments. The Council was granted observer status at the United Nations in 1977, where it presented charges against the American government including injustice, mistreatment, and treaty violations. The U.S. officially rejected the charges.

A major complaint of Native Americans has been the record of treaty violations by state and local governments. Agreements which gave land to Indian tribes many years ago have been broken as the government needed to build highways, reservoirs, and other public facilities. Until recently, such seizures were common, backed by the Constitutional provision of "eminent domain" (5th Amendment). Since 1970, Native-Americans have gone to court over treaty violations and have won most of the time. Officials are now better informed of past treaties when asking for the use of tribal lands.

Enduring Issues 12

In New York State, one of the largest such seizures of tribal land came with the building of the **Kinzua Dam** on the Allegheny River in the early 1960's. The U.S. Army Corps of Engineers told the **Seneca** people that the project would flood most of their reservation in Western New York. The Seneca had signed a treaty in 1794, giving them ownership of the land forever. They brought their case to the United States Congress. After a prolonged wait, Congress voted 15 million dollars in reparations, but it could not replace the loss of a priceless homeland.

Other land seizures affected the **Aknesasne** and **Kanawake Mohawk** peoples in the **St. Lawrence Seaway Project** and the Tuscarora people near the site of the New York Power Authority's **Niagara Power Project.** While compensation was made in both instances, there was little consideration given to the sanctity of treaties.

Questions

1 Which best describes the black experience in the U.S. in the last 40 years?
  1 Little progress has been made in civil rights since WW II.
  2 African American leaders have not employed political power in bringing about reform.
  3 Economic progress has not equaled the achievement of political rights.
  4 The Federal government has strongly resisted the movement for equal rights.

2 Which provision of the U.S. Constitution would be used by groups seeking to justify legislation banning discrimination?
  1 the reserved power clause of 10th Amendment
  2 the 5th Amendment's protection against self-incrimination
  3 Article I's "elastic clause"
  4 "equal protection of the laws" mentioned in the 14th Amendment

3 The Great Society programs of the 1960's,
  1 resulted in increased involvement of the Federal government in citizen's lives.
  2 were usually passed by overriding President Johnson's vetoes.
  3 emphasized increased defense spending to combat recessions.
  4 were designed to pull us out of the "Great Depression."

4 The primary cause of de facto segregation has been
  1 court-ordered busing.
  2 housing patterns.
  3 voting restrictions.
  4 immigration quotas.

5 Which is the most accurate conclusion that can be drawn from a study of the activities of black civil rights groups?
  1 A variety of philosophical approaches have been used to achieve equal rights.
  2 The establishment of a separate society has been a major goal of most groups.
  3 The movement for equality has been dominated by extremist groups.
  4 White Americans have been excluded from joining the civil rights movement.

6 Most major Supreme Court decisions of the past 50 years have
  1 provoked little public controversy.
  2 been unanimously approved by Congress.
  3 reflected changing interpretations of the Constitution.
  4 increased the power of the states at the expense of the Federal government.

7 Great Society programs were designed to help
  1 multinational corporations.   3 poor people.
  2 scientific development.   4 organized religion.

8   A major cause of racial segregation in schools in the Northeastern U.S.
    has been
    1   laws passed by state legislatures and local boards of education.
    2   the refusal of Congress to pass civil rights legislation.
    3   single-group neighborhoods in urban and suburban areas.
    4   Supreme Court decisions on racial quotas.

9   The women's movement in the U.S. in the 20th century
    1   has made the public more aware of sexism.
    2   stresses the natural superiority of women to men.
    3   represents the views of very few women.
    4   has successfully eliminated all discrimination against women.

10 Affirmative action programs are designed to
    1   encourage equal employment opportunities for women and minorities.
    2   increase voter participation in Federal elections.
    3   provide incentive for home construction in ghettoes.
    4   require bilingual ballots in national elections.

11 While more than one half of the U.S. population is female, women are
    often classified as a minority because they
    1   are outnumbered by men in the younger age groups.
    2   hold political views that are distinct from most men.
    3   are numerically dominant in most ethnic minority groups.
    4   have traditionally been denied equal opportunity.

12 Which action could legally override the Supreme Court's 1973 *Roe v.
    Wade* decision on abortion?
    1   Congressional override of a Presidential veto
    2   rejection by a majority of state governors
    3   adoption of a Constitutional Amendment
    4   passage of proper Congressional legislation

13 In which area has the least progress been made by women's rights
    groups?
    1   advancement in higher level executive jobs
    2   voter registration
    3   admission to major colleges and universities
    4   legal ownership of property

14 For the Native-American, one effect of reservation life has been
    1   increased life expectancy.
    2   advanced educational opportunities.
    3   declining economic status.
    4   preservation of treaty rights.

IV. The Limits Of Power:
Turmoil At Home And Abroad, 1965-1972

A. Vietnam:
Sacrifice And Turmoil

The Vietnam War was the longest armed conflict in American history. Except for the Civil War, it was also the most divisive. The war exposed the limitations of American military power when faced with **guerrilla warfare**. The strains which the war placed on American society eventually called into question the Constitutional limitations on the warmaking power of the Executive branch.

Review Of U.S. Involvement In Asia Since 1865

In the latter half of the 19th century, the United States acquired several island possessions in the Pacific (Midway, Wake, Samoa, Hawaii, and the Philippines) in order to protect expanding trade. Subsequently, Secretary of State John Hay's pursuit of an **"Open Door" Policy** in the McKinley-Roosevelt era brought us into competition with major European powers in East Asia. Just as Japan's empire crumbled at the end of World War II, so too did those of the exhausted French, British, and Dutch. Slowly, the latter two withdrew from the region, but France attempted to cling to its possessions in Southeast Asia (Indo-China).

The French-Indochinese War

While France was under Nazi occupation, a nationalist revolution was organized in Indo-China by a Marxist group headed by **Ho Chi Minh**. Non-communist groups joined the independence movement hoping to end French rule. Futile attempts at reaching some accommodation between the rebels and the French colonial government were followed by eight years of sporadic fighting. In 1954, even with aid from the U.S., the exhausted French suffered a final defeat at **Dien Bien Phu**. At a peace conference in Geneva, a cease-fire agreement was worked out in which Vietnam was divided at the 17th Parallel, with Ho and the communists controlling the northern sector and an anti-communist government to the south. The U.S. was to supervise elections to unite the country in 1956. In that year, the government of South Vietnam, under Ngo Dinh Diem refused to participate in the elections. Diem's government was not democratic, but the U.S. supported it, in the hope of containing communism.

When it became apparent that the elections would not be held, Ho Chi Minh gave increasing support to a communist insurgent movement (**Viet Cong**) in the South. President Eisenhower gave military supplies, advisors, and financial support to Diem. Diem's government was unpopular, especially in the treatment of religious groups. Buddhists began open demonstrations.

The Viet Cong had grown into a major threat by the early 1960's, and President Kennedy increased the U.S. commitment by sending 15,000 military personnel as advisors. A coup d'etat in 1963 ended Diem's rule, but the fighting against the Viet Cong continued.

The Domino Theory

First conceived by Dulles and Eisenhower, the "**Domino Theory**" (if one weak nation fell to communism, others around it would similarly topple) continued to dominate the policy makers' thinking in the Kennedy and Johnson years. It was felt that a stand had to be made in Vietnam if the surrounding nations were to survive the communist threat.

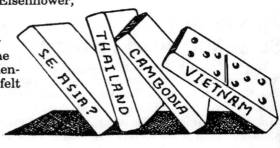

| Enduring |
| Issues |
| **9** |

In 1964, U.S. ships were engaged by North Vietnamese gunboats in the **Gulf of Tonkin**. President Johnson ordered retaliatory bombing of North Vietnamese harbors. In a Gulf of Tonkin Resolution, a nearly unanimous vote in Congress authorized the President to take all necessary action to protect American interests in the region. At this point, most public opinion was supportive of the administration's policy. Bombing continued through 1965, but the Viet Cong appeared to be gaining strength. Johnson's advisors indicated a major effort could stem the tide. The President ordered U.S. combat troops into South Vietnam.

Guerrilla Warfare

Despite heavy bombing, increased troop strength and high communist casualties, the war seemed to be stalemated. Guerrillas attacked towns and villages with no logical pattern, then retreated into the rain forests. So much of the countryside was infiltrated by both Viet Cong and non-uniformed troops, that Americans could not tell friend from foe.

Even the use of toxic chemical defoliants like the **Agent Orange** had little military effect. Communist forces and supplies from the North seemed to be swarming into the South through **Laos** and **Cambodia**.

The "hit-and-run" tactics and the nationalistic spirit of the communists seemed astonishingly effective in offsetting the well trained American forces and sophisticated equipment.

Student Protests At Home

As the war escalated, opposition within the U.S. grew. An increasing number of Americans, nicknamed "doves," demanded immediate withdrawal. The most vocal doves were often young people on college campuses. By 1969, anti-war protests in major cities drew hundreds of thousands of people.

Draft Protesters

As the numbers of young being drafted for service in Vietnam grew, the draft itself became a hated symbol of the war. Many protested by burning their draft cards at campus rallies, some fled to Canada and Scandinavia to avoid the draft, and civil rights leaders protested that a disproportionate number of African Americans were being drafted.

Radical Politics

Radical groups, such as the **Students for a Democratic Society (SDS)**, organized opposition centering on the nation's campuses, as well as civil rights-like marches and demonstrations aimed at the Pentagon and a national student strike on "**Vietnam Moratorium Day**" in 1969.

The Weathermen, an extremist offshoot of SDS, engaged in terrorist tactics, burned buildings, and planted bombs. Demonstrations at the University of California at Berkley and at New York's Columbia University became violent and destroyed millions of dollars in property. In 1970, after President Nixon ordered the bombing of Viet Cong supply routes in Cambodia, a demonstration at the **Kent State** campus of the University in Ohio resulted in National Guardsmen killing four students.

Cultural Radicals: Hippies And Communes

As an offshoot of the radical anti-war movement, some of the nation's youth turned to cultural dissent. They rejected traditional American values, often practiced pacifist religions, adopted outlandish clothes, and experimented with drugs. Some of these "**hippies**" and "**flower children**" rejected society altogether, going off to live in remote rural areas as hermits or in "back-to-nature" communes. They formed enclaves in San Francisco's Haight-Ashbury section and New York's Greenwich Village.

The "Flower Children"

While they were relatively few in number, they had a remarkable influence on the nation's youth. The clothing and music industries were especially quick to publicize their activities and capitalized on their hard-driving protest songs and rebellious image. Critics complained about the negativism, the disrespect for authority, and the increased attraction of youth in general to drug use.

B. President Johnson's Gesture: Abdication And Peace Overtures

In 1964, President Johnson garnered over 60% of the popular vote and excited the nation with his vision of the Great Society. In less than two years, Vietnam made Johnson one of the most unpopular Presidents in U.S. history. "Hawks" criticized him for not mounting an all-out invasion of North Vietnam. "Doves" despised his escalation of the war.

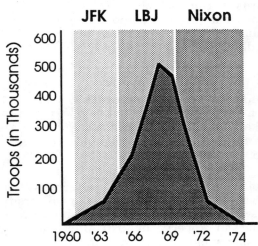

U.S. TROOP ESCALATION IN VIETNAM WAR

Congress continued to appropriate funds for the war, but it was the President who was ultimately accountable for foreign policy. The **Tet Offensive**, launched by the Viet Cong and North Vietnamese during the 1968 New Year holiday, showed that the enemy had been little weakened by three years of American effort.

In March, Johnson announced that he would not seek re-election. At the same time, he ordered a cutback in the bombing of North Vietnam and asked Ho Chi Minh to consider peace negotiations. Peace talks began a few months later in Paris, but the war dragged on for another five years.

The 1968 Chicago Democratic Convention

With LBJ out of the running, Vice-President **Hubert Humphrey** became the logical candidate for the Democrats in 1968. "Doves" rallied behind anti-war **Senator Eugene McCarthy**, but their ranks were split when New York **Senator Robert F. Kennedy**, brother of the slain President, joined the race. Robert Kennedy was assassinated in June, and the anti-war faction lost momentum by the summer convention in Chicago.

Inside the convention, the mainstream Democrats finally nominated Humphrey. Outside, thousands of anti-war protesters demonstrated. As television viewers watched, a violent confrontation unfolded between the frustrated demonstrators and Chicago police. Many criticized the excessive use of force by police, but the net effect was to severely damage the Democrats' chances for holding on to the White House.

Impact Of The War On Society

The Vietnam conflict had a critical impact on America. The Great Society programs suffered as billions of tax dollars were diverted to the military. War spending caused inflation which made everything more costly. Reluctance about the Johnson social program grew as people's incomes became strained.

The American military command was widely criticized for its conduct of the war. Top Generals assured the President and the public that the war was being won while asking for more and more money and troops. As the public began to doubt their leaders, the ranks of war dissenters grew.

Article I, section 8 of the U.S. Constitution specifically gives Congress the responsibility for declaring war, but Article II makes the President Commander-in-Chief of the armed forces. Congress never declared war in the Vietnam conflict. Various executive agreements had put America into a position of defending the Indochinese region after France's exodus.

Enduring Issues 10

As the war became more and more unpopular, demands grew for legal limits on the President's power to involve the country in such situations. While Johnson was to bear the responsibility, it should not be forgotten that the Congress passed the **Tonkin Gulf Resolution** and continued funding the war effort.

In 1973, as we began to withdraw from Vietnam, Congress moved to cut back the war-making power of the President. It passed the **War Powers Act** over the veto of President Nixon. As a result, the President was required to explain to Congress within 48 hours why he was using troops abroad. In addition, the President would have to secure periodic Congressional approval if the troops were to remain in a combat role.

Questions

1 The division of Vietnam in 1954 was
   1 the result of direct popular election.
   2 done without intervention of foreign powers.
   3 based on the principles of self-determination.
   4 worked out as an international compromise.
2 The Domino Theory expressed the fear of
   1 economic collapse in Western Europe.
   2 communist expansion throughout Asia.
   3 proliferation of nuclear weapons in the Third World.
   4 increased famine in developing nations.
3 The Constitutional power by which the U.S. became militarily involved in Southeast Asia was the
   1 Presidential diplomatic power to recognize new governments.
   2 Congressional power to make declarations of war.
   3 Commander-in-Chief role of the President.
   4 Senate's power to ratify treaties and alliances.
4 Conventional warfare failed U.S. commanders in Vietnam because
   1 North Vietnam was closer to its own supply bases.
   2 the Viet Cong guerrilla tactics proved difficult to combat.
   3 U.S. industry could not keep American forces supplied.
   4 the President and his military commanders could not agree on strategy.
5 Protests to military involvement in Vietnam were led by
   1 student activists.   3 Congressional opponents.
   2 veterans organizations.   4 civil rights groups.

6 The greatest troop escalation of the Vietnam war was undertaken by President
  1 Eisenhower.
  2 Kennedy.
  3 Johnson.
  4 Nixon.
7 The Gulf of Tonkin Resolution indicated to President Johnson that
  1 his actions in Vietnam were unconstitutional.
  2 there was full Congressional support for escalation.
  3 the United Nations opposed the American intervention.
  4 student groups would patriotically rally to the American cause.
8 Participation in an undeclared war in Vietnam during the 1960's and 1970's, raised serious questions about the
  1 loyalty of U.S. military commanders.
  2 capacity of the President to involve the country in war.
  3 Supreme Court's role in national security matters.
  4 Congress' capacity to raise war revenues.
9 Public opinion during the Vietnam War was consistently
  1 supportive of the actions of the Johnson administration.
  2 apathetic toward foreign policy matters.
  3 divided between "hawks" and "doves."
  4 in favor of withdrawal from the conflict.
10 A major result of the nation's experience in the Vietnam conflict was legislation to
  1 limit the President's ability to unilaterally make war.
  2 adopt a position of neutrality in international conflicts.
  3 cancel foreign aid programs to Third World nations.
  4 abolish the President's diplomatic powers.

V. Trend Toward Conservatism, 1972 To Present

The period of upheaval and change during the 1960's was followed by a more conservative period in the 1970's and 1980's. The protests and civil disorders convinced many Americans that law and order had broken down. The failure in Vietnam led to increased caution in the area of foreign policy. The momentum of the Civil Rights Movement also evaporated in the domestic turbulence of the late 1960's.

A. Nixon As President, 1969-74

The 1968 election saw the Democratic party in terrible disarray. The Republicans, who had leaned too far to the right with Goldwater in 1964, now saw their chance to capitalize on the divisions racking the opposition and nominated former Vice-President **Richard Nixon.** Promising to restore order to the country, Nixon barely edged Humphrey in the popular vote (43.4% to 42.7%). The results showed a deeply divided electorate, with a staunchly conservative **George Wallace** of Alabama on an American Independent ticket pulling a substantial 13.5% of the popular vote. Analysts indicated that the Wallace vote probably hurt the Democrats more than the Republicans. Once again the Electoral College distorted the true results (Nixon: 301, Humphrey: 191, Wallace: 46). The Democrats retained control of Congress.

Richard Nixon

Domestic Policies And Events
Dismantling The Great Society

The disorientation of the late sixties had led to a pessimistic attitude about Johnson's Great Society. Nixon perceived the public's disenchantment, indicating the programs were ineffective, costly, mismanaged, and had over-expanded the Federal government's power. The **Office of Economic Opportunity** was abolished. Urban renewal, job training, and education programs were reduced or terminated. The Democrats struggled to keep Nixon from cutting even more. Even so, court decisions and new government regulations stemming from them seemed to be increasing the complexity of the Federal government.

Struggling With Inflation

Massive government military and social spending, and the resulting budgetary deficits had badly inflated the American economy by 1970. Only a minor annoyance in the 1950's and early 1960's, inflation had become the leading economic problem. One solution was to tighten the money supply. This could be done through a fiscal policy of raising taxes and cutting government spending, or through a monetary policy of increasing interest rates.

Enduring Issues

12

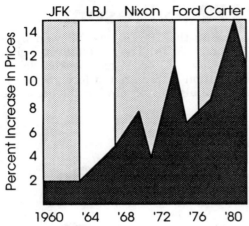

Increases In The Consumer Price Index

JFK LBJ Nixon Ford Carter

Percent Increase In Prices

14
12
10
8
6
4
2

1960 '64 '68 '72 '76 '80

Enduring Issues 2

While Congress and the President were in a stalemate over what to cut in government spending, the Federal Reserve Board's attempt to limit the money supply triggered a recession. Nixon invoked mandatory **wage and price controls**, but they had only a temporary effect. Inflation continued to plague Americans into the next decade.

In trying to limit the growth of the Federal government, Nixon proposed **revenue sharing** in 1971. Instead of providing money for specific programs, this approach gave broad grants to be used at the states' and localities' discretion. While opponents in Congress felt the government would lose control of the funds, the program passed, and billions of unrestricted dollars went to the states. It continued for about fifteen years until phased out under President Reagan.

Environmental And Consumer Legislation

In his State of the Union message in 1970, President Nixon spoke of the need to protect the environment. A major movement had already gained momentum in the late 1960's. The first "**Earth Day**" was held in the Spring of 1970 as a means of educating the public to the general erosion of the natural environment.

Congress authorized Nixon to set up the **Environmental Protection Agency** (EPA) to enforce regulations flowing from the **Clean Air, Resource Recovery,** and **Water Pollution Control Acts.** These measures addressed concerns about offshore oil spills, auto exhaust, industrial discharge, waste disposal, and recycling. The acts were controversial. They had ecological benefits, but businesses and municipalities found it costly to comply. There was a general concern that the acts added to the problem of inflation.

Unsafe products and fraudulent advertising raised the cry for broader consumer protection in the 1960's. A **Consumer Products Safety Commission** was finally created in 1972. Previously, a Federal **Truth-in-Lending Act** (1969) required consistent disclosure of finance charges and **Annual Percentage Rates** (APR) in consumer credit arrangements. In 1971, a controversial measure banned cigarette advertising on radio and television.

Since the 1960's the consumer rights cause has had a strong and intense spokesman in **Ralph Nader.** His legal challenges and writings have exposed a long list of unsafe products and dishonest business practices. His book, *Unsafe at Any Speed* (1965) was highly critical of the lax production methods and unsafe vehicles of the U.S. auto industry, and resulted in several models being discontinued by GM and Ford.

The Burger Court

Enduring Issues **5**

The decisions of the Supreme Court under Chief Justice Warren, which redefined many basic rights, were seen by some critics as having contributed to the disorder and turmoil of the late 1960's. Explicitly defining the rights of accused persons had raised the ire of law enforcement officials. Some indicated that the rising crime rates were the fault of the Court's actions in *Gideon* and *Miranda*. Other critics blamed the moral decay of the nation on the decisions banning school prayer and protecting media obscenity (*Engel v. Vitale* and *Roth v. U.S.*).

Nixon promised to change the High Court's liberalism. He got his chance when Chief Justice Warren resigned in 1969, followed by three other justices within several years. Nixon appointed **Warren Burger** to the Chief Justice's position, and Harry Blackmun, William Rehnquist, and Lewis Powell as associate justices.

The Burger Court exercised **judicial restraint** on the more controversial cases. Conservatives were dismayed that it did not seek to reverse some of the controversial decisions of the Warren years, and they were upset with the new decisions on abortion (**Roe**), busing, and the overturning of many states' death penalty laws.

Pentagon Papers

Enduring Issues **9**

In the 1960's, the Defense Department prepared a confidential study on the progress of the Vietnam War. Daniel Ellsberg, who at one time worked on the study, leaked the information to *The New York Times*. The newspaper published the study, naming it *The Pentagon Papers*. It revealed the misleading and dishonest statements that had been made by the military and the government to gain Congressional and public support for the continued escalation of the war. The Nixon Administration went to court to halt publication of the documents, but lost the case. The ruling was considered a major victory for the 1st Amendment protection of freedom of the press.

Self-determination For The American Indian

The Bureau of Indian Affairs' "termination policy" of the 1950's, which sought to break up tribes and subdivide their land, was a dismal failure. Many Native-Americans wished to remain in the tribal setting, protected but not dominated by the Federal government. In 1970, President Nixon sent a message to Congress proposing a policy of self-determination for American Indians, which would turn over the administration of most of the Federal programs to the tribes. A final version of the measure which passed in Congress did this to some extent, but Native-Americans continued to complain of governmental interference. In a similar action, the administration began to name Native-Americans to management positions in the BIA.

In 1972, the tribes became eligible for the same revenue sharing arrangements as the state governments, releasing significant funds for improvements on reservations. But, these funds increased tribal dependence on Federal money at the same time.

Nixon's Internationalism

Enduring
Issues
9

On taking office, President Nixon appointed **Dr. Henry Kissinger**, a Harvard professor and former foreign affairs aide to New York Gov. Nelson Rockefeller's Presidential campaign, to be a special White House advisor on national security. Kissinger was not part of the Cabinet, but was able to play a very influential role in shaping foreign policy.

Not being tied down to running a major governmental department, Kissinger was able to make frequent trips to Red China and the U.S.S.R. Later, he was appointed Secretary of State by Nixon and continued in that position under Ford, conducting peace missions to the Middle East.

Vietnam Withdrawal

Vietnam posed the most immediate problem for Nixon. In the 1968 campaign, he had promised "peace with honor," an end to the war, but with the "mission accomplished." To that end, Nixon began **"Vietnamization"** of the war, putting more and more responsibility on the South Vietnamese themselves. He began a gradual reduction of U.S. ground forces. Some complained it was too small and too slow. The **Paris Talks** continued, but no major diplomatic progress seemed to be made.

For years, Cambodia was being used as a supply route for communist forces. In 1970, Nixon ordered secret bombing raids on these supply lines. Once made public, numerous demonstrations began, including the deadly incident at Kent State. The massive bombing raids continued into 1973, when the Paris talks finally yielded an agreement. A cease fire was effected, American troops were to be completely withdrawn, and prisoners of war were to be returned.

North Vietnam still had over 100,000 troops in the South Vietnamese countryside. American supplies and financial aid not withstanding, South Vietnam and Cambodia were overrun within months of the American evacuation. After nine years of fighting and more than 50,000 lives sacrificed, America came away disillusioned as to its power and role in the world.

Nixon Doctrine

In the middle of the Indochinese quagmire, the President issued a policy statement which became known as the **Nixon Doctrine**. It stated that the U.S. would continue to honor its treaty obligations in Asia, providing military, financial and humanitarian aid, but actual combat troops would have to be provided by the nation directly involved in the conflict. Nixon hoped to maintain foreign friendship, but wished to avoid another unwinnable war.

Opening To China

Twenty years after Chiang Kai-shek's Nationalist Chinese government was exiled to Taiwan, it was still officially backed by the U.S. Meanwhile it steadfastly refused to establish diplomatic relations with Mao's People's Republic on the Chinese mainland. Early in his Presidency, Nixon investigated the possibility of visiting the mainland nation. China and the Soviet Union were having serious diplomatic problems.

It appeared that communism was no longer an international monolith, posing a single, powerful threat to democracy. Nixon and Kissinger decided on a daring policy toward both nations. A new relationship with communist China might force the Soviet leaders to be more accommodating to America. The hope was that China might be willing to expand trade with the West and perhaps accelerate an end to the war in Vietnam.

No significant agreements resulted from Nixon's trip to China in 1972. However, it served to pave the way for negotiations which would eventually increase trade and cultural exchanges. In 1979, President Carter would open full diplomatic relations. While trade relations were preserved, the mutual defense treaty with Taiwan was ended. Sino-American relations in the Reagan years have continued to be friendly, but the status of Taiwan remains a stumbling block.

Detente: SALT And Grain Deals

After his trip to China, Nixon also made a trip to the Soviet Union in hope of relaxing tensions between the two superpowers and limiting the nuclear arms race. This new policy of **Detente** also widened trade and cultural relations between the two giants.

One result of the Moscow visit was an agreement to allow the U.S.S.R. to buy badly needed American grain for three years. It was beneficial to American farmers, but smaller supplies in the U.S. drove up prices in America and added to inflation.

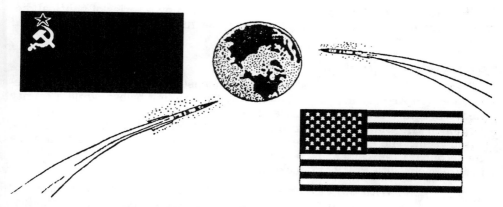

A **Strategic Arms Limitation Treaty (SALT)** also came out of the Kissinger initiatives surrounding the Nixon visit to Moscow. The treaty won overwhelming support in the U.S. Senate. It reduced anti-ballistic systems and froze the expansion of **Intercontinental Ballistic Missiles (ICBM's)**. It did not, however, place limits on multiple warheads, slow construction of long-range bombers, prevent construction of new missile systems, nor provide on-site inspections for verification. The arms race continued in these areas. SALT's supporters hoped these issues could be dealt with in subsequent negotiations. A **SALT II** agreement was reached in 1979, but the Senate never approved it, citing lack of true compliance by the Soviets with the original agreement. Tensions slowly increased between the superpowers after Nixon's resignation.

Seabed Agreement

A proposal by the U.N. to prohibit the placement of nuclear weapons on the ocean floor was signed by the United States, the U.S.S.R. and over one hundred other nations in 1972.

The "Imperial Presidency" In Trouble

Despite a shaky domestic record and continued fighting in Vietnam, Nixon and the Republicans were confident that they would achieve the "Four More Years" of their campaign slogans in the 1972 elections. Nixon based his fortunes on his foreign policy achievements and the gradual de-escalation in Indochina. The Democrats still had not repaired the deep rifts within their party from 1968. They nominated anti-war candidate Senator **George McGovern** of South Dakota, but amid the conservative mood of retrenchment, his liberal philosophy drew little support. In November, Nixon overwhelmed McGovern with more than 60% of the popular vote. In the electoral college, McGovern was only able to carry the District of

| Enduring Issues **11** | Columbia and one state, Nixon took 520 of the 538 votes. McGovern was hoping that he could capture the youth vote which had been increased by virtue of the new **26th Amendment** (1971), allowing 18 to 20-year-olds to vote, but the results |

were disappointing. The Republicans were not able to capture either house of Congress. Analysts interpreted the landslide presidential vote as not so much pro-Nixon, but as the failure of the Democrats to project a positive image in the campaign.

The successes of Nixon's first term were followed by a series of political disasters which would lead to his becoming the first President of the United States to resign from office.

Agnew Resignation

Treasury Department investigations into past activities of Nixon's Vice-President, **Spiro Agnew**, found evidence of his taking bribes while a county executive and Governor in Maryland. Instead of going to trial, Agnew plea-bargained the charges down to income tax evasion and a fine, instead of a prison term. The embarrassment for the administration led him to become the second Vice-President to resign (John C. Calhoun resigned in 1832 in a disagreement with President Jackson).

| Enduring Issues **13** | With the Vice-Presidency vacant, the 25th Amendment (1967) was invoked for the first time. To replace Agnew, the President nominated Gerald R. Ford, the Republican leader in the House of Representatives. He was quickly approved by the required vote of Congress. |

The Watergate Affair

In June of 1972, five men were arrested while attempting to electronically "bug" the Democratic Party headquarters in an office-apartment complex in Washington, D.C., known as officially **"Watergate."** At first it seemed to be a bizarre incident, but investigators soon discovered a pattern of activities by members of the Republican **Committee to Re-elect the President** (CREEP) violating Federal election laws. Nixon repeatedly claimed no knowledge of the activities by anyone in the White House.

In June of 1973, a Congressional investigating committee discovered that President Nixon had routinely made tape recordings of all his conferences and phone conversations. It subpoenaed the tapes. Nixon refused, claiming **executive privilege**, because there were secret, national security matters on the tapes.

Enduring Issues
10

After a protracted struggle, the U.S. Supreme Court ruled (***Nixon v. U.S.***) against "executive privilege" and ordered the President to turn over the tapes to investigators. They revealed that Nixon had knowledge of White House aides being involved in the Watergate affair and had discussed ways of preventing a damaging investigation. (This later became known as "The Coverup.")

Impeachment Proceedings

As Nixon's actions came into question, the Judiciary Committee of the House of Representatives began to consider impeachment charges. After publicly televised hearings in the summer of 1974, the committee voted to recommend Nixon's impeachment on charges of obstructing justice and abuse of executive power. According to the Constitution, a majority vote in the House of Representatives is needed to officially bring charges (**impeach**). The Senate must then hold a trial and vote. (A two-thirds majority is needed to remove a government official from office.)

Nixon Resignation

It was apparent that the Democratic House would vote impeachment. With the Senate vote predicted as close, Nixon would have little chance of surviving the impeachment and removal process. Rather than going through months of debate and paralyzing the government, Nixon resigned 9 August 1974. **Gerald Ford**, who nine months earlier had become the first person ever appointed to the Vice-Presidency, was elevated to the Presidency.

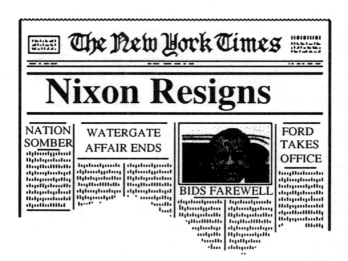

The New York Times

Nixon Resigns

| NATION SOMBER | WATERGATE AFFAIR ENDS | BIDS FAREWELL | FORD TAKES OFFICE |

Questions

1   The goal of President Nixon's Revenue Sharing program was to
1   increase the Federal government role in poverty programs.
2   provide a system for monitoring the use of foreign aid grants.
3   give state and local governments control over programs.
4   provide Federal campaign funds to Presidential candidates.

2   In its "self-determination" policy for the Native-American, the Nixon administration expected to
1   provide the Indians with a separate, sovereign state.
2   increase the Indians' dependence on the Federal government.
3   end segregation practices on the reservations.
4   decrease the Federal controls over Indian's lives.

3   Which is the most accurate definition of "detente" as it was applied to early 1970's relations between the U.S. and the U.S.S.R.?
1   A joint effort to reduce tensions.
2   A U.S. policy seeking to protect Soviet immigrants.
3   An attempt by the U.S. to force the Soviets out of East Berlin.
4   Soviet pressuring for end to U.S. involvement in Southeast Asia.

4   *"Despite all the change in the world, one key reality has remained unchanged: United States participation is still the indispensable condition for a stable, harmonious world order."* In this statement, President Nixon was advocating
1   isolationism.
2   internationalism.
3   imperialism.
4   territorial expansion.

5   Which has occurred in Southeast Asia since the end of the U.S. involvement in the Vietnam War?
1   Democratic governments have replaced military dictatorships.
2   Vietnam continues to be divided between North and South.
3   United States military aid continues to support Vietnamese government.
4   Communist governments have taken over in most of the Indochinese region.

6   Since the early 1970's, the U.S. and the Peoples Republic of China have moved toward establishing better relations because
1   China has become a U.S. supported democratic state.
2   both countries fear the rising industrial power of Japan.
3   the U.S. depends heavily on raw materials produced in China.
4   both wish to balance the power of the U.S.S.R.

7   President Richard Nixon shifted the responsibility of fighting in Vietnam to the
1   United Nations.
2   Soviet Union.
3   South Vietnamese.
4   SEATO alliance.

8   The Burger Court disappointed some conservatives because it
1   continued the activist role of the Court in certain areas.
2   reversed most of the civil rights decisions of the Warren Court.
3   increased the power of the states at the expense of the Federal government.
4   tried to block the impeachment of Richard Nixon.

9   Watergate was the first national political scandal that involved the
    1   conviction of a President on criminal charges.
    2   impeachment of a President.
    3   resignation of a President.
    4   Senate in a trial to remove a President.
10   During the 1970's, worldwide communism experienced
    1   greater unity among nations with Marxist governments.
    2   increased military support from the United States.
    3   cooperation resulting from detente.
    4   division and conflict.

B. Ford And Carter Presidencies

In the wake of Watergate, both **Gerald Ford** and **Jimmy Carter** experienced difficult times as President. Economic woes plagued their tenures, and Carter had the added burden of the **Iranian Hostage Crisis**. Both men lost their bids for re-election, indicating a deep sense of dissatisfaction and disorientation in the nation.

Appointive Presidency: Ford And Rockefeller

Gerald Ford was the first person to occupy the White House by virtue of appointment. When Nixon resigned, President Ford nominated former New York Governor **Nelson A. Rockefeller** to fill the vacant Vice-Presidency, and for the second time in a year, the **25th Amendment** proved its usefulness when Congress approved.

The relationship between the executive and the legislative branch is critical to the success of an administration. Republican **Gerald Ford**'s twenty year experience in Congress helped, but as any President faced with a Congress dominated by the opposing party learns, a working relationship is often modified by partisanship. Democrat **Jimmy Carter**'s campaign stressed he was an "outsider" to scandal-ridden Washington politics. But, it alienated many old hands in Congress, enough to make him seem ineffective.

Gerald Ford

Jimmy Carter

Domestic Policies

The Nixon Pardon

Former President Nixon still faced possible criminal indictment and trial for his actions. He never apologized, and many Americans wished to see justice done. Claiming he wanted to "close the book" on Watergate, President Ford used his Constitutional power to grant a general pardon to Nixon. While Ford's intentions were honorable, the controversial move cost him votes in the 1976 election.

Draft Amnesty

After the final fall of the South Vietnamese government in 1975, many Americans wished to put Vietnam behind them. There remained thousands of "draft evaders" who had left the U.S. to avoid military service in the unpopular war. Ford established a **draft amnesty program** which required those who wanted to return home to take an oath of allegiance to the U.S. and perform community service. Critics charged that Ford's plan asked too much, especially in the wake of his generous pardon of Nixon. Later, President Carter issued an **unconditional pardon** to those who still remained in exile.

Oil Crisis

As the largest energy consumers in the world, Americans had been importing oil in ever increasing quantities in the post World War II period. A seemingly endless supply seemed to be flowing into the U.S. at very low cost. In 1973, Arab members of the world's major oil cartel, the **Organization of Petroleum Exporting Countries (OPEC)**, embargoed oil shipments to nations which supported their enemy, Israel. At the same time, the OPEC nations agreed to increase their prices, eventually raising the price of crude oil from $2.50 to $35.00 a barrel.

While a relatively low percentage of America's oil imports came from the Arab countries, a general disruption in world supplies caused hardships. Shortages and realignment by multinational oil corporations caused prices to rise sharply and continually in the late 1970's. During the embargo, Americans found a new pastime: waiting on long lines to purchase gasoline. In 1979, the revolution in Iran would lead to a second oil shortage.

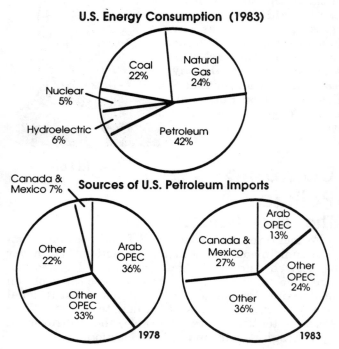

U.S. Energy Consumption (1983)

Coal 22%
Natural Gas 24%
Nuclear 5%
Hydroelectric 6%
Petroleum 42%

Sources of U.S. Petroleum Imports

Canada & Mexico 7%
Other 22%
Arab OPEC 36%
Other OPEC 33%
1978

Arab OPEC 13%
Canada & Mexico 27%
Other OPEC 24%
Other 36%
1983

Measures by Federal, state, and local authorities to ease the energy crisis included temporary gasoline rationing, imposing a highway speed limit of 55 mile-an-hour, and temporary school closings. Both Ford and Carter wished to implement comprehensive national plans for dealing with the crisis, but they were unable to win Congressional approval for many measures.

The completion of the **Alaskan North Slope** pipeline and the development of more fuel efficient American cars reduced foreign dependency somewhat. Revitalizing coal generators and allowing more nuclear power projects helped, but each had environmental drawbacks.

Large scale efforts by Carter included encouraging research on wind and solar power generation, development of synthetic fuels, and urging voluntary cutbacks on power consumption. Most of these programs met with intense opposition from special interest groups. Many efforts fell by the wayside in the 1980's, when Mid-East oil began flowing more freely. Carter did manage to get Congress to create a cabinet level Department of Energy to plan strategies for the future.

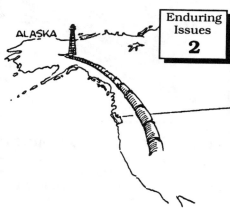

Enduring Issues 2

"Stagflation"

For most of the 1970's, the U.S. was plagued by a stagnant economy, high unemployment, and inflation. Both Ford and Carter failed to solve this dilemma which the media nicknamed **stagflation.**" Ford tried to cut inflation by reducing Federal and consumer spending, but reductions in demand led to higher unemployment. Carter asked for more government jobs and tax cuts to give business incentives, but the increased spending caused inflation to soar. The Federal Reserve Board raised interest rates to cut borrowing and expansion, but this also increased unemployment. Presidential requests to industry to voluntarily hold down prices ("jawboning") were largely ignored.

Enduring Issues 1

The total federal deficit grew in the 1970's. Efforts by both Presidents to balance the budget failed. As the national debt mounted, economists disagreed as to the deficit's impact on the future. Some blamed the deficits for inflation, while others felt they would lead to an eventual economic collapse. Arguments continued throughout the decade as the deficit grew to 100 billion dollars.

Corporate Bailouts

Stagflation began to have significant effects on major corporations. Inflation increased production costs, but demand leveled off or fell as unemployment reduced aggregate consumer demand. Floods of cheaper imported products cut into sales of major American firms. The steel and auto industries were especially hard hit. When **Lockheed Aircraft** and **Chrysler** faced bankruptcy, the Federal government moved to provide them with public loans of several billion each rather than see their collapse cause greater unemployment.

Enduring Issues 12

The Space Program

The fears about government deficits and a decline in public interest led to a more modest space program in the 1970's. The **Skylab** space station was in orbit for several years, permitting astronauts to do research. In 1981, NASA launched a reusable shuttle craft, **Columbia.**

Succeeding shuttle flights placed scientific, commercial, and military satellites in orbit.

However, the program suffered a serious setback in 1986 when the shuttle **Challenger** exploded shortly after takeoff, killing seven astronauts. Unmanned **Explorer** and **Voyager** space probes have also reached other planets, sending back important data and pictures from Venus and Mars.

Legislation For The Bi-lingual And The Handicapped

Several acts passed by Congress during the 1970's provided greater opportunities for foreign language speaking Americans. The 1975 **Voting Rights Act** required bi-lingual ballots in districts with large populations of non-English speaking voters. The **Bilingual Education Act**

Enduring Issues 6

mandated public schools to teach students in their native languages while they were learning English. However, opposition to such costly programs sprang up in the 1980's, as a growing number of Americans sought to make English the official national language.

To meet the needs of the handicapped and disabled, Congress passed the **Rehabilitation Act of 1973**. It forbade discrimination in jobs, education and housing. In 1975, Congress required free public education for all physically and mentally handicapped students. Many communities began providing special vehicle parking facilities and ramps for the disabled.

Environmental Concerns

The **Environmental Protection Agency** was created in the Nixon administration and made significant progress in cleaning up the nation's water and air in the 1970's. New concerns arose over the disposal of hazardous chemical wastes.

In 1977, homes built near a chemical dump called the **Love Canal** near Niagara Falls, New York, had to be abandoned when residents were stricken with illnesses and a high incidence of birth defects. It raised public awareness about the problem of toxic waste. Congress responded with a **"super fund"** of several billion dollars to be used by the Environmental Protection Agency to clean up dangerous sites.

"Mommy, What kind of icebergs are these?"

Over the years, airborne factory pollutants caused by burning of oil and coal were carried high into the atmosphere, eventually returning to earth during rainstorms. This **acid rain** destroyed lakes and forests hundreds of miles from the factories, often in other states and in Canada. Difficulties in determining the sources of such pollution and lobbying by industry slowed efforts at Congressional remedies. In 1986, a meeting between Canadian Prime Minister Brian Mulrooney and President Reagan set up an international effort to seek solutions, but deciding responsibility for cleanup costs is still a problem.

A 1979 accident at the **Three-Mile Island** nuclear power facility near Harrisburg, Pennsylvania increased public awareness of the possible risks of nuclear generators. While no one was killed, and the radioactive release was small, serious concerns emerged. A rash of anti-nuclear demonstrations arose. The **Nuclear Regulatory Commission** tightened safety procedures, and some plants were denied operating licenses, such as the Shoreham facility on Long Island.

Foreign Policies

During the 1970's, it sometimes appeared as though the once mighty United States was at the mercy of international forces beyond its control. Third World nations repeatedly joined forces to block U.S. desires in the United Nations. Arab oil countries seemed be manipulating the economy. The Soviets continued to ignore human rights agreements. Militant Iranian revolutionaries held American officials hostage. American policy makers were lukewarm about containment of communism after the disaster in Southeast Asia. For the struggling President Carter, his brightest and darkest moments came in the area of foreign policy.

Oil Crisis

The oil crisis following the Arab-Israeli War of 1973 heightened awareness of the strategic importance of the Middle East. It also spotlighted America's reliance on energy imports and the growing interdependence of nations. The Soviet Union also began showing more interest in a role in the Middle East.

Human Rights

President Carter was an outspoken critic of human rights violations during his administration. He continually condemned improper and inhumane treatment of political prisoners in Cuba, South Africa, Uganda, and the U.S.S.R.

In 1975, the United States, Soviet Union, and most nations of Europe made several agreements dealing with political boundaries and protocols in Europe. An additional accord was signed which spelled out proper regard for human rights. This **Helsinki Accord** has been a constant source of friction between the United States and the Soviet Union.

Even as the U.S. pointed out violations, the Soviets continued to restrict freedom of speech and the press, and block attempts of those who wished to leave the U.S.S.R., especially Russian Jews.

Afghanistan

Late in 1979, Soviet armed forces invaded neighboring Afghanistan, an impoverished Muslim nation, to support a new Marxist regime fighting a civil war. The move was condemned by western nations, Third World countries, and China. It was seen as an attempt by the U.S.S.R. to influence events in the Middle East. In diplomatic retaliation, President Carter withdrew the SALT II treaty from the Senate, cut sales of U.S. grain to the Soviets, and ordered a boycott of the 1980 Summer Olympics in Moscow. Soviet leaders ignored all protest actions. The U.S. sent aid to Afghan rebels in their mountain strongholds. By 1989, with the rebels still in control of large areas, the Soviets left Afghanistan. Many people compared the Soviet experience in Afghanistan to that of the United States in Vietnam.

Panama

Growing resentment of the U.S. presence in Panama ignited increasingly violent protest riots in the 1960's and 1970's. The U.S. began negotiations to turn the Canal and the U.S. Canal Zone territory over to the Panamanian government. In 1977, President Carter signed a treaty which began a phased turnover to be completed by the year 2000. In the treaty, the U.S. retained the right to intervene in the area to maintain the Canal as a neutral international waterway. There was considerable criticism of the nation's security being compromised, but the Senate ratified the treaty later that year.

Progress on the return of the Canal Zone proceeded well until early 1988, when Panamanian military leader Manuel Noriega, who had been indicted by U.S. officials for drug trafficking, overthrew the civilian government. Panama was wracked by general unrest, strikes, and demonstrations. The Reagan administration levied economic trade sanctions, and Congress cut off aid. Noriega announced a state of war existed with the United States.

In December 1989, after U.S. military personnel were harassed, injured, and one shot by Noriega's forces, President Bush authorized an invasion. In the ensuing skirmishes, a number of Panamanian civilians and U.S. combatants were killed or wounded. Within days Noriega's forces were dispersed, the dictator surrendered and was remanded for trial in the U.S.

Middle East

Efforts begun by Dr. Henry Kissinger in the mid-1970's to bring about a peace settlement in the Middle-East had stalled. In 1978, Egyptian President **Anwar Sadat** and Israeli Premier **Menachem Begin** indicated a willingness to renew the quest for peace. President Carter took the initiative and

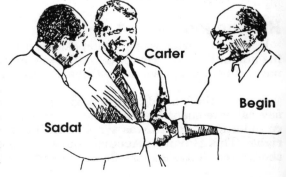

Carter

Begin

Sadat

brought the two leaders together at Camp David, Maryland. The three worked out a peace agreement that was signed at the White House the following year. The **Camp David Agreements** ended thirty years of hostility between the two nations and gave Israel official recognition, as well as, access to the Suez Canal. Israel agreed to evacuate areas of the Sinai Peninsula conquered in the 1973 War. Both parties promised to start negotiations regarding self-determination for the Palestinian refugees in Israel.

Enduring Issues 9

The peace is considered to be President Carter's major achievement in foreign policy. President Sadat was later assassinated by those who felt he had given in to Israel. The Palestinian question remains unsolved, and Israel has been criticized from many corners for its reluctance to deal effectively with the question of the Palestinian refugees in the occupied territories of the West Bank of the Jordan and the Gaza Strip.

Iranian hostages

Ayatollah Khomeini

Carter's most trying experience as President came at almost the same moment as the Israeli-Egyptian accord. Anger with the iron rule of the Shah of Iran boiled over in that country in 1979. A civil war forced the Shah to flee. Resentment grew because of long-time support of the Shah by the U.S. The Shah's harsh government had supplied the U.S. with low cost oil and allowed U.S. military installations. His attempts to "Westernize" the country with the help of U.S. aid had clashed with strong Muslim fundamentalist beliefs. **Ayatollah Rullah Khomeini**, a militant religious leader who had been exiled by the Shah, took control. An "Islamic Republic of Iran" was established which began to purge the Shah's followers and "de-Westernize" the nation.

When the exiled Shah was admitted to the U.S. for cancer treatment at a New York hospital, furious Iranians demanded his return. When the U.S. refused, militant students in Iran attacked the U.S. embassy in Teheran and began holding over 50 U.S. employees hostage.

President Carter's attempts to negotiate for the hostages' release proved futile. Iran was in revolutionary chaos, and the government threatened to put the hostages on trial. Daily newscasts showed thousands of Iranians outside the embassy chanting "Death to Carter - Death to America." As the crisis lengthened, Carter's popularity at home began to wane. A secret rescue attempt failed miserably, and Secretary of State **Cyrus Vance** resigned over the problem.

Enduring Issues 9

By the Fall of 1980, Carter's popularity reached an all-time low. Even before the Iranian situation, Carter's inability to deal with the Soviet invasion of Afghanistan, the energy crisis, inflation, and Congress in general were casting doubt on his leadership ability. When the Iranian Revolution brought about a second oil crisis in 1979, Americans were further demoralized.

The Republicans, devastated earlier in the decade by Watergate, sensed victory as they nominated the conservative Governor of California, **Ronald Reagan.** Promising to reduce the federal bureaucracy and make America strong again, Reagan polled 8 million votes more than Carter and swept the electoral vote 489 to 49.

The Iranians, needing money for their war with Iraq and facing mounting international criticism, released the hostages in the same hour that Reagan was sworn in, and Carter left office on 20 January 1981. The U.S. released frozen Iranian bank accounts in America in return. The hostages were welcomed home with dramatic displays of American patriotism.

Questions

1　The reason the U.S. government used tax dollars to aid certain private corporations on the verge of bankruptcy is that government
   1　used the opportunity to break up monopolies.
   2　pursued a trend toward public ownership of major industries.
   3　wished to avoid the economic repercussions of collapse of these industries.
   4　wished to control the safety and pollution in these industries.

2　In the 1970's, the Federal Reserve Board attempted to reduce inflation by
   1　ordering wage-price controls.
   2　cutting down the size of the Federal budget.
   3　regulating the supply of money and credit.
   4　cutting Federal income tax rates.

3　Several Arab nations have risen in world influence because they have
   1　purchased nuclear weapons from the U.S.
   2　control of a natural resource vital to industrial nations.
   3　formed a strong military alliance.
   4　prohibited Western shipping from using the Suez Canal.

4　The Panama Canal Treaty of 1978 reversed earlier U.S. policy in that region because it
   1　ended U.S. isolation through a military alliance with Panama.
   2　relinquished control of an area long held by the U.S.
   3　recognized a Marxist government in Panama.
   4　accepted European control in the Western Hemisphere.

5　Oil prices increased in the 1970's, primarily due to
   1　economic actions by OPEC.
   2　U.S. government price regulations.
   3　increased costs of exploration and drilling.
   4　competition between consumer and military interests.

6　Ford's pardon of Nixon and Carter's amnesty for draft evaders were both
   1　actions requiring a ⅔ approval of the Senate.
   2　subject to judicial review by the Supreme Court.
   3　legitimate Presidential acts under Article II.
   4　in violation of the principle of checks and balances.

7　A major goal of U.S. foreign policy in the Middle East during the Carter administration was to bring about
   1　a peaceful settlement to the Arab-Israeli disputes.
   2　an end to U.S. cooperation with Arab nations.
   3　private ownership of oil reserves in the region.
   4　permanent U.N. control of disputed territories.

8 "We Americans live in a world we can no longer dominate, but from which we cannot isolate ourselves." The speaker is saying that the U.S. should
   1 become less dependent on other nations.
   2 admit it is no longer a world superpower.
   3 recognize important changes in international relations.
   4 increase its economic and military strength.

9 Which was an underlying cause of the Iranian Revolution of 1979?
   1 ongoing wars between Iran and Israel
   2 Western Europe's control over Iranian oil reserves
   3 Iraq's attempt to overthrow the Shah
   4 repression of political and religious groups by the Shah

10 The problems of acid rain and toxic waste show that
   1 states are not willing to improve the environment.
   2 environmental problems can be traced to developing nations.
   3 the benefits of modern society have their drawbacks.
   4 Congress is unwilling to act on the Federal level.

C. The New Federalism

Ronald Reagan

Ronald Reagan's Presidential victory in 1980 allowed many Republican candidates to ride into office "on his coattails." This resulted in GOP control of the U.S. Senate for the first time in thirty years. Republican victories in Congressional races also reduced the power of the Democrats in the House of Representatives. Although some critics denounced Reagan's domestic agenda and foreign policies, his personal popularity remained high. In the 1984 election, he easily defeated the Democratic challenger, Carter's Vice President, Walter Mondale. Reagan received a record 525 - 13 electoral vote margin and 60% of the popular vote. As with earlier Republicans (Eisenhower, Nixon, Ford), Reagan set a high priority on reducing the growth of the Federal government. He had limited success.

President Reagan called his domestic agenda the **New Federalism**. His goal was to shift Federal programs in education, health, welfare, and transportation to state and local authorities. State officials welcomed control over such programs, but voiced concern about paying for them. Reagan reduced aid to states for the program. The New Federalism had mixed results. The Federal government cut only a few programs and reduced others. The states were unable to finance most of the programs themselves. The Federal government continued massive funding.

Enduring
Issues
2

Supply-Side Economics

Reagan inherited a weak economy. It was one of the nation's most pressing problems. As a solution, the Reagan administration proposed **supply-side**

Enduring Issues 12

economics. Supply-siders pressed Congress to reduce capital gains taxes, individual income taxes for the rich, and corporate income taxes. Supply-side economists pledged to cut expensive government costs. They hoped to free up new investment capital and spur growth. They claimed this would increase supplies of goods and services.

Supply-siders said the general population would eventually prosper as the new growth "trickled down" in the form of new employment. These ideas were similar to those used during Hoover's Administration (chart page 170). Supply-siders theorized the increased employment would expand demand (consumer spending power). Congress supported the basic plan.

First, the rapid economic changes triggered an 18 month recession. The Federal Reserve Board kept bank interest rates high. It feared inflation from the tax cuts. Reagan argued for lower interest rates. The tax breaks eventually increased investments and corporate growth. Critics claimed that the Federal budget cuts harmed millions of poor. They said the rich prospered at the expense of the middle and lower classes.

Tax Cuts And Deficits

A weak Congress bowed to the popularity of Reagan's tax cuts. It passed a 25% tax reduction for individuals, and larger reductions for businesses. A tax simplification program (1986) cut deductions for education, reduced the tax brackets, and simplified payment schedules.

Enduring Issues 12

With reduced **tax revenue** (income), budget **deficits** (imbalance from spending more than its income) soared. Reagan spent more to restore American military power. The government would up borrowing more and more (chart below). The Reagan Administration eventually drove the yearly deficits to record heights. Economists fear that deficits can send the American economy into a prolonged contraction. A serious recession hit the country hard in 1991.

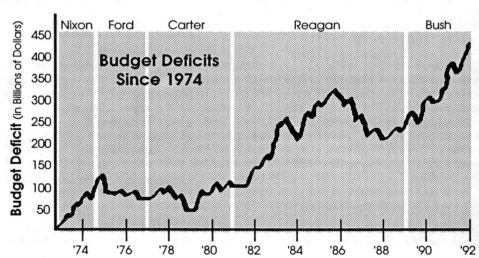

Budget Deficits Since 1974

The President and Congress share responsibility for the deficits. For political reasons, they disagree on where to make necessary cuts in Federal spending. The total Federal debt grew to over $2 trillion in the 1980's, and is now approaching $4 trillion.

The government annually spends well over $100 billion to pay the interest on the **national debt** (money borrowed to cover spending). Economists cannot agree about the seriousness of the situation. Some say the national debt can be reduced over time. Others predict a devastating collapse if the Federal government fails to control the deficit soon. In the 1980's, Congress made several weak tries for a balanced budget, but these efforts ended in failure.

Environmental And Civil Rights Policies

Enduring Issues
1

President Reagan appointed the controversial **James Watt** as his Secretary of the Interior. In trying to promote economic growth, the Interior Department weakened or cut laws giving protection to the environment, endangered wildlife, and national parks. The Reagan Administration also increased the number of permits for offshore oil drilling and strip minin, both potentially dangerous to the environment.

Administration officials claimed that, under the New Federalism, these policies shifted more responsibility to state agencies. Reagan officials said Federal regulations interfered with free enterprise and economic growth. They believed cutting them stimulated the economy. Outraged environmentalists railed against Watt and these policies. They undermined years of ecological work. They said resources, once destroyed, could never be reclaimed.

Reagan also reduced Federal involvement in civil rights. The individual states had to enforce busing, affirmative action, and prosecution of civil rights violations. Civil Rights leaders condemned this approach. They said it abolished progress since the *Brown* decision. Reagan officials argued that these programs broadened economic opportunity and benefited all Americans.

Social Issues: School Prayer And Abortion

Enduring Issues
4

Reagan's actions encouraged a growing conservative movement called the **New Right**. It tried to overturn controversial Supreme Court decisions of the Warren Court (page 240). The banning of prayer in public schools (*Engel*, page 240), and abortion-by-choice (*Roe v Wade*, 1973) were major targets of New Right activists. They also sought stricter censorship of pornographic materials and defeat of the Equal Rights Amendment (page 260).

President Reagan supported attempts to pass Constitutional Amendments allowing school prayer and banning abortions. These proposals did not receive the necessary two-thirds vote in Congress. However, Reagan did manage to reinforce the Supreme Court's conservative direction. He named Justice **William Rehnquist** to replace retiring Chief Justice Warren Burger in 1986. Reagan also named three additional conservatives to Court vacancies: Sandra O'Connor (the first woman to serve on the Court), Antonin Scalia, and Anthony Kennedy.

D. New Approaches To Old Problems
Problems Of Poverty In An Affluent Society

The uneven economic recovery and growth in the 1980's failed to check poverty. Some African Americans and members of other minorities achieved middle class status. However, a significant percentage of the population remained below the poverty line. Growing numbers of elderly people on fixed incomes found it increasingly difficult to survive.

Many critics blamed the problems on the New Federalism. Federal authorities cut many social welfare programs designed to help the poor. Supply-side economics gave tax breaks to the rich and expanded production but did not provide many new jobs. Investment in high tech industrial operations displaced workers.

Unemployment remained especially high among minorities in the inner cities. Federal cuts ended job retraining programs. The new job market provided few opportunities for those with limited education and skills. Poorly administered state programs and inadequate educational systems in many areas also share the blame.

The Reagan cuts forced many states to reduce the patients and staffs of mental institutions. Many former patients became homeless. Others could not afford expensive urban housing and turned to the streets. Drug and alcohol problems added to the problem. Local governments struggled with ways to find housing for the homeless.

Feast And Famine: The Farmers' Dilemma

During the 1970's, inflation drove farm prices to record levels. Demand for food expanded in overseas markets. (Repeated crop failures in the U.S.S.R. drove demand up.) Many farmers expanded. They borrowed for new machinery. In the 1980's, inflation slowed. Domestic and overseas demand fell. Farmers overproduction caused prices to drop.

These factors made it difficult for farmers to pay debts. Foreclosures and bank failures grew in the agricultural regions of the country. The government

Farming In The United States

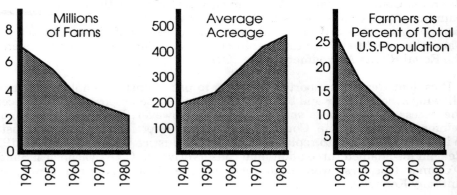

renewed farm subsidy programs, but they provided little relief. In addition, the scientific and technological developments of the Green Revolution affected farming. Increased crop yields result in greater production, but reduce the number of farms and farmers annually.

New Sources Of Immigration

From 1967-1990, American immigration underwent dramatic changes. The **Immigration Act of 1965** tried to deal with newcomers fairly. Congress gave preference to immigrants with needed technical and professional skills. Despite such regulations, millions of illegal aliens continued to enter the country. Most came in search of political freedom and economic opportunity.

To stem the tide of illegal entrants, Congress passed the **Immigration Reform and Control Act of 1986.** The law granted legal status to "illegals" in the country before 1982. However, it also provided strict punishment for employers who continued to hire illegal aliens. Supporters hoped that fewer people would enter if they could not find work. Critics claimed the law was unfair and discriminated against poorer Hispanic groups.

Growing Numbers Of Elderly

In 1900, people over 65 made up four percent of the nation's population. By 1960, the figure doubled. After the year 2000, it will double again. There are many reasons for the rise in the senior citizen population: improvements in medicine, better nutrition, safer working conditions, and the availability of hospital care.

By the year 2000, larger numbers of elderly will pressure the Social Security System to pay more benefits. Society will also have to find ways to deal with the problems of affordable medical care and housing for the elderly.

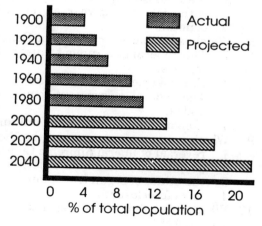

Percent Of Population Over 65

1900, 1920, 1940, 1960, 1980, 2000, 2020, 2040

Actual / Projected

% of total population (0, 4, 8, 12, 16, 20)

Questions

1   Supporters of supply-side economics argue that government should
    1   increase spending on social programs.
    2   give loans to struggling businesses.
    3   raise taxes to increase consumer spending.
    4   reduce taxes to stimulate business expansion.

2   An agricultural trend in the U.S. since 1940 has been the decrease in
    1   the use of machinery.
    2   the size of the average farm.
    3   the number of farms.
    4   the average yield per acre.

3   Farmers prospered during the 1970's because
     1   prices for farm machinery increase.
     2   the number of farms increased.
     3   the government raised tariff rates.
     4   global demand for farm products increased.

4   Which is a characteristic of current U.S. immigration policy?
     1   Special quotas allow more poor and uneducated to enter.
     2   Controlling illegal aliens.
     3   Exclusion of political refugees.
     4   Priority is given to Europeans.

5   In the last 50 years, the amount of food grown on U.S. farms increased, but the total number of farms decreased. These facts show that
     1   farms are larger and more efficient.
     2   imports make unnecessary the need for domestic agriculture.
     3   cities demand greater amounts of food.
     4   farm productivity is decreasing.

6   The annual budget deficits of the Federal government show that
     1   taxes are too high.
     2   consumers over-extend credit limits.
     3   the government spends more that it collects.
     4   Presidents spend money without Congressional approval.

7   By the next century, some critics fear that the U.S. Social Security System may not have enough funds because
     1   fewer workers now volunteer to give to the system.
     2   experts predict that the value of the dollar will decline.
     3   the Defense Department spends money set aside for Social Security
     4   with each passing year, a greater proportion of Americans collect benefits

8   Which is the basis for President Reagan's New Federalism?
     1   The Federal government must take more responsibility for citizens' welfare.
     2   Federal spending programs can solve economic problems.
     3   The Federal government should return some of its power to the states.
     4   Congress should check the military power of the President.

9   Which was a major concern of the "New Right" in the 1980's?
     1   reversal of liberal Supreme Court decisions
     2   proper nutrition for the elderly
     3   the ethics of organ transplants
     4   farm foreclosures

10   Which was a fear of opponents to the New Federalism and supply-side economics?
     1   Growing socialistic influences would undermine individual freedom.
     2   The government would ignore the poor and underprivileged.
     3   The power of the executive branch would expand again.
     4   Military preparedness would suffer.

11   Reagan's administration altered some environmental laws to
     1   provide more land for farmers.
     2   encourage economic growth.
     3   build military installations.
     4   prevent nuclear contamination

E. Renewed U.S. Power Image

Enduring Issues
9

Ronald Reagan promised to restore America's strength and pride on the international front. The President hoped to reverse some of the humiliations of the previous decade.

Central America And Caribbean: Debt And Stability

Reagan opposed communist expansion in Latin America. During the 1970's and 1980's, Cuba secretly supported Marxist revolutions in Nicaragua and Grenada. President Reagan denounced Nicaragua and Grenada as centers of Cuban—Soviet communist influence.

In 1983, Reagan ordered American military forces to join several Latin American nations to stop a communist coup in Grenada. U.S. forces occupied the island. and leaders set up a new, friendly government.

Reagan also struggled with Congress over sending aid to the Nicaraguan **contras** (anti-communist guerrilla group based in Honduras). U.S. aid was sporadic. However, international pressure forced the Nicaraguan government to hold elections. Nicaraguans voted outed Daniel Ortega's communist Sandinistas in 1990. The new democratic leadership under Violeta de Chamorro improved relations with the United States. Reagan also sent aid and advisors to El Salvador. The nation struggled to resist communist insurgents.

Many Latin American nations prospered during the 1970's. High oil prices caused national incomes to jump. Credit was easy, and many booming nations borrowed heavily from American banks. In the 1980's, declining oil prices, reduced demand, and greater global competition caused income to drop. Many nations could not pay their debts. Brazil and Mexico owed over one hundred billion dollars. Argentina and Venezuela also owed tens of billions. Some nations threatened to default completely, which would have been disastrous for American banks. Eventually, most nations refinanced their loans at reduced interest payments. However, continued financial problems mean uneven payments and continued international banking problems.

Middle East: War And Hostages

In the 1980's, Lebanon's civil war between the Muslims and Christians continued. Israel, Syria, the PLO (Palestine Liberation Organization), and various armed Islamic groups entered the struggle. President Reagan sent Marine units to aid the U.N. peace-keeping efforts. In late 1983, Muslim extremists crashed bomb-laden trucks into the Marine headquarters, killing 241 U.S. servicemen. Warring Muslim factions also took Western diplomats, educators, and newsmen hostage at an alarming rate.

Through the 1980's, normal diplomatic channels failed, and the captors released only a few hostages. Tentative peace in Lebanon, and shifting relations in the Middle East helped most hostages regain freedom in 1991 and 1992.

"Get those stars in the right place!"

The war between Iran and Iraq dragged on until the summer of 1989. There was worldwide concern about the effects of the struggle on the vital Persian Gulf oil-production. Both sides bombed of oil tankers to hamper petroleum shipments. President Reagan sent American naval forces to the area in 1987. Other European nations followed the American lead and sent forces to the Gulf region. U.S. Navy ships escorted oil tankers of friendly Kuwait. Reagan arranged for the tankers to fly the American flag while passing through the region. Iranian attacks on the reflagged tankers nearly brought the U.S. into the war.

Terrorism

While relatively few terrorist attacks occurred within the United States, Americans traveling abroad experienced violent episodes in the 1980's. Muslim extremists, backed by the PLO, Libya, or Iran, committed terrorist acts throughout Western Europe. Terrorists bombed a Berlin disco, massacred civilians Rome's airport, and hijacked a TWA plane, holding the passengers hostage for two weeks. A brutal killing of an American took place when terrorists took over the Italian cruise ship *Achille Lauro*. In 1988, 270 died (mostly Americans), when Libyan backed extremists blew up a Pan Am jet over Scotland.

Terrorists usually evaded capture, but U.S. jets managed to capture the *Achille Lauro* terrorists as they escaped. Reagan had U.S. planes strafe terrorist supporter Muammar Quaddafi headquarters in Tripoli.

Drug Trafficking

During the 1980's, there was a steady increase in the quantity of illegal drugs entering the United States. Several foreign governments routinely allowed illegal drug shipments to leave their countries. President Bush traveled to Columbia and met with several Latin American leaders. He pledged to aid efforts to stem the flow of drugs from their Latin American sources.

American law enforcement officials in most communities failed to halt the flow of drugs. FBI anti-crime task forces and drug enforcement units joined police from local areas. Federal agencies worked together to stop drugs from entering the U.S. President Reagan also sponsored drug-testing of Federal employees, a trend which has since spread to private industry.

Enduring Issues 12

F. Trade Imbalance And Divesting

U.S. foreign trade experienced a mounting deficit mounted in the 1980's. A **trade deficit** means the value of imports exceeds exports. Essentially, money flows out of the country. Domestic demand slumps, production slows, and jobs disappear. The deficit grew alarmingly in the 1980's. Reasons for this included:

- a high value for the dollar made imports less expensive and American exports more costly
- lower production costs in foreign nations drove many American manufacturers out of business
- "dumping" of excess products by foreign nations in the U.S.
- trade barriers set up against U.S. products by other nations
- exceptionally high prices of foreign oil in the early 1980's

Japan: Trade Imbalance

Japan exported a flood of autos, cameras, and electronic equipment to the United States. President Reagan was usually an advocate of free trade (no restrictions). However, in the mid-1980's Reagan placed import quota restrictions on some Japanese goods.

The restrictions were too weak to alter the trade deficit. Foreign companies simply cut profits to stay competitive in America. The big foreign automakers (VW, Honda, Toyota) skirted the restrictions. By building auto plants in California, Kentucky, Ohio, Pennsylvania, and Tennessee, they sell their cars here and avoid tariff and quota restrictions.

U.S. consumers benefited from the greater choice of goods at lower prices. However, American workers faced unemployment as domestic producers cut back or ceased production. Reagan and Bush resisted pressure for stronger retaliation against foreign governments. They feared an international trade war, hurting all nations.

United States And South Africa

South Africa's **apartheid policy** (racial separation by law) continued to make relations a thorny problem. Over 70% of South Africa's population is black, yet they are second class citizens. Apartheid restricts their living and working conditions. It limits their civil and voting rights. Throughout the 80's, the white government continued to resist reforms. This led to many violent confrontations.

Nearly all nations condemned apartheid. Some Americans believed that all U.S. based corporations should cease operations in South Africa until the government ended the inequality. They urged stockholders of corporations doing business in South Africa to **divest** (sell off their stock) as a form of protest. Some demanded that the U.S. government sever trade relations to force the abandonment of apartheid.

Others believed that it was best for American corporations to stay in South Africa. These foreign companies were more likely to treat blacks as equals and provide economic opportunity. The Reagan and Bush administrations imposed limited economic sanctions on South Africa, but resisted demands to end all ties.

In 1990, the South African government freed African National Congress leader **Nelson Mandela** after 28 years in prison. A new white minority government headed by **F.W. de Klerk** gradually repealed many apartheid restrictions. In early 1992, a 68% victory in a referendum by white voters encouraged de Klerk, Mandela, and other black leaders to end racial inequality and expand suffrage.

U.S. Returns To Debtor Status

By the mid 80's, trade deficits and other economic conditions caused the United States to become a debtor nation. For the first time since World War I, the U.S. owed more money to others than others owed to it.

Enduring Issues 12

Answers to the problem perplexed the government. Many economists felt the annual Federal budget deficit caused the problem. Some proposed cutting the budget, raising taxes, devaluing the dollar, and restricting trade. These actions were unpopular with the public, and their net effect on the debt problem was uncertain.

G. United States - Soviet Relations

President Reagan opposed the 1970's policy of détente. He took a strong position against Soviet expansionism. He promoted rebuilding U.S. military strength as a deterrent. He spent billions researching the **Strategic Defense Initiative** (nicknamed "Star Wars"). Star Wars' supporters claimed the high tech defensive shield could be built to keep out enemy missiles.

During his first term, Reagan's "hard-line" anti-communism led to a deterioration of relations between the two superpowers. He soundly criticized the shooting down of a Korean airliner which strayed into Soviet airspace, the imposition of martial law in Poland, and Soviet involvement in the war in Afghanistan.

Gorbachev

By Reagan's second term, three Soviet leaders had died. Relations improved in the mid-1980's when **Mikhail Gorbachev** emerged as the Soviet leader. He started economic (*perestroika*) and constitutional (*glasnost*)reforms at home. He reduced the Soviet military presence in Eastern Europe, and allowed the Soviet satellite countries greater autonomy. These reforms ushered in a wave of political upheavals in Eastern Europe and the Soviet Union starting in 1989.

The reforms also signaled a new relationship between the superpowers. Both sides sought new agreements on arms control. Reagan and Gorbachev held frequent summits, and the two superpowers moved vigorously toward significant arms reduction, especially in Europe.

U.S. — Soviet relations improved in the mid–1980's when **Mikhail Gorbachev** emerged as the Soviet leader. Gorbachev instituted economic and constitutional reforms at home. He reduced the Soviet military presence in Eastern Europe and allowed the Soviet satellite countries more autonomy, setting off a wave of political upheavals. U.S. Presidents held frequent summits with the Soviet leader, and the two superpowers began to move vigorously toward arms reduction in Europe.

Gorbachev

"If the President looks for me, tell him he can reach me at 1-800-TEHERAN"

H. Iran-Contra Affair

In 1986, Congressional investigators revealed that members of the Reagan Administration illegally sold weapons to Iran. The officials then diverted the funds to the contra rebels in Nicaragua. Federal courts convicted several White House staff members.

> Enduring
> Issues
> **10**

Congress criticized President Reagan for his unawareness of the illegal activities. President Reagan came under severe criticism for his lax administrative procedures and lack of knowledge about the activities of his staff. Reagan broke no laws, but many critics questioned his lack of control over staff and policy makers.

> Enduring
> Issues
> **1**

Questions

Base your answers to questions 1 through 3 on the quotation below and your knowledge of social studies.

"The United States government should restrict the importation of foreign goods. If we stop importing, Americans will buy American products; that will help the economy and keep the dollar at home."

1 Which group would be most supportive of the above statement?
    1   multinational corporations   3   international bankers
    2   wheat farmers   4   labor unions

2   One way to implement the ideas expressed in the quotation is
     1   expanding loans to foreign nations.
     2   adopting a policy of laissez faire.
     3   raising protective tariffs.
     4   negotiating a reciprocal trade pact.

3   Which is an argument against the policy in the quotation?
     1   It reduces the benefits of international trade.
     2   It validates the laws of supply and demand.
     3   It makes the U.S. less self-sufficient.
     4   It raises the living standards of other nations at our expense.

4   Why do Many nations consider Castro's foreign policy a threat to international peace?
     1   It hinders a free flow of trade among Latin American nations.
     2   It blocks trade with capitalist countries.
     3   It claims to be the major power of the Third World.
     4   It aids Marxist revolutions in Africa and Latin America.

5   South Africa's apartheid policy resulted in
     1   improved conditions for all citizens.
     2   increased dependence on foreign capital.
     3   promotion of world brotherhood and peace.
     4   unjust racial policies.

6   Which is an advantage of a decline in the value of a nation's currency overseas?
     1   Dependence on foreign trade declines.
     2   Exports increase and imports decrease.
     3   Travel abroad is cheaper.
     4   Personal income taxes are reduced.

7   The Reagan Administration became involved in of Latin American affairs because the U.S.
     1   must to protect the rights of U.S. citizens living abroad.
     2   trade in that area is strategically vital.
     3   was in deep financial debt to the nations there.
     4   wished to block communist expansion.

8   Why do authorities find it difficult to prevent terrorism?
     1   Terrorists are better armed than the American military.
     2   Terrorists usually outnumber law-abiding citizens.
     3   Some countries give aid and sanctuary to terrorist groups.
     4   Under U.N. agreement, terrorists have diplomatic immunity.

9   Which was the goal of the Strategic Defense Initiative (Star Wars)?
     1   Drive the Soviets out of Eastern Europe
     2   Protect the U.S. from nuclear missile attack
     3   Settle human rights violations inside the U.S.S.R
     4   Intensify the U.S. military presence in Europe

10   Despite Constitutional authority to control foreign policy, President Reagan had to gain Congressional approval to
     1   cut off diplomatic relations with Libya.
     2   condemn the Soviet invasion of Afghanistan.
     3   invite Gorbachev to the U.S.
     4   send financial aid to the Nicaraguan contras.

VI. America In The 1990's
A. The Bush Presidency

Reagan's Vice President, **George Bush** (Texas) defeated Democratic nominee, Governor Michael Dukakis (Massachusetts) in the 1988 Presidential election. Bush became the first sitting Vice President elected to the Presidency since New York's Martin Van Buren in 1836.

In foreign affairs, the breakup of the Soviet Union and downfall of communism in Eastern Europe ended a generation of Cold War. This presented the Bush Administration with new opportunities and new problems. In the Middle East, Iraq's dictator, Saddam Hussein, began a new threat to the stability of the region.

In domestic affairs, Bush supported most of Reagan's programs. However, he promised some changes. He promised greater emphasis on child care, education, and the war on drugs. Bush's domestic programs lacked vigor. They received lukewarm attention from the Democratic Congress. A recession in 1991-1992 caused high unemployment (7-8%). Economic uncertainty, budget deficits, the S&L crisis (see below) and Congress' own bank scandals nearly stopped legislative activity in the 102nd Congress.

Bush followed the Reagan lead in appointing conservative justices to the Federal bench. Liberals, minorities, and some women's groups criticized these appointments. The Senate approved two Bush nominees to the Supreme Court (Justices Souter and Thomas) only after long and bitter debate.

George Bush

B. Domestic Issues
The AIDS Crisis

AIDS (Acquired Immuno-Deficiency Syndrome) will have an increasing impact on U.S. society in the 1990's. The Federal Center for Disease Control estimated over a million persons have contracted AIDS. It expects a quarter million new cases each year. More than 60, 000 people are dying each year from AIDS related disease. A vaccination against the HIV virus (human immunodeficency virus) eludes researchers. Education on HIV testing, safe sex, and avoidance of contaminated blood is currently the only defense. The infection is usually fatal. Many controversies surround the disease and its victims, including:

- methods of testing to prevent the spread of the disease

- payment for treatment of AIDS sufferers

- rights of confidentiality of individuals with AIDS vs. rights of those with whom they come in contact.

Savings And Loan Failures

Deregulation and lax enforcement of banking rules in the Reagan Administration led to unwise and sometimes dishonest banking practices. Federal investigators implicated several U.S. Senators and many federal and state officials in banking fraud.

By the early 1990's, hundreds of savings and loan associations went bankrupt. The **FSLIC** (Federal Savings & Loan Insurance Corporation) collapsed under the strain of paying off depositors and reorganizing troubled banks. Similar problems affected commercial and savings banks. The **FDIC** (Federal Deposit Insurance Corporation) paid billions to insured depositors of failed banks. Banking officials closed some banks, while others merged with healthier institutions.

To avoid a banking crisis such as that of the Great Depression years, Congress created the **Resolution Trust Corporation** (RTC). The RTC estimated the cost to taxpayers at over five hundred billion dollars before it solves the problem.

Health Care Problems

Affordable health care became a major issue in the 1990's. About half of America's workers receive some form of health insurance protection through their jobs. Government sponsored Medicare and veterans programs provide coverage to others. However, a significant number of individuals have no health insurance. A growing number of workers are losing protection because the high cost of medical care is making insurance too expensive.

Experts debate over the best way to provide affordable health care to all Americans. Some prefer expansion of current programs to cover the uninsured. Others call for a complete overhaul of the insurance system. They believe government should provide universal health coverage. Insurance companies, medical associations, pharmaceutical companies, and consumer advocates are all on different sides of the issue. Providing affordable medical care while containing costs remains an elusive goal.

C. Foreign Issues
The Persian Gulf Conflict

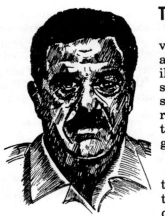

In August 1990, Iraqi dictator **Saddam Hussein** vowed to annex Kuwait. Saddam's well-equipped army quickly overran the tiny, oil rich country. Exiled Kuwaitis and leaders of other Persian Gulf states appealed to the U.S. for help. With Congressional agreement, Bush sent 500,000 troops to the region ("Operation Desert Shield"). He persuaded the U.N. Security Council to condemn Saddam's aggression and set up an economic blockade of Iraq.

Bush organized a **coalition** (alliance) of nations to block any additional Iraqi aggression. He intensified diplomatic pressure to force Iraq to withdraw from Kuwait.

Saddam Hussein

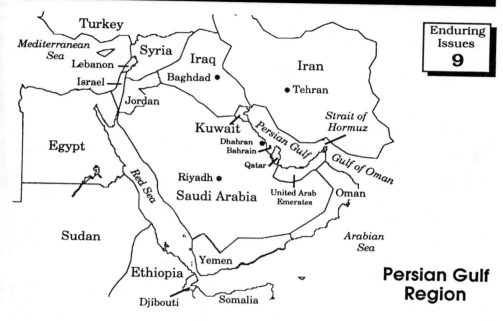

Turkey
Mediterranean Sea
Lebanon
Israel
Syria
Iraq
Baghdad
Jordan
Iran
Tehran
Egypt
Kuwait
Dhahran
Bahrain
Qatar
Persian Gulf
Strait of Hormuz
Gulf of Oman
Red Sea
Riyadh
Saudi Arabia
United Arab Emerates
Oman
Sudan
Arabian Sea
Ethiopia
Yemen
Djibouti
Somalia

Enduring Issues 9

Persian Gulf Region

By early 1991, the international pressure weakened Iraq, but Saddam stubbornly refused to negotiate. In mid-January, coalition air forces began intensive bombing of Iraqi positions ("Operation Desert Storm"). Iraq launched Scud missile attacks on Saudi Arabia and Israel. The delicate stability of the entire Middle East, with its vast strategic oil reserves, was in jeopardy.

After five weeks of the most intense bombing since WW II, Bush ordered ground forces into action. American-led coalition forces invaded southern Iraq, and Kuwait. In four days of fighting, the Iraqis suffered an estimated 100,000 casualties. Large segments of the Iraqi Army surrendered, and coalition troops liberated Kuwait. President Bush ordered a truce, but Saddam Hussein remained in power in Baghdad.

Some criticized U.S. interests in the region as unclear. There were accusations that Bush was protecting the interests of big oil companies. However, the nation as a whole was supportive. Unlike the Vietnam experience, there was no deep divisiveness among the people. The successful military action strengthened Bush's leadership for a time.

The Iron Curtain Falls

During the 1980's, Mikhail Gorbachev's *glasnost* (political) and *perestroika*, (economic) reform programs spread to the U.S.S.R's Eastern European satellites. Inside the **Iron Curtain**, demonstrations for democracy gained momentum. All the Eastern European nations (Poland, Hungary, Czechoslovakia, Rumania, Bulgaria, and Albania) saw their communist leaders ousted. Democratic governments and capitalist reforms began replacing communist systems. Gorbachev allowed the infamous Berlin Wall to be torn down and East and West Germany reunified in 1991.

Collapse Of The Soviet Union

Boris Yeltsin

Inside the U.S.S.R., Gorbachev's economic reforms floundered. He lost support among the Soviet people. Several republics (Ukraine, Lithuania, Latvia, Georgia, and Armenia) demanded greater freedom and self government.

In the summer of 1991, anti-reform Politboro members launched a coup against Gorbachev. While the coup leaders held Gorbachev prisoner in the Crimea, democratic resistance rallied around the Russian Federation President **Boris Yeltsin**. Yeltsin led public demonstrations defying the coup. Red Army commanders and troops refused to fire on their own people. The coup disintegrated. Gorbachev returned and resigned from the Communist Party. However, it was clear he had to share power with Yeltsin.

Gorbachev recognized the independence of Estonia, Latvia, and Lithuania in the Fall of 1991. Ukraine, Belarus, and other republics prepared to leave the Soviet Union. Yeltsin took action on his own. He negotiated a loose military and economic alliance of republics called the **Commonwealth of Independent States** (CIS). After this, Gorbachev resigned.

The **CIS** became a loose alliance of former Soviet republics with little central control. Critics compare it to the weak United States government under the Articles of Confederation (1781-1789). CIS members agree on very few policies.

*The Soviet "Ship of State," the U.S.S.R. sinks into history,
as the former S.S. Republics are set adrift into the "Sea of Uncertainty."*

The U.N. gave Russia the Security Council seat that belonged to the U.S.S.R. Other republics applied for U.N. membership. Yeltsin continued the Gorbachev's pattern of foreign policy. He shares some control of the nuclear arsenal with other CIS members. However, the republics oversee the bases on their soil. Questions about the military, foreign policy, currency, and trade relations remain unanswered.

New governments in Ukraine, Belarus, Kazakhstan and other republics are unstable. Civil struggles plague the Transcaucasian and Central Asian regions. In some areas, the Communist Party retains power. Economic chaos concerns leaders. Market systems work on trial and error. It takes time before consumers and producers achieve price equilibriums. In Russia, the government ended many price controls, but unstable currency and shortages of most products exist. Some Russians demanded a return to the communist system. Some nations sent humanitarian aid. Yeltsin seeks more. Private foreign investors lack confidence to risk long term investment in the region's development.

Most people in the United States supported the changes. The downfall of the Soviet Union meant an end to the Cold War and reduced defense needs. However, as political upheaval threatened stability of the new nations, Americans expressed concern over future control of the thousands of nuclear warheads.

Questions

1 Which best portrays President Bush conservative views?
   1   efforts to abolish most environmental legislation
   2   appointment of Federal judges
   3   use of troops against Saddam Hussein
   4   desire to meet with Russian leader Yeltsin

2 How did the banking crisis of the late 80's and early 90's avoid the widespread public panic as experienced in the 1930's?
   1   By 1985, most people invested their savings in stocks.
   2   Foreign banks intervened to rescue the American banks.
   3   Federal deposit insurance protected most depositors.
   4   The Federal government nationalized the banking system.

3 For Americans, the collapse of the Soviet Union resulted in
   1   a significant decrease in activity of the American Communist Party.
   2   a large increase in the number of Soviet immigrants to the United States.
   3   reductions in American military expenses.
   4   a trade surplus from increased exports to the former Soviet Union.

4 Which act of President Bush stems from the military experience in Vietnam a generation ago?
   1   Asking Congress for a formal declaration of war against Iraq.
   2   Calling for a draft with no exemptions for Operation Desert Storm.
   3   Mobilizing public support for the military operation in the Middle East.
   4   Calling for government control of all defense industries during wartime.

5   Health care concerns in the 1990's centered around
  1   national standards for licensing all doctors.
  2   the shortage of hospitals in urban areas.
  3   the inability of researchers to find a cure for cancer.
  4   available and affordable health care for all.

Essays

1   Describe how each of the methods listed below helped to bring about black equality in the United States. Cite a specific situation in which the method was used and discuss the extent to which the method was successful in bringing about changes. [5,5,5]

Methods
- civil disobedience
- use of the court system
- federal legislation

2   Development of trends often cause problems for societies.

Trends
- Decreasing involvement of the Federal gov't. in domestic affairs
- Decreasing percentage of workers in manufacturing jobs
- Increasing use of computers
- Increasing percentage of older people in the population
- Increasing proportion of women in the work force
- Increasing problems of overproduction on farms
- Increasing concern about the environment

Select THREE of the trends listed above. For EACH ONE chosen, discuss why the trend developed the United States, a problem that has arisen from the trend, and an attempt to deal with the trend. [5,5,5]

3   Many problems today can be considered global problems because their existence in one country or area affects other areas.

Problems
- Terrorism
- Scarcity of energy resources
- Poverty
- Spread of nuclear armaments
- Population explosion

Choose THREE of the problems listed above. For EACH problem chosen, discuss why it is a global problem and an attempt to deal with it. [5,5,5]

4 Show how each of the following government actions has resulted in significant change in the United States society since the end of World War II. Use a different topic for each. [5,5,5]

Actions
- Constitutional amendments
- Supreme Court decisions
- Congressional legislation

5 The provision of equal educational opportunity for all people is a goal of the United States society that has not yet been achieved. Listed below are several groups which have been denied equal educational opportunities at some time in the last 40 years.

Groups
- African Americans
- Native Americans
- Women
- Handicapped
- Immigrants

a Select THREE of the groups. For each one chosen, discuss a problem the group faced in attempting to achieve equal educational opportunity. Use a different problem for each group. [9]

b For ONE of the groups chosen in "a," show how a specific action helped the group. [3]

c For ONE of the groups in part a, discuss a specific reason why the group has not achieved equal educational opportunity. [3]

Issue	Explanation	Example of Enduring Issue
Enduring Issues 1 **National Power - limits and potentials**	Increases or decreases in the amount of power the Federal government exercises.	• Attempts to settle slavery issue by compromise (1820-1860) p. 44 • Federal power in the Great Depression (1929-1939) p. 167-78 • L. B. Johnson & the Great Society(1964-1969) p. 253-63
Enduring Issues 2 **Federalism - the balance between nation and state**	Federalism is the system of power being divided and shared among a strong central gov't. and smaller ones such as 50 states.	• Power over interstate commerce: *Gibbons v. Ogden* (1824) p. 31, *Munn v. Illinois* (1876) p. 83, Interstate Commerce Act (1887) p.83 • School Desegregation: *Brown v. Bd. of Ed.* (1954) p. 241, Montgomery Boycott (1955) p. 242 • Reagan's "New Federalism" p. 287
Enduring Issues 3 **The Judiciary - interpreter of Constitution or shaper of public policy**	Question of Supreme Court's role in broadening governmental power. *Judicial activists* believe court can initiate new policies through decisions. Advocates of *judicial restraint* believe elected officials are source of new policy.	• Marshall Court: *Marbury v. Madison (1803)* p. 26, *McCulloch v. Maryland.(1819)* p.41 • Dred Scott Decision (1857) p. 45 • Race relations: *Plessy v. Ferguson* (1896) p. 67, *Brown v. Bd. of Ed.* (1954) p. 240 • Public morality: *Roe v. Wade* (1973) p. 261
Enduring Issues 4 **Civil Liberties - the balance between the government and the individual**	Basic national civil liberties are found in Bill of Rights & applied to states under the 14th Amendment. They are not absolute. The courts have modified & reinterpreted them in many controversial decisions.	• Clear and present danger rule: *Schenck v. United States* (1919) p.147, *Korematsu v. United States* (1943) p. 201
Enduring Issues 5 **Rights of the Accused and Protection of the Community**	Individual rights in arrest & trial situations are found in Bill of Rights & 14th Amendment, but controversies arise over security of society relative to personal protections.	• Lincoln and Wilson and wartime security p. 48-9, p. 146-47 • McCarthy Era hearings, the Oppenheimer case p. 219 • Warren Court: *Gideon v. Wainwright* (1963) p. 240, *Miranda v. Arizona* (1966) p.240
Enduring Issues 6 **Equality - its definition as a Constitutional value**	14th Amendment guarantees "equal protection of the laws" to all citizens, but actualization of idea has been un-even, controversial.	• Civil Rights Movement (1950-70) p. 241-42, p. 248-49, p. 258-59 • Native-American search for equality (1960's-1970's) p. 261-63

Issue	Explanation	Example of Enduring Issue
Enduring Issues 7 **The Rights of Women under the Constitution**	Legal status of women has changed as a result of laws and amendments.	• Suffrage Movement and the 19th Amendment p. 116, p. 128 • Women's Liberation Movement and struggle for equal rights p. 260
Enduring Issues 8 **Rights of Ethnic and Racial Groups under the Constitution**	Minorities struggle against inequality because of uneven interpretations of the 14th Amendment.	• Nativism and Immigrants p. 98, p. 100 • Civil Disobedience and Dr. King p. 249
Enduring Issues 9 **Presidential Power in Wartime and Foreign Affairs**	Executive power grew as America's role in the world changed.	• Wilson: World War I, and Versailles p. 147-50 • FDR: Edging into World War II, and Summit diplomacy p. 193, p. 207 • Johnson, Nixon & Vietnam p. 265-9
Enduring Issues 10 **Separation of Powers and the Capacity to Govern**	Constitutional relationship of three equal branches is in constant change.	• Congressional and Presidential rivalry over Reconstruction p. 54-56 • FDR and Court Packing p. 177 • Nixon and Watergate p. 276-77 • Reagan Iran-Contra Hearings p. 297
Enduring Issues 11 **Avenues of Representation**	Continuing expansion of American democracy through the 15th, 17th, 19th, 23rd, 24th, 26th Amendments and other voting rights legislation.	• Direct election for U.S. Senators p. 21 • Expansion of suffrage for blacks, women, and youth p. 68, p. 128, p. 276
Enduring Issues 12 **Property Rights and Economic Policy**	Economic function of government has placed Constitution in the center of controversies concerning public welfare v. accumulation of private wealth.	• Hamilton's policies and financial structure p. 29 • Government control of business: anti-trust acts p. 129, consumer protection p. 124-25 • Economic Collapse and New Deal Reform: Social Security, labor rights, deficit spending p. 171-78 • Supply side economic policies under Reagan p. 288
Enduring Issues 13 **Constitutional Change and Flexibility**	Capacity of American government to meet and deal with new situations	• "Elastic Clause" in operation p. 19, p. 41 • "Unwritten Constitution:" political parties, Cabinet p. 28-29 • Judicial Review & key precedents p. 25, p. 30

Constitutional Amendments

Bill of Rights (1791), 17-19

1st Amendment	-	freedom of speech, press, assembly, free exercise of religion **(*4)**, 218, 240, 273
2nd Amendment	-	right to bear arms, Unit 1
3rd Amendment	-	forbids government from quartering of troops in peacetime, Unit 1
4th Amendment	-	protects against unwarranted search **(*4&5)**, Unit 1
5th Amendment	-	protects rights of accused to due process; eminent domain**(*4&5)**, 45, 218, 240, 262
6th Amendment	-	protects rights to fair trial & counsel **(*4&5)**, 240
7th Amendment	-	right of jury trial in civil cases, Unit 1
8th Amendment	-	protects against cruel punishment & excessive bail **(*4)**, Unit 1
9th Amendment	-	rights not specifically mentioned still exist, Unit 1
10th Amendment	-	powers not specified in Constitution left to states and people, 22, 56, 67

11th Amendment	(1795)	-	suits by citizens of one state against a particular state must be heard in the latter's courts not in Federal ones.
12th Amendment	(1804)	-	electors must use separate ballots for President and Vice-President, 23
13th Amendment	(1865)	-	abolishes slavery, 54-55, 116, 241
14th Amendment	(1868)	-	defines citizenship, application of due process, and equal protection **(*6 &7)**, 18, 54, 56, 60-61, 66-67, 82, 126, 240-41, 248
15th Amendment	(1870)	-	defines citizens' right to vote **(*11)**, 54, 66, 68, 241
16th Amendment	(1913)	-	allows Federal income tax, 127
17th Amendment	(1913)	-	direct popular election of United States Senators **(*11)**, 21
18th Amendment	(1919)	-	manufacture, sale, importation, & transportation of alcoholic beverages forbidden in U.S. (repealed by 21st Amend.) **(*1)**, 122, 164
19th Amendment	(1920)	-	right of women to vote **(*7&11)**, 117, 128, 165
20th Amendment	(1933)	-	redefines term of President & sessions of Congress, 20, 23, 25
21st Amendment	(1933)	-	repeal of prohibition amendment(18th), 164
22nd Amendment	(1951)	-	limits Presidential terms, 23, 177
23rd Amendment	(1961)	-	provides presidential electors for District of Columbia **(*11)**, 24
24th Amendment	(1964)	-	abolishes poll taxes: Fed. elections **(*11)**, 259
25th Amendment	(1967)	-	defines succession to presidency & disability of president, 23, 25, 276, 279
26th Amendment	(1971)	-	eighteen year-old citizens may vote in Federal elections **(*11)**, 276

Index — Glossary Of Terms

Abolitionism (anti-slavery movement), 44, 116

Abortion (see Roe v. Wade, 1973), 261, 273, 289

Acculturation (immigrants adapting to their new culture), 99-100

Acheson, Dean (Sec'y. State for Truman), 209-10, 212, 215, 219

Achille Lauro (terrorist incident), 293

Acid rain (airborne industrial wastes in precipitation), 230, 283

Adams, John (2nd President), 8, 10, 13, 32, 186

Adams, John Quincy (6th President; Sec'y. State for Monroe), 34

Addams, Jane (Progressive social worker - Hull House), 121

Adirondack Preserve (conservation, NYS), 126

A.F.L.-C.I.O. (national labor unions), 239

Affirmative action programs (special hiring quotas for minorities), 259

Afghanistan (and U.S.S.R. invasion), 284-85

African immigration, 98

African National Congress (prior to 1990, an outlawed revolutionary group in South Africa that opposes the apartheid government rule), 295

Age of Reason (European Enlightenment's impact on U.S. gov't.), 8

Agent Orange (toxic chemical defoliants used in Vietnam War), 266

Agnew, Spiro (Vice-President under Nixon; resigned), 276

Agrarian protest (see Grange, Populist Party), 108-09

Agricultural Adjustment Act (AAA- New Deal farm relief), 173-74, 176

AIDS (Acquired Immuno-Deficiency Syndrome) 299

Aknesasne Indian Peoples (treaty disputes with NYS), 263

Alaskan North Slope pipeline, 281

Albany Plan of Union, 9

Alcatraz (occupation by Native American protest groups), 262

Alger, Horatio (stories of industrial era heroes), 79, 94

Alliance for Progress, 250

Allied Powers in WW I (Britain, France, Russia, and Italy), 143, 159

Amendment process (means of changing the U.S. Constitution), 17-18 [*13]

American Bar Association, 118

American Communist Party, 179

American Dream, 159, 167

American Expeditionary Force (AEF - U.S. in World War I), 145, 156

American Federation of Labor (AFL), 84, 175

American Independent Party, 2741

American Indian Movement (AIM - civil rights group), 261-63

American Liberty League, 175

American Party - "Know-Nothings" (anti-immigrant nativist group), 98

American Protective Association (anti-immigrant nativist group), 100

American Railway Union (see Pullman Boycott), 85

American Revolution, 116

American Telephone and Telegraph Corporation (AT&T), 78

American Women Opposed to the League of Nations, 148

American Woolen Company, 85

Americanization Process (see acculturation), 99
Amnesty Act (1872 - pardon for Confederate officials), 67
Anarchists (advocating the abolition of all government), 164
Anglo-Conformity (see acculturation), 100
Anglo-Saxon (dom. ethnic/cultural group in U.S. legal system), 8-9, 97
Annual Percentage Rates (APR - see Truth-in-Lending Act), 272
Anti-Klan Law, 67
Anti-Federalists (opponents of U.S. constitution), 15
Anti-Red crusade (see McCarthyism), 218
Anti-trust suits (stopping monopolies), 125, 160 [*12]
Antiquities Act (1906), 126
Apartheid policy (So. African policy of total separation of races), 294
Apollo 11 (moon landing), 255
Appalachian Mountains, 105, 254
Appeasement Policy (European countries conciliatory to Hitler), 191
Arab-Israeli War (of 1973), 280
Arbitration (third party dictates settlement in labor-management or
    international disputes), 86
Argonne Forest (WW I battle), 145
Aristotle (ancient Greek political philosopher influenced American ideas on
    government), 8
"Arkies" (victims displaced by 1930's Dust Bowl disaster), 178
Armour, Philip (meat-packing industry), 78
Articles of Confederation (first U.S. government), 9
"Arsenal of Democracy" (FDR pre-WW II speech), 193
Assembly-line patterns, 160
Assimilation (to take in immigrants and make them part of society), 97, 100
Astair, Fred (Hollywood entertainer), 179
Aswan Dam (Egypt), 236
Atlantic Charter (World War II aims for U.S. and Britain), 194
Atomic Energy Commission, 202, 219
Atoms for Peace program (Eisenhower era), 235
Axis Alliance (Italy, Germany, and Japan in World War II), 189, 193

Baby boom (post WW II population explosion), 244-45
Backlash (negative reaction to Civil Rights Movement of 1960's), 60
Baker v. Carr (1962) - (Congressional apportionment), 240, 259
Bakke v. the Regents of the University of California, (1978) (questioned use of
    racial quotas in affirmative action programs), 259
Bank Holiday (FDR action suspending banking operations), 172
Bank of the United States (Jackson's controversial veto), 29-30, 41
Banking, regulation of, 172 [*12]
Baron de Montesquieu (ideas influential in U.S. Constitution), 8
Baruch, Bernard (financier, managed WW I economy), 156
Batista, Fulgencio (Cuban dictator overthrown by Castro), 250
Battle of the Bulge (WW II battle), 197
Bay of Pigs in Cuba (CIA attempt overthrow Castro), 250
Begin, Menachem (Prime Minister of Israel, 1970's), 284
Bell, Alexander Graham (inventor: telephone), 78
Bell Telephone Company, 78
Bellamy, Edward (early socialist reform work: *Looking Backward*), 210

Belligerent nations (countries at war), 189

Berlin Blockade and Airlift (Cold War confrontations), 211

Berlin Wall (divides communist and free sections of Germany), 251

Bessemer, William (steel processing), 58, 71-72

Bethune, Mary McLeod (1930's civil rights activist), 178

Bicameral legislature (lawmaking body divided into 2-houses), 11, 26

"Big Bull Market" (wild speculation before 1929 stock market crash), 161, 167

"Big Four" (U.S., U.S.S.R., Britain, and France WW II alliance), 235

Big government, 176

"Big Stick, The" (Theodore Roosevelt's foreign policy), 139 [*9]

"Big Three" (U.S., Britain, & U.S.S.R.-World War II summit meetings), 200

"Big Three" of American auto industry (Ford, GM, and Chrysler), 244

Bilingual Education Act, 282

Bills of attainder (laws declaring persons guilty without right of trial), 22

Bill of Rights (1791 - U.S. Constitutional amendments 1-10 stating
    fundamental personal rights of citizens), 17-19, 26

Birth control (see Margaret Sanger), 121

Birthrate (high increase in period after WW II, see baby boom), 230

Black Codes (Southern state restrictions on blacks after Civil War), 54

Black Friday (financial panic of 1869), 62

Black Muslims (religious group; advocates of separatism, 1960's), 257

Blacklist (lists of undesirable employees), 218

Blackmun, Harry (U.S. Supreme Court justice; Roe decision), 273

Blacks (and racial discrimination), 60, 67, 121, 202

Black Panthers (militant civil rights group), 257

"Black Power" (militant civil rights activities), 256

Blitzkrieg (lightning war; Nazis - WW II), 193

Blue-collar jobs (industrial workers), 225

"Blue Eagle" symbol (see National Industrial Recovery Act), 174

Bolsheviks (communists led revolution in Russia), 101, 145, 147, 164

Bond rallies (World War II home front), 199

Bonus Army (veterans' march on Washington 1932), 169

Border states (slave states that did not rebel against the Union), 48

Boston Manufacturing Company, 72

Boxer Rebellion, The (anti-imperialist movement in China, 1900), 136

Boycott (organized abstaining from doing business with someone to force
    them to accept a condition), 242

Bradley, Omar (U. S. commander WW II), 197

"Brains Trust, The" (New Deal advisors), 172

Brandeis Brief (form of legal presentation containing social statistics), 126

Brandeis, Louis (U.S. Supreme Court - judicial activist), 126

Bread and Butter Unionism" (AFL's idea of negotiating for basic conditions
    of employment - hours, safety, wages), 84

Brinkmanship" (confrontational Cold War diplomacy; see Dulles), 234

Brooklyn Bridge, 91

Browder, Earl (U.S. communist leader), 179

Brown v. Board of Ed. of Topeka (1954 - school desegregation), 67, 240-41,
    248, 256, 258-59

Bryan, William Jennings (Populist/Democratic leader), 109, 164

Buchanan, James (15th U.S. President during Southern secession), 45

Budget cuts, Reagan (see supply-side economics), 288

Buffalo, 33

Bullitt, William (first U.S. ambassador to U.S.S.R.), 188
Bunche, Ralph (1940's civil rights leader, U.N. activist), 178
"Bundle of compromises" (structure of U.S. Constitution), 14
Bureau of Indian Affairs (BIA) ("termination policy" of '50's), 261, 273
"Bureaucracy" (power concentrated in an immense hierarchy of governmental
    agencies), 26, 176
Burger Court (judicial restraint), 273
Burger, Warren (Chief Justice - advocate of judicial restraint), 273
Burns, George & Gracie Allen (radio/TV entertainers), 179
Burr, Aaron, 26
Bush, George (41st President), 299
Business cycle (the ebb and flow of demand which causes the economy to
    expand and contract at intervals), 82, 167

Cabinet, The (collective heads of the various executive agencies functioning
    as an advisory group to the President), 29
Calhoun, John C. (Sen., Vice-Pres., Southern rights spokesman), 32, 40, 276
Call of the Wild (Jack London story - realism of industrial era writers), 94
Cambodia, 266, 274
Camp David Agreements (Egyptian-Israeli accords), 285
"Camp David, Spirit of" (Eisenhower-Khrushchev agreements), 285
Campaign (candidates running for political office), 23
Canada, 33, 45, 107, 193, 267, 283
Captains of industry (big business leaders of the industrial era), 78
Carmichael, Stokley (militant civil rights leader), 256
Carnegie, Andrew (steel industrialist), 79, 91
Carnegie Steel Company (monopoly), 77, 85
Carter, Jimmy (39th President), 275, 279-86
Cartels (internat'l trade organizations with monopolistic power), 70
"Cash and carry" amendment (pre-WW II neutrality acts allowed sale of U.S.
    arms only if buyers paid cash and picked up themselves), 189
Castle Garden (early U.S. immigration depot in NYC), 97
Castro, Fidel (communist leader of Cuba), 250
Cattle Kingdom, The, 106
Caucus (gathering of political leaders often to choose candidates), 23
Cease-and-desist orders (court orders to stop a group from continuing an
    action - an injunction), 128
Central America and Caribbean, 292
Central Intelligence Agency (CIA) (U.S. espionage), 203, 250
Central Pacific Railroad Company, 62
Central Powers (Austria, Germany, Turkey WW I alliance), 143, 156
Century of Dishonor, A by Helen Hunt Jackson (1881), 106
Challenger space shuttle, 282
Chamberlain, Neville (British Prime Minister, c. 1939), 191
Chambers, Whittaker (accused communist spy), 218
"Charleston" (1920's dance), 164
Chateau-Thierry and Belleau Wood (WW I battles), 145
Checks and Balances (grants of power to various branches to keep other
    branches within specific bounds), 15 [*10]
Chemical dumping, 230
Cherokee Nation (confiscation of land - forced removal by U.S. gov't), 43

Cherokee Nation v. Georgia (1830), 43, 105
Chicago Democratic Convention (1968), 268
Chicago, Milwaukee & St. Paul Railway Co. V. Minn. (1889), 108
Child labor (industrial era exploitation of children), 84
China Policy, 216, 236, 274-75
China trade, 135
Chinese Exclusion Act,1882 (immigration restriction), 101
Chinese Nationalists (Party of Chiang Kai-shek), 216, 236
Chiang Kai-shek, China's Generalissimo, 200, 215, 236, 274
Chrysler bail-out, 281
Churchill, Winston (British WW II Prime Minister), 194, 200, 209
Cigarette advertising banned, 272
Civil disobedience (intentional public breaking of laws deemed unjust), 249
Civil liberties (basic personal rights and protections in U.S. Constitution, Bill
    of Rights, and other amendments), 19, 48, 148 [*4 & 5]
Civil Rights Acts, 242, 258, 260
Civil Rights Cases, 61
Civil Rights Commission (1947), 204, 242
Civil Rights Movement, 241-42, 248-49, 258-59 [*6]
Civil service (distribution of governmental jobs through fair competitive
    examinations; see Pendelton Act), 117
Civil War, 46-49, 54, 58-60
Civil Works Administration (CWA), 1933-34, 173
Civilian Conservation Corps (CCC)1933-1942, 173
Clay, Henry (compromiser of the sectionalist era), 32, 40-41, 44
Clayton Anti-Trust Act (1914), 127
Clean Air Act of 1970 254, 272
"Clear and present danger rule" (government can suspend civil liberties in
    time of national stress), 147, 201 [*4]
Clemenceau, Georges (French WW I leader), 148
Cleveland, Grover (22nd and 24th President), 24, 26
Clinton, DeWitt, 26
Clinton, Gov. George (NY anti-Federalist leader), 13, 15, 26
Closed-shops (workplaces where a union must be joined as a condition of
    employment), 202
Coal, 77, 125
Coalition (an alliance of small groups to achieve majority control of a
    government or organization), 202
Co-ed schools and colleges (admit men and women), 165
Collective bargaining (labor-management negotiation), 83, 86, 175
Collective security, 212
College enrollments (increase as result of baby boom), 244
Cold war (intense competition between international powers), 201
Colonial experience as influence on U.S. constitutional government), 9
Columbia Space Shuttle, 281
Command economy (basic economic decisions by government), 156
Commerce clause (Constitutional grant of power to Congress to regulate trade
    among various states), 120
Commerce Department (1903), 124
Committee on Public Information (World War I), 157
Committee on the Status of Women (springboard for Women's Liberation
    Movement), 260

Committee on Un-American Activities (U.S. House of Representatives investigations on communism and subversive activities), 218

Commonwealth of Independent States (CIS – joint economic/military administration body for former Soviet republics, 1991), 302

Communications, 78

Communism (follows basic Marxist brand of socialism), 101, 179, 265

Compromise, The Great (Constitutional Convention), 14

Compromise of 1850 (slave v. free territory), 44

Computers, 225

Concurrent power (power shared by several divisions of gov't.), 21

Confederate States of America, 45

Confederation (union of sovereign states retaining power locally), 9, 11

Confederacy, 9, 11

Conglomerates (large, highly diversified corporations), 226

Congress, The (federal legislative body of U.S.), 20-22

Congress of Industrial Organizations (CIO-major nat'l labor union), 175

Congress of Racial Equality (CORE- civil rights organization), 256

Congressional elections of 1946 (Republicans returned to power after 12 years), 202

Congressional Power (17 delegated powers plus elastic clause), 21

Consensus (general agreement of large group), 164

Conservation (attempts to preserve the natural environment), 125

Conspicuous consumption (lavish indulgence by the very rich seen as a duty of status), 92, 118

Constitution (fundamental law of United States), 9, 14-15, 20-27

Constitution- Comparison to New York State Government, 26

Constitution - Comparison to Other National Governments, 27

Constitution - The Preamble (basic statement of Am. political values), 14

Constitutional Convention (1787), 9, 13-15

Consumer Products Safety Commission, 271 [*12]

Consumers' Union (consumer rights advocates), 86

Consumerism (movement - laws protecting buyers rights), 124, 163, 271 [*12]

Containment policy (post World War II foreign policy to restrain growth of communism on global scale), 203, 210-13, 215-17 [*9]

Continental Congress (American Revolution), 8

Coolidge, President, 151, 160

Cooperatives (farmers organization to combat high railroad shipping charges), 84, 107

"Copperheads" (Lincoln's critics), 48

Coral Sea (WW II battle), 197

Corporate bail-outs (see bail-out), 281

Corporations (business organization drawing capital from large group of share holding owners), 72-73

Coughlin, Charles E. (critic of FDR), 179-80

Council of National Defense, 156

Counterrevolution (reactionary group seeking to undo revolution), 250

"Court Packing Plan" (FDR's influence in Supreme Court), 177 [*10]

Cox, James M., 170

Craft unions (labor organizations for skilled trades), 83-84

Crane, Stephen (realist author of industrial era works: Red Badge of Courage; Maggie, Girl of the Streets), 94

Credit Mobilier Scandal (Grant era railroad scandal), 62

Creel, George (WW I propagandist), 157

Crime of '73 (refusal of gov't. to increase silver coinage issue), 109
"Criminal syndicalism" laws (laws making support for violent protest and anarchism illegal), 146
"Critical Period" (1781 to 1789 - near collapse under Articles of Confederation), 11
Crop lien system (mortgaging future crops to pay for present expenses), 59
Crosby, Bing (singer-actor, radio, cinema, TV), 177, 179
"Cross of Gold" (William. J. Bryan's 1896 campaign speech in favor of free silver), 109
"Crow, Jim" (nickname for Southern segregation laws), 60, 67, 121, 241
Cuba (as U.S. protectorate after Spanish American War), 137-38
Cuban Problems (Kennedy v. Castro conflicts), 249
Cuban-Soviet alliance (see missile crisis), 250
Cultural pluralism (society made up of a blend of numerous cultures), 100
Cultural paternalism (groups viewing themselves as superior seeking to act as guardians of others), 100, 133
Cumming v. County Board of Education (1899 - Southern school segregation upheld), 61
Cycle of demand (see business cycle), 167
Czechoslovakia, 191

Dartmouth College v. Woodward (1819, legal sanctity of contracts), 31
Davis, Jefferson (President of Confederate States, Civil War), 45
Dawes General Allotment Act (1887 - attempt to distribute lands and resettle Native Americans), 106
Debs, Eugene V. (industrial era labor union and Socialist Party leader), 85-86, 147
Debtor nation (one that owes others), 295
Declaration of Independence, 10-11, 44, 116
Declaration of Sentiments, 116
De Klerk, F.W. (President of South Africa), 295
De facto segregation (racial separation by informal means - as in neighborhood settlement patterns), 258
Deficit spending (going into debt to cover expenses), 176, 281, 288 [*12]
DeGaulle, Charles (French WW II leader), 193, 200
De jure segregation (racial separation by legal statutes), 60, 67, 241, 258
Delegated Power (specifically assigned in Constitution), 21, 41
Demagogue (political agitator), 179
Demobilization (disband military structures), 158
Democratic-Republicans (early U.S. political party organized by Jefferson & Madison), 30
Dennis v. U.S. (questioned freedom of speech rights for communists), 218
Department of Defense (formed, see National Security Act of 1947), 203
Department of Transportation (DOT), 255
Department stores (mass marketing - Wanamaker's, Macy's), 73, 91
Depression (severe economic contraction characterized by low production and high unemployment), 159
Depression, The Great (1929-1941), 167
Desert Shield and Storm, Operations (see Persian Gulf Conflict), 300
Destroyers-for-Bases Deal (WW II aid to Britain), 193
Detente (a relaxation of tense diplomatic relations between adversaries), 275

Developing nations of Asia, Latin America, and Africa (U.S. policy), 228
Dewey, Thomas E. (NY prosecutor, Governor, Presidential contender), 26, 172, 204
Diaz, Porfiro (Mexican dictator), 140
Dien Bien Phu (battle in which French were forced out of Vietnam 1954), 265
Dime novels (inexpensive adventure stories popular c.1900), 94
Direct taxes (taxes levied directly on the individual), 22
Disabled (see Rehabilitation Act of 1973), 282
Displaced persons (World War II refugees), 208
Disputed election of 1876, 66
"Divine mission" (see U.S. imperialism), 133, 135
Dix, Dorothea (crusader for rights of mentally ill, prison reform), 117
"Domino theory" (feeling that if one small country in a region succumbs to communist insurgency, others will quickly fall), 234, 266
"Do-Nothing 80th Congress," 204
Dos Passos, John, (1920's author, work: U.S.A.), 165
Douglass, Frederick (anti-slavery leader), 44
"Doves" (anti-war activists, pacifists), 267-8
Draft amnesty program (drop charges against Vietnam draft evaders), 279
Draft (military conscription), 48, 146-7, 193, 267, 279
Drago Doctrine (anti-American interventionism in Latin America, 1903), 140
Dred Scott v. Sanford (slaves declared property), 45
Drieser, Theodore (industrial era realist, work: Sister Carrie), 94
Drug trafficking, 294
Drug Summit, Latin American (1989, held in Columbia with President Bush and the leaders of several Latin American nations), 294
DuBois, W. E. B. (civil rights leader; founder of NAACP), 61, 121, 256
Due process (proper and fair admin. of legal procedures), 18, 60-61, 164, 201
Due process clause (14th Amendment), 55, 60-61, 67, 108
Dukakis, Michael (Gov. of Mass., unsuccessful Pres. candidate), 297
Dulles, John Foster (Sec'y. State for Eisenhower), 234, 266
Dust Bowl, The (natural disaster on Great Plains in 1930's), 177
Duties (tariffs - taxes on imported goods), 161

Earth Day (ecology movement rally, 1970's), 272
Economic contraction (decline - see depression and recession), 158
Economic imperialism (seeking to use economic power to dominate another nation or group), 132
Economic sanctions (using economic actions such as protective tariffs or boycotts as weapons), 295
Edison, Thomas Alva (practical use of electricity, inventor), 78
Education, changing patterns and reforms, 84, 260
Eisenhower Doctrine (containment in Middle East), 237
Eisenhower, Dwight D. (34th President, WW I supreme commander-Europe), 196, 234, 266
El Alamein in Egypt (WW II Allied victory), 197
"Elastic clause" (Article I sec. 8,18 gives Congress power to stretch meaning of its assigned powers to meet new situations), 19, 21, 29, 41, 48 [*13]
Elastic currency (measures which allow government to increase or decrease money supply to stabilize the economy), 128
Elderly, care of, 254, 291

Electors of the President (same as Electoral College), 24, 42

Electricity, applications to daily life in industrial era, 78

Elementary and Secondary Education Act of 1965, 254

Elevated railroads ("Els" - urban mass transit), 90

Eliot, T. S. (disillusion after WW I - poems, The Hollow Men and The Waste Land), 165

Elkins Act (1903 - expanded power of Interstate Commerce Commission), 124-25

Ellis Island (industrial era immigration depot in NY harbor), 97

Emancipation Proclamation (Lincoln declares slaves free in Confederate States), 49

Embargo (action by gov't. or group halting economic activity), 193

Embargo Act (Jefferson's attempt to keep U.S. from being drawn into Napoleonic wars), 32

Emergency Banking Act (1933 - New Deal attempt to stop bank closings), 172

Emergency Quota Act (1921 - discriminatory immigration quotas begun), 101

"Eminent domain" (under the 5th Amendment personal property can only be taken by the government if fair compensation is made to the owner), 261

Engel v. Vitale (1962 - school prayer decision), 240, 273, 289

Enlightenment thought (an influence on framers of Constitution), 8

Enumerated Power (specifically assigned in Constitution), 21

Environmental concern (ecology movement), 125, 272, 289

Environmental Protection Agency (EPA), 272, 282

Equal Pay Act (women's rights), 260

Equal protection of law (see 14th Amendment), 18, 67

Equal Rights Amendment (women's rights), 117, 261 [*7]

Equality in the workplace (see women's rights), 261 [*7]

"Era of Good Feeling" (c.1820's), 39

Erie Canal (transportation improvement), 33

Escapism (lively forms of entertainment-cinema, radio- helped ease the problems of the Great Depression), 179

Espionage Act of 1917 (to limit WW I dissent), 146

Ethnic distribution c. 1870 (cultural or national groupings), 97

Europe, 143-45, 210

European Coal and Steel Community, 210

European Economic Community, or "Common Market", 210

European Imperialism and Missionary Impulse (19th century struggles for control of Asia, Africa, & Pacific), 133

European Parliament, 211

European Recovery Act (aid after WW II; The Marshall Plan), 210

Evans, Walker (photographer of 1930's life), 179

Evers, Medgar (assassinated civil rights leader), 249

Excise Tax (tax on luxuries), 29

Ex parte Milligan (1866- limits of Presidential power in wartime), 48

Exports, 58

Ex post facto laws (retroactive legislation- making something a crime after the act has been committed-forbidden in Constitution), 22

Executive privilege (presidents refusing to share information with Congress or the courts by claiming it would compromise either national security or the principle of separation of powers; see Nixon v. U.S.), 277

Fascist (aggressively nationalistic totalitarian gov't. system), 179, 186

Fascist Italy, (WW II; see Mussolini) 186

"Fair Deal" (domestic program of Truman), 204

Fair Labor Standards Act (1937- Federal minimum wage, other labor rights), 175 [*12]

Fall, Albert (Sec'y. Interior for Harding; Teapot Dome scandal), 160

Farm problems, 107-09, 161, 290

Faubus, Governor Orville (defies Brown desegregation order in Little Rock crisis), 242

Federal Bureaucracy (see bureaucracy), 26

Federal Deposit Insurance Corporation (FDIC- New Deal bank depositor's insurance), 175, 300

Federal Emergency Relief Act (FERA- New Deal relief measures), 172

Federal guarantees (payment for crops under AAA), 174

Federal Housing Administration, 174

Federal Reserve Board, 160, 175, 281, 288

Federal Reserve System (banking regulation, reorganization), 128, 175

Federal Savings and Loan Insurance Corporation (FSLIC), 300

Federal Theater Project (New Deal aid for arts), 178-79

Federal Trade Commission, 127-28, 160

Federal union (see federalism), 9

Federalism (a union with a strong central government with some power shared among smaller components), 9, 15 [*2]

Federalist Papers, The (essays in defense of new U.S. Constitution by Hamilton, Jay, and Madison, 1788), 15

Federalists (supporters of the Constitution in ratification struggle, also early U.S. political party founded by Hamilton and John Adams), 15, 30, 40

Female emancipation (broadening of social, political, and economic status of women), 165

Ferdinand, Austrian Archduke Franz (assassination causes WW I), 225

Fiber optics, 225

Filibuster (blocking legislation in U.S. Senate by exercise of the privilege of unlimited debate), 121, 248

Fillmore, Millard (13th President, NY), 26

"Fireside Chats" (FDR's radio messages to the nation), 177

First Continental Congress, 10

Fisk, Jim (industrial era businessman), 62

Fitzgerald, F. Scott (post WW I disillusion; works: This Side of Paradise, The Great Gatsby, and The Beautiful and the Damned), 165

Fletcher v. Peck (Federal courts can review state laws), 31

Flynn, Elizabeth (Populist/Progressive reform leader), 86

Foraker Act (Puerto Rican colonial status, 1900), 137

Force Acts (early anti-KKK laws, c. 1870), 67

Ford, Gerald R. (38th President), 276-77, 279-81, 286

Ford, Henry (developed U.S. mass market for autos), 77, 79, 160

Formosa Strait (Chinese-American relations strained, c.1960), 236

Foster, William Z. (leader of American Communist Party), 179

Four Freedoms Speech (FDR voices U.S. WW II aims), 194

Fourteen Points (Wilson's plan for post-WW I world peace), 148

France, 32, 147-50, 186, 191, 207, 265

Franco, Francisco ("El Caudillo" - Fascist dictator of Spain, 1937-73), 189

Franklin, Benjamin (American colonial leader and diplomat), 9, 10
Free French government (WW II resistance to Nazi occupation), 193
Free Soil Party (anti-slavery political group), 45
Free trade (no national restrictions international commerce), 133
Freedom Riders (civil rights voting registration campaigns of 1960's, 242
French and Indian War (1756-63: French driven out of North America), 10
French-Indochinese War (1946-54), 265
Frick, Henry C. (industrial era steel magnate), 85
Friedan, Betty, work: The Feminine Mystique (Women's Liberation
    Movement), 260
Frontier closing (1890), 103, 109
Fugitive Slave Law (required capture and return of runaway slaves), 44

Gandhi, Mohandus (non-violent independence leader in India), 249
Garfield, President (20th President - assassinated), 117
Garland, Hamlin (agrarian nostalgia, work: Son of the Middle Border),94
Garland, Judy (film actress, singer in The Wizard of Oz), 179
Garrison, William Lloyd (abolitionist), 44
Garvey, Marcus (civil rights-separatist leader in 1920's), 121
Gas tax (federal charge for usage), 171
General Agreement on Tariffs and Trade (GATT), 133
General Assembly (see United Nations), 207
General Electric Company, 78
Geneva Disarmament Conference of 1932-34, 188
Gentlemen's Agreement (1907- restrictions on Japanese immigration), 101
George, David Lloyd (British WW I leader), 148
George, Henry (industrial era philosopher/author), 110
Geographic population distribution (c.1870), 103
Germany, 70, 136, 143-45, 149, 159, 186, 191-92, 195, 200-01
Gerry, Eldridge (Constitutional Convention delegate), 13
Ghetto (racial / ethnic settlement area), 99
"G.I. Bill of Rights" (aid for returning veterans and post WW II economic
    recovery), 203, 244-45
Gibbons v. Ogden (1819 - upheld Congressional power to regulate interstate
    commerce), 31 [*2]
Gideon v. Wainwright (1963- rights of poor to legal defense), 240, 273 [*5]
Gilded Age (Mark Twain's name for Industrial Era), 76-77, 91, 118
Glass-Steagle Banking Act (sets up federal bank examinations, FDIC), 175
Glasnost (U.S.S.R. internal political and economic reform program initiated
    by Gorbachev), 296
Glenn, John (astronaut), 251
Gold market, 62
Goldman, Emma (WW I radical dissenter), 147
Goldwater, Barry (conservative President- candidate, 1964), 253, 271
Gompers, Samuel (founder American Federation of Labor), 84, 156
Good Neighbor Policy (FDR improves of U.S.-Latin American relations), 187,
    250
Gorbachev, Mikail (Soviet leader), 296, 301-302
GOP (name for Republican Party), 287
Gospel of Wealth, The (Andrew Carnegie's social philosophy), 91
Gould, Jay (railroad financier of industrial era), 62

Government controlled banking system (see Fed. Reserve reform), 128
Government regulation, 83
Graduated income tax (individual taxes scaled to income; see 16th
     Amendment), 127
Grain sales to the Soviets, 284
Grandfather clauses (South's voting restrictions on former slaves), 60
Grange laws (see Grange Movement), 83, 107
Grange Movement (agrarian reform group), 107
Grant, Gen. Ulysses S. (18th President, Civil War commander), 49, 62
Great Atlantic & Pacific Tea Company, The (mass marketing of food products
     - the supermarket), 73
Great Britain, 27, 32, 135-36, 143-45, 150, 186, 191, 207, 265
Great Compromise (settled issue of representation in the national
     legislature), 14
Great Depression (1929-1941), 167-87 [*1]
Great Society program (Lyndon Johnson's social welfare reforms), 253-63,
     268, 271 [*1]
Greeks (classical influence on American constitutional government), 8
Green Revolution (agricultural technological movement), 228, 290
Grenada invasion (Reagan administration intervention in Caribbean), 292
Gross National Product (GNP) (statistical compilation of all nation's
     production of goods and services in a given year), 167, 169, 176
Guadalcanal (WW II battle), 197
Guerrilla warfare (small band hit-and-run fighting tactics), 265-66
Gulf of Tonkin Resolution (Congressional permission for Johnson to escalate
     troops in Vietnam), 266, 269

H-Bomb, 235

Hamilton, Alexander (Sec'y of Treasury for Washington), 13, 15, 29, 30, 82
Hamilton's Financial Plan (establishes credit for the new nation), 29 [*12]
Hancock, John (American Revolution leader), 13
Handicapped Americans (see Rehabilitation Act of 1973), 282
Harding, Warren G. (29th President - died in office), 150-51, 158, 159-60, 160
Harriman, Averill (diplomat of WW II and Cold War era, ambassador to
     U.S.S.R., Governor of NY), 209
Harris, Joel Chandler (post Civil War southern author, work: Uncle Remus
     Stories), 94
Harte, Bret (western frontier journalist, work: Luck of Roaring Camp), 94
Haudenosaunee Union (see Iroquois Confederacy), 9
"Have v. Have Not" Nations, 231
Hawaii, acquisition of, 136, 265
"Hawks" (pro-war groups), 268
Hawley-Smoot Act (1930), 161, 168
Hay, John, (Sec'y of State for McKinley and Roosevelt), 136, 265
Haymarket Affair (violent labor confrontation of 1880's), 84
Hayes, Rutherford B. (19th President), 66
Hayne, Robert Y. (U.S. Senator, defender of states rights concept), 40
Haywood, William "Big Bill" (leader of International Workers of the World),
     86, 147
Hearst, William Randolph (newspaper publisher- c. Spanish American War,
     see yellow journalism), 94

Helsinki Accords (agreements on human rights and defense perimeters of Europe, 1975), 283

Hemingway, Ernest (post WW I author; work: The Sun Also Rises), 165

Hepburn Act (1906 - continues civil service reforms), 125

Henry, Patrick (American Revolutionary leader), 13, 15

"Hesitant Colonialism" (reluctance of U.S. to become an imperialist world power), 137

Higher Education Act (expanded minority rights, opportunities), 260

Highway Beautification Act (improvement of national landscape), 254

"Hippies" and "flower children" (1960's counter culture/youth revolt), 267

Hirohito, Japanese Emperor (role as WW II leader), 198

Hiroshima (US nuclear bombing), 198

Hiss, Alger (sensational McCarthy Era spy case), 218

Hitler, Adolph (German leader), 186, 191, 194, 197

Ho Chi Minh (Vietnamese leader), 265-66, 268

Hoffa, James R. (controversial Teamster's Union president), 240

Holding companies (form of monopoly), 83

Hollywood (as form of escape from realities of Great Depression), 179

"Holocaust, The" (Nazi treatment of Jews in WW II), 201

Home front (domestic World War II efforts), 199-200

Home Owners Loan Corp. (HOLC - New Deal housing assistance), 174

Home rule (local political control for a political unit), 67

Homestead Act (1862 - free land to induce settlement of the American West), 103

Homestead Strike (1892- Bloody strike against Carnegie Steel Co.), 84

Homesteaders (western pioneer settlers), 103, 106

Hoover, Herbert (31st President), 156, 161, 167-71, 188

Hopkins, Harry (domestic and foreign policy aid to FDR), 171-73, 178

Hot Line (direct telephone line between U.S. and U.S.S.R. to be used to prevent accidental nuclear war), 251

House of Representatives, U.S., 20-22

Housing and Urban Affairs, Department of (HUD), 255

How a Bill Becomes a Law (chart), 22

How the Other Half Lives (1890- analysis of urban poverty, Jacob Riis), 120-21

Howe, Louis (political manager and aide to FDR), 171

Huckleberry Finn (1884- M. Twain novel of Mississippi boyhood), 94

Hull, Cordell (Sec'y of State to FDR), 187

Hull House in Chicago (1889- settlement house), 121

Human rights (see Helsinki Accords and Carter foreign policy), 283

Humphrey, Hubert (Senate leader & Vice Pres. under LBJ), 253, 268, 271

"Hundred Days, The" (whirlwind New Deal legislation of first three months of FDR's administration in 1933), 172

Hungarian Revolution (1956), 236

Hussein, Saddam (Iraq's dictator) (see Persian Gulf Conflict), 300

Hydrogen bomb, 219, 235

I Have a Dream speech, Dr. King (height of civil rights era), 249

Illegal aliens (as an immigration problem), 290

Immigration, 97-101, 104, 245, 290

Immigration Act of 1965, 245

Immigration, general reasons for, 97
Immigration Reform and Control Act of 1986, 290
Immigrants, 84, 97-101, 104, 109
Impeachment (accusation of, and removal procedures for officials), 23
Impeachment Proceedings against Nixon, 277
Impeachment of Andrew Johnson, 56
Imperialism (see "Hesitant Colonialism"), 132-41
Implied power (not specific but broadly hinted at in Constitution) (see elastic
    clause), 19, 21, 41, 48
Inauguration of President, 25
Indentured servants (immigrant contract laborers, colonial era), 97-98
Indian Removal Act of 1830 (see Cherokee nation), 43, 105
Indian Reorganization Act (Wheeler Act), 1934, 178
Indian reservations, 104
Indian Service scandal (1876), 62
Indian Territory (Oklahoma), 43, 105
Indian Wars (1850-1890), 105
Industrial - Colonial Connection, 132
Industrial nations, 228
Industrial revolution (production becomes mechanized), 70-113
Industrial unions, 83, 84
Industrial Workers of the World, (IWW), (see Wobblies), 86, 147
Inflation (significantly rising prices not balanced by rising productivity),
    271-72, 281
Initiative (Progressive reform in some states which requires action by
    legislature on demand of certain percentage of electorate), 124
Injunction (court order forbidding an action - employers use injunctions to
    avoid strikes by unions), 85
Inland Waterways Act (1907- conservation measure), 126
Installment plan (paying for an item in small graduated payments over
    extended period), 163
Insular Cases (1901- governing overseas territories), 138
Interlocking Directorates (form of monopolistic management), 82
"Intolerable Acts" (1774 - cause of American Revolution), 10
International Brotherhood of Teamsters (transportation union), 240
Internationalism (foreign policy in which full participation in world affairs is
    sought), 132-151
International Ladies Garment Workers Union (ILGWU), 84
International Longshoremen's Association, 240
International Peace Efforts, 207
Interstate Commerce Act (regulates power of railroads), 83, 108, 160
Interstate Commerce Commission (ICC), 108, 124-25
Interventionism (interfering with the internal affairs of another sovereign
    nation), 188
Investment capital (resources used to expand business operation), 228
Iran, 209, 283, 285, 286, 293
Iran-Contra Affair (activities in Reagan administration), 297
Iran-Iraq War, 293
Iranian hostages (Carter administration), 285
Iron Act (1750 - colonial industry curtailed by British), 71
Iron Curtain (separation of Eastern and Western Europe into communist and
    free nations), 209, 301

Iroquois Confederation (loose union of the five nations in NY), 9
Isolationism (foreign policy which seeks to keep a nation in neutral and unaligned status), 186, 187
Iwo Jima (bloody WW II battle in Pacific), 198

J ackson, Andrew (7th President), 40, 42, 105 [*2]
"Jacksonian Democracy" (expansion of popular participation in gov't), 42
Japan, 70, 101, 135, 145, 150, 161, 189, 191, 193, 195, 197-98, 201, 215, 265, 294
Jay, John, 15, 32
Jay's Treaty (1794- kept infant U.S. out of war), 32
Jazz music (in Roaring Twenties), 165
Jean-Jacques Rousseau (Enlightenment influence on U.S. gov't.), 9
Jefferson, Thomas (colonial leader, 3rd President), 8, 10, 13, 15, 29, 30, 32, 186
Jefferson's Embargo (1807- attempt to keep U.S. out of Napoleonic Wars), 32
Jews, 97-100, 201 [*9]
Jim Crow laws (see de jure segregation), 60, 67, 121, 241
Job Corps (Great Society employment retraining & youth assist.), 254
Jodl, Field Marshall Alfred (German WW I commander), 197
Johnson, Andrew (17th President, impeached), 54-56
Johnson, Lyndon B. (36th President), 248, 253-268, 266-69, 271 [*9]
Joint Chiefs of Staff (combined U.S. military command), 203
Joint Defense Board, 193
Jones Act (1917- U.S. citizenship for Puerto Ricans), 137
Judicial activism (initiating public policy through court decisions with broad interpretations of constitutional law), 45, 240 [*3]
Judicial Branch, The (Federal court structure), 25-26
Judicial restraint (curtailing the courts practice of broadening public policy), 273 [*3]
Judicial review (Supreme Court power to declare acts of Congress, President, Federal agencies or state laws and actions unconstitutional), 25, 30 [*13]
Judiciary Committee of the House of Representatives, 277
Jungle, The (1906- muckraking Sinclair novel led to Meat Inspect. Act), 120
Justice Department, 29

K anawake Mohawk Indian peoples (and NY treaty violations), 263
Kellogg-Briand Pact in 1928 (attempt to outlaw aggression among nations), 151
Kennan, George F. (State Dept. official in Truman administration, worked out containment policy), 209
Kennedy, John F. (35th President, assassinated), 248-252, 266
Kennedy, Robert F. (U.S. Attorney General for JFK, presidential advisor, U.S. Senator from NY, Presidential candidate, 1968, assassinated), 258, 268
Kent State (anti-Vietnam protest, students killed), 267, 274
Kerner Commission (investigated race riots of late 1960's), 257
Keynsian economics (permanent role for government in stabilizing the economy), 202

Keynes, John Maynard (British economist: General Theory on Employment, Interest, and Money), 171

King George III of England (and American Revolution), 11

King, Jr., Martin Luther (1950's-'60's non-violent civil rights leader, assassinated), 242, 249, 256, 258 [*8]

Kinzua Dam on the Allegheny River, 262

Kissinger, Dr. Henry (presidential advisor and Sec'y of State for Nixon, Ford), 274-75, 284

Knights of Labor (early national labor union), 84

Knox, Henry (Sec'y of War for Washington), 29

"Know-Nothings" (anti-immigrant organization), 98

Korean Conflict, 215-17, 234

Korematsu v. U.S. in 1944 (suit against internment of Am. citizens of Japanese ancestry during WW II, see "clear & present danger" rule), 201 [*4]

Khomeini, Ayatollah Rullah (Islamic fundamentalist leader of Iranian Revolution), 285

Khrushchev, Nikita (Soviet Leader, 1956-63), 235, 250-51

Kremlin (center of governmental power in U.S.S.R.), 235

Ku Klux Klan (racist, nativist group), 60, 66, 100, 164

Kuwait (U.S. protection of oil tankers in Persian Gulf), 293

Labor (difficulties in industrial era), 59

Labor mediation (settling disputes by a neutral third party), 125

Labor rights, 175 [*12]

Labor unions (early), 83

Labor unrest, 239

Ladies' Home Journal, 84

LaFollette,Robert (Progressive leader), 121, 123

LaGuardia, Fiorello (reform mayor of NY, 1930's and '40's), 172, 175

Laissez-faire (economic philosophy which seeks to minimize governmental interference with the economy), 79, 82, 91, 160-61

"Lame-duck" President (weakness of retiring president between election and inauguration of new president; see 20th Amendment), 45

Landon, Alf (Kansas Gov., 1936 Presidential candidate), 175

Landrum-Griffin Labor Management Reporting and Disclosure Act (1957 - control of corruption in labor unions), 240

Landslide vote (an overwhelming victory in an election), 177

Lange, Dorothea (photographic artist- Depression images), 179

Lansing, John (NY anti-Federalist leader), 13, 15

Laos, 266

Latin America, 138-141, 187

Lawrence Textile Strike (1912), 85

League of Nations (post-WW I world peace organization - U.S. never joins), 148-50, 186, 190

Lebanon, 237, 293

Lee, Richard Henry (VA anti-federalist leader), 10-11

Leisure, 94

Lend-Lease Act by Congress (U.S. aid to Britain v. Nazis), 193, 196

Lethal pesticide residues, 230

Letter From a Birmingham Jail (statement of philosophy of social justice by Dr. Martin Luther King), 249

Levittown, 245

Lewis, John L. (leader of United Mine-workers Union), 175

Lewis, Sinclair, novels: Main Street, Babbitt, Elmer Gantry, 165

Liberator, The (anti-slavery newspaper), 44

Lighter metals and alloys, 225

Limited economic opportunity (treatment of ex-slaves), 60

Limited government (political principle of restricting gov't power), 15

Lincoln, Abraham (16th President, Civil War leader), 45-49, 54 [*2, 5]

Line-item veto (executive power to reject parts of a bill), 26

Literacy tests (citizens must pass exam to vote - used to keep poor blacks from voting in the South), 60

Literacy Test Act (1917 - immigration restricted to those literate in native language), 101

Little Rock Crisis (desegregating Southern schools), 242

Livingston, Robert (NY colonial leader, diplomat, Federalist supporter), 15

Lloyd, Henry Demerest (Progressive era social philosopher), 110

Lobbying (groups organized to influence legislation), 31

Lochner v. New York (1905- constitutionality of working conditions legislation questioned), 126

Locke, John(English Enlightenment political philosopher, influenced U.S. Constitutional framers heavily), 8, 10

Lockout, 86

Lodge, Henry Cabot (Senate leader- anti-League of Nations), 149-50

Log-rolling (legislators voting on a bill as a favor to other legislators), 29

London International Economic Conference (1933), 187

London, Jack (realist writer of early 1900's works: The Seawolf, Call of the Wild), 94

Long, Huey (controversial Louisiana Senator, opponent of FDR), 179

Looking Backward (1888- socialist proposal of industrial era philosopher Edward Bellamy), 110

Loose constructionists (believers in broadly flexible interpretations of the Constitution's ideas), 21, 29

Louisiana Purchase (first major addition of territory constitutionality of addition questioned), 33-34 [*1]

Love Canal, (NY toxic waste controversy), 282

Lowell System (textile manufacturing in early U.S.), 72

Lower-class (the poorest level of economic or social status), 90

Loyalty oaths (citizens being required to pledge allegiance to their country as a condition of employment), 218

Loyalty Review Board (Truman era anti-communist program), 217

Luck of Roaring Camp, The (Brete Harte frontier story), 94

Lusitania (controversial torpedoing of British ship as cause for U.S. entry into WW I), 144

MacArthur, Douglas (WW II Pacific commander, military governor of occupied Japan, Korean War commander fired by Truman), 169, 197, 201, 215, 217

Macy, R. H. (originator of early department store), 73, 91

Madison, James (4th President, major force at Constitutional Convention), 8, 13, 15, 17, 30, 32, 40, 186

Maggie, Girl of the Streets , (Stephen Crane story of industrial era), 94

Mahan, Alfred(advocate of U.S. sea power c. 1890's), 132
Mail order (mass retailing - Montgomery Ward and Sears-Roebuck), 73
Malcolm X (Black Muslim minister, civil rights activist, assassinated), 254
Manchuria (site of Japanese aggression in 1930's), 187
Mandela, Nelson (leader of African National Congress; imprisoned for 28
    years in South Africa), 295
Manhattan Project(develops atomic bomb), 198
"Manifest Destiny" (emotional drive for territorial expansionism), 33, 135
Mao Zedong (communist Chinese revolutionary leader), 215
Marbury v. Madison (established power of judicial review), 26, 30 [*3]
"Margin" (buying stocks on some sort of credit arrangement), 161
Marines (ordered to Lebanon), 293
Market economy (system wherein key decisions are made through the
    interaction of buyers and sellers), 156, 167
Marshall Field (originator of early department store), 73
Marshall Plan (European post WW II economic recovery), 210
Marshall, George C. (WW II commander, Sec'y of State and Defense under
    Truman), 196, 210, 216
Marshall, John (Chief Justice, U.S. Supreme Court), 26, 31, 41, 105, 210
Marxist Bolsheviks, see Bolsheviks, 101, 145, 147, 164
Mass advertising campaigns, 160
Mass communication media (emerge with urban-industrial era), 118
Mass transportation (emerge with urban-industrial era), 76
Massive retaliation (to deter aggression by major military buildup), 234
Materialism, 94
Maximum Employment Act of 1946 (adopts Keynsian economics), 202
Maximillian Affair (Europeans attempt takeover of Mexico, 1860's), 137
McCarthy, Eugene (U.S. Senator, 1968-72 anti-war Presidential candidate),
    268
McCarthy, Joseph R. (U.S. Senator, controversial anti-communist crusade in
    early 1950's), 219
McCarthyism (widespread, emotional, and largely ungrounded leveling of
    communist subversive activities), 219 [*5]
McCarran Internal Security Act (anti-subversive), 218
McClure's (early popular magazine, carried muckraker articles in
    Progressive Era), 94, 120
McCulloch v. Maryland (power of state to tax federal institution overturned),
    31, 41
McGovern, George (Senator, anti-war Presidential candidate, 1972), 276
McKinley, William (25th President, assassinated), 109, 137, 265
Meany, George (labor leader of AFL, 1940's through 1960's), 239
Meat Inspection Act, The (1906- first major consumer legislation; see The
    Jungle), 120
Medicaid (public welfare system providing medical treatment of poor), 254
Medicare (public welfare system providing medical treatment of elderly), 254
Mediation (settlement of disputes by neutral third party), 86
Mellon, Andrew (Sec'y of Treasury for Hoover), 161
Melting Pot (a theory of immigrant assimilation), 100
Mentally ill (reforms for), 117
Mercantile system (closed trading system involving immense profit for
    mother country, while using colonies as market for goods), 10, 71, 132
Mergers (two or more businesses forming single larger corporation), 82

Meredith, James (civil rights leader, 1st black to enter University of Mississippi), 248-49
Mesabi iron deposit, 72
Metropolitan Museum of Art (New York City), 94
Mexico, 137, 140-41, 293
Midway (Pacific battle- WW II turning point), 197
Middle-class (usually the average level of economic or social status), 93-94, 167
Middle East, 236, 283, 293
Middle Passage (trip from Africa in slave ships), 98
Military Conscription Act (draft law), 48
Military occupation of Germany & Japan (by U.S. after WW II), 200-01
Military occupation of the South (by North after Civil War), 54, 66
Military Reconstruction Plan by Congress (1867), 55
Minimum wage and maximum hour laws, 171
Minority groups (treatment in New Deal), 171
Miranda v. Arizona (1966) (rights of accused clarified), 240, 273 [*5]
Missile bases (Cold War crisis in Cuba, 1962), 250
Mission Oak (industrial era furniture style), 95
Missouri Compromise of 1820 (slavery issue), 44
"Model T" (mass production popular middle class Ford auto), 77, 79
Moley, Raymond (aide to FDR), 172
Mondale, Walter (U.S. Vice-Pres.), 287
Monopoly, 83
Monroe Doctrine, The, 34, 137, 139, 186, 250
Monroe, James (5th President), 34, 39
Montevideo Conference, (1933), 187
Montgomery, Bernard L. (British WW II commander), 197
Montgomery Movement (desegregation of city buses led by Dr. King), 242
Montgomery Ward (early mail-order business), 73, 107
Moon Landing, 255
Moratorium (suspension of activities), 168
Morgan, J.P. (Wall St. financier), 77, 78, 79, 125
Morganthau, Henry (Sec. Treasury to FDR), 171, 172
Morrill Land Grant Act of 1862 (agricultural colleges), 107
Morse, Samuel F.B. (telegraph), 78
Moses, Robert (NYS parks and highways aide to Governor FDR), 172
Mott, Lucretia (early women's rights advocate), 116
Muckrakers (journalists who expose corruption and scandal), 120-21
Muir, John (conservationist), 126
Muller v. Oregon (1908- working hours), 126
Multinational corporations (worldwide operations - widely diversified), 226
Munich Conference (1938 - Hitler appeased; given Czechoslovakia), 191, 234
Munn v. Illinois (1876 - states could regulate railroads), 83, 108 [*2]
Mussolini, Benito (fascist dictator of Italy), 186, 191, 197

NAACP (National Association for the Advancement of Colored People (major civil rights group; c. 1909, Niagara Falls, NY), 61, 256
Nader, Ralph (consumer rights spokesman), 272
Nagasaki (nuclear bombing by U.S., 1945), 198
Napoleonic Wars (U.S. tries to remain neutral), 32, 186

Nasser, Gamal Abdul (Egyptian nationalist leader; c.1956), 236

Nast, Thomas (industrial era political cartoonist and anti-corruption crusader), 62-63

National nominating convention (as method of selecting Presidential candidates; c. 1830), 42

National Conservation Congress (1908), 126

National Consumers League, 118

National Defense Education Act, 237

National Forest Service, 126

National Guard, 193

National Grange of the Patrons of Husbandry (1867), 107

National Industrial Recovery Act (NIRA - New Deal stimulation), 173, 176

National Labor Relations Act (1935 - Wagner Act: right of organization and collective bargaining for unions), 175, 203

National Park System in 1891, 126

National Recovery Administration (NRA), 174

National Road (or Cumberland), 33

National Organization of Women (NOW- women's civil rights group), 260

National Origins Act in 1924 (immigration restriction), 101, 164 [*8]

National security (defense against aggression), 131-32

National Security Act of 1947, 203

National Socialists (Nazi), 186

National Union for Social Justice (see Fr. Coughlin), 180

National Youth Administration (New Deal aid for underprivileged youth), 178

Native Americans (struggles for human rights), 43, 104-06, 261-63, 273 [*6]

Nativist (organized opposition to immigrants), 98, 100

Nazi death camps: Auschwitz, Belzec, and Treblinka, 201-02

Nelson, Donald (industrialist who managed WW II military production for FDR), 199

Neutrality (foreign policy of nonalignment started under Washington in 1790's), 31-33, 142, 144, 186

Neutrality Acts of 1935,'36,'37 (pre-WW II isolationist sentiment), 188-89

New Deal (FDR's reform programs to help in Great Depression), 67, 171-78

New Deal Philosophy (pragmatic and optimistic), 171-78

New Freedom (Wilson's domestic Progressive reform program), 127

Newlands Act (1902 - national parks), 126

"New Federalism" (Reagan's policy of shifting more welfare responsibilities on local government), 287

"New Frontier" program (JFK's legislative program), 248

"New" Immigrants (predominance of Asian and Hispanic groups coming after 1965 legal revisions), 245, 290

"New" Immigration (Southern and Eastern European groups coming in large numbers after 1890), 100

New Nationalism (Teddy Roosevelt's general legislative program), 124

New Right (ultra conservative groups in current U.S. politics), 289

"New South" (seeking industrial development after the Civil War), 59-61

New York State Government (comparison to U.S. gov't. forms), 26

New York State Forest Preserve, 126

New York State Treaty Violations (against Native-Americans), 262

Newspaper sensationalism (emphasizing stories on vice, crime, violence, corruption; see "yellow journalism"), 94

Ngo Dinh Diem (South Vietnamese leader 1954-61), 265-66

Niagara Movement (founding of NAACP), 61

Niagara Power Project (New York Power Authority v. Native American peoples), 263

Nicaragua (Latin America and Reagan administration), 292, 297

Nicaraguan Contras (anti-communist guerrilla group), 292, 297

Nimitz, Admiral Chester (WW II Pacific commander), 198

Nine-Power Treaty of 1922 (reduction of naval armaments), 189

Nisei: aliens and American citizens of Japanese ancestry, 201

Nixon Doctrine (curtailing American use of power against communist insurgency after Vietnam), 274

Nixon, pardon by Ford (after Watergate & resignation), 277

Nixon, Richard M. (37th President),121, 218, 248, 267, 269, 271-79

Nixon v. U.S. (Supreme Court rules against "executive privilege"), 277

Non-violent, direct action(protest tactics of the civil rights movement), 242

Noriega, Manuel (Panamanian dictator, indicted by U.S. for drug trafficking and overthrowing the elected Panamanian government), 284

Normandy, France (WW II D-Day invasion in 1944), 197

Norris, Frank (muckraker, work: The Octopus, The Pit), 120

North emerges as an Industrial Power, 58

North Atlantic Treaty Organization (NATO- first U.S. peacetime defense alliance, 1949), 211-12

North Korea (Soviet satellite attacks South Korea, 1950), 215

Northern Securities Co. v. U.S. (first Federal prosecution and breakup of a monopoly), 125

Northwest Ordinance of 1787 (procedures for admission of states), 11, 105

Nuclear family units (smaller family in industrial society), 93

Nuclear power plant (first opened, 1957), 224

Nuclear Regulatory Commission 283

Nuclear Test-Ban Treaty (U.S.-U.S.S.R.), 251

Nuclear testing in atmosphere, 230

Nullification (individual states deciding a Federal Law is invalid and refusing to enforce it), 40

Nye Committee report in 1935 (leads to new neutrality laws), 188-89

Oakies (farmers displaced by 1930's Dust Bowl disaster; see Steinbeck's Grapes of Wrath), 178

Octopus, The (1901- Norris' muckraking novel on railroads), 120

Offshore oil (allow more state management under Eisenhower), 239

Office of Economic Opportunity (OEO- major Great Society job retraining and anti-discrimination agency), 254, 271

Office of Price Administration (administered WW II rationing), 199

Ohio Gang (corrupt politicians in Harding Era), 160

Oil, 77

Oil Crisis (economic sanctions used against Western nations), 280, 283

Okinawa (WW II Pacific battle), 198

Old-age insurance (see Social Security), 171

Old Folks' Crusade (New Deal Era campaign by Dr. Townshend), 179

"Old" Immigrants (predominance of WASP-related groups before Civil War), 97

Olney, Richard (Sec'y of State and Attorney Gen. for Cleveland), 140

Olympics (U.S. boycott of the1980 Summer Games in Moscow), 284

O'Neill, Eugene (20th c. plays: Emp. Jones, Mourning Becomes Electra), 165

OPEC (oil boycotts of the mid-1970's), 231, 280
Open Door Policy (U.S. & China trade, 1900), 136
Operation Desert Shield (1990-91 protection of Saudi Arabia, preparation for invasion of Kuwait), 300
Operation Desert Storm (1991 invasion of Kuwai–Persion Gulf Conflict), 300
Operation Overlord (WW II - largest amphibious invasion in history; see Normandy), 197
Oppenheimer, J. Robert (atomic scientist - security risk affair in McCarthy Era), 198, 219
Organization of American States (peace organization), 250
Organization of Petroleum Exporting Countries (OPEC- price setting cartel of oil producers), 280
Orlando, Vittorio (Italian Premier at Versailles, 1918-19), 148
Oswald, Lee Harvey (JFK assassin), 252
Over-producing (as a cause of the Great Depression), 167

Palestinian refugees in Israel, 285
Palestine Liberation Organization (PLO), 293
"Palmer Raids" ("Great Red Scare" against anarchists, 1919), 101, 164
Pan-American Union (inter-American peace organization, predecessor of Organization of American States), 193
Panama Canal Zone, 139, 284
Panama Invasion (December 1989, U.S. armed forces remove dictator Manuel Noriega and restore elected government), 284
Panmunjom peace talks (Korean War, 1950-53), 215-17, 234
Paris summit (fails because of U-2 incident, 1960), 235
Parks, Rosa (triggered Montgomery Movement, 1956), 242
Parkchester (privately-funded housing project in Bronx during Great Depression), 172
Paris, Treaty of (1783- gives U.S. independence), 11
Paris talks (on ending Vietnamese War), 274
Partisan politics, 30
Partisans (underground resistance), 197
Partnerships (limited business organization), 72-73
Party caucuses (small leadership group picks candidates), 42
Patton, Gen. George S. (WW II commander in Europe), 197
Payment-in-kind (Reagan farm aid program), 289
Peace Corps (JFK international volunteer group to personally aid people in underdeveloped nations), 250
Pearl Harbor (naval base in Hawaii- attack draws U.S. into WW II), 195
Pendleton Act (civil service examination system initiated, 1881), 117
Pentagon Papers , The (intensifies anti-Vietnam War demonstrations), 273
Peoples' Republic of China (falls to communists,1949), 216
Perestroika (U.S.S.R. internal political and economic reform program initiated by Gorbachev), 296
Perkins, Frances (Sec'y of Labor under FDR, first female cabinet member), 171, 178
Perry, Commodore Matthew (opens trade with Japan 1854), 135, 265
Pershing, General John (WW I commander), 141, 145
Persian Gulf (U.S. involvement in protecting oil shipping), 293
Persian Gulf Conflict (Operations Desert Shield and Storm), 297-298

Pétain, Field Marshall Henri (surrenders France to Nazis, 1940), 193

Philanthropy (wealthy persons making gifts to public works and charities, Carnegie & Gospel of Wealth), 91

Philippines (fall to U.S. in Spanish-American War; fall to Japan in WWII), 138, 195

Pillsbury, Charles (industrialist, flour milling), 78

Pinchot, Gifford (conservationist for T. R.), 126

Pinckney, Charles (diplomat under Washington), 32

Pinckney's Treaty (1795- gains right of deposit from Spain in Louisiana for western farmers), 32

Pinkerton guards (used by industrialists as strikebreakers), 85

Pit, The (1903- muckraking novel by Norris), 120

Plastics, 225

Platt Amendment (1901 - U.S. grants Cuban independence), 137

Plato (classical Greek influence on governmental institutions), 8

Plessy v. Ferguson (1896 - allows de jure segregation, sets "separate but equal" rule), 61, 67, 241 [*3]

Pluralistic society (multiple ethnic and cultural groups), 93

Point Four Program, 212-13

Poland (freedom in question at Yalta Conference), 192

Polarization of world affairs (U.S.-U.S.S.R. cold war rivalry), 209

Police powers (gov't. regulation of business for social welfare), 124

Polish Revolution (anti-Soviet revolt), 236

Political bosses (individuals who dominate a political system), 62

Political parties (organizations of common political interest), 30

Political reform (see reform), 116-17

Poll taxes (fees charged in order to vote, see 24th Amendment), 60

Pollution (environmental contamination), 230

Pools (monopolistic management structures), 82-83

Popular Sovereignty (territorial slavery decided by each state), 44

Populism (see Populist Party), 108-09

Populist (People's) Party (1892 - western reform group primarily agrarian), 108-09

Post-war contraction (1919-21: natural recession when stimulus of war production ceases), 160

Potsdam, Germany (WW II summit meeting Stalin-Churchill-Truman), 200, 203, 208-09

Powderly, Terence (leader of Knights of Labor), 84

Prayer, school (see Engle v.Vitale), 240, 273, 289

Preamble, 14

Presidency, 23-25

President Pro Tempore of U.S. Senate, 24

Presidential Disability and Succession Amend. (see 25th Amend.), 25

Presidential election process (see Electoral College), 42

Presidential powers, 25

Presidential Succession Act (1947), 24

Press, 18, 94

Precedents (initial actions in government which become basic pattern for subsequent actions of similar nature), 28 [*13]

Price ceilings (World War II gov't. management of economy), 199

"Prime the pump" theory (New Deal/Keynesian approach: government spending to generate demand in the economy), 170-71

Primogeniture (all inheritance rights given to first-born son), 116

Prisoners of war (problems of return after Vietnam War), 274

Proclamation of 1763 (British curtailed settlement beyond Appalachian Mts. - angered homesteaders, and land investors), 105

Proclamation of Neutrality (1793- Washington seeking isolation from European wars), 32

Proclamation of Neutrality of 1914 (Wilson seeking isolation from WWI in Europe), 142

Progress and Poverty (1879 - social commentary on new American socio-economic patterns), 110

Progressive income tax (see 16th Amendment), 127

Progressive Party in 1948 election, 127, 203

Progressivism (general reform spirit c. 1900 to readjust society to industrial era), 117-28

Prohibition (see 18th Amendment), 122, 164 [*1]

Project Head Start (Great Society program for pre-school help for minority children), 254

Propaganda (information managed and disseminated by an agency to promote a particular set of ideas), 163

Proprietorships (single-owner businesses), 72-73

Protectionists (high-tariff advocates), 133

Protective tariffs (Fordney-McCumber,1922), 29, 161

Public utilities (government franchised and regulated electric, gas, telephone, transit companies), 171

Puerto Rico (taken as U.S. colony in Spanish-American War), 137

Pulitzer, Joseph (newspaper publisher; yellow journalism), 94

Pullman Boycott (1894- bloody national railroad strike), 84

Pullman, George, 76, 84

"Pump-Priming," 170-71

Pure Food and Drug Act (1906- Progressive consumer reform), 120

Qaddafi, Muammar (Lybian leader, proponent of terrorism attacked by U.S. under Reagan), 294

"Quarantine" Speech of 1937 (FDR's), 189

Quotas (ethnically biased immigration restrictions of 1920's), 101

Race to the Moon, 250

Radical Republicans (lead Reconstruction Era), 54-56, 66

Railroads, 58, 76-77, 104, 107

Randolph, A. Philip (labor and civil rights leader), 178

Randolph, Edmund (leader at Constitutional Convention), 13, 29

Rankin, Jeannette (U.S. Representative, opponent of WW I), 121, 148

Ratification (battle to accept the U.S. Constitution), 15

Rationing program (WW II government controlled consumer supplies of critical goods), 199

Ray, James Earl (assassin of Martin Luther King, Jr.), 258

Reagan, Ronald (40th President), 271, 275, 287-300

Real wages (actual purchasing power of dollars earned), 59, 84

Recall (a public election to remove an official from office; reform sought by Populists & Progressives), 124

Reciprocity Act (1934, New Deal- to reduce trade barriers), 187, 188

Reconstruction of South after Civil War, 54-56, 66-68 [*10]

Reconstruction Finance Corporation (RFC - Hoover's attempt to stimulate economy in Great Depression to business loans), 168

Reconversion and "Normalcy" 1918-1920 (restoring U.S. economy to peacetime productivity), 158

Red Scare - 1918-1919 (paranoiac response to fear of socialist and anarchist activities after WW I; see Palmer Raids), 147, 164

"Redeemer" governments (Southern white-supremacists regain control after Reconstruction), 60, 66

Redemptioners (see indentured servants), 97-98

Referendum (to decide a public issue in a general election; democratic reform sought by Populists and Progressives), 26, 124

Reforestation and flood-control (conservation), 173

Reform in America (survey of major movements), 116-17

Rehabilitation Act of 1973 (federal law providing improved public access and facilities for the handicapped and forbidding discrimination against them), 282

Rehnquist, Chief Justice William, 273

Religion, 93, 97

Reparations and war debts (as a cause of economic difficulties in Europe after WW I), 149

Representative government (see republic; republican forms), 15, 26

Representatives, House of, 14

Republic of Korea (attacked by North Korea in 1950), 216-17

Republican Party, 45, 204

Reserved powers, 19, 55

Resignation of Nixon (1st President to resign, 9 August 1974), 277

Resolution Trust Corporation (RTC) (created by the U.S. Congress (1989) to replace the collapsed Fed. Savings and Loan Insurance Corporation), 300

Resource Recovery Act (environmental action under Nixon), 271

Revenue Act of 1913 (began Fed. income tax under the 16th Amendment), 127

Revenue sharing (Pres. Nixon's financial aid to states, 1971), 272

Revolution of Rising Expectations (desire among developing nations for improved quality of life after WW II), 228

"Right to Life" and "freedom of choice" (opposing sides in abortion question), 261

Right to petition (privilege of citizens to formally request government action, see 1st Amendment), 17

Riis, Jacob (investigative journalist of the industrial-Progressive Era), 120, 121

Robber barons (derogatory name for ruthless industrialists), 78

Robinson, Jackie (first black player in major league baseball), 241

"Rock'n'Roll" (music style begun in 1950's), 245

Rockefeller, John David (oil industry monopolist), 77-79, 91

Rockefeller, Nelson (Governor of NY, appointed Vice-President under Ford), 26, 274, 279

Roe v. Wade (1973 - controversial abortion decision), 261, 273, 289

Rogers, Ginger (Hollywood actress-dancer), 179

Romans (classical influences on American government), 8

Rommel, Gen. Erwin (legendary WW II German tank commander, "Desert Fox"), 197

Roosevelt Corollary to the Monroe Doctrine (U.S. acts as protector of the Western Hemisphere, adopts interventionist approach), 140
Roosevelt, Eleanor (influence on FDR, U.N. delegate), 171, 178
Roosevelt, Franklin D. (Governor of NY, 32nd President), 26, 137, 151, 169-200, 207
Roosevelt, Theodore (Governor of NY, 26th President), 26, 120, 121, 124, 127, 139-40, 187, 265
Rosenberg case (atomic secrets espionage case of early 1950's), 219
"Rosie the Riveter" (fictional American heroine - symbolic of women's role in the WW II production effort), 199
Roth v. U.S. (1957 - obscenity ruling), 273 [*3]
Rousseau, Jean-Jacques (impact on Constitution), 9
Ruby, Jack (murdered JFK assassin Lee Harvey Oswald), 252
Roycroft Movement (anti-industrial craft movement in NY), 95
"Rule of reason" (judicial concept used in determining monopoly violations), 125, 160
Russian Revolution in 1917, 145
"Rust Belt, The" (decaying industrial centers of Northeast and Mid-west), 246

S acco-Vanzetti trial (due process questions), 164
Sadat, Egyptian President Anwar, 284
Saddam Hussein (Iraqi leader, defeated in Persian Gulf Conflict), 300
"Salary Grab Act" (1873 - Grant Era scandal), 62
Samoa (taken for naval base in era of U.S. imperialism), 136, 265
Sanger, Margaret (advocate of birth control, planned parenthood), 121
S & L Crisis (see Savings & Loan failure) 299
Saturday Evening Post, The (influence of mass media), 94, 163
Savings & Loan Failures (bank deregulation crisis - Reagan and Bush), 299
"Scabs" (strikebreakers), 84
Schechter Poultry Corp. v. United States (1935 - court strikes down New Deal's Nat. Industrial Recovery Act), 176
Schenck, Charles (a leading WW I Socialist), 147
Schenck v. United States (1919- civil rights in wartime; see clear and present danger rule), 147, 201 [*4]
School aid (FDR programs while Governor of NY), 172
Schuman, Robert (Post WW II European economy), 210
Scientific American (reports on inventions in industrial era), 58
Scopes "Monkey Trial" (1925 - controversy over teaching evolution), 164
Seabed Agreement (control of undersea nuclear weapons), 276
Sears Roebuck, 73, 107
Second Continental Congress (issues Declaration of Independence), 10
Secret ballot (reform sought by Populists & Progressives), 124
Secretary of State (cabinet officer in charge of foreign affairs), 24
Sectionalism (loyalty to state or region over nation), 39
Securities and Exchange Commission (SEC - regulation of stock market), 175
Security Council (major power arm of U.N.), 194
Sedition Act in 1918 (concern for wartime security and dissent), 146
Segregation (racial separation), 178, 204
Selective Service Acts (military conscription, draft laws), 146, 156, 200
Senate (power as upper chamber of Congress), 20-22
Senate Committee on Government Operations (see McCarthyism), 219

Senators, direct election of U.S. (see 17th Amendment), 304 [*11]

Seneca people (resist NY state dam project on tribal land-1960's), 262

Sensationalism, 94

"Separate but equal accommodations" (see Plessy v. Ferguson), 67

Separation of Power (three branches of U.S. government to avoid tyranny), 8, 15

Service industries (as major employment in U.S.), 226

Servicemen's Readjustment Act (see "GI Bill"), 202

Settlement houses (aid for immigrants, industrial poor), 121

Seven Years' War with France, 10

Shah of Iran, 283

"Share Our Wealth" program (campaign slogan of Sen. Huey Long in Great Depression), 179

Sharecropping (payment of land rent with agricultural produce), 59

Sherman, Roger (delegate to Constitutional Convention, Great Compromise), 13-14

Sherman Anti-trust Act (1st gov't attempt to regulate monopolies), 83-84

Significance of the Frontier in American History, The (Turner), 103

Silicon chip of the 1980's (impact of modern technology), 225

Simpson-Mazzoli Immigration Act (1986 - illegal aliens), 289

Sinclair, Upton (muckraker, work: The Jungle), 120

Sirhan, Sirhan (assassin of Sen. Robert F. Kennedy), 258

Sister Carrie - An American Tragedy (Theodore Dreiser), 94

Sit-ins (non-violent civil rights protest tactic), 242

Skylab space station, 281

Skyscrapers (industrial era urban architecture), 90

Slater, Samuel (1st U.S. textile factory), 72

Slaughterhouse Cases (question of Fed. rights guarantees on state level), 61

Slave revolts, 44

Slave Trade (abolished by Constitution), 14, 43

Smith Act (WW II anti-subversion law), 193, 218

Smith, Al (Governor of NY, 1st Catholic Pres. candidate, 1928), 26, 171, 248

Social Darwinism (application of "survival of fittest" to human behavior, justification for ruthless business practices of industrial era), 91

Social Security System, 174, 179, 291

Socialist Party, 179

Soil Bank Plan (farm conservation), 239

Solid South (predominance of Democratic Party after Civil War), 63

Son of the Middle Border (Hamlin Garland story, mid-western farm life), 94

South Africa (problem of apartheid), 295

South Carolina Exposition and Protest (Calhoun's statement on states rights), 40

South Vietnamese government (U.S. withdraws, falls in1975), 274

Southern Christian Leadership Conference (SCLC- Dr. King's civil rights group), 256

Southeast Asia region (French Indo-China: anti-colonial revolts), 265

Southeast Asia Treaty Organization (SEATO - U.S. backed regional collective security arrangement, 1953), 234

Sovereignty (national independence), 11, 149-50

Soviet Union (U.S.S.R.), 187, 191, 192, 235, 250, 275, 283, 301-302

Space Program, 281

Space shuttles Columbia, Challenger , 281

Spanish Civil War (1930's- as rehearsal for WW II), 189

Spanish-American War (U.S. imperialism), 137-38

Speaker of the House (presiding officer of the U.S. House of Representatives), 21, 24

Spencer, Herbert (British, theory of Social Darwinism), 91

Sputnik I and II (seen as Soviet challenges to American technology), 237

Square Deal (Theodore Roosevelt's Progressive philosophy), 124

St. Lawrence Seaway Project, 263

"Stagflation" (problem of stagnated growth, with inflation), 281

Stalin, Joseph (U.S.S.R. dictator), 188, 193, 195, 200-03, 207, 209-11, 235

Stalingrad (Nazi invasion of U.S.S.R.), 197

Stamp Act (1765 - cause of American Revolution), 10

Standard Oil Trust, 77, 78, 79, 125

Stanton, Elizabeth Cady (early women's rights leader), 116

Stanton,Edwin (Secretary of War under Lincoln and Johnson), 56

States' rights (opposition to power of Federal government), 39

States' Rights Party, nicknamed the Dixiecrats (Southern opposition to Truman's civil rights program), 203

Steffans,Lincoln (muckraker), 120

Steinbeck, John (classic novel of Dust Bowl, The Grapes of Wrath), 178

Stephens, Uriah (early U.S. labor leader-Knights of Labor), 84

Stereotyping (form of prejudice), 100

Stevenson, Adlai (Democratic Presidential Candidate, 1950's), 238

Stewardship Theory of Presidency, The (see Theodore Roosevelt), 124

Stickley, Gustav (Mission Oak furniture), 95

Stimulation measures (government "pump-priming" to move the economy, see New Deal), 173

Stock brokers (over-speculation as a cause of Great Depression), 168

Stock Market Crash, The (connection to Great Depression), 168

Straits of the Dardenelles, 210

Strategic Arms Limitation Treaty (SALT), 275, 284

Strategic Defense Initiative (Reagan's "Star Wars"space missile defense system proposal), 296

Streetcars (industrial era mass transit), 76

Strict constructionists (believers precise interpretations of the Constitution's ideas), 21, 29

Strikes, 85

Strip mining, 230, 289

Strong, Rev. Josiah (pro-imperialist of 1880's), 133

Student Non-violent Coordinating Committee (SNCC), 256

Students for a Democratic Society (SDS- radical anti-Vietnam group), 267

Submarine warfare (as a cause of U.S. entry into WW I), 143-44

Submerged Lands Act (1953), 239

Suburbia (new lifestyle caused by automobile), 163

Suburbs (growth after WW II), 245

Subversion (to plot and take secretive actions to overthrow a gov't.)

Subway systems (industrial era urban mass transit), 90

Sudetenland (region of Czechoslovakia taken by Hitler), 191

Suez Canal (nationalized by Nasser, 1956), 236

Suffrage (the right to vote), 42, 55, 116

Suffragettes (crusade for women's right to vote), 116-17 [*7]

Summit meetings (personal diplomacy among world leaders), 19, 200, 235-36, 296 [*9]

Sumner, William Graham (Social Darwinist writer), 91
"Sun Belt" (South and West), 245
Superconductivity, 225
"supply side" economics (gov't stimulus through tax incentives), 288 [*12]
Supreme Court, 25, 240, 259
Sussex Pledge (Germans agree to stop sub. attacks on neutrals, WW I), 144
Suzuki (Japanese Premier, WW II), 198
Swan v. the Board of Education of Charlotte-Mecklenburg (1971- busing as desegregation technique), 259
Sweatshops (factory with poor working conditions), 91

Taft, William Howard (27th President), 127, 140
Taft-Hartley Labor Management Relations Act (cuts power of labor unions), 202, 239
Taiwan (Republic of China), 274-75
Talented Tenth (W.E.B.DuBois theory for social equality for Blacks), 61
"Talkies" (talking motion pictures introduced in the late 1920's), 163
Tammany Hall (New York City Democratic political club), 100
Tarbell, Ida (muckraker work: History of the Standard Oil Co.), 120
"Tariff of Abominations" (1828 - subject of Southern protests), 40-41
Tariffs (duties, taxes on imports), 14, 29, 30, 40-41, 48, 58, 175
"Tax simplification" program (1986-Reagan reform of income tax system), 288
Taylor, Frederick Winslow (1920's industrial efficiency expert), 160
Tea Act (1772 - as cause for American Revolution), 10
Teapot Dome Affair (1920's Harding era scandal), 160
Technology, 71, 90, 106-07
Telegraph, Telephone, 78, 118
Television, 244
Teller Resolution (1898 - promise of Cuban independence), 137
Temperance (see prohibition movement), 122
Temporary Emergency Relief Agency (TERA- NY predecessor of New Deal, c. 1930), 171
Tenement houses, 91
Tennessee Valley Authority (New Deal conservation/power projects), 239
Tenure of Office Act (used as ploy to impeach Andrew Johnson), 55
Terrorism (use of acts of violence for political purposes), 293
Territorial expansion (U.S. land acquisitions), 34 [*1]
Tet Offensive (massive Viet Cong attack 1968 leads to question's about U.S. role), 268
Textiles (first major U.S. industry), 72
"Third World" Countries (underdeveloped nations of Asia & Africa), 212, 283
Thomas, Norman (socialist leader), 179
Three-Fifths Compromise (slavery question in Constitutional Convention), 14
Three R's (Relief, Recovery, Reform [in New Deal]), 171-75
Three Mile Island (nuclear accident, 1979), 225, 283
Thurmond, Governor Strom (leads opposition wing of Democrats against Truman in 1948), 203
Tilden, Samuel (Gov. of NY, Democratic Presidential candidate,1876), 26, 66
Title VII (Civil Rights Act of 1964), 260
Title XI (equal educational access - women, minorities), 260
Tojo, General (Japanese WW II commander), 195

Tom Sawyer (1876 - work by Mark Twain), 94

Townsend, Dr. Charles (leader of 1930's old folks crusade), 179

Townshend Acts (1767- cause of American Revolution), 10

Trade Agreements Act of 1934 (allowed Pres. to negotiate tariffs), 175

Trade deficit (U.S. - mounted alarmingly in the 1980's), 294

"Trail of Broken Treaties" (civil rights of Native Americans), 262

"Trail of Tears" (forced government relocation of Native Americans under President Jackson), 105

Trans-oceanic telegraph cables, 132

Transportation, Dept. of, 255

Transistors, 225

Treaty of Ghent (1814), 33

Treaty of Paris (1783 - ends American Revolution), 11

Treaty of Versailles (ends WW I, creates League of Nations, U.S. Senate rejects), 147-50 [*9]

Triangle Shirtwaist Co. fire (NYC disaster spurs factory safety reforms), 84

"Trickle-down theory" (government stimulation of sluggish economy through loans to business under President Hoover), 170-71 [*12]

Triple Alliance (WW I alliance, Central Powers: Germany, Austria-Hungary, and Italy), 143

Triple Entente (WW I alliance: France, Great Britain, Russia), 143

Truman Doctrine (containment of communist expansion in Europe), 210

Truman, Harry S. (33rd President), 198, 200, 202, 204-19, 237

"Trust Busting" (T. Roosevelt - anti-monopoly crusades), 124-25

Trusts(monopolies), 82, 124-25

Truth-in-Lending Act (1969 - consumer protection: banking, installment buying), 272

Tubman, Harriet (abolitionist, organized "Underground Railway"), 45

Tugwell, Rexford G. (advisor to FDR), 172

Turner, Frederick Jackson (frontier theory), 103

Turner, Nat (led early slave revolt in 1830's), 44

Tuscarora Indian people (NY treaty problems), 263

Tuskegee Institute (Booker T. Washington's technical training school for blacks), 61

Twain, Mark (industrial era author, humorist; works: Tom Sawyer, Huckleberry Finn), 91, 94

Tweed Ring (NYC political corruption in Glided Age), 62

Tweed, William Marcy (see Tweed Ring, Thomas Nast's cartoons), 62, 92

Two Treatises on Government (British enlightenment philosopher John Locke's work - influenced framers of Constitution), 8

Tydings-McDuffie Act of 1946 (U.S. grants Philippines independence), 138

U-2 incident (U.S. spy plane shot down in U.S.S.R.), 235

Uncle Remus' Stories (post Civil War Southern literature - Joel Chandler Harris), 94

Uncle Tom's Cabin (abolitionist novel: Harriet Beecher Stowe), 44

Unconditional pardon of Vietnam draft evaders, 279

"Underground Railway" (abolitionists aided slave escapes), 44

Underwood Tariff (Progressive era attempt to lower tariffs), 127

Unemployment relief (New Deal actions to relieve economic misfortune), 169, 171

Unicameral legislature (having only one House in government), 11
Union Pacific Railroad (Transcontinental railroad), 62, 77
Union Party (New Deal right-wing opponents; see Fr. Couglin), 180
Universal Declaration of Human Rights (backing for basic rights; see Eleanor
     Roosevelt), 208
Universal Negro Improvement Association (Marcus Garvey's separatist
     back-to-Africa movement in 1920's), 121
U.N. Appeal by Native Americans (1977- civil rights protest against U.S.
     government mistreatment), 262
U.N. Security Council, 207, 217
U. S. v. Cruikshank (early interpretation of 14th Amendment), 61
U.S.S.R. (see Soviet Union), 27, 187, 207, 216
United Nations, 194, 200, 207
United States Steel Corporation (J. P. Morgan buys out Carnegie, 1900), 77
United States-Soviet Relations, 295
United States v. Butler (Supreme Court strikes down New Deal's
     agricultural program), 176
United Steel Workers, 84
Unsafe at Any Speed (Ralph Nader book on U.S. auto industry), 272
Unwritten constitution (precedents, judicial decisions, expansions of legal
     power and procedure not officially in Constitution), 28, 29
Upper-class (the highest level of economic or social status), 91
Urban League (civil rights group), 256
Urbanization (process of the society's central activities taking place in cities),
     90-95, 99

V-2 rockets (used in WW I by Germans), 197
Valentine, Lewis (crusading NYC Police Commissioner under Mayor
     LaGuardia), 172
Van Buren, Martin (8th President, NY), 26
Versailles Peace Conference (ends WW I), 147-50, 186
Veterans' Bureau (involved in Harding era corruption), 161
Veto power (executive power to nullify legislation), 41, 207
Vice-President (takes over when president dies, is incapacitated, or resigns,
     also is presiding officer of U.S. Senate), 24, 25
Victorian ideal, The (idealized vision of women as delicate, weaker members
     of the society c. 1890's), 93, 165
Viet Cong (communist insurgent forces in Vietnamese War), 265-66
"Vietnam Moratorium Day" (1969- massive anti-war rally), 267
Vietnam War, 265-69, 274 [*9]
Vigilante groups (sought unofficial law and order in old west), 106
Villa, Pancho (Mexican revolutionary leader c. 1913), 141
Volkswagen "Beetle," (imported cars popular in U.S. in 1950's), 244
Voltaire (French Enlightenment thinker whose views influenced framers of
     Constitution), 8
Volunteers in Service to America (VISTA) program (Great Society gov't
     sponsored aid to underprivileged), 254
Voting Rights Acts of 1965, 1970, 1975 (insured proper procedures against
     racial discrimination), 259, 282

Wabash, St. Louis, and Pacific Railway v. Minn. (1886 - states could regulate railroads), 108

Wage Slavery, 92

Wagner Act (major rights for labor unions), 175

Wall Street (financial center - home of NY stock market), 161

Wallace, George (Gov. of Alabama, ran for President in 1968), 271

Wallace, Henry A. (Vice President under FDR, ran for President against Truman in 1948), 203

Wanamaker, John, 73

War of 1812, 32-33, 39

War bond drives (WW II patriotic pressures to finance war effort), 199

"War crimes" (Nazi leaders put on trial in 1946), 202

War economy (WW I management by Wilson), 156-59

"War Hawks" (land-hungry pro-war Congressmen in 1812 era), 33

War Labor Board (WW I and II management of labor force), 156, 199

War on Poverty, The (see Great Society), 254

War Manpower Commission (WW II management of labor), 199-200

War Powers Act (post Vietnam Congressional move to limit Pres. power), 269

War Production Board (WW II command structure under Donald Nelson), 199

War reparations (vindictive penalties assessed against Germany after WW I), 149, 159

War's impact on gender roles and on blacks (women and blacks participation in WW I changes status), 157

Warren Commission (investigates JFK assassination), 252

"Warren Court" (followed a policy of judicial activism), 240 [3]

Warren, Earl (Chief Justice of the Supreme Court), 240

Warsaw Pact (Soviet alliance of Eastern European nations; gave Soviet commanders control over the satellite's armies; ended in 1991), 296

Washington Conference (attempts to stop naval arms race after WW I), 150

Washington, Booker T. (post Civil War black leader), 61, 121

Washington, George (1st President), 13, 29, 32, 142

Washington Post (major role in exposing Watergate scandal), 121

Washington's Farewell Address of 1796 (recommended neutrality), 142, 186

WASP (white, Anglo-Saxon, Protestant as majority ethnic/cultural group in U.S.), 97

Water Quality Control Act (anti-pollution and environmental reform), 254

Water Pollution Control Act (environmental reform), 272

Watergate Affair (election scandal - Nixon resignation), 276-77, 279, 286

Watkins v. U.S. (personal rights during McCarthy Era), 218

"We Shall Overcome" (hymn of Civil Rights movement), 249

Wealth Against Commonwealth (1894- Henry D. Lloyd: socialist proposal attacking tactics of big businessmen, see "robber barons"), 110

Weathermen (a radical offshoot of SDS in Vietnam era), 267

Weaver, Robert (Sec'y of Housing under Lyndon Johnson), 178

Webster, Daniel (Senator, crusader for Union in pre-Civil War Era), 40

West Indian Protectorate (Teddy Roosevelt's "Big Stick" interventionist policies), 139

Western Union Telegraph Company, 78

Westinghouse, George, 76

Whiskey Rebellion, The (Pennsylvania farmers protest Hamilton's excise tax, 1792), 30

Whiskey Ring (scandal in Grant era), 62
White Armies (anti-communist Russian groups aided by Allies in 1918), 145
"White Man's Burden" (racist-imperialist concept of WASP as custodians of
    civilization), 133
Wilderness Act (environmental preservation measure), 254
Wilson, James (influential at Constitutional Convention), 13
Wilson, Woodrow (28th President, Progressive Governor of NJ), 121, 127,
    140-50, 156, 186, 187
"Wildcat" state banks (unregulated independent banks of Jacksonian era
    helped cause collapse in late 1830's), 41
"Wobblies" (see "Industrial Workers of the World"), 86, 147
Women, 93, 157
Women's Christian Temperance Union (1876 - prohibitionists), 122
Women's International League for Peace and Freedom (WW I pacifists), 148
Women's Movement (1960's), 260
Women's Suffrage Movement (crusade to gain the vote), 116, 128 [*7]
Women's Trade Union (early women's rights group), 86
Worcester v. Georgia (1830 - Court ruling in favor of Cherokee against
    Georgia's confiscation of tribal lands), 43
Working conditions, 92, 124, 126
Work-relief (government projects to give work to indigent in Great
    Depression), 171
Works Projects Administration (WPA) see "work-relief," 173, 178
World Court (U.S. isolationists kept U.S. from joining international peace
    organization in 1920), 151
World Health Organization (U.N. branch that studies health-related
    problems in countries of the world and works to solve them), 297
World population growth, 229
World War I, 142-51
World War II, 195-205
Wounded Knee (1973- civil rights demonstration at site of 1890's massacre),
    105, 262
Writs of habeas corpus (constitutional protection that accused be informed of
    charges against them or released), 22, 48-49

Xenophobia (fear of foreigners), 164

Yalta Conference (WW II leaders summit), 200, 207, 208-09
Yates, Robert (New York State delegate to Constitutional Convention,
    Anti-federalist), 13, 15
Yates v. U.S. (1957- Court redefines subversive activities), 218
Yellow Dog Contract, 86
Yellow journalism (sensationalist press activities), 94, 137
Yeltsin, Boris (Russian leader), 302

Zimmerman note (inflamed U. S. anti-German sentiment before WWI), 144

Examination Strategies

How you approach the final exam and how you use your time can often affect your success.

- Take the full amount of time. You've spent a great deal of time and effort getting ready for the exam. A few minutes taken at the end can help you spot errors and make appropriate adjustment.

- **First Reading**: Skim over the whole examination quickly. Answer only those Part I questions of which you are absolutely sure. Skip the rest. When you get to Part II, read the questions and jot down on scrap paper any factual data that you think you could use to answer the question. Do this for all questions on Parts II and III. It will help you decide which questions to choose to write.

- **Second Reading**: Read Part I again, but more slowly this time. Answer as many questions as you can, but don't be afraid to leave an answer blank for now. As you again go through Part I, be alert for ideas which you might use on Part II and Part III answers. Jot them down on scrap paper as they come to mind. Choose the Part II or Part III question about which you feel most confident and write the answer. Be brief. Let the point values guide you on how much to write. Written answers should not be more than two pages. Be sure to label the parts of the answer *exactly* as they are on the examination.

The final exam lists these ideas about Part II and Part III:

1) include specific factual information wherever possible.
2) keep to the questions asked; do not go off on tangents.
3) avoid over-generalizations and sweeping statements which are difficult to prove.
4) keep these general definitions in mind:
   a) **discuss** means "to make observations about something using facts, reasoning, and arguments; to present in some detail"
   b) **describe** means "to illustrate something in words or tell about it"
   c) **show** means "to point out; to set forth clearly a position or idea by stating it and giving data which support it"
   d) **explain** means "to make plain or understandable; to give reasons for or causes of; to show the logical development or relationships of"

- **Third Reading**: Go back to Part I and work briefly on the remaining questions, then write out the other Part II or III answers.

- **Fourth Reading**: Finish Part I. Take your best guess on any questions of which you are unsure. *Do not leave any answer spaces blank.* Re-read your answers on Parts II and III carefully and make corrections and alterations neatly. Make sure all parts of each answer are properly and *distinctly* labeled.

Practice Exam 1 — *June 1991*

Part I (55 credits) Answer all 48 questions in this part.

1 Which issue discussed at the Constitutional Convention of 1787 continues to be a major concern in the United States?
1 relationship of states to each other
2 power to regulate foreign trade
3 balance of power between state and national governments
4 location of the national capital

2 The United States Constitution is best described as a
1 statement of rules and procedures for governing
2 summary of governmental customs and traditions
3 guarantee of prosperity for all citizens
4 justification for rebellion against Great Britain

3 The Bill of Rights was added to the U.S. Constitution primarily to
1 protect citizens from state governments
2 guarantee economic equality to all people living in the United States
3 expand the delegated powers of the Federal Government
4 protect citizens from excessive power of the Federal Government

4 Cases that reach the United States Supreme Court from lower courts are generally cases that concern
1 constitutional law
2 property rights
3 conflicts between corporations
4 civil lawsuits

5 Which fact best illustrates separation of church and state in the U. S.?
1 Congress seldom meets on Sunday.
2 Religious chaplains serve in the armed forces.
3 Organized prayer in public schools is prohibited.
4 Only one Catholic has been elected President.

6 "The individual can be free only when the power of one governmental branch is balanced by the other two."

-Baron de Montesquieu, 1735 (adapted)

The idea expressed in this quotation is best illustrated by which aspect of the United States Government?
1 existence of a Cabinet
2 separation of powers
3 elastic clause
4 executive privilege

Base your answers to questions 7 and 8 on the next page on this quotation from the 14th amendment to the Constitution and on your knowledge of social studies.

"All persons born or naturalized in the United States, and subject to the jurisdiction thereof, are citizens of the United States and of the state wherein they reside. No state shall make or enforce any law which shall abridge the privileges or immunities of citizens of the United States; nor shall any state deprive any person of life, liberty, or property, without due process of law;..."

7   An important effect that the principle stated in this quotation had on
     the United States legal system was to
     1   extend the protections of the Bill of Rights to include actions of state
          governments
     2   permit states to define United States citizenship in their own ways
     3   reduce the control of Federal Government over legal rights of states
     4   make state governments less democratic

8   An important application of the "due process of law" clause in this
     quotation has been its use in Supreme Court cases involving
     1   income taxes   3   prayers in the public schools
     2   rights of the accused   4   freedom of speech and press

Base your answers to questions 9 and 10 on the statements below and on
your knowledge of social studies.

Booker T. Washington:
To those of my race who depend on bettering their condition in a foreign
land or who underestimate the importance of cultivating friendly
relations with the southern white man ... I would say: Cast down your
bucket where you are ... Cast it down in agriculture, in mechanics, in
commerce, in domestic service, and in the professions. No race can
prosper until it learns that there is as much dignity in tilling a field as
in writing a poem.

W.E.B. Du Bois:
Mr. Washington asks that black people give up, at least for the present,
three things, political power, insistence on civil rights, and higher
education. As a result, what has been the return? In these years there
have occurred: 1. the disenfranchisement for the Negro, 2. the legal
creation of a distinct status of civil inferiority for the Negro, 3. the
steady withdrawal of aid ... for the higher training of the Negro.

9   W.E.B. Du Bois believed that Booker T. Washington's advice to blacks
     1   widened the gap of inequity between blacks and whites
     2   was correct, considering the times in which they lived
     3   significantly helped blacks to gain civil rights
     4   was an excellent means for blacks to become accepted by white
          society

10   The statements of both Booker T. Washington and W.E.B. Du Bois
     reflect their commitment to
     1   preventing differences of opinion between blacks and whites in
          American society
     2   obtaining government aid for black Americans
     3   improving the position of blacks in American society
     4   helping blacks to adjust to the rapid industrialization of the nation.

11   The power relationship that changed most as a result of the Civil War
     was the increase in the power of the
     1   individual over the state
     2   military over the civilian population
     3   Congress over the President
     4   Federal Government over the states

12 What was a major cause of labor-management conflicts in the last half of the 19th century?
1 Public opinion sided with labor rather than management.
2 The Federal Government actively encouraged labor unions to strike.
3 Most labor union members were also stockholders.
4 Business leaders opposed the efforts of labor unions to organize and improve conditions.

13 Antitrust laws attempted to protect the public against the activities of big business by
1 maintaining competition
2 encouraging government ownership of business
3 establishing government ownership of business
4 confining business activities to a single state

14 During the 19th century, the United States placed few restrictions on immigration mainly because
1 the birthrate was low
2 organized opposition to immigration did not exist
3 a steady demand for cheap labor existed
4 most immigrants were easily assimilated into American society

15 A main characteristic of third parties in United States political history is that they have generally
1 embraced a broad range of issues
2 addressed issues that have been avoided by the major parties
3 gained support by ignoring controversial issues
4 taken enough votes away from one major party to assure victory to the other major party

16 During the latter part of the 19th century, which two groups would most likely have agreed that the Federal Government should regulate industry?
1 railroad owners and homesteaders
2 environmentalists and Native American Indians
3 laborers and farmers
4 bankers and industrialists

17 The Progressive movement was most concerned with
1 helping the nation adapt to the social and economic changes resulting from industrialization
2 expanding the civil rights of minorities
3 healing the split caused by the Civil War and Reconstruction
4 controlling the swings in the business cycle

18 As a result of Progressive Era politics, the United States became more democratic with the adoption of a constitutional amendment that
1 restricted the President's control over the military
2 gave 18-year-old citizens the right to vote
3 eliminated the poll tax
4 provided for direct election of United States Senators

19   A major reason the United States began to seek colonies during the late
     1890's was that the
     1   Monroe Doctrine required such action
     2   expansion of American industry made acquiring new markets and
         additional resources desirable
     3   population pressures within the United States had become more
         severe
     4   cold-war rivalry between the United States and the Soviet Union had
         heightened

20   One motivation for the passage of the immigration quota acts of 1921
     and 1924 was
     1   congressional support for free, unlimited immigration
     2   the industrialists' need for workers from southern and eastern
         Europe
     3   the prevailing mood of welcome to new foreign ideas
     4   a recurrence of nativist attitudes following World War I

21   In an outline of major developments in United States foreign policy
     during the late 19th and early 20th centuries, which entry would be the
     main topic?
     1   Emerging Global Involvement
     2   Expansion in the Pacific Ocean
     3   Building a Two-Ocean Navy
     4   Intervention in Latin America

22   "The chief opponents of the Versailles Treaty were dead men:
     Washington, Jefferson, and Madison." This statement suggests that
     opposition in the United States to the Versailles treaty was based on the
     1   rejection of Woodrow Wilson's Fourteen Points
     2   fear that the treaty would violate the tradition of noninvolvement
     3   belief that the treaty was too harsh on the Central Powers
     4   unhappiness of citizens with U.S. participation in World War I

23   The return to "normalcy" during the 1920's can best be described as an
     attempt to
     1   expand social welfare programs
     2   show greater tolerance toward immigrant groups
     3   reduce the role of government in regulating the economy
     4   increase United States intervention in European political affairs

24   The U.S. supported the Open Door policy toward China mainly to
     1   construct military bases
     2   bring about democratic government
     3   encourage European nations to leave
     4   increase trading opportunities

25   Which major trend characterized the 1920's and continues today?
     1   retail buying on installment credit
     2   legal discrimination against eastern European immigrants
     3   the steadily increasing power of established churches
     4   the mass migration of northern blacks to southern rural areas

26   In the United States, a major cause of the Great Depression was
  1   excessive government spending on the military
  2   the rapid decrease in consumer demand and purchasing power
  3   the large deficits resulting from World War I
  4   increased government spending on social welfare programs

27   A major idea in the philosophy behind the New Deal was that
  1   the states should accept more responsibility for the funding of social programs
  2   individual citizens should solve their own problems
  3   private organizations are best equipped to solve social problems
  4   the resources of the Federal Government should be used to solve social problems

28   In the U.S., a major effect of the Great Depression of the 1930's was to
  1   reinforce traditional beliefs in rugged individualism
  3   give political control to the Socialist Party
  3   make increased governmental intervention in the economy more acceptable
  4   strengthen the demand for the acquisition of overseas territories

29   President Franklin D. Roosevelt's clashes with the United States Supreme Court over his New Deal programs best illustrate
  1   federalism that was carried to extremes
  2   separation of powers in operation
  3   refusal of the Supreme Court to engage in judicial review
  4   weaknesses in the constitutional amendment process

30   The New Deal was similar to the earlier Progressive movement in that both
  1   attempted to reform the economic system
  2   aimed to overcome severe economic depression
  3   emphasized the need to control the evils of organized labor
  4   made strong efforts to fight racial segregation

31   The Neutrality Acts of 1935 and 1937 were based upon the United States desire to
  1   be militarily prepared for the approaching war in Europe
  2   change the basic nature of the foreign policy it had followed since the end of World War I
  3   avoid participation in a European war
  4   become immediately involved in any future European war

32   The experience of Japanese Americans during World War II was most similar to that of which other group in United States history?
  1   Chinese Americans during the Progressive Era
  2   Native American Indians during the period of the closing of the frontier
  3   British Americans during the World War I period
  4   Asian Americans during the Korean conflict

Base your answers to questions 33 and 34 on the passage below and on your knowledge of social studies.

"From Stettin in the Baltic to Trieste in the Adriatic, an iron curtain has descended across the Continent. Behind that line lie all the capitals of the ancient states of central and eastern Europe .... all are subject, in one form or another, not only to Soviet influence but to a very high and increasing measure of control from Moscow." -Winston Churchill

33 When did the situation described in the passage occur?
   1   toward the close of WW I   3   soon after WW II
   2   during the Great Depression   4   during the Vietnam War

34 This observation by Winston Churchill is often regarded as the symbolic start of
   1   detente
   2   balance-of-power politics
   3   the United States policy of neutrality
   4   the cold war

Base your answers to question 35 on the passage below and on your knowledge of social studies.

The restructuring of the United States economy, especially in the explosive rise of the electronic industry, created new jobs that industry was desperate to fill with men or women. The United States found itself threatened with a declining place in the world marketplace unless it could strengthen its high-tech industries. In doing so, it could not afford to waste the talents of half its population.

35 According to the passage, a principal motivation for the changing role of women in the American workplace over recent decades has been
   1   feminist demands for equality
   2   new trends in industrialization
   3   the increase in single-parent households
   4   the need for two incomes to support a family

Base your answer to question 36 on the cartoon at the right and on your knowledge of social studies.

36 The main idea of the cartoon is that
   1   the war on drugs can be won through the criminal justice system
   2   the war on drugs is slowed down by an unwillingness to pay for solutions
   3   members of Congress will take unpopular steps to solve the drug problem
   4   citizens want the war on drugs won regardless of costs

37   The general nature of United States foreign policy since 1945 can best be
     described as
     1   providing the leadership of the Western bloc of nations
     2   continuing a policy of expansionism to acquire new colonies
     3   remaining firmly committed to isolationism
     4   seeking peace at any price

Base your answers to questions 38 and 39 on the speakers' statements below
and on your knowledge of social studies.

   Speaker A: The United States has no right to interfere in South Africa's
   internal policies. We should mind our own business and not get involved
   with other countries. If every country did the same, we would all be
   better off.

   Speaker B: The United States Government has a moral obligation to
   speak out against the atrocities being committed by the government in
   South Africa. We should cut off diplomatic and trade relations with
   South Africa and urge all of our allies to do the same.

   Speaker C: The United States Government should aid the rebel forces in
   South Africa, who are fighting to overthrow the government. Force is
   the only effective way to push the current government out of power.

   Speaker D: If it were the whites in South Africa that were being treated
   so poorly, the United States Government would be doing more to change
   the situation. Our country never has treated people of color fairly,
   whether at home or overseas.

38   The speakers held conflicting opinions about how the United States
     Government should respond to the South African Government's policy of
     1   communism
     2   expansionism
     3   apartheid
     4   democratic socialism

39   Which policy did speaker *A* support?
     1   isolationism
     2   socialism
     3   internationalism
     4   imperialism

40   United States foreign policy toward the Soviet Union during the 1970's
     was designed mainly to
     1   match Soviet economic aid to Eastern European nations
     2   address the question of neutrality rights for navigation in the Persian
         Gulf
     3   forge a joint peace resolution leading to successful Soviet withdrawal
         from Afghanistan
     4   shift relations from the confrontation of the cold-war era to
         negotiations in an era of better understanding

41 Which statement most accurately describes the exercise of power by the three branches of the United States Government?
1 Executive power has decreased significantly during periods of war.
2 Periods of strong Presidential leadership have alternated with periods of strong congressional leadership.
3 The legislative branch has consistently held the most power because it authorizes spending and taxation.
4 The relative power exercised by each branch of government has not changed since Federal Constitution was ratified.

42 "Basically, the United States today has only a one-party political system." This viewpoint is most likely based on the belief that
1 a one-party system simplifies the task of governing
2 political parties no longer play an important role in the democratic process
3 few significant differences exist between the two major political parties
4 democracy is best preserved by eliminating conflicts between political parties

43 **"Lincoln Suspends Habeas Corpus Rights in Maryland"**
"FDR Supports Relocation of Japanese Americans"
"Wilson Refuses To Pardon Eugene V. Debs"
Which is a valid conclusion based on these headlines?
1 Restrictions on people's rights may occur during wartime.
2 Congress tends to expand the power of the states during wartime.
3 Great Presidents seldom take controversial actions.
4 The status of minority groups often improves during wartime.

44 As related to the United States Constitution, Thomas Jefferson's purchase of Louisiana and Franklin D. Roosevelt's Hundred Days legislation are both examples of
1 strict construction
2 States rights
3 loose interpretations
4 judicial review

45 One similarity between the United States Articles of Confederation and the League of Nations Covenant was that the organizations created by both plans
1 were overwhelmingly supported by the American people
2 concentrated great power in a central government
3 lacked the power to enforce their decisions on sovereign members
4 achieved most of their major goals

46 United States immigration laws have generally reflected
1 the social and economic conditions within the U.S. at a given time
2 a preference for immigrants from the Eastern Hemisphere
3 the desire to help other nations solve their population problems
4 the government's goal of developing a pluralistic American society

Base your answers to questions 47 and 48 on the charts below and on your knowledge of social studies.

FARM POPULATION IN THE UNITED STATES

Year	Farm Population (in millions)	Farm Population as a Percentage of Total U.S. Population
1880	22.0	44%
1900	29.9	39%
1920	32.0	30%
1970	9.7	4.7%
1980	6.0	2.7%

UNITED STATES PRODUCTION OF FOODSTUFFS

Year	Corn (millions of bushels)	Wheat (millions of bushels)	Beef (millions of pounds)	Pork (millions of pounds)
1880	1,700	500	*	*
1900	2,600	600	5,600	6,300
1950	3,000	1,000	9,500	10,700
1970	4,100	1,400	21,700	14,700
1980	6,600	2,400	21,700	16,600

47 Which statement is most clearly supported by the information in the charts?
1 Most farms in the United States are owned by corporations.
2 The United States Government is not doing enough to help farmers.
3 The nation will need more farmers in the near future.
4 The number of farmers declined while farm output increased.

48 The trends shown in the charts were most likely caused by
1 failure to use the latest farm technology
2 increases in productivity
3 changes in consumer tastes
4 competition from imported food products

Part II
ANSWER ONE QUESTION FROM THIS PART. [15]

The powers and functions of the United States Government have changed greatly since the ratification of the United States Constitution. Much of this change has been brought about by the actions such as:

Presidential decisions   Supreme Court rulings
Congressional legislation   Custom and usage
            Constitutional amendments

Choose *three* of the actions listed. For *each* one chosen:
· Describe a specific example of the use of this action
· Describe the circumstances that led to this action
· Show how this action changed the powers or functions of the United States Government   [5,5,5]

2   The President of the United States has many roles. Some of these roles are listed below.

Presidential Roles

Chief executive   Chief diplomat
Chief legislator   Head of state
Political party leader

a   Choose *two* of the roles listed. For *each* one chosen, explain how the President carries out this role. Describe a specific example of a Presidential action that illustrates this role.   [10]

b   Select *one* of the roles listed and discuss how the power of a specific President exercising this role has been limited.   [5]

Part III
ANSWER TWO QUESTIONS FROM THIS PART.   [30]

3   During the period from 1865 to 1920, the industrialization of the United States led to many changes. Some areas of change include:

Production techniques   Labor
Immigration patterns   Energy sources
Urbanization   Business organization

Choose *three* of the areas of change listed and for *each* one chosen:

- Show how that area was changed as a result of industrialization during the period from 1865 to 1920 [Include a specific example of a change.]
- Discuss *one* positive and *one* negative effect of the change on American society   [5,5,5]

4   During the period from 1865 to the present, certain groups have not fully participated in the "American dream of opportunity." Some of these groups include:

Native American Indians   Women
Hispanics   Asian Americans
Persons with handicapping conditions

Choose *three* of the groups listed and for *each* one chosen:

- Show how the group has been left out of the "American dream of opportunity" at some period in United States history since 1865 [Provide a different reason for each group you choose.]
- Explain how a specific government action attempted to expand the group's participation in the "American dream of opportunity" [Use a different specific action for each group you choose.]   [5,5,5]

5   Certain works of literature are important in understanding American society. Some of these works include:

   Uncle Tom's Cabin by Harriet Beecher Stowe
   A Century of Dishonor by Helen Hunt Jackson
   The Jungle by Upton Sinclair
   Main Street by Sinclair Lewis
   The Grapes of Wrath by John Steinbeck
   The Crucible by Arthur Miller
   To Kill a Mockingbird by Harper Lee
   The Femine Mystique by Betty Friedan

   Choose *three* of the works listed. For *each* one chosen, describe the major ideas in the work and discuss why the work is important in understanding American society.   [5,5,5]

6   In August 1990, Iraq's invasion of Kuwait forced President George Bush to make a number of significant decisions.

   a Discuss the extent to which President Bush's initial decision to send forces to the Persian Gulf area reflected major United States interests.   [6]
   b Discuss the impact of President Bush's actions in the Persian Gulf of United States relations with Western Europe, the Middle East, and the Soviet Union.   [9]

7   Since 1960, various areas of concern have aroused some Americans to action. Some areas of concern are listed below.

                         Areas of Concern

   Environment   Abortion   Substance abuse
   Health care   Crime

   Choose *three* of the areas of concern listed and for *each* one chosen:

   ·   Describe a problem in the area of concern
   ·   Show how a public or private group of Americans has taken action in an attempt to deal with the problem
   ·   Discuss the extent to which this action has been successful in dealing with the problem   [5,5,5]

Answers, Explanations, and Page References
Part I

(Students should note the variety of instances in which material from Part I questions can be useful in answering Parts II & III and vice versa.)

1 (ans. 3) Because Congressional use of the "elastic clause"and precedents set by the Presidents and the Federal Courts national power have expanded national power, state power has been eroded. The other three answers are false because they were either settled at the 1787 Convention or not discussed at all. (Details on pgs. 14, 287)

2 (ans. 1) Answer 1 is the most basic definition of a constitution - a framework of government. *The Declaration of Independence* (1776) justified the rebellion, and the other two items do not exist. (Details on pgs. 14-15)

3 (ans. 4) The first 10 Amendments ("Bill of Rights") specifically address citizens' rights in regard to the Federal government. Court decisions in the last 150 years, based on the 14th Amendment have extended the Federal Bill of Rights guarantees to state governments. (Details on pg. 18)

4 (ans. 1) The U.S. Sup. Court is essentially an appellate court dealing with interpreting and clarifying the principles underlying the U.S. Constitution. (D. on pg. 25)

5 (ans. 3) Answers 1,2,4 indicate a connection between religion and government. The idea of separation is clear in answer 3 and is based on *Engle v. Vitale* (1962). (Details on pgs. 240, 289)

6 (ans. 2) Montesquieu's comment indicates checks are necessary to keep a governmental branch from becoming too powerful. The quotation refers more specifically to the concept of checks and balances than to separation, but answer 2 is closest to Montesquieu's line of thinking. (Details on pgs. 15, 20-25)

7 (ans. 1) The second half of the quotation forbids states from "abridging" (changing, diminishing) or "depriving" citizens' rights. The Amendment repeats items listed in the Bill of Rights. State power is diminished by the Amendment. (See explanation for question 3 above.) (Details on pgs. 18, 240)

8 (ans. 2) The legal "process" the citizen is "due" (owed) is fair and equal treatment (under the Bill of Rights) when criminal charges are leveled by the state and Federal governments. (Details on pg. 18)

The Washington/DuBois quotations require students to see the contrast in ideas, but it is important that the central idea they are arguing be identified as the basic status and position of black Americans after the Civil War. Some hint of a date or time period would have been helpful.

9 (ans. 1) DuBois indicates the return for Washington's recommended sacrifices was a loss of political and civil rights. (Details on pgs. 60-61)

10 (ans. 3) DuBois and Washington were divided on tactics, not on goals. Both wanted to improve life for black Americans. (Details on pgs. 60-61)

11 (ans. 4) The defeat of the rebelling Southern states in 1865 strengthened the chain of ideas of Marshall, Jackson, Webster, Lincoln, etc. - the Federal Union is stronger than the will of any state or group of states. (Details on pg. 68)

12 (ans. 4) The capitalist system holds the right of private property very highly. Allowing others to negotiate the use of one's property was alien to the society. Compromising on this principle with employees was unthinkable for most business owners. (Details on pgs. 84-85)

13 (ans. 1) Pools, trusts, etc. created monopolies which eliminated competition and gave one group a dictatorship in the market. The Sherman Antitrust Act (1890) forbid these "combinations in restraint of trade." (cf. details on pgs. 83, 128)

14 (ans. 3) While 19th century Americans were fecund, the labor demands of the industrial revolution went beyond even the normally high birth rate. Overseas sources of labor were desperately needed. Business interests opposed most laws reducing the flow of immigrant labor. (Details on pg. 99)

15 (ans. 2) No third party has ever controlled the Federal government, but they have been influential in pressing for reforms on the state and local levels ignored by the Democrats and Republicans. The Populists of the late 19th Century, for instance, were so influential that both the major parties began adopting their reforms. (cf. details on pgs. 108, 127)

16 (ans. 3) Factory laborers and farmers were suffering at the hands of powerful monopolies by the end of the 19th Century. Laborers were treated inhumanely with long hours, low pay and unsafe conditions. Farmers were being charged exorbitant freight rates and storage fees. Both groups wanted government regulation of big business. (See next answer. Details on pgs. 83-86, 106)

17 (ans. 1) The Progressive Era focused on controlling the negative effects of the Industrial Era. Excesses of business trusts (monopolies) and political corruption were key targets for reformers. Industrialization brought women into the work force in greater numbers and resulted renewed demands for equality. (See answer to preceding question. Details on pgs. 120, 128)

18 (ans. 4) Progressive reformers achieved more direct power for people. State party bosses & business interests lost the power to put their own agents into the Senate seats. (See preceding questions. Details on pgs. 21, 304)

19 (ans. 2) Raw materials and market expansion were often used as justification for imperialism. The Roosevelt Corollary to the Monroe Doctrine (ans. 1) was an underpinning for nationalistic intervention in Latin American countries' affairs, but not to establish colonies. The other two answers are false. (Details on pg. 132)

20 (ans. 4) The post-war depression and disillusion created an unsettled time of fear and violence in America. In such settings, prejudice and extremism such as nativism thrive. A great deal of the intolerance was aimed at non-Anglo-Saxon groups of newcomers. (Details on pg. 101)

21 (ans. 1) The rise of the U.S. as an industrial power broadened its overseas economic interests. These interests often brought contact with other major powers, forcing the U.S. out of its more comfortable non-involvement policies. (D. on pgs. 132, 145)

22 (ans. 2) Isolationists always indicated that early presidents had advised against involvement in European power politics. The truth was that all three of these early presidents were deeply entangled in European problems. (cf. details on pgs. 31-32, 144, 186)

23 (ans. 3) Harding's term "normalcy" contained the idea that the Progressive Era reforms had gone too far. Restoring laissez-faire appealed to an emotionally drained public and especially to business interests. (Details on pgs. 158, 160-161)

24 (ans. 4) John Hay's idea of fair and equitable trading rights in China was an attempt to broaden U.S. trade. The U.S. was limited by the European territorial claims to exclusive commercial "spheres of influence." These were informal colonial structures. (Details on pg. 136. Also see question 21.)

25 (ans. 1) Retailers did promote installment contracts. To define the technique as a "major trend" is debatable. Uneven distribution of wealth by the mid-1920's meant the public lacked the purchasing power to continue the boom in durable goods. This expansion of consumer credit may have postponed the economic collapse until the end of the decade. Of course, it is the only answer to which "continues today" applies. (Details on pg. 163)

26 (ans. 2) Questionable premise. Decreasing purchasing power was a result of other economic malfunctions, rather than a "major cause". While answers 1 and 4 are fallacious, a case could be made for answer 3: European nations' deficits did not allow repayment of large war debts to U.S. financiers. This did contribute to the economic collapse here. (Details on pgs. 167-168.

Also see answer to preceding question.)

27 (ans. 4) The Progressive Era experiences of most New Dealers was the source of their beliefs that government had a social responsibility. (D. on pgs. 171-175, 180)

28 (ans. 3) During the Depression, the attitude of the American public toward the role of the Federal government in economic affairs changed. After 1929, the public began to look to the government to regulate, repair, and maintain the economic health of the country. (See pg. 180. Also see answer to preceding question.)

29 (ans. 2) The hostile political struggle between the Court and the President over the Constitutionality of New Deal laws illustrates the power of one branch to block excessive power moves by another. (Details pgs. 176-177) **30 (ans. 1)** Remember the New Deal's "3Rs": Relief, Recovery, and Reform. The other three answers contain fallacies. (Details on pgs. 127-128, 175, 180. Also see answer for question 27.)

31 (ans. 3) The nature of neutrality is to avoid being drawn into problems concerning others. (Details on pg. 188)

32 (ans. 2) While racism is present in three answers, the "similar experience" appears to be concept of geographic isolation, physically separating both groups from the society-at-large. In that sense, the experiences of the Native American and Nisei are most similar. (cf. details on pgs. 104-105, 201)

33 (ans. 3) The "Soviet influence" and "control from Moscow" phrases would indicate the period after the Red Army's sweep through E. Europe in 1945. (Details on pg. 209)

34 (ans. 4) Churchill's views helped convince American leaders of the need for countermoves to check Soviet influence and the spread of communism. (Details on pg. 209)

35 (ans. 2) The passage reduces the gains made by the women of America to a matter of mere economic expediency. (Details on pgs. 84, 93, 259-260)

36 (ans. 2) The real cost of legislating desired social ends is a rise in taxes. The cartoon emphasizes that leaders lack the courage to take such politically unpopular steps. (Details on pg. 294)

37 (ans. 1) Due to the weakened state of Britain and France, the U.S. shed previous isolationism and assumed leadership of the Western bloc. Informal protectorates were established, but not formal colonies. Pre-WW II appeasement, hinted in answer 4, was generally rejected. (Details on pgs. 208-212)

NB: On "Speaker" questions, it is suggested students always take two steps. *First*, identify the common thread among the statements (e.g., here it is U.S. reaction to racial policies of South Africa). *Second*, classify the positions of speakers (e.g., A -"against intervention," B - "moralist," C - "pro-rebel force," D - "concerned with racial influence on policies") and write the label next to them.

38 (ans. 3) The major bone of contention with South Africa in the modern era has been its racial policies. (Details on pgs. 294-295)

39 (ans. 1) Noninvolvement is sometimes used as a synonym for isolationism. (Details on pgs. 186-187)

40 (ans. 4) Chronology is critical here. Answers 1-3 involve issues of the 1980's. Answer 4 applies to Nixon Era détente which broke down in the latter half of the 1970's. (Details on pgs. 274-275)

41 (ans. 2) Answer 2 reflects a defensible general observation in U.S. government not generally stressed in the state syllabus. Answers 1, 3, and 4 are contrary to fact. Considering the question's reference to exercise of power by three branches, answer 2's omission of the judicial branch makes it somewhat misleading. (Details on pgs. 20-25)

42 (ans. 3) While answer 3 reflects an arguable general observation, the terms "viewpoint" and "belief" create an ambiguity which make it hard to use the process of elimination. Answer 1 reflects totalitarian beliefs contrary to democratic traditions. Students aware of the rising number of independent voters in New York might choose 2. Political scientists who stress compromise as critical to democracy might make a case for 4.

43 (ans. 1) The three headlines involve controversies basic rights. The three presidents were war leaders. (cf. details on pgs. 48, 146, 201)

44 (ans. 3) The Jefferson reference is specific and the Roosevelt reference is not. The answer has to be based on the Jefferson example, an action was taken not mentioned in the Constitution (territorial expansion). (cf. details on pgs. 21, 176)

45 (ans. 3) Both these organizations were ineffective because they were loose confederations in which the members gave up minimal sovereignty. (cf. d. on pgs. 11, 149)

46 (ans. 1) A history of immigration indicates that the laws are made more restrictive in times of stress and less restrictive in times of economic expansion and reform. (Details on pgs. 84, 97-101, 290)

47 (ans. 4) The general trends in the two charts are in opposition. Farm population declines, while productivity rises. (Details on pgs. 106-107, 290)

48 (ans. 2) Production and productivity appear to be used synonymously here. (Details on pgs. 106-107, 290)

Part II

Students should note the variety of instances in which material from Part I questions can be useful in answering questions on Parts II and III vice versa. Also, it is useful to compare questions on this exam to others in this book.)

Writing Strategy: Each of the 3 actions selected must be described by using a specific example - name individuals, laws, Court cases, amendments, or other specific actions. Describing the circumstances means that the events and reasons surrounding the action must be discussed. Finally, you must clearly show how the power or function of the United States Government was changed. (*Important:* the action must have changed the power or function of government - how the government operates)

Presidential decisions: Franklin Roosevelt and the New Deal. Prior to the Great Depression, the government generally did not play an active role in pulling the country out of periodic depressions. During the 1930's, Franklin Roosevelt realized the great need for drastic action during the Depression. His New Deal Programs of Relief, Recovery, and Reform were intended to prevent such a serious depression from occurring again. Since then, the Federal government has taken a much more active role in the regulation of the business cycle, trying to lessen the effect of recession and depression. (Details on pgs. 172-178)

Congressional Legislation: The War Powers resolution. During the Vietnam War, many were critical of the vast military powers used by Presidents Johnson and Nixon. Mounting public pressure in opposition to the war eventually led Congress to pass the War Powers resolution in 1973. This resolution was passed in hope that it would limit the power of the President to wage war. As a result, the President must now inform Congress of his deployment of troops in combat situations and seek Congressional approval if they remain overseas for an extended time. (Details on pg. 269)

• *Supreme Court rulings: Gibbons v. Ogden* and the interpretation of Interstate Commerce. The Constitution's description of interstate commerce is rather vague. The invention of the steamboat and its use in trade and travel increased conflict between the states in the area of commerce. In 1824, the Supreme Court gave a broad interpretation of interstate commerce, saying the Federal government controls all commercial activity between states. This paved the way for Federal regulations of railroads and communications in later years. (Details on pg. 31)

• *Constitutional Amendments:* 22nd Amendment - Two term limit. Until 1940, all Presidents followed the precedent set by George Washington of serving no more than two terms (8 years) as President. In 1940, President Franklin Roosevelt broke this precedent by winning election to a third, and later a fourth term as President. Many were critical of Roosevelt's continued leadership, fearing that he was becoming too powerful. The 22nd Amendment passed in 1951 has limited Presidents since then to two terms in office. Presidents who have been elected to a second term since then (Eisenhower, Nixon, and Reagan) have found their Presidential power weakened as Congress knew their time in office would soon be up. (Details on pg. 177)

• *Custom and Usage:* Establishment of the two party system. The Constitution mentions nothing of political parties, but since the earliest days, there have been two major political parties in the United States. These two political parties emerged from the political differences between the supporters of Alexander Hamilton and Thomas Jefferson in the 1790's. The two party system changed the function of the electoral college in American government, from a group of independent electors to electors pledged to a party and candidate before the election. (Details on pg. 30)

2 *Writing Strategy:* In part *a*, you should define each role selected, in other words, what is meant when the President is described as chief executive. (General information on pg. 23.) Then, give some specific information surrounding a particular President's use of that role. In part *b*, you are being asked to show how Presidential power is checked - from the concept of checks and balances. Show the President's power being checked in a specific historical example.

Suggested part *a* answers:
• *Chief executive:* This means that the President is in charge of running government programs and enforcing laws. It is up to the President to enforce the laws made by Congress and the decisions of the Federal Courts. In 1957, President Eisenhower used Federal troops in Little Rock, Arkansas, to enforce the Court decision calling for an end to segregated schools. (Details on pg. 242)

• *Chief legislator:* This means that the President can propose and suggest laws and programs to Congress. In 1933, President Franklin Roosevelt proposed a vast amount of New Deal legislation to Congress during his first "hundred days". (Details on pg. 172)

• *Chief diplomat:* This means that the President is responsible for the over all conduct of foreign relations. The President appoints ambassadors and makes treaties with foreign nations. In 1919, President Woodrow Wilson went to Europe to take part in the Versailles Peace Conference, which led to the Treaty of Versailles and creation of the League of Nations. (Details on pgs. 148-149)

• **Head of State:** This means that the President is the ceremonial leader of all the American people, and serves as a source of unity. The President is the person who represents the nation to the rest of the world. In 1989, President Bush went to Japan to represent the United States at the funeral of Japanese Emperor Hirohito.

• **Political party leader:** The means that the President is leader and most important person of his political party. The Constitution does not mention political parties, but this role of the President has evolved through custom and tradition. Republican President's Reagan and Bush put great pressure on Republican members of Congress to uphold a number of Presidential vetoes.

Suggested part *b* answers on limitations on Presidential roles:
• **Chief executive:** Presidents appoint Cabinet officers to help run the daily affairs of government, and provide expert advice. Appointees have to be approved by the Senate. In 1989, President Bush's choice for Secretary of Defense was rejected by the Senate. (Details on pg. 29)
• **Chief legislator:** In the years following the Civil War, President Andrew Johnson faced a hostile Congress and was unable to get his programs for Reconstruction passed. (Details on pgs. 54-56)
• **Chief diplomat:** After Woodrow Wilson negotiated the Treaty of Versailles, Wilson was unable to convince the Senate to pass the Treaty by the required a $2/3$ majority. (Details on pgs. 149-150)
• **Head of state:** The President's role as head of state is largely symbolic. The President does not gain any extra powers and is still subject to Constitutional checks. At the height of his popularity, Franklin Roosevelt proposed a plan to add additional justices to the Supreme Court. The plan met much public opposition and was defeated by Congress. (Details on pg. 177)
• **Political party leader:** There is no Constitutional requirement that the members of a party follow the lead of the President. Despite being leader of his party, President Carter experienced difficulty in gaining Democratic support in Congress for some programs. (Details on pgs. 279)

3 Writing Strategy: When you describe the changes caused by industrialization, check that it took place in the time period 1865-1920. Be sure to explain both a positive and negative effect of the change.
• **Production techniques:** As industrialization progressed, more and more workers worked in large factories of hundreds or thousands of workers. The need for the production of large amounts of goods as quickly as possible led Henry Ford to introduce the assembly in automobile production in the early 20th century. A positive effect was the greater efficiency with which goods were made, which led to lower prices. A negative effect was the poor conditions and long hours imposed on many workers in large factories, which were much more impersonal than factories of the early 19th century. (Details on pgs. 78-79)
• **Immigration patterns:** Factories needed cheap labor. Many Americans saw opportunities out West and did not want to work in the poor conditions of the factories. American businesses encouraged large numbers of unskilled im-

migrants to come to America, especially from southeastern Europe. These new immigrants were hired for very low wages. A positive effect of this change was the increased diversity of the American population, and the talents brought by the newcomers. A negative effect was the rise of nativism in the early 20th century, as many saw the new immigrants as inferior. (Details on pgs. 97-101)

• **Urbanization:** Industrialization required large numbers of workers and extensive transportation facilities. Immigrants were attracted to New York City because of its job opportunities, and businesses located in New York City to take advantage of its transportation network. A positive effect of urbanization on American society was the increase in job opportunities available to Americans. A negative effect was the overcrowding and generally poor conditions experienced by city dwellers in slum areas. (Details on pgs. 90-91)

• **Labor:** Industrialization led to larger factories and more impersonal relationships between employee and employer. Employees were subject to dangerous working conditions and low wages. In 1886, the American Federation of Labor was formed in an effort to organize workers and end abusive conditions. By 1900, millions of workers were represented by labor unions. A positive effect of the change was the improved conditions which unions slowly gained for their workers. A negative effect of this change was the violence which often accompanied strikes in the late 19th century. (Details on pgs. 83-86)

• **Energy Sources:** Large scale production in the industrial period was impossible with the water power methods of the early 19th century. To power the new factories, coal was the major energy source of the 19th century. It was plentiful and easily mined. A positive effect on society was the enormous number of jobs created by mining and related industries. A negative effect was the pollution caused by the burning of large quantities of coal. (Details on pg. 77)

• **Business organization:** Industrialization led to the creation of businesses with nationwide distribution networks and the need for larger amounts of capital. Through creation of corporations, businesses sold stock to shareholders and raised needed capital for business expansion. By the end of the 19th century, large corporations dominated the oil industry (John D. Rockefeller) and the steel industry (Andrew Carnegie). A positive effect of corporate growth was the use of efficient business methods which resulted in greater quantities of goods and wider distribution capabilities. A negative effect was the tendency of many of these large corporations to form monopolies in order to reduce competition. Lack of competition eventually resulted in higher prices for consumers. (Details on pgs. 72-73, 78-79)

4 *Writing Strategy:* Key theme here is the "American Dream" of opportunity - the desire of all citizens to partake in the democratic process and achieve economic well being. The groups listed found it difficult to attain this dream at various times. Divide your answer into 3 paragraphs, each one containing discussion of a different group seeking to participate fully in the "American dream." Each paragraph must contain *a)* one way in which that group was disadvantaged in the time period since 1865; *b)* how a specific *government* action was designed to help them participate in the American dream of opportunity. **INFORMATION and GOVERNMENT ACTIONS must not be repeated.**

· *Native American Indians:* a) Starting after the Civil War, the Federal government placed Native Americans on reservations, usually on poor land with little economic value. As a result, Native Americans had little opportunity to achieve the American dream. Those living on isolated reservations were plagued by poor health and high unemployment. b) In an attempt to expand participation in the American dream, legislatures and courts in recent years have given Native Americans compensation for land taken by the government long ago. In the 1970's, the Seneca people were given $15 million in compensation for land illegally taken for a state dam. (Details on pgs. 105-106, 261-262)

· *Women:* a) Though citizens, women were not guaranteed the right to vote, the most basic dream in a democratic society. Throughout the 19th century, suffragettes sought to gain voting rights for women. b) Finally in 1920, the 19th Amendment to the Constitution was ratified gave women voting rights. (Details pgs. 116-117)

· *Hispanics:* a) The limited English of many Hispanic immigrants shut them out of many political and educational opportunities. Many Hispanics were reluctant to exercise their right to vote, and Hispanic children fell behind their English counterparts in school. b) During the 1970's, the Federal government passed the Voting Rights Act (Details on p. 259), which required the use of bilingual ballots. Also, the Bilingual Education Act (Details on pg. 282) led to the use of school instruction in languages other than English.

· *Asian-Americans:* a) During World War II, Japanese Americans were denied the American dream of opportunity when hundreds of thousands were rounded up by the Federal government and placed in detention centers out west. Though guilty of no crime, many lost their homes and businesses. b) A belated government action to allow this group to achieve the dream of opportunity was taken in 1988, when Congress agreed to pay $20,000 to each survivor as restitution for the earlier detainment. (Details on pgs. 201-202)

· *Persons with handicapping conditions:* a) For many years, those with physical disabilities were denied equal educational opportunities and faced discrimination in employment. The reason given was that it was too difficult to provide the necessary facilities with the physically disabled, and many believed the disabled would be unable to keep up with the demands of modern life. b) To correct this discrimination and provide disabled Americans with the American dream of opportunity, the Rehabilitation Act of 1973 forbade discrimination in jobs, education and housing. The Education Act of 1975 made mandatory equal education for all children with handicaps. (Details on pg. 282)

5 *Writing Strategy:* Divide your answer into 3 paragraphs of equal length. Each paragraph will focus on a different work of literature and contain two main points: a) the major ideas contain in the work; b) why the work is important in understanding American society.

Uncle Tom's Cabin by Harriet Beecher Stowe - a) Written in the 1850s this novel sought to publicize the harsh and brutal treatment of slaves in the American south. Stowe was a northern abolitionist who had not visited a southern plantation. b) Public outrage over the portrayal of slavery in this novel increased abolitionist feeling in the North. Although the Kansas-Nebraska Act was designed to let the citizens of territories seeking to enter the Union decide whether they would enter as slave or free states, opposing groups met in bloody conflict over this issue. (Details on pgs. 44)

• *A Century of Dishonor* by Helen Hunt Jackson - *a)* Jackson described how the federal government had mismanaged Indian affairs during the established and expansion of the United States. *b)* The attention brought to Indian affairs by this book led in part to the Congressional passage of the Dawes General Allotment Act of 1887. This act gave Indian heads of household a 160 acre farm and American citizenship when they 'civilized'. It did not work. The Native Americans involved were not used to farming. Much reservation land was lost as surplus land was sold to non-Indians. (Details on pgs. 106)

• *The Jungle* by Upton Sinclair - *a)* Sinclair was one of a series of writers at this time known as "muckrakers." Although written by Sinclair to show the poor working conditions and treatment of immigrants in the Chicago meatpacking industry, the public fixed its attention on the graphic descriptions of how sausages and other meat products were made. The descriptions were often nauseating accounts of the uses of rancid meat and other fillers used to make sausages. *b)* Public outrage over the quality of meat led to the passage of Progressive Era laws, the Meat Inspection Act and later the Pure Food and Drug Act. Sinclair was one of a series of writers at this time known as "muckrakers." (Details on pg. 120)

• *Main Street* by Sinclair Lewis - *a)* Written in 1920, *Main Street* portrayed the dullness and sameness of middle class life during the age of consumerism. Businessmen were portrayed as narrow minded, boring, and unhappy. *b)* Lewis was one of the "lost generation" of American writers who were dissatisfied with the materialism and consumerism of the 1920s. Other writers of this group were F. Scott Fitzgerald and Ernest Hemingway, and T.S. Elliot. (Related ideas on pg. 165)

• *The Grapes of Wrath* by John Steinbeck - *a)* *Grapes* chronicles the life of an Oklahoma family during the Depression as they leave their farm for a new life in California. Their few joys and major disappointments and setbacks are set down. *b)* Steinbeck's novel, written during the Depression, traces a common path followed by one group of people during this time period. The forces of economy and geography forced many people from the dust bowl states to relocate westward hoping to find work and betterment. (Details on pg. 178)

• *The Crucible* by Arthur Miller - *a)* Using the Salem Witch Trials of the 17th century as a setting, Miller attacked Senator Joe McCarthy's communist witch hunt. *b)* The conservatism and fear of communism during the 1950s reached their apex with the actions of Senator McCarthy. McCarthy and the witch hunt mentality fell out of favor, but not before the lives of many Americans were disrupted and in some cases ruined. (Background on pgs. 218-219)

• *To Kill a Mockingbird* by Harper Lee - *a)* This novel explored racial attitudes and class structure in the South during the end of the Depression years. The central plot involves the trial of a black man for rape and the resulting impact for him and his white defense attorney. Intolerance and racism provide the focal conflict. *b)* The dual class structure described in this book illustrates the life in the South prior to the civil rights actions of the mid 20th century. Life in the South before the impact of the 1954 Brown v. Board of Education is one of de jure segregation. (Background on pgs. 241-243)

• *The Feminine Mystique* by Betty Friedan - *a)* This 1963 book states that women were pressured by society into finding their roles and themselves in the home. Therefore, when the children are grown and off on their own, these same women have no sense of self worth and identity. *b)* Friedan's work spurred on the modern women's movement. Feminists formed the National Organization for Women and worked for ratification of the Equal Rights Amendment. (Details on pg. 260) *(Ed. note: The perspective above was written in mid-1990.)*

6 *Writing Strategy:* (This essay is narrow in scope and focuses on one current event. Students should exercise caution if they do not have factual information to support the opinions they will express here.) In Part *a)*: carefully identify the political and economic interests of the U.S. in the Middle East and in the Persian Gulf. In Part *b)*: Describe the long term results of the "Desert Shield" and "Desert Storm" operations with regard to our relationships with Western Europe, the Middle East and the U.S.S.R.

• ***Part a):*** Political and economic interests of the U.S. in the Middle East and in the Persian Gulf: The United States has been actively interested in the events in the Middle East since World War II. Strategic oil supplies for Japan and other Western European allies, open traffic in the Suez Canal, and protection of Israel have been among the greatest priorities in the region. President Bush's decision to send troops to the Persian Gulf was a response to perceived threats to these interests. In mid-1990, Saddam Hussein of Iraq threatened and invaded Kuwait, a small oil-rich Persian Gulf state. The U.S., rallied the United Nations and other countries to use economic sanctions then force against Saddam. He was perceived to be an aggressive dictator whose actions threatened the delicate balance of peace. Saddam Hussein also threatened Israel and the sovereignty of Saudi Arabia. In addition, the United States does have a history of opposing, with force, the actions of aggressive dictators. (Background and details pgs. 297-298)

• ***Part b):*** Long term results of U.S.-led military operations with regard to our relationships: The full impact of the Persian Gulf War and its aftermath have not yet been sorted out. Some general statements can be made regarding the crisis' effect on U.S. relations with other areas.

• ***Western Europe***: The United States led a coalition of forces against the aggression of Saddam Hussein. Major military support for the coalition came from France and Great Britain. Other European nations in pledged a variety of aid. Not all of these pledges have been met. Congress has requested this money be paid promptly.

• ***Middle East***: Although coalition forces included many Middle Eastern countries, their inclusion generated much controversy within the region. Saddam's SCUD missile attacks on Israel prompted concerns that Israel would take action against Iraq thereby threatening the existence of the coalition. United States' diplomatic efforts helped to prevent the coalition's breakup. However, since the end of military action in the Persian Gulf, there has been no resolution to the 'problem' presented by Saddam Hussein. There is still great dissension between fundamentalist Muslims (Shi'ite) and moderate Muslims (Suni). U.S. Secretary of State James Baker tried to bring the nations of the Middle East together to discuss longstanding issues, including recognition of Israel and lack of a Palestinian homeland.

• ***Soviet Union***: In the midst of great political realignment and upheaval at home, the U.S.S.R. tried a series of initiatives designed to prevent the outbreak of the Gulf War. These included introducing United Nations resolutions. The United States did not agree with the Soviet actions. While critical of Saddam Hussein's actions, the Soviets did not supply active military assistance to the coalition forces. In fact, the Soviets had been the main suppliers of Iraqi military prior to the outbreak of the war. (Background information on pg. 283, 293)

7 *Writing Strategy:* Divide your essay into three paragraphs of equal length. Each paragraph will focus on one of the three areas of concern you chose. Within each paragraph, a) describe a problem within the area of concern, b) discuss how a public or private group of Americans is attempting to deal with the problem, and c) discuss to what extent their actions have been successful.

• ***Environment:*** a) The disposal of waste materials generated by millions of Americans each day presents a huge problem. The nation's landfills are rapidly filling up. b) Local governments are passing a number of laws calling for citizens to reduce their garbage poundage in a number of different ways. Recycling of glass, aluminum, and other metals is mandatory in most municipalities now. Container deposits exist in many states. c) Although the total amount of garbage produced per person continues to increase, more material is being recycled. Answers to the nation's garbage problem involve more than recycling.

• ***Abortion:*** a) Many people oppose the *Roe v. Wade* decision of 1973 which in effect legalized abortion in the United States. A vocal percentage of those people are trying to get this decision overturned. b) The Right to Life Party is a third political party. Its main goal is to elect officials who are against legalized abortion. They campaign actively on all governmental levels. c) The actions of the Right to Life Party have resulted in their candidates getting elected. A number of states have passed stricter abortion laws, but the *Roe v. Wade* decision of the Supreme Court still stands.

• ***Substance Abuse:*** a) Alcohol is probably the number one substance abused in the United States. b) Students Against Drunk Driving chapters were organized in schools all across the United States in an effort to decrease the amount of alcohol abuse, especially when combined with driving. c) The actions of groups such as SADD combined with stricter penalties for drunk driving have had some impact on related statistics, but major problems still exist.

• ***Health Care:*** a) The cost of adequate health care in the United States continues to skyrocket. b) In many cities across the United States, groups of physicians and other health care workers have opened up free or low cost health clinics to provide minimum health care to the poor. Children are especially targeted. c) Congress and other groups are looking for ways to provide some sort of minimum health care to all those living in the United States at a reasonable cost. So far there has been no answer.

• ***Crime:*** a) Crime of any sort has always been of major concern to Americans. Since 1960 there has been an increase in the frequency of crime. b) Local neighborhoods have organized Neighborhood Watch groups to patrol local areas. These patrols are on the lookout for suspicious activity and are to report it to the police. c) Neighborhood groups have fostered closer ties within the neighborhood. Certain types of crimes have gone down in these areas.

Practice Exam 2 — *January 1992*

Part I (55 credits) Answer all 48 questions in this part.

Directions (1-48): For each statement or question, write on the separate answer sheet the *number* of the word or expression that, of those given, best completes the statement or answers the question.

1 According to the Declaration of Independence, the purpose of government is to
 1 establish separation of church and state
 2 secure natural rights for the people
 3 provide for the defense of the country
 4 encourage economic expansion

2 At the Constitutional Convention of 1787, serious differences about representation were resolved by creating
 1 a judicial system
 2 an electoral college
 3 a bicameral legislature
 4 a strong executive branch of government

3 The United States Constitution includes both the Bill of Rights and a description of treason. These provisions illustrate that the Constitution
 1 attempts to balance the need for liberty and the need for order
 2 emphasizes the importance of personal liberties
 3 gives greater weight to national security than to other concerns
 4 outlines the distribution of ruling powers among government leaders

4 In United States history, the development of the Cabinet, political parties, and judicial review indicates the
 1 need to limit the power of the three branches of government
 2 growth of government based on the unwritten constitution
 3 failure of the Constitution to adapt to political change
 4 continuing importance of the States rights principle

Base your answers to questions 5 through 7 on the statements below and on your knowledge of social studies.

Speaker A: The framers of the United States Constitution deliberately made the amendment process difficult so that Congress and individual state legislatures would have the opportunity to experiment with solutions to problems.

Speaker B: Constitutional amendments give citizens a sense of correcting injustices. We need many more amendments to define our freedoms fully.

Speaker C: Constitutional amendments are to be ratified sparingly. Historically, the Constitution has been changed more by reinterpretation than by amendments.

Speaker D: We have to remember that constitutional amendments must reflect a national consensus. Citizens will ignore an amendment if they think it interferes with their personal freedoms.

5   Which speaker refers most directly to the principle of federalism?
   (1) *A*   (3) *C*
   (2) *B*   (4) *D*

6   Which speaker refers to the United States experience with prohibition?
   (1) *A*   (3) *C*
   (2) *B*   (4) *D*

7   Which speaker refers to the role of the Supreme Court in bringing about constitutional change?
   (1) *A*   (3) *C*
   (2) *B*   (4) *D*

8   The main purpose of granting life tenure to Federal judges is to
   1   help bring about impartiality in their decision making
   2   permit them to obtain judicial experience
   3   assure that they will follow the President's wishes
   4   reward them for their political party loyalties

9   Presidents Abraham Lincoln and Franklin D. Roosevelt had a similar impact on government in that they both
   1   urged Congress to enact legislation to aid the unemployed
   2   reduced the authority of the National Government over the states
   3   changed the role of the United States Supreme Court
   4   furthered the idea of a strong chief executive

10 The best evidence that the Civil War greatly increased the power of the Federal Government over the states was the
   1   reelection of Abraham Lincoln in 1864
   2   passage of the black codes
   3   impeachment of President Andrew Johnson
   4   ratification of the 14th amendment

11 The philosophies of Booker T. Washington and of W.E.B. Du Bois differed *most* with regard to the
   1   effects of Reconstruction upon the South
   2   best response of African Americans to racial segregation
   3   policies pursued by the United States Government toward African nations
   4   desirability of the migration of African Americans from the rural South to Northern cities

12 In the South, Jim Crow laws passed during the late 19th century were designed to
   1   make sure that the 14th amendment would be enforced
   2   provide employment opportunities for the newly freed African Americans
   3   create separate societies for whites and African Americans
   4   guarantee civil rights for African Americans

13 Labor groups in the United States supported the Homestead Act of 1862 because this act
1 encouraged surplus labor in the Eastern states to move west
2 reduced immigration from the poorer countries of Europe
3 ended slavery in the territories
4 established a minimum wage

14 *"Every contract, combination in the form of trust or otherwise, or conspiracy, in restraint of trade...is...illegal."*
The law from which this quotation was taken was passed to enable the Federal Government to control
1 tariff rates
2 monopolistic business organizations
3 large-city political machines
4 farm cooperatives and unions

15 Which situation was a direct result of the industrialization of the United States during the period from 1865 to 1900?
1 organized labor successfully using strikes to achieve gains in the status of labor
2 technological growth creating controversial issues such as death with dignity and living wills
3 the population shifting from urban to rural areas as agriculture became more productive
4 an expanding job market creating a need for immigrant labor

16 One reason for United States imperialistic expansion abroad in the late 19th century was to gain new sources of raw materials and markets. This statement shows that
1 United States economic and foreign policies often complement each other
2 the United States has sometimes given large amounts of aid to poor countries
3 the United States has often been unable to set clear policy goals
4 United States national security has sometimes been sacrificed for economic gain

17 In the 1880's and 1890's, the efforts of farmers to obtain the passage of favorable legislation led to the
1 establishment of government price-support programs
2 elimination of most tariffs
3 formation of the Populist Party
4 prohibition of land speculation

18 The primary stimulus to social and economic reforms during the Progressive Era came from
1 the Supreme Court
2 authors and social activists
3 the leadership of the two national parties
4 bankers and industrialists

19 Progressives favored the direct election of Senators because the Progressives wanted
1   political machines to become more powerful
2   state legislatures to become stronger
3   political corruption to lessen
4   the power of Congress to increase

20 In the United States, the belief in manifest destiny was most similar to later demands for
1   restrictions on immigration   3   regulation of interstate commerce
2   a laissez-faire economic policy   4   imperialistic expansion

21 During the latter part of the 19th century, United States industrialists generally urged the Federal Government to
1   control the price of raw materials
2   levy high protective tariffs
3   pass laws to insure fair business competition
4   adopt immigration restrictions

22 United States foreign policies toward Latin America during the early 20th century resulted in
1   a lasting resentment and distrust of the United States
2   long periods of economic prosperity in most Latin American nations
3   a period of little economic involvement with the United States
4   the establishment of stable democratic governments in Latin American nations

23 A basic function of the Federal Reserve System is to
1   increase the Federal supply of gold
2   increase Federal revenue
3   regulate the amount of money and bank credit available
4   provide the nation with additional commercial banks

24 In the United States during the late 1800's, nativist reactions to immigration were intensified by
1   difficult economic conditions
2   a declining urban population
3   corruption scandals at all levels of government
4   an increasing disregard of basic civil rights by the government

25 The 14 Points proposed by President Woodrow Wilson inspired hopes for a fair settlement of World War I because this program called for
1   an agreement among nations to establish military alliances
2   the return of Europe to its prewar political status
3   establishment of economic sanctions against the Central Powers so that they would be powerless to start another war
4   the establishment of a world peace organization to guarantee political independence for all nations

26 The racial segregation and poverty experienced by African Americans in the South during the 1920's led them to
1   move to the North in great numbers to find factory jobs
2   join with whites in strong national movements to protest unjust laws
3   evolve their own strong labor movement
4   support Federal programs that gave them their own farmland

27 A characteristic of United States immigration laws passed during the 1920's is that they
1 permitted unlimited immigration
2 favored immigration from Eastern Europe
3 prohibited immigration from the Western Hemisphere
4 were more restrictive than prior laws

Base your answer to question 28 on the cartoon below and on your knowledge of social studies.

Herbert Johnson in *Saturday Evening Post*, January 8, 1938

"Samuel! You're not going to another lodge meeting!"

28 The main idea of this 1930's cartoon is that the United States should
1 take a very cautious attitude toward involvement in foreign affairs
2 join the League of Nations
3 form strong collective security agreements with European allies
4 begin a program of military and economic aid to nations threatened by aggression

29 Which was an immediate effect of the use of new production techniques during the period from 1900 to 1929 in the United States?
   1   a loss of commitment to the work ethic
   2   a flood of consumer products on the market
   3   an increase in the rate of unemployment
   4   a sharp decline in business profits

30 One lasting impact of the New Deal is that the Federal Government has
   1   taken control of many corporations
   2   worked to discourage the growth of organized labor
   3   assumed more responsibility for the care of the needy
   4   lessened its role in the economy

Base your answer to question 31 on the cartoon below and on your knowledge of social studies.

31 The main idea of the cartoon is that the passage of Social Security legislation would result in
   1   a loss of individual identity
   2   the bankruptcy of the Federal Government
   3   large-scale unemployment
   4   the end of the free enterprise system

32 Which statement accurately describes conditions in the United States during both World War I and World War II?
   1   Civilian lifestyles were unaffected by the war.
   2   Women assumed new roles in the workforce.
   3   Few Americans supported the war effort.
   4   Congressional leaders controlled military policy.

33 Which was a major purpose of the United States and its wartime Allies at the World War II summit conferences held in Yalta and Potsdam?
1 to plan the political future of defeated nations
2 to reveal the events of the Holocaust to the world
3 to establish the rules of conduct for the cold war
4 to coordinate the development and use of the atomic bomb

Base your answer to question 34 on the cartoon below and on your knowledge of social studies.

HERE I AM — TO STAY!

ALL THE LATEST REFORMS

BUILT BY ... WASHINGTON

ANTI-3RD TERM WALL

?

— Denver Post, 1912

WHERE WILL HE LAND ?

34 The issue pictured in the cartoon was resolved in the 20th century by
1 a Supreme Court decision
2 an act of Congress
3 a constitutional amendment
4 an executive order

35 President Harry Truman decided to use the atomic bomb in World War II mainly to
1 satisfy Allied demands for a quick end to the war in Europe
2 gain valuable information for future peacetime use of atomic power
3 increase the prestige of the United States
4 bring an immediate end to the war

36 Following World War II, the Nuremburg Tribunal established the principle that
1 citizens charged with war crimes must be given a trial in their home country
2 only a nation's leader can be charged with war crimes
3 military leaders are more responsible for war crimes than civilian authorities are
4 obedience to a nation's wartime policies does not excuse guilt for crimes against humanity

37 A cause of public controversy in the United States during both the Korean War and the Vietnam War was that in each conflict
1   a President fired a popular general
2   the United States used atomic weapons
3   no declaration of war was authorized by Congress
4   guerrilla warfare frustrated military and civilian leaders

Base your answer to question 38 on the cartoon below and on your knowledge of social studies.

38 According to the cartoon, the growth of Federal social programs has led to
1   new conflicts over States rights
2   a shift in the financial responsibility for government-funded social programs
3   the revival of the "war on poverty" program of the 1960's
4   increased congressional control of the budget process

ase your answer to question 39 on the raph at the right and on your nowledge of social studies.

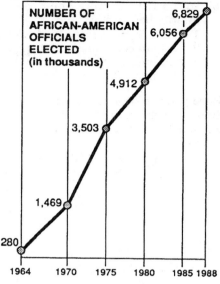

NUMBER OF AFRICAN-AMERICAN OFFICIALS ELECTED (in thousands)

6,829
6,056
4,912
3,503
1,469
280

1964   1970   1975   1980   1985 1988

Source: Joint Center for Political Studies

9 Which factor has contributed most to the trend shown in the graph?
1 Recent constitutional amendments have allowed African Americans to run for election.
2 Congressional legislation has helped to increase African-American participation in government.
3 Technological advances allow African-American candidates to campaign more effectively.
4 African Americans have gained the resources necessary to pay poll taxes.

0 The basic purpose of affirmative action programs has been to
1 bring about equal opportunities for minorities and women
2 encourage more people to vote in elections
3 make the tax laws fairer
4 reduce the Federal budget deficit

1 In the U.S. today, full equality for women is most often limited by
1 legal restrictions enacted by state legislatures
2 Supreme Court decisions
3 the decline in manufacturing jobs
4 anti-feminist attitudes based on customs and tradition

2 *"We will match your capacity to inflict suffering with our capacity to endure suffering.... We will not hate you, but we cannot obey your unjust laws...."*   - Dr. Martin Luther King, Jr.

This quotation most strongly advocates
1 segregation   3 prohibition
2 anarchy   4 civil disobedience

3 An accurate description of labor unions today is that they
1 continue to limit themselves to "bread-and-butter" issues
2 place heavy emphasis on violent confrontation with management
3 place a high priority on job security
4 have no interest in social problems that do not affect their members

4 At the present time, most of the immigrants to the United States come from
1 the Middle East   3 Latin America and Asia
2 southern and eastern Europe 4 western Europe and Africa

45 In the 1980's, many Americans began to resent Japan's economic strength mainly because
  1 the United States trade deficit with Japan increased significantly
  2 Japan controlled strategic oil reserves
  3 Japanese products were inferior to American products
  4 many American companies built factories in Japan

Base your answer to question 46 on the graph at the right and on your knowledge of social studies.

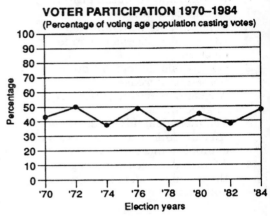

VOTER PARTICIPATION 1970–1984
(Percentage of voting age population casting votes)

Source: U.S. Bureau of the Census

46 Why did voter turnout change throughout the period from 1970 to 1984?
  1 The number of citizens eligible to vote decreased dramatically.
  2 Presidential elections attracted more voters than "off-year" elections did.
  3 Increases in voter registration resulted in greater voter turnout.
  4 Many Americans still could not vote because of poll taxes.

47 Due to recent shifts in population, which section of the United States has experienced the greatest gain in the electoral college?
  1 Northeast   3 Pacific Northwest
  2 Midwest   4 Southwest

48 *"The public mood zigzagged from one extreme to the other: first hysteria over radicalism, then complacency over good times, and finally gloom when economic catastrophe occurred."* Which decade is being described?
  (1) 1860's   (2) 1890's   (3) 1920's   (4) 1930's

Students Please Note:
In developing your answers to Part II and III, be sure to
    (1) include specific factual information and evidence whenever possible
    (2) keep to the questions asked; do not go off on tangents
    (3) avoid overgeneralizations or sweeping statements without sufficient proof; do not overstate your case
    (4) keep these general definitions in mind:
        (a) discuss means "to make observations about something using facts, reasoning, and argument; to present in some detail"
        (b) describe means "to illustrate something in words or tell about it"
        (c) show means "to point out; to set forth clearly a position or idea by stating it and giving data which support it"
        (d) explain means "to make plain or understandable; to give reasons for or causes of; to show the logical development or relationships of"

Part II

ANSWER TWO QUESTIONS FROM THIS PART. [15]

1 The United States Supreme Court has interpreted the constitutional guarantees contained in amendments to the United States Constitution. Some of these guarantees are listed below.

Constitutional Guarantees

First amendment guarantee of freedom of religion
First amendment guarantee of freedom of speech
First amendment guarantee of freedom of the press
Fourth amendment guarantee concerning search and seizure
Sixth amendment guarantee of the right to counsel
Fourteenth amendment guarantee of equal protection of the law

Choose *three* of the constitutional guarantees listed and for *each* one chosen:

· Identify a United States Supreme Court case in which the decision was an interpretation of the guarantee

· Discuss the issue involved in the case

· Show how the ruling of the Court in that case has had a significant impact on United States society [5,5,5]

2 Critics of government in the United States have suggested reforms to improve the operation of government. Some of these suggested reforms are listed below.

Suggested Reforms

Finance all political campaigns for public office from government funds.

Provide the President with a line-item veto in the Federal budget.

Pass a constitutional amendment to require a balanced annual Federal budget.

Replace the present system of selecting Presidential candidates with a national direct primary.

Reduce the powers of the United States Supreme Court.

Limit the number of terms that a legislator may serve.

Choose *three* of the suggested reforms and, for *each* one chosen, discuss *one* reason to support the proposed change and *one* reason to oppose the proposed change. [5,5,5]

Part III

ANSWER TWO QUESTIONS FROM THIS PART. [30]

3 In the 20th century, the United States has become an active participant in world affairs.

Areas of the World

Africa   Asia
Europe   Latin America
Middle East

From the list, choose *three* areas and for *each* one chosen:

· Identify a specific example of United States involvement in that area during the 20th century
· Discuss reasons for that involvement
· Discuss the extent to which this involvement furthered the national self-interest of the United States   [5,5,5]

4 At times in United States history, the actions or contributions of certain individuals have had an impact upon American society. Some of these individuals are listed below.

Neil Armstrong   Andrew Carnegie
Rachel Carson   Charles Lindbergh
Jackie Robinson   Eleanor Roosevelt
Jonas Salk   Upton Sinclair
Harriet Tubman

Choose *three* of the individuals listed and for *each* one chosen:

· Describe the actions or contributions of the individual
· Discuss the impact of the actions or contributions on American society   [5,5,5]

5 The people and government in the United States are confronted with numerous social problems. Various proposals have been made to deal with these problems.

Proposals

Require random drug tests for American workers.
Enact a national law legalizing euthanasia (mercy killing).
Place censorship restrictions on literature, the arts, and entertainment.
Eliminate the use of capital punishment.
Enact laws to protect the rights of homosexuals.
Enact laws requiring equal pay for equal work.

Choose *three* of the proposals listed and for *each* one chosen:

· Describe the problem that the proposal addresses
· Explain how the proposal attempts to deal with the problem   [5,5,5]

At various periods in United States history, groups of people have been affected by specific actions or events.

Groups - Periods
Native American Indians - 1865-present
Factory workers - 1865-1920
Women - 1900-1925
Farmers - 1929-present
Japanese Americans - 1941-1945
African Americans - 1950-present

Choose *three* of the groups listed and for *each* one chosen:
- Identify a specific action or event that had an impact on the group during that time period
- Discuss a positive *or* a negative impact of the action or event on the group during that time period
- Discuss the extent to which the condition of the group has changed since the action or event   [5,5,5]

The words of United States Presidents offer insight into their goals, accomplishments, and regrets. Several Presidential statements are listed below.

Presidential Statements
"Should the time ever arrive when Northern agitation and fanaticism shall...render the domestic firesides of the South insecure, then...will the Union be in danger."   -James Buchanan

"With malice toward none, with charity for all,...let us...bind up the nation's wounds..."   -Abraham Lincoln

"Speak softly and carry a big stick."   -Theodore Roosevelt

"...the only thing we have to fear is fear itself..." -Franklin D. Roosevelt

"...ask not what your country can do for you-ask what you can do for your country."   -John F. Kennedy

"This administration here and now declares an unconditional war on poverty."   -Lyndon B. Johnson

"I regret deeply any injuries that may have been done...if some of my judgements were wrong,...they were made in what I believed at the time to be the best interest of the Nation."   -Richard Nixon

Select *three* of the Presidential statements listed and for *each* one chosen:
- Describe a historical situation that led the President to make the statement
- Discuss the impact on United States history of the idea that is expressed in the quotation   [5,5,5]

Answers, Explanations, and Page References

Part I

1 (ans. 2) Answers 1,3,4 are not part of the *Declaration,* they are issues related to the Constitution. The key is to remember the *Declaration* is a proclamation of democratic ideals of the Enlightenment, especially those of Locke and Rousseau. (Details on pgs. 10-11)

2 (ans. 3) A two house (bicameral) solution allowed one house based on population (House of Rep) and the other on equality among the states (Senate). Each could check the other. (Details on pgs. 11, 13-15)

3 (ans. 1) Article III is very specific and a clear statement of behavior that will not be tolerated tempers the Bill of Rights' broad assurances of liberty. (Details on pgs. 17-19)

4 (ans. 2) Early activities inside and outside the government led to patterns of political behavior not covered by the Constitution. (Details on pgs. 29-31)

N.B.: On "Speaker" questions, students should always take *two* preliminary steps: 1) identify the common thread among the statements (e.g., This one is on views of the amending process.); 2) classify the positions of speakers (e.g., *Speaker A* -"deal locally with problems," *B* - "more amendments," *C* - "broad interpretation of existing amendments," *D* - "cautious about public support for amendments") and write a label next to them.

5 (ans. 1) *Speaker A* is talking about federalism - the idea that the central government addresses the broad national issues while states focus on local issues. (Details on pg. 15)

6 (ans. 4) *Speaker D* is reflecting on the idea that small groups in each state pushed for the 18th Amendment (1919), and later most Americans willfully ignored it. The result was that it became the only amendment to be repealed by another - the 21st in 1933. (Details on pg. 164)

7 (ans. 3) The U.S. Supreme Court is essentially an appellate court which deals with interpreting and clarifying the principles underlying the U.S. Constitution. (Details on pgs. 25, 240)

8 (ans. 1) By making Federal judgeships non-elective and lifelong, the writers of the Constitution hoped to remove them from political influences. This enables them to focus on the principles of justice. (Details on pg. 25)

9 (ans. 4) Chief executives that have had to serve during national emergencies have often expanded the power of the Presidency. (Cf. details on pgs. 49, 173-177, 196-198, 200)

10 (ans. 4) The 14th Amendment gave a broad, national Constitutional guarantee of equal protection and due process for all citizens. This meant state laws denying such guarantees would be null or void. (Details on pgs. 56, 68)

11 (ans. 2) The central idea of both Washington & DuBois concerns the basic status and position of African Americans. They disagreed on tactics, not on goals. Both wanted to improve life for African Americans. (Details on pgs. 60-61)

12 (ans. 3) After the removal of Northern occupation armies in 1877, a series of legal moves in the South established de jure segregation. These moves resulted social, political and economic separation of the two races. (Details on pg. 60)

13 (ans. 1) There was some union hostility toward immigrants. Unionists theorized that immigrants accepted low wages to survive. This competition undermined labor's efforts to raise wages and improve conditions. Logically, unions supported legislation which drew immigrants away from the cities. (Details on pg. 84)

14 (ans. 2) Pools, trusts, etc. created monopolies which cut competition and gave industrialists a dictatorial power in the market. The Sherman Antitrust Act (1890) forbid these "combinations in restraint of trade." (cf. details on pgs. 83, 128)

15 (ans. 4) While 19th century Americans were fecund (prolific), the labor demands of the industrial revolution went beyond even the normally high birth rate. Industries desperately needed overseas sources of labor. Business interests did what they could to increase the flow of cheaper immigrant labor. (Details on pg. 99)

16 (ans. 1) The rise of the U.S. as an industrial power broadened its overseas economic interests. These interests often brought contact with other major powers, forcing the U.S. out of its more comfortable non-involvement policies. Imperialists often used raw materials and market expansion as justification for colonialism. (Details on pgs. 132, 145)

17 (ans. 3) No third party has ever controlled the federal government. However, they have been influential in pressing for reforms on the state and local levels ignored by the Democrats and Republicans. The Populists of the late 19th century were very influential in pressing for agrarian reform. (Details on pgs. 108 -109)

18 (ans. 2) Muckrakers of the 19th and early 20th centuries called public attention to corruption and unsavory business practices. Their work certainly aided the crusading individuals who had long labored for political and social reform. Whether their activities were the "primary" stimulus of Progressivism is arguable. (Details on pg. 120)

19 (ans. 3) In the Gilded Age, industrialists bribed state legislators to do their bidding. In the original Constitution, U.S. Senators were chosen by their state's legislators. Therefore the Senate was full of indirectly chosen to protect special interests. Progressives eventually succeeded in getting the 17th Amendment ratified. It required direct popular election of Senators.

20 (ans. 4) The idealistic (and ethnocentric) belief that America's role was to spread democracy westward led to a crusade to expand territory in the early 19th century. In the late 19th c., imperialists revived the idea. They claimed America's mission was to democratize the world. (Details on pgs. 132-141)

21 (ans. 2) In the early stages of industrialization, domestic businesses advocated high taxes on goods imported from industrially advanced nations. High tariffs were supposed equalize emerging U.S. industries' chances to compete. By the late 19th century, most U.S. industries did not need the protection, but still wanted the protective wall. (Details on pg. 133)

22 (ans. 1) The Roosevelt Corollary to the Monroe Doctrine was an underpinning for nationalistic intervention in Latin America. (Details on pgs. 132, 145 and essay 7 of this exam)

23 (ans. 3) The "Fed" was a Progressive reform to help regulate commercial banking. (Details on pg. 128)

24 (ans. 1) Nativists traditionally thrive in troubled times such as economic contractions. It is psychologically appealing to select weak members of the society and have them serve as scapegoats. (Details on pgs. 100-101)

25 (ans. 4) The most famous of the 14 Points and the one President Wilson most wanted was the League of Nations. (Details on pgs. 148-149)

26 (ans. 1) (Time frame creates a questionable premise here.) In the segregated South, social, political and economic justice were denied to African Americans. Historians say they began a "Northern Migration" in the late 19th century. It accelerated as jobs opened in the North in World War I industries. In the early 1920s, the post war depression saw a decline available jobs, but the desire for a better life kept the momentum of migration going. (Details on pgs. 60, 157)

27 (ans. 4) The early 1920's were a time of depression, and fear of subversion. A history of immigration shows that the laws become more restrictive in times of stress. (Details on pgs. 84, 97-101, 290)

28 (ans. 1) The activities of fascist regimes in the 1930's has Uncle Sam looking wistfully at his Wilsonian ("Make the World Safe for Democracy") uniform from World War I. His wife (the American People) expresses anti-involvement doubt and concern in the caption. (Details on pgs. 186-188)

29 (ans. 2) A generalized cause-effect question. The key word is immediate. Answer 2 is the most immediate effect. Answers 1 and 3 are can be validly argued as long range effects of mechanization and automation.

30 (ans. 3) During the Depression, the attitude of the American public toward the role of the Federal government in economic affairs changed. Remember the New Deal's "3Rs": Relief, Recovery, and Reform? The public began to look to the government to repair and maintain the economic health of the country. Part of that expectation included aid to the needy. (Details on pgs. 127-128, 175, 180.)

31 (ans. 1) The numerical references in the cartoon characters' dialog involve anonymity. The massive government record keeping brought on by the Social Security System fostered an impersonal feeling.

32 (ans. 2) Both wars called for large conscriptions of men, leaving women and minorities to fill homefront positions. (Details on pgs. 157, 199)

33 (ans. 1) No general peace conference ended World War II. Thus, many of the Allied leaders' decisions at strategy conferences laid down the general patterns for the post war world. (Details on pg. 200)

34 (ans. 3) This cartoon is inappropriate to illustrate the accompanying question. The 22nd Amendment (two term limit) was ratified in <u>1951</u>. The Amendment was more a reaction to FDR being elected four times than to Theodore Roosevelt's 1912 attempt to seek an additional term.

35 (ans. 4) Truman always claimed his decision rested on saving Allied and enemy lives by not an invading the Japanese home islands. (Details on pgs. 198-199)

36 (ans. 4) Nuremburg opened the whole question of individual moral responsibility in modern military situations. (Details on pg. 202)

37 (ans. 3) Involves some detailed knowledge of both wars. Truman fired MacArthur during Korea, but there was no such controversy during Vietnam. Guerrilla warfare was not prevalent in Korea. Current accounts do not show any use of nuclear weapons in either war. However, students should be aware that the Congress last declared war in 1941. (cf. details on pgs. 217, 265-266, 268-269)

38 (ans. 2) A face value reading of the cartoon has Uncle Sam (Federal Government) returning the responsibility for social programs to the states. Its basis is the "New Federalism" of the Reagan administration. (Details on pg. 287)

39 (ans. 2) The graph's trend stems from the Civil Rights and Voting Rights legislation of the 1958-mid 1970s period (Details on pgs. 249, 256-259. Also, note that graph data could be useful for essay 6.)

40 (ans. 1) Straight recall. Students must know the definition of affirmative action. These programs involve a conscious effort to employ groups frequently victimized by discrimination. (Details on pg. 259)

41 (ans. 4) As with all prejudice, anti-feminism is psychologically ingrained in many individuals. Laws can curb more overt forms of discrimination, but attitudes are harder to reverse. (Details on pgs. 260-261)

42 (ans. 4) Dr. King's words "...cannot obey..." convey disobedience. "We will not hate you, ..." shows his promotion of a non-violent passive resistance. (Details on pgs. 242, 256-258)

43 (ans. 3) Current corporate trends have led to "downsizing" and increased automation. These trends place jobs in jeopardy. Unions have had to take a defensive position on jobs for their members.

44 (ans. 3) In the late 1960's, Congress lifted restrictive national quotas. Since then, the major flow of immigrants has come from less developed areas. (Details on pgs. 245, 290)

45 (ans. 1) Non restrictive U.S. government policies have allowed Japan to export large quantities of high quality goods at competitive prices. Japan's policies have tightly restricted imports. A serious trade deficit has resulted. (Details on pg. 294)

46 (ans. 2) The graph shows the general range of voter participation remained relatively constant. This eliminates the kind of dramatic shifts mentioned in answers 1,3,4. The "change" the question refers to is the fluctuations within the range. Those fluctuations occur in "off-year" election years. You are expected to know which years were Presidential election years.

47 (ans. 4) In the late 20th century, population shifted away from the old manufacturing centers of the Northeast and Midwest ("the Rust Belt"). The movement has been to the "Sunbelt" regions of the South and West.

48 (ans. 3) Students would have to have a broad historical perspective here. The 1950's and the 1980's showed similar patterns. However, they are not offered as answers. The Red Scare, Booming Prosperity, and onslaught of the Great Depression make the 1920's the proper answer. (Details on pgs. 159-167)

Part II

(Students should note how often material from Part I questions can be useful in answering Part II and III questions and vice versa. Also, it helps to compare answers on this exam to the other sample exams in this book.)

1. *Writing Strategy:* This question tests your knowledge of the 13 Enduring Constitutional Issues. Review the chart on pages 302-303. Divide your answer into *three* paragraphs. In *each* paragraph: *a)* identify a specific case, *b)* discuss the constitutional issues in the case, and *c)* show how the ruling had an important effect on United States society

- ***Freedom of Religion*** - (Enduring Issue 4) *a)* Before the 1960's, it was commonplace for public school students to say a morning prayer along with the Pledge of Allegiance. *Engel v. Vitale* (1962) challenged that activity. *b)* Did the New York State Regents' Prayer conflict with the First Amendment's guarantee of separation of church and state? The challengers argued that public schools are institutions created for all citizens. They could not promote specific religious beliefs through this government decreed prayer. The Supreme Court, under Chief Justice Earl Warren, decided that the Regents' Prayer was unconstitutional. *c)* No matter how generic, public school prayers have been disallowed since that time. This decision has led some people to protest the "moral decay" of the nation. Some seek alternatives for the prayer ceremony, such as a moment of silence. Some seek a Constitutional Amendment to allow school prayer . (Details on pgs. 240, 273)

- ***Freedom of Speech*** (Enduring Issue 4) - a) In 1918, the government arrested an anti-war (WW I) protester. Socialist leader Schenck violated the Espionage Act banning resistance to the military draft. *b)* The issue in *Schenck v. the United States* (1919), was whether or not the United States government could suspend freedom of speech. The Supreme Court decided that the right to encourage disobedience in the "clear and present danger" of a national emergency (WW I) jeopardized society safety. *c)* The "clear and present danger" ruling is still one of the free speech tests used by the courts today. (Details on pg. 147)

- ***Freedom of the Press*** (Enduring Issue 4) - a) *New York Times v The United States* (1971) involved freedom of the press. *b)* The *Times* wished to print a series of documents known as the "Pentagon Papers." The "Papers" were a confidential study of government actions in fighting the Vietnam War. They showed misleading and dishonest statements made to gain public and Congressional support. The Nixon Administration went to court to halt the publication. The *Times* stated this was a violation of the First Amendment. The Supreme Court ruled against the government. *c)* Many loose constructionists considered this a major victory for freedom of the press.

- ***Search & Seizure Guarantees*** (Enduring Issue 5) - *a)* In *Mapp v. Ohio* (1961), the Supreme Court ruled on Fourth Amendment guarantees against unreasonable search and seizure. *b)* With proper evidence, authorities can get warrants for search. In *Mapp*, however, questions arose over evidence found while police were routinely conducting an investigation and not searching a home with a warrant. The Court ruled police were limited in getting evidence without warrants. *c)* Arguments continue over whether the Court's ruling hampers police too much, especially in drug related cases.

Right to Counsel (Enduring Issue 5) *a) Gideon v. Wainwright* (1963) involved a poor man convicted under state law without the benefit of a lawyer's help. *b)* At issue was a Florida law which guaranteed a lawyer to poor persons only for a felony. The Sixth Amendment guarantees accused persons legal counsel. This right, and the Fourteenth Amendment's right to due process, were at issue in this case. The Supreme Court declared the Florida restrictions to counsel invalid. The Court declared the right to counsel guaranteed in all criminal proceedings. *c)* Critics argued that this decision led to an increase in crime. They claimed made it more difficult for states to try cases in a timely manner. (Details on pg. 273)

Equal Protection of the Law - (Enduring Issue 6) - *a) Brown v. Board of Education of Topeka, Kansas* (1954) involved local laws segregating of schools on the basis of race. *b)* The basic constitutional issues were the rights of the state (reserved powers - 10th Amendment) versus equal treatment of students (14th Amendment). The Supreme Court ordered state and local education agencies to abolish racially segregated schools. *c)* This was a turning point in the legal and political struggle to integrate American society. This "separate is inherently unequal" ruling led to later decisions disallowing racial, religious, age-based and sexual segregation of airports, train stations, playgrounds, and public facilities. (Details on pgs. 240-41)

Writing Strategy: The focus of this essay is government reform. Some suggestions deal with U.S. Constitutional provisions, others with political tradition. A review of general government structures (pgs. 20-27) will help. Divide your answer into *three* paragraphs. In *each* paragraph: *a)* discuss one reason to support the reform *(FOR)* and *b)* one reason to oppose such a reform. *(AGAINST)*.

Government Finance of Political Elections - *a) FOR* : The race for political office today is time consuming and costly. Besides travel and staff expenses, a large amount of money goes for advertising. Requiring candidates to raise their own campaign funds keeps qualified people out of races. Providing more government funds for elections might aid more people in running. Also, placing a money limit on campaigns would keep costs from skyrocketing. *b) AGAINST* : The government has enough trouble providing money and programs for people who need its services to survive. The Federal Government has been running a deficit for several years. Instead of looking for new ways to spend government funds, we should be looking for ways to cut costs.

Presidential Line Item Veto - *a) FOR:* With the help of the Office of Management and Budget, the President prepares the budget and sends it to Congress for approval. Before Congress sends it back, much discussion, adjusting, and amending takes place. Final approval for the President is all or nothing. He cannot single out any of the added

Congress programs. With an item veto, he could decrease spending. *b)* *AGAINST:* While other officials (such as the Governor of New York) have a "line item veto," the President should not. It would give him too much power to veto specific programs or items just for political reasons.

- ***Constitutional Amendment for Balanced Budget*** - *a) FOR:* The U.S. budget deficit is our most significant national problem. The interest on the national debt alone exceeds two trillion dollars. Forcing the President and Congress to balance the budget would help us regain financial control. In the 1980's, President Reagan called for such an amendment. Congress never acted. *b) AGAINST:* A balanced budget amendment would be too restrictive. It ignores emergency situations or fluctuations in the economic cycle. The Federal Government would not be able to deal with crises in a timely manner. Cuts would be required regardless of the need of people. Congress and the President need to work out such decisions.

- ***National Direct Primary System*** - *a) FOR:* Today, not all voters have equal access to the candidates. The number of candidates in the first primary (New Hampshire) differs from the number in later primary states such as New York. Holding one national primary lets candidates focus on issues of national importance. They can spend more time on their positions on issues instead of traveling. *b) AGAINST:* The current method of choosing Presidential candidates takes several months. Although it is a costly and grueling, it allows voters to see how the candidates deal with the stress and issues. Those who can withstand the pressure have the qualities to become President. It also allows for diversity within the federal system. Individual states decide the procedures for each primary or caucus.

- ***Reduce the Powers of the Supreme Court*** - *a) FOR:* Supreme Court decisions have not always reflected the current thinking of the public and its elected leaders. Due to life appointment, the thinking of the members of the Supreme Court may become out of step with the rest of the nation. Sometimes they may make decisions that should be in the hands of state governments. *Roe v. Wade* legalized abortion in the United States. Attempts to overturn that decision have been unsuccessful. *b) AGAINST:* To be a co-equal branch, the Supreme Court must have its power of judicial review. Because they are not elected, Supreme Court justices can be neutral in assessing laws and actions involving the United States Constitution.

- ***Limit Legislators Terms*** - *a) FOR:* It is not easy to remove incumbents from office. Some legislators have served in Washington for decades. These professional politicians have lost touch with the people they represent. Congressional power is in the hands of the few senior members. This is not because they are fine legislators, but because they have simply been there the longest. By limiting the number of terms a legislator can serve, we can break this strangle-hold on political power. *b) AGAINST:* Legislators with long-term experience are a valuable asset to the nation. The Congress has existed for over 200 years in its present form. Despite problems with the system, it is up to the voters to choose their representatives. If the voters of this nation keep electing the same individuals to office, who is to tell them that they may not?

PART III

3. Writing Strategy: The United States has been very active in world affairs throughout this century. This essay will illustrate your understanding of this statement. Divide your answer into *three* paragraphs. In *each* paragraph: *a)* give an example of U.S. involvement in the 20th century, *b)* discuss reasons for that involvement, and *c)* discuss how United States' self interests were served.

- **Africa** - *a)* During the 1980's and earlier, the U.S. placed several economic sanctions on the Republic of South Africa. This was in response to the South African policy of apartheid or discrimination of its black majority populace. *b)* At that time, the U.S. took a stand against policies it found offensive, but was reluctant to require stricter sanctions. *c)* South Africa supplies U.S. corporations with important products such as diamonds and gold. American corporations, doing profitable business in SA, wanted the U.S. government to play a low profile. (Details pg. 295)

- **Asia** - *a)* A significant conflict in Southeast Asia involved the U. S. from the late 1950s to 1973. U. S. involvement in the Vietnam War was an attempt to prevent Southeast Asia from falling to communist rule. *b)* It created a divisive conflict at home. America pulled out in 1973 and South Vietnam quickly fell to the communists; *c)* This episode dealt a severe blow to the U.S. interest in protecting and fostering democracy. The government reevaluated its role in active military defense against communism in the world. (Details pgs. 265-66, 268-69, 274)

- **Europe** - *a)* World War II devastated Europe. Concerns about losing Western Europe to communism led President Harry Truman to develop the Marshall Plan. *b)* It gave economic aid to the nations of Europe to aid their recovery from the war. The Marshall Plan succeeded. Western Europe did not go communist. The European economy became stabilized over time. *c)* It achieved a national interest to contain the spread of communism. (Details pg. 210)

- **Latin America** - *a)* In 1904, the Dominican Republic had problems repaying loans to its European creditors. Concerned over the action that the European nations would take to see their loans repaid, President Theodore Roosevelt announced his corollary to the Monroe Doctrine. *b)* The Roosevelt Corollary states that the U.S. alone could intervene in Western Hemisphere affairs if necessary. The U.S. collected the debt money from the Dominican Republic and paid off the European creditors. *c)* These actions made the U.S. "guardian of the Western Hemisphere." This role protected America's economic and strategic interests. It also protected vulnerable Latin American nations from Europe. (Details on pg. 140)

- **Middle East** - *a)* In January of 1991, the United States tried to liberate the nation of Kuwait from Iraqi control. *b)* Iraq invaded Kuwait seven months earlier to gain control of its oil and port facilities on the Persian Gulf. A U.S.-led coalition, under the auspices of the United Nations, attacked Saddam Hussein's forces. *c)* The U.S. national self-interest included protection of Kuwait's and Saudi Arabia's oil for itself and its western allies. (Details on pgs. 297-298)

Part III

4. *Writing Strategy*: These individuals were either the first to do something unique, or made a significant contribution affecting the lives of many Americans. Divide your answer into *three* paragraphs. In *each* paragraph: *a)* Describe in some detail the contribution, and *b)* Show how this contribution affected American society.

- *a)* On 20 July 1969, ***Neil Armstrong*** became the first person to set foot on the moon. The voyage of the Apollo 11 astronauts marked the pinnacle of America's space achievements. *b)* After the Soviets successfully launched the Sputnik satellite in 1957, Americans wondered if their nation was falling behind the Soviets in technical ability. The achievement of Armstrong gave Americans the sense that the nation was still vital, and that this was just the beginning of new advances in space. (Details on pg. 255)

- *a)* At the end of the 19th century, ***Andrew Carnegie*** made millions in the steel industry by monopolizing many aspects of production. *b)* He then gave much of it away for philanthropic and peace pursuits, especially the construction of libraries. Americans continue to enjoy the benefits of these contributions. (Details on pg. 79)

- *a)* In 1962, ***Rachel Carson*** wrote *Silent Spring*. It described the terrible toll that industrial wastes and chemical pollution were taking on the environment. *b)* Environmental concerns among Americans grew, and the Federal Government passed a wide range of legislation to protect the environment. Efforts included the Clean Air Act in 1970, and creation of the Environmental Protection Agency. (Details on pgs. 255, 272)

- *a)* ***Charles Lindbergh*** was the first to fly non-stop across the Atlantic Ocean. In 1927, he flew solo from Roosevelt Field on Long Island to Paris. *b)* America hailed him as a hero for his success. His trip had significant impact. It made Americans realize that Europe, and the rest of the world, was now much closer. Eventually, passenger air transportation was developed. Pan American Airlines was one of the first commercial carriers.

- *a)* ***Jackie Robinson*** became the first African American player in Major League Baseball. He signed with the Brooklyn Dodgers in 1947. He broke baseball's "color line" (the owners' unwritten agreement to keep African-Americans out of professional baseball). Despite prejudice from opposing teams and fans, his playing abilities overcame opposition. *b)* His achievement opened the way for other African Americans to enter Major League Baseball. It rallied people to fight for acceptance and equality in other areas of employment. (Details on pg. 241)

- *a)* In the 1930's, ***Eleanor Roosevelt*** spoke and wrote against the unequal treatment of minorities and women. She urged her husband, President Franklin Roosevelt, to begin Federal efforts to stop the inequality. *b)* Her efforts built support for laws to end discrimination. This goal became a reality during the Civil Rights Movement of the 1950's and 1960's. After FDR's death, she spearheaded the efforts of the United Nations to create the *Universal Declaration of Human Rights*. She provided a role model for women in the United States. She symbolized drive for human rights throughout the world. (Details on pg. 178)

*a) **Jonas Salk*** invented the polio vaccine in the 1950's. *b)* This medical procedure saved thousands from this deadly and debilitating disease. It also led to millions of inoculations of children, with hopes of eventually wiping out the disease.

a) In 1904, **Upton Sinclair** wrote *The Jungle*. This novel described the horrible conditions of immigrant workers in general, and the meat packing industry in particular. It characterized the actions of individuals and groups to correct and control the abuses of big business. *b)* "Muckrakers" such as Sinclair raised awareness of problems during the Progressive Era (1900-1917). Knowledge of such conditions outraged the public. In response, Congress passed legislation which included the Meat Inspection Act, and Pure Food and Drug Act. (Details on pg. 120)

*a) **Harriet Tubman*** was a fugitive slave who operated the underground railroad in the years before the Civil War. *b)* With her help, hundreds of slaves escaped north into Canada. Abolitionists praised her actions but she outraged Southerners. (Details on pg. 45)

5. *Writing Strategy*: Many advocate proposals such as these to solve problems in America today. They are controversial, not supported by all Americans. Divide your answer into *three* paragraphs. In *each* paragraph: *a)* describe the specific problem, and *b)* explain how the proposal will deal with the specific problem.

Require random drug tests for American workers - *a)* This proposal tries to deal with the problem of illegal drug use in the United States. Drug use accounts for much of the crime in this country, decreases the productivity of the workforce, and in many cases, presents a danger to the public. *b)* Tests can be given at any time. Employees could be fired if found to have recently used illegal drugs. Proponents of random tests say they would encourage employees to stay away from drugs. (Details on pg. 294)

Enact a national law legalizing euthanasia (mercy killing) - *a)* With new medical technology, people can live longer and longer on life support systems. *b)* A law would make clear the use of euthanasia . At present, state laws and judicial rulings have created a confusing pattern of laws and precedents. A national law could clarify an issue which is now quite vague. It would lessen uncertainty for family members.

Place censorship restrictions on literature, the arts, and entertainment - *a)* Some books, movies, and artwork are sexually explicit. Opponents see them as offensive. *b)* Censoring them would discourage the artists and writers from producing such works, and keep the public from viewing them. Censorship would also send a message to the community at large that these things are unacceptable. (However, such laws can often conflict with 1st Amendment Rights)

Eliminate the use of capital punishment - *a)* It is possible for an innocent person to be found guilty by a jury. *b)* If a death sentence is imposed and carried out, such a wrong cannot be corrected. Life sentences are reasonable substitutes for serious crimes. They allow a flawed verdict to be reversed if new evidence becomes available.

Enact laws to protect the rights of homosexuals - *a)* Civil rights legislation of the 1950's tried to end racial and religious discrimination.

However, the laws made no mention of sexual preference. Homosexuals are often denied equal opportunity because of their lifestyle. They are sometimes subject to harassment and physical abuse. *b)* Extending civil rights laws to homosexuals would provide equal opportunity and basic rights to another group of Americans.

- *Enact laws requiring equal pay for equal work* - *a)* Women often perform the same or similar job as men. However, they are given different job titles, with lower pay. *b)* Comparable Worth laws (equal-pay-for-equal-work) would determine what jobs are of equal difficulty, and require the same pay. Such laws would help to end pay differences between men and women. (Details on pgs. 260-261)

6. *Writing Strategy:* The groups listed in this question have all at one time or another faced difficulty in American society. Divide your answer into *three* paragraphs. In each paragraph: *a)* identify a specific action or event that affected that group, *b)* indicate why that specific event was positive or negative, and *c)* discuss how the condition of the group has changed since the event. (Be sure to stay within the given period.)

- *Native American Indians:* 1865 - Present. *a)* In 1887, Congress passed the Dawes Act. *b)* It attempted to move Native Americans off the reservations and assimilate them into American society. The effort harmed the Indians. They were pressured to give up their traditional lifestyle for an unknown one. After decades of confusing Federal policies, Native Americans today are encouraged to live on reservations and maintain aspects of traditional culture. (Details pg. 106)
- *Factory workers:* 1865-1920. *a)* New York City's worst fire took place in 1911 at the Triangle Shirtwaist Company. *b)* Over 100 died due to unsafe conditions in the factory. Improved fire regulations and codes resulted. Today, while not perfect, the workplace is safer than in previous years. Workers face fewer dangers than in the past. (Details on pg. 84)
- *Women:* 1900 - 1925. *a)* In 1920, the states ratified the 19th Amendment to the Constitution. It gave women the right to vote. *b)* Up until this time, only some states allowed women to vote, and only in certain elections. Passage of the amendment had a positive impact. Women gained voting equality with men, and make up a majority of the electorate. Since then, women fought for equality in other areas of life, such as employment and education. The Women's Movement has made progress in seeking equality for women. (Details on pgs. 128, 259-261)
- *Farmers:* 1929 - present. *a)* As part of the New Deal, Congress passed the Agricultural Adjustment Act. *b)* This act aided farmers by helping to stabilize farm prices and regulate production. While the Supreme Court declared the original AAA unconstitutional, similar programs emerged<. Today, the government continues to subsidize certain farm products, but most benefits go to large agricultural firms. The small farmer has found it increasingly difficult to stay in business. (Details on pgs. 174, 290)
- *Japanese Americans:* 1941 - 1945. *a)* After the 1941 attack at Pearl Harbor, the U.S. government rounded up and relocated Japanese Americans on the West Coast to internment camps scattered throughout the West. *b)* Thousands of Japanese Americans lost their homes, their businesses, and their freedom during the years in which they were

isolated. In recent years, Congress has apologized for the internment and granted some monetary compensation to those still alive. (Details on p. 201)

- *African Americans:* 1950 - present. *a)* During the 1960's, Congress passed several Civil Rights Acts (1964 and 1968). *b)* These legislative measures helped African Americans by prohibiting discrimination in voting, employment, education, and housing. By the 1990's, African Americans held many leadership positions in society, but many leaders claim that full equality has not yet been achieved. (Details on pgs. 256-259)

7. *Writing Strategy:* Each Presidential statement is a response to an important issue of the time. Divide your answer into *three* paragraphs. In *each* paragraph: *a)* describe the circumstances that led the President to make the statement, and *b)* show how it affected history

- *a)* **James Buchanan** won election to the Presidency in 1856, a time of bitterness over the future of slavery. He hoped that the issue of slavery would fade, and this was a warning to Northern abolitionists to put less pressure on the South. During Buchanan's term, fighting in Kansas, John Brown's raid, and the Dred Scott decision fueled the conflict. Voters elected Abraham Lincoln in 1860 and the Southern states left the Union. Buchanan claimed he lacked constitutional authority and did nothing to stop them. *b)* No action was taken until Lincoln's inauguration in 1861. (Details on pgs. 44-45)

- *a)* **Abraham Lincoln** anticipated the reconstruction of the South after the Civil War. He wished to re-admit the Southern states as quickly as possible. He opposed punishing the South any further for the rebellion. Tragically, Lincoln fell victim to an assassin's bullet at the end of the war. Radical Republicans in Congress then imposed harsh military reconstruction upon the South. *b)* As a result, even more animosity between the North and South. (Details on pgs. 64-65)

a) At the start of the 20th century, **Theodore Roosevelt** made this statement in response to America's growing involvement in foreign affairs. By brandishing a 'big stick' (strong military), the U.S. would be able to get its way in dealing with other countries. *b)* The result was the frequent use of military forces in Latin America (Panama, Dominican Republic, Cuba, Nicaragua). (Details on pgs. 139-141)

a) **Franklin Roosevelt** expressed this idea at his inauguration in 1933. The country was in the midst of the Great Depression. It was an effort to restore confidence in America. Roosevelt urged Congress to pass a wide array of economic and social programs, aimed at "Relief, Recovery, and Reform." *b)* As a result, the nation slowly recovered, and many of the reforms are basic to American life today. (Details on pgs. 167-178)

a) **John F. Kennedy** urged Americans to give something back to their country - to help others, and not always look to the government for solutions. Kennedy urged Americans to search for "New Frontiers" in domestic and foreign policies. *b)* As a result, Congress created the Peace Corps in 1961. This volunteer program encouraged Americans to use their technical and educational abilities to aid developing nations. (Details on pgs. 248-250)

- *a) Lyndon Johnson* expressed this view in the mid 1960's, as studies showed that nearly 20% of the American public lived below the poverty line. *b)* As a result, Johnson declared a "War on Poverty." He convinced Congress to pass programs such as Head Start and Medicare to reduce poverty. Johnson's "Great Society" programs reduced, but did not wipe out poverty. (Details on pgs. 254-255)
- *a) Richard Nixon* made this statement in response to the Watergate break in and subsequent cover up during his administration. Despite tapes which indicated guilt, Nixon claimed he had done no wrong. Congress and the public didn't believe Nixon. When Congress moved to impeach him, he resigned in August of 1974. (Details on pgs. 276-277)

Practice Exam 3 — June 1992

Part I (55 credits)
Answer all 48 questions in this part.

Directions (1-48): For each statement or question, write on the separate answer sheet the number of the word or expression that, of those given, best completes the statement or answers the question.

1 The government that was created under the Articles of Confederation lasted only a few years because the government
   1 supported the extension of slavery into the Northwest Territory
   2 lacked the ability to enforce its authority
   3 circulated a uniform paper currency
   4 compelled the states to abide by its treaties

2 At the Constitutional Convention of 1787, the Great Compromise settled the issue of representation in Congress by
   1 giving each state two senators and a number of representatives based on population
   2 allowing all states to have equal representation in Congress
   3 having both houses of Congress chosen by the state legislatures
   4 having both houses of Congress elected directly by the people

3 The Preamble of the United States Constitution was written to
   1 outline the organization of the government
   2 protect the people from abuses of the Federal Government
   3 describe the purposes of the government
   4 provide for ways to amend the Constitution

4 The United States Constitution places no time limit on the terms of Supreme Court Justices mainly because
   1 the framers of the Constitution could not agree on the length of a Justice's term of office
   2 qualified people will not seek the job without lifetime tenure guarantees
   3 screening and selection of candidates is too time consuming for short-term appointments
   4 Justices should be free from political or economic pressures that might influence their decisions

5 Before the Civil War, one example of increased democracy was the
   1 elimination of property ownership as a requirement for voting in national elections
   2 granting of the right to vote to women
   3 elimination of the electoral college system for electing the President
   4 extension of suffrage to most African Americans

Base your answer to question 6 on the chart at the right and on your knowledge of social studies.

THE UNITED STATES SUPREME COURT	
Periods	Number of Overrulings of Previous Decisions
1789 – 1835	3
1836 – 1910	25
1911 – 1957	62

6   The most accurate explanation of the information in the chart is that the Supreme Court has
   1   generally dominated the other branches of government
   2   increasingly reinterpreted the Constitution to meet changing needs
   3   often limited the use of judicial review during economic or military crisis
   4   usually tried to ignore established legal precedents

7   Which action increased the opportunity for public participation in the political process?
   1   passage of Jim Crow laws
   2   passage of legislation in the late 19th century that required poll taxes
   3   changing the month of the Presidential inauguration from March to January
   4   ratification of the 17th amendment, concerning the election of United States senators

8   Which statement about the Supreme Court is an opinion rather that a fact?
   1   Supreme Court decisions are responsible for the recent decline in law and order.
   2   Supreme Court decisions have affected the apportionment of state legislatures.
   3   A dissenting view in one Supreme Court can become the majority view of a later Court.
   4   The Supreme Court has broadened the interpretation of "equal protection of the law" clause.

9   The Supreme Court under Chief Justice John Marshall was similar to the Court under Chief Justice Earl Warren in that both
   1   strengthened the power and influence of business
   2   increased the President's war powers
   3   changed public policy through broad interpretation of the Constitution
   4   increased the rights of the accused under the fifth and sixth amendments

10   Which statement concerning the President's Cabinet is most valid?
   1   Its members are elected by voters.
   2   It has become part of the U.S. Government by custom and tradition.
   3   Its members have little real responsibility or authority.
   4   It makes decisions that the President must follow.

11 Which opinion contributed to the restrictive immigration legislation of the 1920's?
1 Religious differences are not important.
2 Well-educated immigrants should be kept out of the country.
3 Only skilled workers are needed for factory jobs.
4 Some immigrant groups will never be assimilated.

12 Which historic period was marked by the military occupation of a portion of the United States, attempts to remove the President from office, and major constitutional revisions?
1 Reconstruction
2 Roaring Twenties
3 Depression and New Deal
4 Vietnam War Era

13 Which situation resulted from the laissez-faire economic policies followed by the Federal Government between the Civil War and 1990?
1 Government regulation of prices in the oil and steel industries benefited consumers.
2 Employers used their financial gains to improve wages and working conditions for their employees.
3 Trusts and monopolies were created by entrepreneurs to maintain control of the market.
4 Lower tariffs stimulated foreign trade and promoted the sale of United States goods abroad.

14 Native Americans have traditionally believed that the
1 Federal Government has the right to manage their affairs
2 settlement and development of western lands is essential to economic well-being
3 ownership of land is a basic individual right
4 environment and people are interrelated

Base your answer to question 15 on the statements below and on your knowledge of social studies.

- *The public be dammed...I don't take any stock in this silly nonsense about working for anybody's good but our own.*
- *They were aggressive men...nearly all of them tended to act without moral principles...these men were robber barons.*

15 The attitudes reflected in these statements were important because these attitudes
1 improved the moral reputation of big business
2 helped to establish the industrial power of the United States
3 helped reduce the economic gap between the owners of industry and the workers
4 improved relations between the United States and European nations

16 A major complaint of western farmers in the late 19th century concerned the
1 increase in the number of immigrant settlers in the west
2 restrictive land policies of the United States
3 heavy military expenditures of the Federal Government
4 power of banks and railroads over the farm economy

17   The history of the Populist and Progressive movements illustrates the
   1   supremacy of agriculture in the economy of the nation
   2   ultimate powerlessness of the middle class
   3   ability of organized groups to influence government policy
   4   success of third parties in electing Presidents

18   Jacob Riis' photographs and the Settlement House movement led by Jane Addams drew attention to the needs of the
   1   freedmen immediately after the Civil War
   2   farmers in the 1880's and 1890's
   3   urban poor in the late 19th and early 20th centuries
   4   Japanese and Chinese laborers in the late 1800's

19   The views of William E.B. Du Bois clashed with those of Booker T. Washington because Du Bois insisted that African Americans should
   1   seek immediate equality of all types and resist any form of second-class citizenship
   2   pursue a policy of gradual integration
   3   accept racial segregation laws because they were constitutional
   4   learn a trade before pursuing political equality

20   In the United States, many of the reform movements of the early 1900's were primarily the result of
   1   the growth of States rights as a political issue
   2   the increase in taxation
   3   the continuing decline in immigration
   4   industrialization and the growth of cities

21   Cartoons by Thomas Nast were urban political machines as *The Jungle* by Upton Sinclair was to
   1   railroad monopolies
   2   the meatpacking industry
   3   lumber and logging companies
   4   public utilities

22   Which belief was the basis of President Theodore Roosevelt's foreign policy in the Western Hemisphere?
   1   The United States can intervene in the Western Hemisphere to protect political stability and American interests.
   2   Each nation in the Western Hemisphere is entitled to full respect for its sovereign rights.
   3   The Monroe Doctrine has outlived its usefulness and should be ignored.
   4   European nations should be allowed to protect their interests in the Western Hemisphere.

23   One major result of the Spanish-American War was that the United States
   1   established many foreign-aid programs
   2   obtained overseas colonies
   3   abandoned the principles of the Monroe Doctrine
   4   settled disputes by relying on international peace organizations

24 At the beginning of World War I, President Woodrow Wilson continued
    the traditional foreign policy of the United States by
    1   asking Congress to declare war against Germany
    2   refusing to allow trade with either side
    3   adopting a policy of neutrality
    4   sending troops to aid Britain and France

25 The "clear and present danger" principle stated in the Supreme Court
    case *Schenck v. United States* upheld the idea that
    1   constitutional freedoms can be limited
    2   foreign affairs do not justify civil rights restrictions
    3   government powers cannot expand during national emergencies
    4   the rights of the accused should not be endangered to facilitate police
        work

Base your answer to question 26 on the cartoon below and on your knowledge
of social studies.

W. A. Rogers in *Harper's Weekly*, November 18, 1899

Uncle Sam: "I'm out for commerce, not conquest!"

26 Which goal of United States foreign policy is pictured in the cartoon?
    1   allowing China the right to follow a policy of isolation
    2   establishing a United States colony in China
    3   assisting in the growth of China's industrialization
    4   increasing opportunities for the United States to trade with China

27 The "boom" years of the 1920's were characterized by
    1   decreases in both agricultural surpluses and farm foreclosures
    2   limited investment capital and declining numbers of workers in the labor force
    3   widespread use of the automobile and an increase in buying
    4   increased regulation of the marketplace by both Federal and state governments

28 In the United States, attempts to enforce laws relating to Prohibition led to a public awareness that
    1   violators of Federal laws inevitably receive severe punishment
    2   unpopular laws are difficult, if not impossible, to enforce
    3   government should limit itself only to actions clearly defined in the Constitution
    4   government action determines social behavior

29 Which characteristic of the 1920's is best illustrated by the Red Scare, the trial of Sacco and Vanzetti, and the activities of the Ku Klux Klan?
    1   increased nativism
    2   belief in unlimited progress
    3   growth in humanitarian causes
    4   faith in big business

30 The primary purpose of President Franklin D. Roosevelt's Good Neighbor policy was to
    1   give the United States the right to intervene in Latin America
    2   improve relationships between the United States and Latin America
    3   decrease social and economic ties with Latin America
    4   encourage European nations to renew their colonial interests in Latin America

31 Until the New Deal, the basic approach of government in the United States for handling a depression was to
    1   allow the economy to adjust itself
    2   ask other nations for economic aid
    3   establish massive deficit-spending programs
    4   try a variety of approaches from inaction to intervention

32 The United States Government placed Japanese Americans in interment camps during World War II. This action illustrates that
    1   Presidents generally uphold the constitutional rights of minorities
    2   ethnic minorities often have uncertain loyalties during wartime
    3   unpopular groups should be placed in custody
    4   violations of civil liberties tend to increase in times of national stress

33 The history of Woodrow Wilson's New Freedom, Franklin D. Roosevelt's
New Deal, and Lyndon Johnson's Great Society illustrates that
1   domestic reform programs can be reduced by involvement in war
2   proposed reforms can be blocked by a Congress controlled by the
opposition party
3   United States citizens are generally hostile to reform programs
4   Presidents are rarely interested in domestic reform movements

34 The most immediate goal of the New Deal programs proposed by
President Franklin D. Roosevelt was to
1   have the states assume responsibility for relief programs
2   control wages and prices
3   conserve natural resources
4   provide work for the unemployed

35 In the period after World War II, the North Atlantic Treaty Organization
(NATO) was formed to
1   supervise the government of West Germany
2   establish a common trade market for Western European nations
3   provide collective security against communist aggression
4   create a new world court

36 The "domino theory," popular in the 1950's and 1960's, assumed the
expansion of
1   South African apartheid into other African nations
2   totalitarianism throughout Latin America
3   communism into Southeast Asia
4   Soviet influence into China

37 Ethnic and racial groups in the United States have often objected to the
ways in which they are treated by the popular media because these
groups
1   believe that the media use prejudicial stereotypes in portraying
minorities
2   are ignored in their demands for compensation by the media
3   are frustrated by the refusal of the media to hire any minority
workers
4   have not had any of their members achieve celebrity status

38 "You express a great deal of anxiety over our willingness to break laws.
This is a legitimate concern....The answer is found in the fact that there
are two types of laws: there are just and there are unjust laws. I would
agree with St. Augustine that an 'unjust law is no law at all.' "
This statement best justifies the idea of
1   acculturation
2   checks and balances
3   socialism
4   civil disobedience

Base your answer to question 39 on the cartoon below and on your knowledge of social studies.

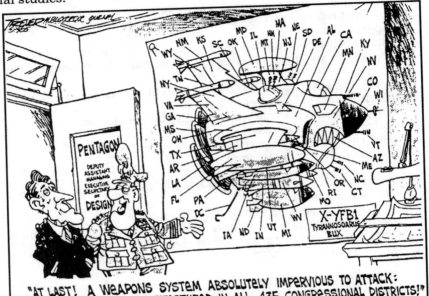

"AT LAST! A WEAPONS SYSTEM ABSOLUTELY IMPERVIOUS TO ATTACK: IT HAS COMPONENTS MANUFACTURED IN ALL 435 CONGRESSIONAL DISTRICTS!"

39 The main idea of the cartoon is that
1   the Pentagon and Congress work closely together on the defense budget
2   politics play a large role in determining how the defense budget is spent
3   the nation needs a strong defense establishment
4   new weapons systems are expensive

40 Which situation best illustrates a conflict between the function of a free press and the power of government?
1   A reporter who write a false story about someone is sued for slander.
2   During wartime, reporters voluntarily censor their stories at the request of the President.
3   A reporter is jailed for contempt of court rather than endanger a source of information by revealing the source's identity.
4   A President who refuses to hold press conferences is criticized.

41 Presidential nominations of Supreme Court Justices can lead to controversy because
1   Congress consistently refuses to approve candidates who are not members of the majority party
2   Congress claims that it has the sole right to nominate Justices
3   Presidents most often nominate their friends rather than persons with judicial experience
4   the President and Congress sometimes have different views on the judicial philosophy that a proposed Justice should hold

42 Which action could legally change a ruling of the U. S. Supreme Court?
 1 congressional debate on the ruling
 2 ratification of a constitutional amendment
 3 a decision by a Federal district court
 4 a rejection of the ruling by a majority of the state governors

43 Which action would most reduce the dependence of elected officials on special-interest groups?
 1 giving free postage to all candidates
 2 limiting campaigns and providing full public funding for these campaigns
 3 permitting unlimited campaign spending
 4 increasing the number of Federal election inspectors

44 Which statement best explains why Presidential power has increased since World War II?
 1 Supreme Court rulings have increased judicial authority in both domestic and foreign affairs.
 2 Amendments to the Constitution have resulted in increased power for the executive branch.
 3 Both national and international events often require the personal diplomacy of the President's office.
 4 Congress has legally turned over much of its constitutional power to the President.

45 The purpose of the War Powers Act (1973) was to
 1 limit the President's ability to involve United States forces in battle without the participation of Congress
 2 limit the role of the people in foreign affairs
 3 give military leaders more freedom to make decisions about placing troops in areas of conflict
 4 allow the Secretary of State more control in foreign affairs

46 Despite gains made by the women's movement, many women in the United States still do *not* have
 1 the same earning power as men
 2 legal protection against job discrimination
 3 the right to sue for sexual harassment in the workplace
 4 the right to hold high political offices

47 Which conclusion is most accurate based on the United States experience in the Vietnam War?
 1 War is the only way to contain communism.
 2 Superior military technology does not guarantee victory.
 3 Unpopular Presidents are frequently impeached.
 4 Public opinion does not affect national policy.

48 During the 1980's, which factor was a major problem in the relationship between the United States and Canada?
 1 Canada continued to encourage the flow of illegal aliens from Canada to the United States.
 2 Canada formed alliances with several nations that were hostile to the United States.
 3 Trade between the United States and Canada declined drastically.
 4 Acid rain caused by United States industries polluted the Canadian environment.

Students Please Note:

In developing you answers to Parts II and III, be sure to
   (1) include specific factual information and evidence whenever possible
   (2) keep to the questions asked; do not go off on tangents
   (3) avoid overgeneralizations or sweeping statements without sufficient proof; do
       not overstate you case
   (4) keep these general definitions in mind:
       (a) <u>discuss</u> means "to make observations about something using facts,
           reasoning, and argument; to present in some detail"
       (b) <u>describe</u> means "to illustrate something in words or tell about it"
       (c) <u>show</u> means "to point out; to set forth clearly a position or idea by stating it
           and giving data which support it"
       (d) <u>explain</u> means "to make plain or understandable; to give reasons for or
           causes of; to show the logical development or relationships of"

Part II

ANSWER ONE QUESTION FROM THIS PART.   [15]

1   The United States Constitution incorporates a number of significant
features.

Features of the United States Constitution

    Federalism
    Checks and balances
    Elastic clause ("necessary and proper" clause)
    Electoral college
    Amending process

Choose *three* of the features listed and for *each* one chosen:
   ·   Explain why the feature was incorporated into the United States
     Constitution
   ·   Discuss the use or application of the feature by referring to a
     specific situation in United States history   [5,5,5]

2   The United States Supreme Court has dealt with important issues and
has made decisions that have had major impact on American society.
Listed below are several cases and the issue involved in each case.

Supreme Court Case - Issue

   Marbury v. Madison (1803) — power of judicial review
   McCulloch v. Maryland (1819) — Federal-state relationship
   Gibbons v. Ogden (1824) — interstate commerce
   Korematsu v. United States (1944) — equal protection of the law
   Engel v. Vitale (1962) — separation of church and state
   Miranda v. Arizona (1966) — rights of the accused
   New York Times v. U.S.(1971)
          (Pentagon Papers case) — freedom of the press
   Roe v. Wade (1973) — right to privacy

Choose *three* of the Supreme Court cases and issues listed and for *each*
one chosen:
   ·   Explain how the case dealt with the issue
   ·   Discuss the impact of the Supreme Court's decision on American
     society   [5,5,5]

Part III

ANSWER TWO QUESTIONS FROM THIS PART. [30]

3 . Since 1860, the United States has experienced economic situations that have resulted in problems.

Economic Situations

Growth of industry (1865-1920)
Agricultural overproduction (1930-today)
Energy crisis (1970-today)
Foreign competition (1970-today)
Increased Federal budget deficit (1980-today)

Choose *three* of the economic situations listed and for *each* one chosen:

- Describe a problem that resulted from the economic situation during that time period

- Discuss a specific government action that was taken to deal with the problem

- Discuss the extent to which the government action was successful in dealing with the problem [5,5,5]

4 Since 1945, a number of foreign policy situations have been responded to by the United States. Listed below are several of these situations and a Presidential administration that dealt with each situation.

Foreign Policy Situation - Presidential Administration

Communist expansion - Harry Truman
Placement of missiles in Cuba by the Soviet Union - John F. Kennedy
Vietnam War - Lyndon Johnson
Tensions between the United States and China - Richard Nixon
Iran's seizure of American hostages - Jimmy Carter
Latin American intervention - Ronald Reagan
Persian Gulf crisis - George Bush

Choose *three* of the foreign policy situations listed and for *each* one chosen:

- Describe the historical background that led to the situation

- Discuss the response of the United States to the situation

- Discuss a major result of the United States response to the situation [5,5,5]

5   In United States history, many individuals have been influential in reform movements. Each reform movement listed below is paired with a reformer.

Reform Movements - Reformers

Women's rights — Susan B. Anthony
Institutional reform — Dorothea Dix
Abolition — Harriet Beecher Stowe
Labor reform — Samuel Gompers
Progressivism — Ida Tarbell
Conservation — Theodore Roosevelt
Environmentalism — Rachel Carson
Consumerism — Ralph Nader

Choose *three* of the pairs listed and for *each* pair chosen:
- Describe the conditions that prompted the reformer to take action
- Discuss the efforts of the reformer to improve these conditions
- Describe a change in the United States that resulted from the efforts of the reformer and his or her followers   [5,5,5]

6   In the United States today, people hold different viewpoints concerning controversial issues. Some of these areas of controversy are listed below.

Areas of Controversy

Capital punishment   Right to die
Affirmative action   Censorship
Health care funding   Homelessness

Choose *three* of the areas of controversy listed and for *each* one chosen:
- State an issue involved in the controversy
- Discuss *two* different points of view concerning the issue
- Describe a specific action taken by government or a group to deal with the issue   [5,5,5]

7   Many reform measures established during the New Deal had lasting effects on American life. Some of these reform measures are listed below.

Tennessee Valley Authority
Social Security Administration
Federal Housing Administration
Federal Deposit Insurance Corporation
Securities and Exchange Commission
National Labor Relations Board

Choose *three* of the reform measures listed and for *each* one chosen:

- Explain the purpose of the measure
- Describe a specific way the measure was implemented
- Discuss one impact of the measure on American life   [5,5,5]

Answers, Explanations, and Page References
Part I

1 (ans. 2) The states retained most power in the 1781-1789 confederation. Rules required 2/3rds majority to pass laws, and there was no executive to enforce them. The states pursued them as they saw fit. (Details on pg. 11)

2 (ans. 1) The Great Compromise created a bicameral solution. One house based on population (House of Rep.) and the other on equality among the states (Senate). Each could check the other. (Details on pgs. 11, 14)

3 (ans. 3) Traditionally, a preamble is a preface or introduction which states the purpose of a document. (Details on p. 14)

4 (ans. 4) The writers of the Constitution made Federal judgeships non-elective and lifelong to remove them from political influences and enable them to focus on the broad principles of justice. (Details on pg. 25)

5 (ans. 1) The early westward movement resulted in new state constitutions (OH, KY, TN, IN, LA, AL) which dropped property requirements. Women (ans. 2) and African Americans (ans. 4) did not receive the right to vote until after the Civil War, and the electoral college (ans. 3) still exists. (Details on pg. 42)

6 (ans. 2) The chart shows a rising trend of cases reconsidered. However, no text shows why. A reader has use logic to eliminate illogical answers. Ans. 1 is fallacious because the Court clashed with, but never dominated the other branches. Ans. 3 is fallacious because there is no limit on judicial review and the chart numbers run contrary to this statement. Ans. 4 is fallacious because Anglo-Saxon law's equity system builds on precedent. This would leave ans. 2 as the only logical choice.

7 (ans. 4) In the original Constitution, U.S. Senators were chosen by their state's legislators. In the Gilded Age, industrialists bribed state legislators to do their bidding. Therefore, the Senate was full of indirectly chosen to protect special interests. Progressives eventually succeeded in getting the 17th Amendment ratified. It required direct popular election of U.S. Senators.

8 (ans. 1) Separating opinion from fact involves a knowledge of the certainty of an action or event. Answers 2,3,4 are factual, and actually occurred. Answer 1 however, places total responsibility on the Court, ignoring other possible causes for the decline.

9 (ans. 3) The basic common denominator is that the Court employed a philosophy of judicial activism. Its decisions allowed new interpretations of the phrases in the Constitution, setting precedents for future cases. (Details on pgs. 30-31, 41, 240)

10 (ans. 2) The Cabinet emerged under Washington (and Hamilton) as an unofficial executive advisory council. Its model was the British Cabinet which has political power. In the American system, it has no Constitutional validity. Its influence as a body varies from one Presidential administration to another. (Details on pg. 29)

11 (ans. 4) Stereotyping was a major weapon used by the nativist groups that lobbied for the Emergency Quota Acts. Groups such as the KKK cited religious differences and illiteracy as major reasons for rejecting newcomers. (Details on pgs. 98-101, 164)

12 (ans. 1) Recall question creating a combination of events relating to the aftermath of the Civil War. (Details on pgs. 54-56)

13 (ans. 3) Laissez-faire allowed industrialists to create monopolies (pools, trusts, etc.) which cut competition and gave them near-dictatorial power in the market. The Sherman Antitrust Act (1890) later forbid these "combinations in restraint of trade." (cf. details on pgs. 82-83, 127-128)

14 (ans. 4) Sociological background on the clashes between Native Americans and the U.S. Government shows the values of the two sides toward nature and the environment were in opposition. Answers 1-3 were all the beliefs of the government rejected by Native Americans. (Details on pg. 104)

15 (ans. 2) The statements clearly reflect the self-interest and competitiveness that drove the industrialists of the 19th century. (Details on pgs. 78-79, 82)

16 (ans. 4) Monopolistic control of transportation and finance kept fares and interest rates so high that framers began to organize (Grange, Farmers Alliance, Populists) against them. (Details on pgs. 107-109)

17 (ans. 3) No third party has ever controlled the Federal government. However, they have been influential in pressing for reforms ignored by the Democrats and Republicans. The Populists and Progressives of the late 19th and early 20th centuries were very influential in pressing for general reforms needed because of by industrialization. (Details on pgs. 108-109, 117-128)

18 (ans. 3) The Progressive Reform Movement included literary exposés (Riis) and direct actions (Addams) which focused attention on the growing numbers of urban industrial poor. (Details on pg. 120)

19 (ans. 1) Both Washington & DuBois wanted to improve life for disadvantaged and disenfranchised African Americans. They disagreed on how quickly to achieve social equality. Washington opted for a gradual form of integration. (Details on pgs. 60-61)

20 (ans. 4) Changes in the nature and quality of life wrought by the Industrial Revolution led to movements to realign and adjust government and legislation. (Details on pgs. 116-118, 120)

21 (ans. 2) While Nast preceded Sinclair and the Muckrakers of the Progressive Era by a generation, the analogy is valid. Attacks on political corruption through the media is a common tactic which connects them. (cf. details on pgs. 62, 120)

22 (ans. 1) The Roosevelt Corollary to the Monroe Doctrine was an underpinning for nationalistic intervention in Latin Am. (Details on pgs. 139-140)

23 (ans. 2) Debates over foreign relations throughout the 19th century reflect many calls for overseas colonialism. It was not until the Spanish-American War that imperialists achieved success. (Details on pgs. 137-138)

24 (ans. 3) From the days of Washington, Americans embraced the idea that avoiding European military and political conflicts served the national nterest. Although groups were sympathetic toward both sides in WW I, most mericans favored the perception that tradition warranted neutrality. Details on pg. 144-145)

5 (ans. 1) Federal authorities tried Schenck during WW I for anti-draft ctivities. He claimed his conviction under the Espionage Act violated his 1st mendment right of freedom of speech. The Court said individual rights ield if the society is in peril. (Details on pg. 147; Also see answer to ques. 32)

6 (ans. 4) The rise of the U.S. as an industrial power broadened its verseas economic interests. These interests often brought contact with other 1ajor powers, forcing the U.S. out of its traditional non-involvement policies. Details on pgs. 132, 142)

7 (ans. 3) Sales of automobiles and the expansion related industries aided he business prosperity of the 1920's. Consumer credit (installment loans) ccelerated the boom enabling people to pay for durable goods over time. The ther answers are all in opposition to conditions in the expansion phase of the usiness cycle. (Details on pg. 163)

8 (ans. 2) While a dedicated group of temperance advocates convinced 'ongress and 3/4ths of state governments to ratify the 18th Amendment, 1ost people lacked enthusiasm for Prohibition. Widespread violations of the 'olstead Act proved the difficulty of legislating enforcing moral behavior. :atification of the 21st Amendment (1933) repealed 18th. (Details on pg. 164)

9 (ans. 1) Nativists traditionally thrive in troubled times such as economic epression after World War I and the social change of the Roaring 20's. It is sychologically soothing to those distraught by change to have weak ewcomers serve as scapegoats for problems. (Details on pgs. 100-101)

0 (ans. 2) For a generation, from the Spanish-American War through 'oolidge's interference in Nicaragua, U.S.-Latin American policies were haracterized by interventionism. Hoover laid some groundwork for FDR to hange to a more cooperative emphasis. (Details on pg. 187)

1 (ans. 1) Adam Smith's laissez-faire philosophy dominated classical conomic thinking. Except in wartime, government officials largely frowned pon fiscal policy before the 1930's. Government "tampering" with the usiness cycle was tantamount to heresy. (Details on pgs 168, 171)

2 (ans. 4) Victims of internment challenged the government in *Korematsu U.S.* (1944). The Supreme Court applied the "clear and present danger" recedent from the *Schenck* decision in WW I (see ques. 25 above). It said 1at individual rights become less sacrosanct in perceived peril. (Details on g. 201)

3 (ans. 1) The question contains obscure cross-chronology analysis. The mbiguous phrase "...can be reduced..." in answer 1 confounds readers. [owever, ans. 1 contains the only true statement. It is true these reform 1ovements did lose momentum because wars diverted public attention.)etails on pgs. 128, 180, 268)

4 (ans. 4) During the Depression, the New Deal's "3Rs"(Relief, Recovery, nd Reform) led to an expectation of aiding the most needy with jobs. (Details 1 pgs. 172-173)

35 (ans. 3) NATO is the oldest and strongest of the collective security agreements which "Cold Warriors" advocated as part of a global containment policy. (Details on pgs. 212-213)

36 (ans. 3) The fear of a "chain collapse" of weak nations strengthened the arguments of "Cold Warriors" to pursue a global containment policy. (Details on pg. 266)

37 (ans. 1) An obscure question, hardly viable considering the syllabus' strong emphasis on legal and constitutional issues of social inequality. Some teachers might allude to media bias in class discussions on prejudice, but it is not generally emphasized. The question might be more valid if considering Hollywood productions prior to the Civil Rights Movement. However, such criticism of today's media treatment is rare. (Details on pgs. 256-257)

38 (ans. 4) The references to "unjust law" and a religious tradition of higher justice among civil rights advocates are key phrases here. Civil disobedience is an act of public protest in which the protesters accept punishment to call attention to the injustice of a law. (Details on pg. 242)

39 (ans. 2) Caption indicates the General (Pentagon) is trying to please Congress and avoid political "attack." While answer 1 has validity, the "attack" phrase, although subtle, gives answer 2 preference.

40 (ans. 3) Key word in stem is *conflict*. Answer 3 portrays a clear constitutional conflict over basic rights. The other answers contain equivocal words such as *false, voluntarily,* and *criticized.*

41 (ans. 4) Philosophical differences have defined the confirmation process from Congress' rejection of Washington's nomination of John Rutledge (pro-slavery) to the rejection of Reagan's nomination of Robert Bork (rightist). (Additional discussion: pgs. 289, 299)

42 (ans. 2) Once the Supreme Court defines the Constitutionality of an issue it rarely reconsiders its opinion. The only immediate recourse for opponents is to rewrite (amend) the Constitution itself. (Additional discussion on pgs. 25, 17)

43 (ans. 2) Special interest groups (lobbies) organize Political Action Committees (PACs) to ask for contributions from members for candidates friendly to their causes. Successful candidates become beholden to these PACs and fall under their influence. This thwarts democratic action. Full public funding from taxpayers is a possible solution to eliminating PACs (See details on lobbying pg. 31)

44 (ans. 3) Instantaneous communication and rapid modes of travel allow direct involvement by the president in events once handled by bureaucrats and diplomatic officers. (Details on pg. 200)

45 (ans. 1) The instant retaliation needed with intercontinental missile technology and the military commitments of collective security treaties combined to broaden the President's power. The War Powers Act was Congress attempt to check the modern war making power of the President. (Details on pg. 269)

46 (ans. 1) Unusual to find a negative question on a Regents exam, but current statistics show that women make up one half of the American workforce. Yet their incomes lag those of men by nearly 33% in most major occupational fields. (Details on pgs. 260-261)

47 (ans. 2) Technology and strategies geared to traditional battles proved frustratingly inadequate against the Viet Cong's hit-and-run guerrilla tactics. (Details on pgs. 266, 274)

48 (ans. 4) Air pollution from cities such as Chicago and Detroit drifting eastward into the Canadian population centers of Ontario became a serious source of friction in the 1980's. (Trade agreements worked out in the 1980's actually promoted U.S.-Canadian trade.) (Details on pg. 283)

Part II

(Students should note how often material from Part I questions can be useful in answering Part II and III questions and vice versa. Also, it helps to compare answers on this exam to the other sample exams in this book.)

1. *Writing Strategy:* This question tests your knowledge of the 13 Enduring Constitutional Issues. Review the chart on pages 302-303. Divide your answer into *three* paragraphs. In *each* paragraph discuss: *a)* why the feature was needed, *b)* give an example of the feature being used.

* *Federalism* - (Enduring Issue 2): *a)* <u>why needed</u>: Federalism is a method of limiting governmental power by dividing authority between the national (federal) and state governments. The Constitution gives the Federal government certain powers and reserves the rest for the states; *b)* <u>example of use</u>: The national government has delegated powers, including the ability to raise an army, establish post offices, control interstate commerce. The state governments have reserved powers guaranteed under the 10th Amendment. (control of commerce, licenses and charters, schools, law enforcement). (Details on pgs. 9, 15)

* *Checks and balances* - (Enduring Issue 10): *a)* <u>why needed</u>: Montesquieu's checks and balances is an idea based separating power among three branches. The branches check one another resulting in a near balance of power. No one branch will take over the others. *b)* <u>example of use</u>: The President may negotiate treaties, but the Senate must ratify them. President Wilson negotiated the Versailles Treaty ending WW I. The Senate objected to the League of Nations provision as a loss of Congressional war making power. It rejected the treaty. President Carter negotiated the SALT II Treaty with the Soviet Union. After the Soviets invaded Afghanistan in late 1979, the Senate refused to ratify the SALT II agreement. (Details on pgs. 15, 20-21, 149, 284)

* *Elastic clause* - (Enduring Issue 13): *a)* <u>why needed</u>: The Constitution's elastic clause (Art. I,8,18) allows Congress implied power to respond to changing needs of the society. *b)* <u>example of use</u>: During the early years of the republic, Alexander Hamilton came up with a plan for the financial health of the nation. As the cornerstone of his financial plan, he wished Congress to create a national Bank of the United States. A controversy followed. Opponents said it was not specified the in the Constitution. Proponents of the Bank said the elastic clause would allow its creation. In 1819, the Supreme Court later upheld the constitutionality of the bank in *McCulloch v. Maryland.* (See answer to Essay #2 below.) (Details on pgs. 21, 31, 41)

- *Electoral College* - (Enduring Issue 11): *a)* <u>why needed</u>: The electoral college chooses the President and Vice-President as part of an indirect election system . States are allotted electors based on their total number of representatives in Congress. The drafters of the Constitution believed by presidential candidates who were unworthy of the office might sway the uneducated voters. They believed that an indirect election would provide a safeguard against this happening. *b)* <u>example of use</u>: The electoral vote count may appear to give a presidential candidate an overwhelming victory. However, this may not be truly reflective of the popular vote count. Ronald Reagan received the most popular votes of the presidential candidates in 1984. He took 59% of the popular vote, but won 49 of 50 states in the electoral vote. Less than 50% of the eligible voters voted in this election. (Basic concepts on pgs. 23-24)

- *Amending process* - (Enduring Issue 13): *a)* <u>why needed</u>: The amending process allows the Constitution to adapt to meet changing times. It was successfully used in 1791 for the group of 10 amendments known as the Bill of Rights, but since then, the states ratified only only 16 other amendments. The founding fathers realized that change would occur. The amendment process is a mechanism that would allow the Constitution to change. It is not an easy process. Three-fourths of the states are must agree to ratify amendments. *b)* <u>example of use</u>: During the Progressive Era, the United States ratified the 18th Amendment to the Constitution calling for prohibition of alcohol. A few years later in 1933, the states ratified the 21st Amend. repealing the 18th. (Details on pgs. 17, 18, 164)

2. *Writing Strategy:* This essay is about the Supreme Court's power. Divide your answer into *three* paragraphs. In *each* paragraph: *a)* give the background of the case and show the connection to the issue, *b)* show the long range effect of the decision on the nation. (Indicate the *precedent* it set.)

- *Marbury v. Madison* (1803) - *power of judicial review: a)* <u>case background / connection to issue</u>: In *Marbury*, the Marshall Court assumed for itself the power of judicial review. The Court declared an act of Congress, the Judiciary Act of 1789, unconstitutional. This power gave the Court a coequal check on the other branches of government. *b)* <u>long range effect of decision / precedent set</u>: The Supreme Court's power of judicial review has put it in the center of controversy throughout the nation's history. In 1857, it ruled that slaves were not citizens and had no legal standing (*Dred Scott v. Sanford*). In addition, the Court declared Congress' Missouri Compromise Act (1821) unconstitutional. The *Scott* case is considered one of the causes leading to the Civil War. (Details on pg. 45)

- *McCulloch v. Maryland* (1819) - *Federal-state relationship: a)* <u>case background / connection to issue</u>: In *McCulloch*, the Marshall Court defined part of the Federal-state relationship. At issue was the constitutionality of the Bank of the United States. (See ans. to Essay #1 above.) Maryland levied a tax against the Baltimore branch of the Bank of the United States. The Federal bank manager refused to pay the state tax. In the decision, the Supreme Court reasoned "the power to tax is the power to destroy." This decision upheld Congress' use of the elastic clause and the implied power to create the Bank. *b)* <u>long range effect of decision / precedent set</u>: *McCulloch* increased the power of the Federal government to regulate economic affairs, including the later Federal Reserve System. In addition, the Supreme Court upheld "loose construction of the Constitution" allowing Congress to use a broad range of implied powers. The growth of federal power has sometimes come at the expense of state power. For example, federal civil rights legislation of the 1960s curtailed some states' actions in the treatment of its citizens. (Details on pgs. 41, 128, 241-242)

- *Gibbons v. Ogden* (1824) - *interstate commerce: a)* case background / connection to issue:In *Gibbons*, the Marshall Court ruled in favor of a Federal license granting a ferry boat service between two states. This decision disallowed a state-granted monopoly. The Court's reasoning stated that operating interstate service across or between state lines cannot be a reserved power of the states. Rather, it is a delegated power of the Federal government. *b)* long range effect of decision / precedent set: The broad language of the *Gibbons* decision allowed the Federal government to later issue regulations to the railroad and airline industries, as well licensing the airwaves for radio and television use. (Details on pg. 31)

- *Korematsu v. United States* (1944) - *equal protection of the law: a)* case background / connection to issue: The internment of Japanese Americans during WW II as a result of an executive order was at issue in *Korematsu*. Fred Korematsu claimed that the government violated his14th Amendment right to equal protection. Prejudice, rather than a documented threat, led to him being sent to a camp. The Court ruled in favor of the U.S. government. It reasoned that in a wartime emergency, the government may curtail civil liberties. *b)* long range effect of decision / precedent set: Congress voted to give survivors of the internment camps a token amount of money as a show of remorse from the nation. However, during the Gulf Crisis, the FBI questioned members of the Arab communities in the U.S. The government's actions met with censure, but the extent of civil liberties during wartime continues to be an issue. (See ques. 25 and 32 on Part I of this exam. Details on pgs. 201, 147)

- *Engel v. Vitale* (1962) - *separation of church and state: a)* case background / connection to issue: New York State's Board of Regents' rule requiring a non-denominational school prayer be said daily prompted the *Engel* decision. Offended parents challenged the state's right to pass such a regulation. They claimed it violated the lst Amendment's separation of church and state clause. The Supreme Court upheld this reasoning and declared the Regents' rule unconstitutional. *b)* long range effect of decision / precedent set: Today, the issue is still controversial. In June 1992, the Rehnquist Court used the *Engel* precedent to ban invocation prayers at public school commencement exercises. Conservative groups wish the schools to reestablish a prayer component. The New Right also wishes to overturn decisions such as *Engel* and the *Roe* case which they believe have threatened the ethical values of the U. S. (Details on pgs. 240, 289)

- *Miranda v. Arizona* (1966) - *rights of the accused: a)* case background / connection to issue: Criminal rights are the subject of the *Miranda* decision. The Supreme Court ruled that the authorities must inform accused persons of their "due process" rights guaranteed under the 5th and 6th Amendments to the Constitution. The 14th Amendment protects these rights from contrary acts by state governments. *b)* <u>long range effect</u> <u>of decision / precedent set</u>: As a result, police now must immediately inform accused persons of their "Miranda Rights." Several of the criminal rights decisions of the Warren Court expanded the rights of the criminally accused. Since that time, the Supreme Court has narrowed some of the rights of the accused, but the Miranda decision still provides an important legal protection. (Details on pg. 240)

• *New York Times v. United States* (1971) - *freedom of the press: a)* <u>case</u> <u>background / connection to issue</u>: The issue of freedom of the press and the ability of the government to censor articles before print was at issue in *New York Times v. USA*, or "Pentagon Papers Case." After secretly receiving the Pentagon Papers, a series of papers dealing with government policy in fighting the Vietnam War, and the NY *Times* planned to publishing them. The Federal government sought aprior restraint order to stop publication. The Supreme Court ruled that the government had not shown good reason for a prior restraint order and that a free press is a valuable part of a democracy. *b)* <u>long range effect of</u> <u>decision / precedent set</u>:Although free press was upheld, censorship is still an issue. During the Persian Gulf Crisis, constraints placed upon the press by the military leadership of the coalition forces upset them. Lack of travel permits and the pool reporting system were sources of irritation for the press. (Details on pg. 273)

• *Roe v. Wade* (1973) - *right to privacy: a)* <u>case background / connection to</u> <u>issue</u>: *Roe* addressed the right to privacy, specifically a woman's right to have an abortion. The Supreme Court invalidated all state laws which prohibited abortion and ruled that within certain guidelines, the decision on abortion should be left up to a woman and her doctor. *b)* <u>long range</u> <u>effect of decision / precedent set</u>: Disagreements between abortion supporters and opponents continue to spark violence. It is an issue in local, state, and federal elections. An amendment banning abortion has been a proposed and backed by Presidents Reagan and Bush. Although the Supreme Court has not overturned *Roe*, some states have passed laws challenging it. Under Reagan and Bush, the Federal gov't has cut the use of Medicaid funding for abortions. (Details on pgs. 261, 273, 289)

PART III

3. *Writing Strategy:* This question tests your knowledge of economic events in U.S. history. Divide your answer into *three* paragraphs. In *each* paragraph: *a)* give the details of the problem, *b)* indicate a government action in response to the problem, *c)* discuss success of the government action.

• *Growth of industry* (1865-1920): *a)* <u>problem</u>: Industry grew larger during this period and monopolies formed. The factory system developed and the workplace became larger and more mechanized. The workers, many of them unskilled labor, suffered from long hours and poor working conditions, including unsafe workplaces. Unions, such as the American Federation of Labor developed. *b)* <u>government action</u>: Initial government reaction to unions was often negative. The government used early antitrust legislation, including the Sherman Anti-Trust Act (1890), to prosecute union leaders. *c)* <u>action's success</u>: These responses slowed the growth of organized labor in the U.S. It wasn't until the 1930s, during the

New Deal Era, that organized labor received legislative support from the Federal government. (Details on pgs.83-86, 92,175)

· *Agricultural overproduction* (1830-today): *a)* problem: The productivity of the American farmer is among the highest in the world. This has led to a decrease in the income received by some farmers. The cost of the machinery and fertilizers used is high. Huge surpluses depress the prices of these farm commodities. During the 1920's, farmers did not enjoy the general prosperity, and they were hard hit by droughts and dust storms in the 1930's. *b)* government action: Congress passed the New Deal's the Agricultural Adjustment Act, a program for increasing farm income by offering subsidy payments to decrease production. *c)* action's success: The Supreme Court declared the AAA unconstitutional in *U.S. v. Butler* (1936). (Details on pg. 174)

· *Energy crisis* (1970-today): *a)* problem: The 1973 Arab Oil Embargo made Americans realize that reliance on foreign oil had increased dramatically and oil reserves are a finite resource. *b)* government action: During Carter's presidency, the government allocated money for alternative fuel sources. The Alaskan North Slope Pipeline supplied the West Coast with a new source of oil. Congress passed stricter regulations for auto engines' fuel consumption. *c)* action's success: Although Congress discussed and enacted many measures, there is still lack of a comprehensive policy to deal with the energy problems. The U.S continues to use a disproportionate share of the world's energy. Under Reagan and Bush, there have been some reductions on fuel economy regulations on auto manufacturers. (Details on pgs. 280-281)

· *Foreign competition* (1970-today): *a)* problem: During the 1980's, the U.S. trade deficit climbed alarmingly. Skyrocketing crude oil costs, trade barriers, some nations "dumping" their excess products in the U.S. led to this problem. Japanese trade patterns caused concern for Americans. Japan exported a flood of electronic goods. U.S. workers lost manufacturing jobs while the number of choices for American consumers increased. *b)* government action: Congress allowed President Reagan to place import quota restrictions on Japanese goods. In 1992, President Bush traveled to Japan to work out trade problems. *c)* action's success: After much discussion, not much concrete happened. Agreements on allowing more U.S. goods into Japan have met with mixed success. Japan agreed to allow more larger American cars into the Japanese market, but are already considering cutting quota numbers. (Details on pg. 294)

· *Increased Federal budget deficit* (1980-today): *a)* problem: Currently, the U.S. government faces annual budget deficits in the $400 billion range. In part, this resulted from Reagan Administration tax cuts not offset by reductions in total government spending. *b)* government action: Presidents Reagan and Bush and Congress have tried to make spending cuts. Congress passed the Gramm-Rudman-Hollings Balanced Budget Act(1985) ordering spending cuts of $36 billion annually to balance the budget by 1991 *c)* action's success: As of now, Bush and Congress have never met the Gramm-Rudman limits. The deficit has doubled since it was passed. (Details on pgs. 288, 299)

4 . *Writing Strategy:* This question tests your knowledge of U.S. behavior as a world power since WW II. Divide your answer into *three* paragraphs. In *each* paragraph: *a)* give dates and events in discussing the historical background for each situation; *b)* the form of U.S. response is usually an action taken by the President or Congress, since they deal most directly with foreign policy; *c)* the results must describe the effects of the action either in the foreign nation or in the United States.

- *Communist expansion - Harry Truman: a)* background: As the Soviet Army advanced on Germany in 1944-1945, the Soviets occupied many of the nations of Eastern Europe. After the War ended, the Soviet authorities helped create communist governments in most of Eastern Europe. In 1947-1948, the Soviets tried to exert their influence over the governments of Greece and Turkey. *b)* response: President Truman issued the Truman Doctrine, which pledged to give weapons and money to those who resisted communism in Greece and Turkey. *c)* effects: A result was that the eastern Mediterranean did not come under Soviet influence, and Greece and Turkey eventually became members of the North Atlantic Treaty Organization (NATO-1949). (Details on pg. 210)

- *Placement of missiles in Cuba by the Soviet Union - John F. Kennedy: a)* background: A revolution in Cuba brought Fidel Castro to power in the late 1950's. He soon announced his intentions to show friendship with the Soviets. In 1962, the Soviet Union used this opportunity to place missiles with nuclear capabilities in Cuba. *b)* response: U.S. spy planes showed proof of the missile bases, and Kennedy announced his intentions to quarantine (blockade) Cuba until the Soviets removed the missiles. *c)* effects: As a result, Soviet leader Khrushchev decided to remove the missiles from Cuba. Later, the Nuclear Test Ban Treaty was signed and was the White House and the Kremlin set up a direct line of communication. (Details on pg. 250)

- *Vietnam War - Lyndon Johnson: a)* background: In 1954, the French left their colony of Vietnam. A peace conference temporarily divided it in two: North Vietnam was to be Communist, and South Vietnam would stay anti-communist. Elections to unite the two never took place, and the communists from the North began to infiltrate the South. *b)* response: Concerned over the Domino Theory, the U.S. first sent military advisors, then began bombing the North, and finally sent in ground forces in 1965. By 1968, Johnson escalated the war so over 500,000 American troops were in Vietnam. *c)* effects: A result of this was the deep division of the American public over U.S. involvement in Vietnam. Anti-war protests grew dramatically as the war progressed, and Lyndon Johnson decided not to run for re-election in 1968. (Details on pgs. 265-269)

- *Tension between the United States and China - Richard Nixon: a)* background: After the communist takeover of China in 1949, the U.S. refused to recognize the communists as the legal government of China. *b)* response: The United States recognized the Nationalists on Taiwan as the legitimate government of China. In 1972, President Nixon and his National Security Advisor, Henry Kissinger visited Communist China in the hopes of improving relations. *c)* effects: Friendship between the two nations increased, and the U.S. officially recognized China in 1979. Trade between the two nations grew as a result. (Details on pgs. 274-275)

- *Iran's seizure of American hostages - Jimmy Carter: a)* background: For over 20 years, Shah Muhammed Reza Pahlevi ruled Iran. Despite some undemocratic features of the Shah's government, the U.S.

maintained close relations with Iran. In 1979, the Shah resigned and Islamic Shi'ite fundamentalists took over the government. *b)* <u>response</u>: When President Carter admitted the Shah to the U.S. for medical treatment, Islamic fundamentalist students took over 50 hostages at the U.S. Embassy. Carter used economic sanctions, secret diplomacy, and military action to free the hostages, all without success. *c)* <u>effects</u>: The hostage crisis contributed to the defeat of Jimmy Carter in the 1980 election. (Details on pgs. 285-286)

- *Latin American intervention - Ronald Reagan*: *a)* <u>background</u>: In Nicaragua, a 1979 revolution resulted in the overthrow of the ruling dictator. A communist group, the Sandinistas, gained power. The new government set up ties with Communist countries. Reagan opposed communist expansion in Latin America. The United States had a longstanding history of intervention in this area under the strained auspices of the Monroe Doctrine. *b)* <u>response</u>: Reagan denounced Marxists revolutions in Grenada and Nicaragua. He charged the Sandinistas with trying to provoke communist uprisings in other nations. Reagan struggled with Congress to give aid to the Nicaraguan 'Contras', a group trying to overthrow the Sandinista government. In all, U.S. Contra aid was sporadic, due to weak Congressional support. Congress was still wary after the Vietnam experience of the 1960's and 1970's. *c)* <u>effects</u>: Continuing U.S. pressure forced the Sandinistas to call for elections, which resulted in their defeat in 1989. (Details on pgs. 292-293)

- *Persian Gulf crisis - George Bush*: *a)* <u>background</u>: Iraqi leader Saddam Hussein invaded neighboring Kuwait in August 1990, and threatened the stability of the entire Middle East. *b)* <u>response</u>: President Bush organized a coalition of nations with U.N. support, to isolate Iraq and use military force to end the occupation of Kuwait. In early 1991, this military coalition overwhelmed Iraqi troops. Kuwait was freed, but Saddam remained in power in Iraq. *c)* <u>effects</u>: The War also brought about greater cooperation between the United States and several Arab nations. (Details on pgs. 298-300)

5. *Writing Strategy*: This question tests your knowledge of American reformers and reform movements. Divide your answer into *three* paragraphs. In *each* paragraph: *a)* give dates and events in discussing the historical background for the movement; *b)* describe action(s) taken by the reform leader; *c)* describe the change resulting from these actions.

- *Women's rights - Susan B. Anthony*: *a)* <u>historical background</u>: Throughout the 19th century, women lacked equality with men. This was especially true in the area of voting rights. Susan B. Anthony was President of the National American Woman Suffrage Association. *b)* <u>action(s) taken</u>: They demanded a woman's suffrage Amendment to the Constitution. *c)* <u>change</u>: Women gained voting rights in several western states in the late 19th century. In 1920, the 19th Amendment to the Constitution guaranteed the right of women to vote everywhere. (Details on pgs. 116-117)

- *Institutional reform - Dorothea Dix*: *a)* <u>historical background</u>: The insane lived in sub-human conditions in the early 19th century, sometimes chained and poorly clothed. *b)* <u>action(s) taken</u>: Dorothea Dix investigated the conditions in Massachusetts (1840's), and urged state legislators to build better facilities. *c)* <u>change</u>: As a result, states and some cities built public institutions to care for the insane. (Details on pg. 117)

- *Abolition - Harriet Beecher Stowe:* a) <u>historical background</u>: Slavery in the Southern states meant a life of brutality and hopelessness for many blacks. *b)* <u>action(s) taken</u>: Stowe wrote *Uncle Tom's Cabin*, a novel about slave life in the South. Her book graphically exposed the evils of slavery. *c)* <u>change</u>: Her efforts strengthened the abolitionist movement in the North. and made others question their apathy. Eventually, the 13th Amendment in 1865 ended slavery. (Details on pg. 45)

- *Labor reform - Samuel Gompers:* a) <u>historical background</u>: Workers in the late 19th century were subject to long hours and low wages. Large corporations worried little about the safety of workers. *b)* <u>action(s) taken</u>: Gompers formed the American Federation of Labor, made up of skilled workers. Its goals were to pursue basic goals of labor - wages and hours, and strengthen worker's rights. *c)* <u>change</u>: The AFL increased in membership, and in the 20th century successfully guaranteed for workers the right to form unions. They also helped passage of the Clayton Act, which exempted unions from anti-trust laws. (Details on pgs. 83-84)

- *Progressivism - Ida Tarbell:* a) <u>historical background</u>: Large corporations in the late 19th century employed ruthless business practices to reduce competition and increase sales. John D. Rockefeller's Standard Oil Company was one of the largest. *b)* <u>action(s) taken</u>: Tarbell, one of many muckrakers of the Progressive Era, wrote a series of magazine articles highly critical of the business practices of the Standard Oil Company. *c)* <u>change</u>: As a result, government enforcement of anti-trust laws grew, and the Progressives gained passage of a wide range of laws to protect consumers. A Court ruling ordered the breakup of the Standard Oil Company in 1911. (Details on pg. 120)

- *Conservation - Theodore Roosevelt:* a) <u>historical background</u>: Westward expansion in the 19th century led to the growing destruction of limited natural resources. *b)* <u>action(s) taken</u>: Roosevelt placed the power of the presidency behind the outcries of conservationist Gifford Pinchot and naturalist John Muir to increase public awareness of conservation. *c)* <u>change</u>: As a result of Roosevelt's efforts, the government protected millions of acres of forest land, and through the Newlands Act, began irrigation projects in the west. (Details on pgs. 125-126)

- *Environmentalism - Rachel Carson:* a) <u>historical background</u>: Industrialization resulted in growing amounts of air, land, and water pollution. *b)* <u>action(s) taken</u>: Rachel Carson wrote *Silent Spring*, which described the deadly effects of chemicals on the environment. *c)* <u>change</u>: It resulted in increased awareness of the environment, as shown by the Clean Air Act and the creation of the Environmental Protection Agency. (Details on pg. 272)

- *Consumerism - Ralph Nader:* a) <u>historical background</u>: In the years after World War II the American Automobile industry tried to sell cars with only a limited concern for passenger safety. Highway deaths and injuries grew each year. *b)* <u>action(s) taken</u>: Nader wrote *Unsafe at Any Speed* in 1965, which described the dangers in a particular General Motors model. *c)* <u>change</u>: Federal regulations now require many safety features on cars, such as automatic seat belts or air bags. the government also tests cars in crash situations for safety. (Details on pg. 272)

6. *Writing Strategy:* This question tests your knowledge of current events and contemporary issues. Divide your answer into *three* paragraphs. In *each* paragraph: *a)* describe the problem over the issue; *b)* describe opposing viewpoints on the issue; *c)* describe actions government or groups have taken on the issue.

- ***Capital punishment:*** *a)* <u>problem</u>: The issue revolves around the question of whether the government has the right to take a human life. *b)* <u>opposing viewpoints</u>: Supporters of capital punishment say that the death penalty would send a message to criminals and that it would cut down on violent crime. Opponents say that the death penalty is cruel and unusual punishment, and that the chance exists that an innocent person could be put to death. *c)* <u>actions taken</u>: In New York, the State Legislature passes a death penalty bill every year, but Governor Cuomo vetoes it.

- ***Right to die:*** *a)* <u>problem</u>: The issue is whether those near death have a right to die without being kept alive by extraordinary means of life support. *b)* <u>opposing viewpoints</u>: Supporters of the right to die say that keeping people alive with virtually no chance of recovery prolongs the agony for both patient and family. Opponents say that no one has the right to determine when a life is not worth saving. *c)* <u>actions taken</u>: Some states allow patients to sign statements saying that no extraordinary means should be used to keep then alive in case of an irreversible illness.

- ***Affirmative action:*** *a)* <u>problem</u>: The issue is whether minority groups and women should be given preference in employment and education to make up for past discrimination. *b)* <u>opposing viewpoints</u>: Supporters say that these groups have been denied equality in the past, and giving them preferences to increase their numbers now is an important way to make up for past discrimination. Opponents say that it is a form of reverse discrimination, where people are chosen not on their ability, but on the basis of race or sex. *c)* <u>actions taken</u>: In some civil service jobs, the gov't has actively stepped up recruiting in minority communities, without actually setting racial quotas for job placement. (Details on pg. 259)

- ***Censorship:*** *a)* <u>problem</u>: The issue revolves around the question of what is morally offensive and subject to government censorship. Recently, the National Endowment of the Arts, a government funded organization, has come under criticism. *b)* <u>opposing viewpoints</u>: Some say the NEA supports pornographic art, and public money should not go to such endeavors. Others condemn the government for interfering with artistic freedom. *c)* <u>actions taken</u>: Under public pressure, the government in recent years withdrew public funds from controversial art exhibits, but continues to support most NEA projects. (Details on pg. 289)

- ***Health care funding:*** *a)* <u>problem</u>: The controversy centers on the issue of who should pay for health care. *b)* <u>opposing viewpoints</u>: Some say it is the responsibility of the individual to pay for medical care. Others argue that high costs prevent many from paying out of their own pocket. *c)* <u>actions taken</u>: As a result, they go without health care. Medicare and Medicaid are programs that help those unable to pay for adequate medical care. (Details on pg. 254)

- ***Homelessness:*** *a)* <u>problem</u>: The 1980's saw an increase in the number of homeless people, especially in urban America. The question centers on who is responsible for these people. *b)* <u>opposing viewpoints</u>: Some argue that providing housing is not the role of the government. Others cite the lack of affordable housing in many urban areas, and say the government has a responsibility to provide adequate housing for all. c) <u>actions taken</u>: In New York State, Andrew Cuomo (the Governor's son), has led efforts to construct temporary housing for the homeless. (Details on pgs. 289-290)

7. Writing Strategy: This question tests your knowledge of New Deal reforms. Divide your answer into *three* paragraphs. In *each* paragraph: *a)* state why the act was needed; *b)* show how the act worked; *c)* state how the act changed society.

- **Tennessee Valley Authority:** *a)* <u>need</u>: The purpose was to provide cheap, available electricity to the rural south, and by doing so, improve economic and social conditions. *b)* <u>how it worked</u>: To do this, the government built a series of dams along rivers in the south to harness hydroelectric power. *c)* <u>social change</u>: As a result, electrification in the south improved the living standards of many residents, and flood control was also a byproduct of the dam construction.

- **Social Security Administration:** *a)* <u>need</u>: Social Security Administration: to provide the elderly with a source of income for their retirement. FDR proposed it in 1935. *b)* <u>how it worked</u>: To pay for it, taxes are deducted from the workers' wages. *c)* <u>social change</u>: It has resulted in greater financial security for elderly people in America. (Details on pg. 174)

- **Federal Housing Administration:** *a)* <u>need</u>: to boost housing construction and help the country out of the Great Depression. *b)* <u>how it worked</u>: The FHA did this by encouraging mortgaging lending by banks and providing banks with protection from potential losses. *c)* <u>social change</u>: FHA loans helped individuals achieve the American dream of home ownership. (Details on pg. 174)

- **Federal Deposit Insurance Corporation:** *a)* <u>need</u>: to protect depositors money in banks if the bank failed. *b)* <u>how it worked</u>: The FDIC collects a fee from each bank which goes into the insurance fund. *c)* <u>social change</u>:It has given people confidence that their money is safe, even if the bank itself fails. (Details on pg. 175)

- **Securities and Exchange Commission:** *a)* <u>need</u>: The decade of the 1920's saw wild swings in the stock market. This was often the result of fraud and dishonesty in the Market. The purpose of the SEC is to regulate the Stock Market, and prevent unwise and dishonest practices. *b)* <u>how it worked</u>: The SEC forbid buying on margin (credit). *c)* <u>social change</u>: The SEC increased confidence in the stock market, and created more stability in the institution. (Details on pg. 168, 175)

- **National Labor Relations Board:** *a)* <u>need</u>: In 1935, the National Labor Relations Act (Wagner Act) provided for creation of the National Labor Relations Board. Its purpose was to promote fairness in disputes between unions and employers. *b)* <u>how it worked</u>: The NLRB acts as an arbitrator in labor disputes, and can demand the end to unfair labor practices of employers. *c)* <u>social change</u>: An impact was the strengthening of unions, and a dramatic increase in union membership between 1935 and 1955. (Details on pg. 175)